Francis Arthur Fahy

Ireland in London

Francis Arthur Fahy

Ireland in London

ISBN/EAN: 9783742809735

Manufactured in Europe, USA, Canada, Australia, Japa

Cover: Foto ©ninafisch / pixelio.de

Manufactured and distributed by brebook publishing software (www.brebook.com)

Francis Arthur Fahy

Ireland in London

Evening Telegraph Reprints—VII.

IRELAND IN LONDON

BY

MESSRS. F. A. FAHY & D. J. O'DONOGHUE

Reprinted from the "Evening Telegraph."

Dublin:
"EVENING TELEGRAPH" OFFICE: 83 MIDDLE ABBEY STREET,
1889.

IRELAND IN LONDON.

INTRODUCTION.

THOROUGH investigation into the history of the Irish race in London, such as is attempted in the following papers, cannot fail to be of the keenest interest to our compatriots, wherever they may be. Perhaps no city out of Ireland has been so much influenced by Irish genius, Irish character, and Irish achievement. The inquiry: "How far has that influence been exercised, and to what purpose?" can only be answered—first, by a glance at their position among the other various races in England, and its tremendous difficulties; and, secondly, by a study of their achievements in literature, art, science, military genius, and statesmanship, as exemplified in the metropolis of the world. London teems with memories of Irishmen—famous in all the various walks of life—and of their works, and the truly great part they have taken in making London what it now is—the most extensive as well as the most solidly intellectual city of the world—can be unerringly traced through every step of its history, literary and otherwise, from the remotest period of its literary and mechanical activity down to the present day. The task is not unattended with difficulties, some of them unexampled and unique, for there have been times when it would have been folly and even madness in any Irishman to boast of or even admit his Irish birth or descent, and consequently many brilliant Irishmen have either changed their names or so Anglicised them

BYRON.

as to prevent the student from judging precisely of their Celtic origin. When James Montgomery, the poet (who, though born in Scotland, was of Irish parentage), pleasantly remarked that he had had a narrow escape from becoming an Irishman, he doubtless echoed the words of others who more seriously thought it a lucky thing for them to have been born on English soil. Many of those Irishmen whose names occasionally appear in the annals of English literature or art, like beacons, to show the surrounding darkness, or to point out the direction in which Irish genius has proceeded, have left no record of their connection with Ireland, other than that furnished by their names. But these names, though they conclusively prove that Irishmen won their way to eminence in early times, and in spite of all disadvantages, cannot show positively how far Celtic influence extended. The nature of early English literature is a more decided criterion still, although, as Matthew Arnold and Ruskin have both admitted, there can be no exact knowledge as to the extent of the unquestionably immense influence of the Celtic genius over English literature alone. The former great writer has even expressed the opinion that it would probably account for what is best in the greatest of all writers, Shakespeare.

As already hinted, however, it is perfectly obvious that in those times, so far as England was concerned, Celtic genius had to conceal itself, so to speak, under an English exterior, and that, with respect to the Irish in England, unless under very special circumstances—

Undistinguished they lived if they shamed not their sires.

To begin at the beginning, it may at once be said that London itself, according to the testimony of many authorities, is derived from two Celtic words, signifying "Stronghold of Ships," and that its first inhabitants were Celts, such as now dwell in Ireland. Moreover, the earliest artistic work of England is purely Celtic, and Irish; the illuminated and other work, termed Anglo-Saxon, executed in the monasteries, being chiefly done, or at least inspired or taught, by Irish monks. Miss Margaret Stokes's fine work on "Early Christian Art" deals very fully with the subject, and renders of it will find therein proofs of what is here advanced. In those times Irishmen were held in as high repute for their learning as for their valour, and various famous Englishmen, notably Alfred the Great and the Venerable Bede, ungrudgingly praised them ; but as time went on, and the struggle for national existence on the one hand, and for increase of territory on the other, became more violent, English feelings naturally became more embittered, and the attitude of the English people towards the Irish is pretty plainly discerned in the great writers of succeeding times. But it was the Reformation that really intensified the bitterness to its sharpest degree ; for England, suddenly (in a sense), becoming Protestant, made the terrible mistake of trying to force another nation to also change its creed ; and it was in this attempt to impose their newly-formed religion upon the Irish people that the English acted most unjustifiably, and caused the bloodiest and most persistent conflicts. That it was mostly, at one time, if not always, a religious matter between the conqueror and the conquered is proved by the fact that those Irishmen who elected to become Protestants always received better treatment than the Catholics, being considered, in short, almost as good as Englishmen. Throughout the whole sad history of the English connection with Ireland, the very worst excesses have been those committed in the name of religion, and the severest penalties have always attached to the profession of Catholicism. That is to say, where an Irish Protestant was tolerated, an Irish Catholic was not. It may very safely be said that the prejudice against the Irishman's religion has at all times been stronger than against his mere nationality. During Queen Elizabeth's reign more than one writer advocated the utter extermination of the Irish—as, for instance, Harrington in his "Oceana ;" while others, such as Spenser and Raleigh, did their very best towards that end, practising rather than preaching. But they had a respect for the valour and some other qualities of the Celts ; it was the persistency of the latter in refusing to be annihilated that really roused the strongest ire of the courtly writers and soldiers of Queen Bess. English ignorance of the real people of Ireland was then abysmal, and is expressed in the writings of Shakespeare and his contemporaries. Shakespeare's Captain Mac-

Shane is a pure savage, who talks only of cutting throats as a mere pastime. At this time, it should be noted, the Scotch were held somewhat in great esteem by the best English writers ; a feeling that did not apparently last very long, for we find them heartily detested in the eighteenth century, while the Irish gradually grew in the estimation of the same writers, until they reached the highest point of good opinion at the beginning of this century. Even by Pope and writers of his time Irishmen were highly thought of although Pope could have known very little about them, and when he spoke of Ireland as "the mother of sweet singers," he was undoubtedly ignorant of the genuine poetry of Ireland.

But in spite of persecution, the Celtic genius could not be repressed, and at the very time when all kinds of projects were being mooted as to the best manner of exterminating the Irish people, and actually in the very midst of the would-be exterminators, Irish talent was silently winning its way into various branches of literature and art. Lodowick Barry, the dramatist, a contemporary of Shakespeare, and Duffet, Southerne, &c, among succeeding writers, are instances of this. The authors just mentioned were unquestionably Irish; but what of those writers and artists whose names are clearly Irish, but of whom no particulars as to Irish origin are recorded ? William Walsh the poet, John Tobin the dramatist, Byrne the engraver, Riley the painter, and, some time after, Heaphy and Hearne, two very eminent watercolour painters, are all probably lost to Ireland on account of this absence of definite information regarding their true origin. Perhaps they found it to their advantage to keep their Irish origin secret ; but it is also likely enough that English biographers purposely placed their birth in England, as it is supposed they have done in the case of a much greater man, William Congreve.

Apparently, also, the Irish were to the front in the agitations of early days, for most of the desperate characters of those times, curiously enough, turn out to be of Irish birth—as Jack Cade, the leader of the rebellion of the Kentishmen, who is said to have been an Irish physician, whose real name was Aylmer. Although decried by almost all historians, however, Cade was evidently leading a legitimate agitation ; for most of the reforms he demanded are moderate enough, in all conscience.

Up till the end of the eighteenth century the working classes of England had not been appre-

Ireland in London.

ciably augmented by Irish emigration; although various causes, such as the Williamite Wars, the Periodical Famines, and the destruction by the British Government of many Irish Industries, had necessarily driven some Irishmen to England as to all other corners of the earth, in search of a livelihood. But perhaps the army had swallowed the best part of them; for as Wolfe Tone bitterly remarked, " The army of England is supported by the misery of Ireland." It may therefore be said that up to this date the Irishman in London was generally what is termed by English writers a " literary or military adventurer." There were many of them in England in the eighteenth century, and, as might be expected, they attained the very highest positions in literature, art, and the drama. Sheridan and Goldsmith, Burke and Malone, Macklin, Murphy, O'Keeffe and Kelly, are but a few of the great literary Irishmen of the time; Tresham, Hone, Garvey, Peters and Barrett. all Irish painters of note, reached the coveted distinction of election as R.A.; M'Ardell, Burke, Egan, Murphy, Sullivan and Fry, but particularly the first and last, carried the art of steel engraving to its highest pitch of excellence; whilst in the art of the actor, Irishmen and women were, as ever, unsurpassable as will afterwards appear. While Grattan's Parliament lasted, Irishmen were indispurably highly respected in England, and it is probably due to the fair play they received in the last century that they succeeded so admirably in all the professions they chose to exercise their genius upon.

Coincident with this esteem for the Irish people, there existed a bitter feeling against the Scotch. There are few writers of the last century who do not show more or less of this animosity, which may be due to envy at the superior shrewdness of the Scotchmen in London. The famous satirist, Churchill, wrote a bitter but amusing satire on Scotland, entitled " The Prophecy of Famine: a Scot's Pastoral;" while in his " Rosciad " he extols the abilities and the character of the Irish people. Dr. Johnson's strong antipathy to Scotchmen is well known, and instances of it are impartially related by the sly Boswell, who when he first met Johnson, was mortally afraid lest the latter should discover his nationality. Of Ireland and Irishmen Johnson had a very high opinion; his most intimate friends were amongst the latter; and over and over again he denounced with indignation the actions of the Protestant minority in Ireland, backed up by the English Government, and had " great compassion for the Papists;" " let the authority of the English Government perish," said he, " rather than be maintained by iniquity." And when an Irish Bishop expressed a fear that if Johnson went to Ireland he might treat the Irish people as badly as he did the Scotch, he replied : " Sir, you have no reason to be afraid of me. The Irish are not in a conspiracy to cheat the world by a false representation of the merits of their countrymen. No, sir; the Irish are a *fair people*." As for the Union, which was then only hinted at. Johnson spoke as follows to an Irishman who asked him his opinion on the subject : " Do not make a Union with us, sir. We should unite with you only to rob you. We should have robbed the Scotch, if they had any-

DR. JOHNSON

thing of which we could have robbed them." And again, to conclude these quotations as to the opinion of English writers on the relative merits of Scotchmen and Irishmen, even " Junius " used these words : " I own I am not apt to confide in the professions of gentlemen of Scotland; and when they smile, I feel an involuntary emotion to guard myself against mischief." Of course Scotchmen can well afford to despise and to laugh at such prejudices —the only reason for quoting them afresh is to show, at least relatively, the esteem in which Irishmen were held a hundred years ago.

Irishmen were warmly welcomed in any profession they chose during the last century, but they received a special welcome in those professions where Englishmen were not too abundant or not of the highest excellence. Nearly all the great writers of the latter part of the eighteenth, and the earlier part of this century. have had a good word, to say of Ireland, and she has had no truer friends, among Englishmen, than Byron, Shelley, Sydney Smith, Dickens, and Thackeray; and among Scotchmen, Scott, Campbell, Brougham, Jeffrey, and Chalmers. Byron's friendship for Ireland is too well known to need proof; Shelley deeply sympathised with the Irish people, as his visit to Ireland and his works prove; Thackeray, though some of his Irish characters are not very flattering, has spoken of Irish intelligence in the highest terms; and Sydney

Smith more than once feelingly refers to the "brave, generous, open-hearted peasants of Ireland." To the same effect, Brougham and Chalmers might be quoted ; and Jeffrey, who called Ireland pre-eminently " the land of genius ;" but it is not so well known that Dickens also expressed his admiration for the character of the Irish people ; and the following passage from his "American Notes," where he relates his meeting with two Irish emigrants in New York, will perhaps be new to many readers :—

"Let us see what kind of men are those two labourers in holiday clothes, of whom one carries in his hand a crumpled scrap of paper from which he tries to spell out a hard name, while the other looks about for it on all the doors and windows. "Irishmen both! You might know them if they were masked, by their long-tailed blue coats and bright buttons, and their drab trousers, which they wear like men well used to working dresses, who are easy in no others. It would be hard to keep your modern republics going without the countrymen and country women of these two labourers. For who would dig, and delve, and drudge, and do domestic work, and make canals and roads, and execute great lines of international improvement? Irishmen both! and sorely puzzled, too, to find out what they seek. Let us go down and help them, for love of home, and that spirit of liberty which admits of honest service to honest men, and honest work for honest bread, no matter what it may be."

The poems of Scott and Campbell are full of evidence as to their appreciation of their brother Celts. Other writers, such as Landor and Leigh Hunt, might have been quoted also, but the above testimony will doubtless suffice. Such

REV. SYDNEY SMITH.

sympathy was rare in the sixteenth and seventeenth centuries, and most of the prejudice and ill-feeling prevalent at that time was owing to the ignorance of English people respecting the Irish. This ignorance was fostered and encouraged by interested persons, and sometimes by the Governments of the time. Strong prejudice, but chiefly religious, was the result, and this was not sensibly diminished for some time. The ignorance was not dissipated in Swift's day, as a passage, somewhat ironical, but doubtless true enough, will show. He says :—

" As to Ireland, they know little more of it than they do of Mexico ; further than it is a country subject to the King of England, full of bogs, inhabited by wild Irish Papists, who are kept in awe by mercenary troops sent from thence. And their general opinion is, that it were better for England if this whole island were sunk into the sea. For they have a tradition that every forty years there must be a rebellion in Ireland. I have seen the grossest suppositions pass upon them ; that the wild Irish were taken in toils, but that, in some time, they would grow so tame as to eat out of your hands. I have been asked by hundreds . . . . whether I had come from Ireland by sea: and, upon the arrival of an Irishman to a country town, I have known crowds coming about him, and wondering to see him look so much better than themselves."

That the above passage fairly describes the ignorance of English people concerning Ireland in Swift's time, will hardly be disputed by those who have read the polemical literature of that period. When Englishmen really know the Irish character intimately, they rarely fail to admire and respect it. It may be truthfully said that, personally, the Irish people are greatly esteemed in England, and are preferred to other nationalities. That charm which so many English writers have remarked, and which has taken so many English settlers in Ireland captive, and made them "more Irish than the Irish themselves," to quote a hackneyed saying, attracts Englishmen in London as well as at its source. Of its power over the settlers already alluded to, proofs are hardly required, but two facts, little known, but startling in their significance, may be noted. One is that the grandson of the poet Spenser was an " Irish rebel," another is the equally important fact that a descendant of Swift became a United Irishman, and was also attainted as a rebel. But at certain times the English prejudice against Irish people has been furiously revived—as, for instance, after the events of 1867, the Manchester rescue and the Clerkenwell explosion, and during those days of fierce excitement the Irish in England have led an unenviable life. As their influence grows greater in political and municipal matters, they are more carefully studied, and their suffrages more sought after. As the late A. M. Sullivan said :—

"As long as the working classes of England were unenfranchised, these vast bodies of Celtic material accumulated between the Tay and the Thames, were of little account. But as every day the influence of these classes increases—as the franchise is extended, and schoolboard, poor-law, municipal, and Parliamentary elections admit the masses of the people to the exercise of public power—the men whom Irish landlordism swept in thousands from their native valleys in the Western island will, as a consequence, be heard from They are placed in all the great centres of public opinion and political activity: and some of the most momentous issues of the near future will be largely determined, one way or another, by their aid."

The foregoing words hold as good to-day as they did in 1877, when they were written; and in the succeeding chapter we shall endeavour, by a careful consideration of their numbers and political status, to indicate the exact extent to which the influence of the Irish in London on public questions may be felt.

CHAPTER I.

UNTIL the end of the last century the growth of the Irish population in Great Britain was very gradual. There has been at all times a comparatively small number of them scattered throughout England, particularly since Elizabethan days, and it may be here mentioned that the parish of St Giles's, London (of which the Seven Dials is the most thickly-populated part) was noted as a favourite residence of the Irish two hundred and fifty years ago. It would be impossible to give their exact numbers in those days, as no particulars are recorded of the various nationalities which formed the England of the period. But by studying the Catholic population statistics of the end of the seventeenth century and onwards, we may get a fairly correct idea of the proportion of Irish among them. The following table gives the number of the Catholics of England and Wales at various intervals between 1699 and 1845 :—

Year.	Numbers.	Proportion to Total Population.
1699	27,696	Less than ½ per cent.
1767	67,916	Less than 1 per cent.
1780	69,380	Less than 1 per cent.
1845	284,300	1.70 per cent.

Though the exact proportion of Irish cannot be stated, it is certain that at least one-half of those Catholics enumerated in 1699 were Irish, and that their proportion gradually increased, until they were considerably more than one-half in 1845. From the beginning of the eighteenth century there has been a continual, yet thin, stream of Irish emigration into England, but previous to 1841 no official return of their numbers had been made. In that year, however, and in every succeeding decade, an official record has been taken of Irish-born in this country, and in the following table the results are shown, their proportion to the populations of England and of Ireland, and indicating also the approximate number of the Scotch. Only those born in Ireland are given as Irish in the returns—their children, if born in England, being considered as English natives.

TABLE OF IRISH AND SCOTCH-BORN PERSONS IN ENGLAND AND WALES.

Year.	Numbers.	Proportion to population of England.	Proportion to population of Ireland.	Approximate No. of Scotch.
1841	290,891	1 in 54	1 in 28	103,000
1851	519,959	1 in 3½	1 in 13	130,000
1861	601,634	1 in 35	1 in 9	140,000
1871	566,540	1 in 40	1 in 8	169,000
1881	592,734	1 in 46	1 in 8	213,000

In the last-named year (1881), of every 1,000 Scotchmen in England and Wales 195 were in London, while only 144 out of every 1,000 Irishmen were in the capital.

The increase in the number of Irish-born people in England and Wales between 1841 and 1851 is an eloquent though sad indication of the ravages committed in Ireland during the famine years; but a few details will still more clearly show the terrible sufferings of our countrymen during that fateful period. Thus, in one year alone (1848), no fewer than 296,231 Irish people landed at Liverpool. Nearly half of this enormous number proceeded direct to the United States; about 50,000 others had come to England on ordinary business, unconnected wi'h the famine; while, saddest fact of all, over 100,000 men, women, and children, more than a third of the entire number, were absolute paupers, in a terrible condition, who were destined to drag out what was, in most cases, a miserable existence in the slums of the great English towns. A great many of them perished from want of food and the effects of fever, in spite of all efforts to save them; and in those efforts, 10 Catholic priests, one Protestant clergyman, and many parochial officers and medical men paid the price of their devotion by death. During those years great numbers of Irish people came to England, via Newport, having been brought from Ireland in coal-vessels, "as return cargo," the highest fare amounting to only 2s 6d. Few were brought direct to London, most of those who reached that city having gradually made their way up from the country ports. In one year alone, 8,794 poor persons were admitted into one of the London Asylums for the Houseless Poor, and of that number 2,455 were Irish-born. The same asylum admitted within its doors during the fourteen years succeeding the famine 130,000 destitute people, and of these 34,000 were Irish. It is almost certain that most of these Irish emigrants were natives of Cork, for the relieving officer of Cardiff at the time stated, of his certain knowledge, that of every 100 who came to England via Newport 99 were Corkmen. Meanwhile those of our countrymen who could manage it proceeded to London in one continuous stream for some years, and, as the following table shows, formed a large proportion of the total population of that city:—

TABLE OF IRISH-BORN IN LONDON.

Yr.	Total No.	Prop. to Pop. of Lond.	Proportion to Pop. of Ireland.
1841	40,000*	1 in 41	5 in London to every 1000 in Ireland
1851	108,548	1 in 22	16 " " 1000 "
1861	106,879	1 in 26	18 " " 1000 "
1871	91,171	1 in 3	17 " " 1000 "
1881	80,778	1 in 4	16 " " 1000 "

* Approximately

The above figures do not include, of course, the children of Irish parents, born in London. The number of Irish-born and their immediate descendants in London must at least amount to *a quarter of a million*, which would be about one in twenty of the present total population—nearly five millions.

The several tables given above show a decrease of Irish-born persons in this country, a fact that can be easily explained. In the famine years the people came over in enormous quantities, and the emigration would have to keep to its then level in order to show an increase. Irish men generally have largely increased in numbers, but as the tide of emigration gradually subsided, and the number of those who came over during the famine period was slowly diminished by death, the number of Irish-born consequently decreased.

The Irish who came to London went always to those districts or localities where Irish colonies were already settled, and where lodgings were cheapest—partly because they were poor, but also because many of them understood little English

THE LATE LORD CAIRNS.
(From a Photograph.)

and in some cases, none at all. The following are those districts, in their order of density, most favoured by the Irish exiles:—St Olave's (South wark), where, in 1861, they numbered 1 in every 6 of the total population of the district; Whitechapel (1 in 8), St Giles's (1 in 9), Holborn

(1 in 11), St George's in the East (1 in 13), Stepney (1 in 15), Greenwich (1 in 16), Lambeth East and West London, Westminster, Marylebone, Poplar, St Saviour's (Southwark), Bermondsey, and Rotherhithe — and with the exception of one or two of these localities, where many street improvements have been carried out, they are those to which the poorer Irish even to this day resort. They do not choose these districts from mere inclination; from their circumstances they are obliged to settle in the lowrented neighbourhoods, where the scum and dregs of London generally live. But though compelled to dwell in the midst of the concentrated villany of London, it may happily be said that they escape almost unscathed from the fierce ordeal. It is the universal testimony of Englishmen that the Irish are greatly superior in morality to their English neighbours in the courts and alleys. They are more honest, more chaste by far, and less brutal. Naturally enough, now and then they fall into temptation, but, generally, it is their proud distinction that, in spite of all allurements to the contrary, they live industriously, honestly, and religiously. They would be more than human if they did not occasionally err and wander into wrong courses; and one sees Irish names in the "police news" not infrequently; but it is mostly for trivial offences they are there, and not for the serious crimes which are so common in the modern Babylon. When sober and industrious, they are greatly preferred to people of other nationalities by the more respectable of the artisan class among whom they live and move. They are never absorbed into the general population, but preserve their national characteristics through all circumstances. As the distinguished antiquarian writer, Mr. E. Walford, says, they "live in various parts of London, apart and amongst themselves, carrying with them the many virtues and vices of their native land, and never becoming absorbed in the nation to which, for years, they may be attached. Swindlers, thieves, and tramps may surround them, but do not in general affect them." Another excellent English author, Mr Diprose, says on the same subject:— "It would be a curious investigation for the philosopher how far the interest and progress of this most gallant and interesting nation have been affected by what, in the absence of a better definition, we shall designate the absence of merging power."

Respecting the callings and occupations of the Irish in London a great deal might be said, but a brief glance at the most important of those they do and do not follow will be doubtless more interesting than a mass of detail.

They undoubtedly form the largest proportion of the building trades, especially the unskilled branches. In a very literal sense, they have built London, for, according to good judges, they number about 70 per cent. of the whole of the building classes. Contrary to usual custom, however, the more intellectual work connected with building has not been, to any large extent, done by Irishmen. The labours of the great Irish engineers, such as Dargan and M'Neill, O'Shaughnessy and Benson, are more closely connected with their own country and with the British Colonial possessions than with London, and the same remark applies to the Tobins, Deanes, and Morrisons, among Irish architects. It is Scotchmen who have done a great part of the brain work employed in the material formation of London. James Gibbs, the two Smirkes, and Norman Shaw, among other Scotch architects, have built, or rather designed, some of the finest parts of London; while the greatest bridges over the Thames have been erected by John Rennie and Thomas Telford, two great Scotch engineers But although Irishmen have, generally speaking, performed the greater part of the manual work required, and comparatively little of the brainwork, it must not be supposed that there has been no Irish genius concerned in the making of London. A most distinguished Irish architect Captain Francis Fowke, designed the Albert Hall one of the most remarkable buildings in London, and the splendid buildings of the South Kensington Museum were also erected from his designs. Two other great architects, Sir Charles and E. M. Barry, R.A., father and son, are intimately associated with the greatest triumphs of modern architectural genius in London. Ireland may not unfairly, by reason of their descent, claim them as her own. Another son of the first-named, John Wolfe Barry, is a very distinguished engineer, now erecting the great bridge over the Thames at Bermondsey.

It is very probable that the occupation which attracts the majority of the London Irish is what is known as street-selling. At one time the orange trade was altogether in the hands of Jews, but gradually they have been superseded by Irishwomen and girls, and a Jew orange-seller is in these days a curiosity—at any rate, so far as street-selling is concerned. The "costermonger" proper is mostly purely Eng.lish—though this was apparently not always the case. According to Charles Knight, the well-known scholar, it is clear, from references in the old dramatists, that he used to be an Irishman. The present term is derived from "costard-monger," a seller of costards or apples, and at the present day most of these are Irish by birth or parentage. Most of the flower-girls are also of Irish origin, few of them, however, being Irish-born. Many of these Irish street-sellers of fruit have been very successful in their occupation, and now own some of the largest retail businesses in London. As near as we can judge, the following are the principal callings of the Irish, male and female, in London, apart from those already mentioned:—Tailoring, shoemaking, domestic service, the work connected with gas factories, he laundry, and unloading at the docks. The extent to which certain nationalities favour certain occupations is remarkable. While a great number of the milkmen of London are Welsh, the milkwomen are mostly Irish: the majority of the bakers of London are German—and in this trade the Irish are conspicuous by their absence; while in other occupations they are few and far between. For example, there are exceedingly few Irishmen among the cabmen of London, that class being peculiarly English in its habits and general mode of life—and it may also be mentioned that there are very few Irish barbers in London

They are only thinly scattered through the higher class trades, such as engineering, cabinet-making, &c, these trades requiring generally a severe technical training, which they are mostly too poor to get, or which they are unable to take advantage of from other causes. It should also be mentioned that most of the market-gardeners of the western suburbs of London are Irishmen, the original colony having been brought over in the famine days and planted there by the Society of Friends. The position of the Irish in their respective callings is generally high. When a recent French writer made the sweeping assertion that nearly all the foremen of London were Scotchmen, he showed unusual inaccuracy. There are a great number of them, it is true, but it is also a fact that a goodly proportion of the managers and foremen of the most successful businesses in London are Irishmen, especially in those trades they most affect. Besides those Irishmen who come over specially for harvesting purposes in the summer, there are also many Irish people, generally of the poorest class, who flock in thousands to the Kentish and other hop-fields in early autumn, and from this visit they generally manage to bring back sufficient to help them through the winter. Such are the chief occupations of the Irish in London; and in concluding this part of the present paper we need only add that where the hardest and most dangerous work is to be done, work which Englishmen cannot or will not do there is to be found the Irishman.

As regards religion, the Irish population of London is overwhelmingly Catholic, and the enormous sacrifices they have made for their creed might be dilated upon at great length if there were any need. The indignities they have suffered for it, the churches they have built by their hard-won pence, and the many other good and pious works they have performed for the religion they deem their best guide and consolation in this world, would all furnish plenty of material for such a thorough investigation. Suffice it to say here that, when the history of Catholicism in modern England comes to be written, it will be found that, as in America, its strongest support and stoutest defender has been always the exiled Celtic Irish race. Concurrent with this wide extension of Catholicity, chiefly, as has been said, aided by Irishmen, has occurred the great impetus given to the temperance movements by the countrymen

FATHER MATHEW.
(After Haverty's Picture)

of the greatest of modern crusaders against vice—Father Mathew. A good deal of his great work in London had become practically undone in the particularly bitter fight of the Irish for a bare existence—when national and religious prejudices were stronger than they are now—but the formation of the League of the Cross in 1873 by Cardinal Manning gave fresh opportunity to the Irish in London of renewing the famous discipline and conduct which they evinced so strongly in Father Mathew's day. The League, which numbers some 35,000 members, was formed out of six persons who had taken (and kept) the pledge from the great Apostle of Temperance. It now has 40 branches, 46 large banners, 18 brass and 23 drum and fife bands, and about 95 per cent of its members are Irish. So Irish is it, in fact, that its regalia is the traditional green-and-gold shamrock-besprinkled silk, while its banners are genuinely National in colour and in pictorial representation. Though, comparatively speaking, it is small in numbers, there is no telling the great benefits this organisation has conferred upon society in general, and especially upon the Irish working classes in London. Its work has been silent but beneficial, steady but sure, and its promoters deserve all the credit and all the satisfaction which every good work brings in its train.

The Irish in London are, unfortunately, so far as the majority are concerned, not in very affluent circumstances. The uncertainty of employment, in the first place, added to the expenses of bringing up large families; and, moreover, the many appeals to their patriotism, their religious feelings, and their general benevolence, all combine to make their position less enviable than it might otherwise be. Their political status is higher than many people imagine. In certain districts their voting power is so strong as to enable them to turn the scale to their own liking, but the exact figures cannot be stated precisely, pending the present registration.

Hitherto we have spoken only of those Irishmen who go to swell the working classes, but, as everywhere else, the irrepressible Celts are to be found in all professions, from the lowest to the highest. At one time, especially when the Peninsular War was being fought, the army was two-thirds Irish, according to Sir E. Lytton Bulwer, afterwards Lord Lytton. In 1807, according to Dr. M'Nevin, the well-known United Irishman, the proportion of Irishmen in the British army was "about one-half." It is much less favoured by Irishmen of the present day, but still, even now, it contains great numbers of them, probably one-fourth of the service being Irish born. It is likewise largely officered by Irishmen, and a bare list of the famous Irish officers of the last 200 years would require a column in itself. They are not so numerous in the navy, but they are by no means scarce in that profession. There are large numbers of them in the police force also, though not so many as formerly, for it will be found that while most of the veterans are Irish, the younger members are chiefly recruited from the class to which Hodge belongs—the English farm labourer. In the various Civil Service departments throughout the country (especially in the Customs and Excise) there are thousands of Irishmen—in fact, they seem to be more successful in this profession than in any other, judging by their numbers and their relatively high position in it. Again, the Irish medical men of London are another important body, large in numbers, and perhaps superior in status to their English rivals. Many of the greatest physicians at the leading London hospitals are now, and have hitherto been, largely recruited from the medical men of Ireland. There is no need to mention more than one hospital—St. Bartholomew's, for example, which has had among its most famous physicians such men as John Abernethy (of Irish parentage), Dr. Walter Moxon, and many others of equal or more renown, and which, at the present moment, counts among its most distinguished men Dr Norman Moore, celebrated as a Celtic scholar as well as a physician. Other Irishmen hold also very important appointments: the head of the Army Medical Staff is an Ulsterman—Sir Thomas Crawford—while another great practitioner intimately connected with London, Sir William M'Cormac, is, like the foregoing, also an Ulsterman.

To mention the Bar to those acquainted with Irish history is like saying the proverbial "word to the wise." There is no profession more remarkable for its Irish associations than that of the lawyer, unless, indeed, it be that of the soldier. Therefore, it will very easily be believed that some of the greatest of modern English lawyers have been Irishmen. One of the greatest of recent Lord Chancellors of England was the late Lord Cairns—an Irishman, needless to say, as great as an orator as he was learned in the law. It is not so well known that the present Lord Chancellor, Lord Halsbury, is also an Irishman, or at least of Irish descent. He is the son of an eminent Irish journalist, Dr Stanley Lees Giffard. One or two others among the famous Irish lawyers connected with London may be mentioned. Chief among them are Baron Huddleston and Mr Justice Mathew, two of the most highly respected occupants of the Bench. As an advoate, moreover, there is none greater than Sir Charles Russell (a native of county Down), who is doubtless destined for a much higher position than he now holds. To notice only one other

SIR CHARLES RUSSELL, M.P.
(Late Attorney-General for England.)

name, we may instance Mr. Geoghegan, one of the most distinguished of living exponents of the criminal law. In every other department of public life they have as admirably succeeded. There have been two Irish Prime Ministers during this century alone, not including Lord John Russell (who considered himself an Irishman) or Lord Palmerston, who was of Irish descent, though not primarily. It would, of course, be of little use to enumerate all the distinguished Irishmen who have held the highest positions in the land at various times; but at the present moment some very important posts are held by them, and may be mentioned. For instance, the Director of the National Gallery (Sir F. W. Burton) is an Irishman; the Director of the Science and Art Department (General Donnelly) is another; the Assistant Commmissioner of Police (Mr. Anderson) is another (just as was the first Chief Commissioner of the London Police, Sir Richard Mayne); and, lastly, the Chief of the Metropolitan Fire Brigade (Captain Shaw) is likewise an Irishman; and although the present Lord Mayor of London is not Irish, yet even that most exclusive of exclusive offices in the British Empire has been held by an Irishman—namely, Sir William M'Arthur. They have succeeded in every capacity, and have filled all exalted positions, with the single exception, perhaps, of the English throne. There need be no reasonable limit to their ambition or to their successes. If, as the poet says :—

Too low they build who build beneath the stars,

Irishmen need have no fear of being over-ambitious. They will doubtless continue to win their way to the chief positions in the empire they have helped so materially to build up. Strictly speaking, Englishmen are only its nominal rulers for it may be truly said that the greatest and best of their colonial and other administrators have been and are natives of the once-despised island. As for the future capabilities of the Irish race, let the testimony of an English writer, John Foster, the brilliant essayist of the last century testify :—

"It would be the utmost want of candour, we think, to deny that they are equal to any nation in the earth in point of both physical and intellectual capability. A liberal system of government and a high state of mental cultivation would make them the Athenians of the British Empire."

CHAPTER II
FLEET STREET.

"How often have I fancied, if the walls by which thousands now daily pass without a glance of recognition or regard, if those walls could speak, and name some of their former inmates, how great would be the regret of many at having overlooked houses which they would perhaps have made a pilgrimage of miles to behold, as associated with the memory of persons whose names history, literature, or art has embalmed for posterity, or as the scene of circumstances treasured up in recollection."

T. C. CROKER.

LONDON is full of such memories as those to which the above quotation from Crofton Croker refers. Many of the places hallowed by the reminiscences of great Irishmen remain as "silent witnesses of the past," but some of them have, naturally enough, given place to modern edifices and thoroughfares. To know the exact position once occupied by those departed relics, however, is in itself valuable. FLEET-STREET, strange to say, does not, as might be supposed, greatly abound in memories of eminent Irishmen—at any rate, not to the extent that other London streets do. At the same time, since Fleet-street has been the home of journalism, Irishmen have necessarily had many close connections with it. Indirectly, every publishing house has had its Irish associations, and every newspaper office its Irish contributors among its staff. With these we do not now propose to deal, as the Irish journalists of London will be discussed as adequately as possible in separate articles of the present series.

When Charles Lamb spoke of the "impossibility of feeling dull in Fleet-street," he referred only to those who looked at it from a historical or literary point of view, and in describing the Irish landmarks of London to our readers (who for the nonce may assume the rôle of visitors), we shall stop only at those places which have a strong interest for Irishmen, and which call up memories mostly creditable to their character and genius. We shall follow the only feasible rule of taking a certain street or neighbourhood and dealing with it separately. By the accompanying sketch-map it will be seen that Fleet-street begins at Ludgate Circus, from which point we propose to start. A short distance on the left will bring us to a narrow passage, with the "Punch" Office at the corner, leading to St. Bride's Church, one of the finest of Wren's works. Its name (St. Bride or Bridget) clearly implies that it is a relic of pre-Reformation days—as is also the name of a prison which once stood behind it, and was called "Bridewell," from a holy well known as St. Bridget's well. The Church of St. Bride was originally built in the Middle Ages, but was destroyed by the Great Fire, and rebuilt in 1680 by Sir Christopher Wren. Within its precincts is buried a Countess of Orrery, probably the wife of that Earl in whose honour the instrument known as the "oriery" was named.

Nearly opposite St. Bride's is SHOE-LANE, where Samuel Boyse, the unfortunate Irish poet of the eighteenth century, died. Shoe-lane has, however, other and more important Irish associations. In this narrow turning was started the famous debating club and resort for politicians, known as "Cogers' Hall." It was founded by one Dan Mason in 1755, and till very recently was situated in Shoe-lane. Now, however, it occupies another part of Fleet-street, and even now is a kind of oratorical school for Irish politicians of various grades. Among its most famous past members were three Irishmen — Daniel O'Connell, John Philpot Curran, and Judge Keogh. The word "coger" does not mean a drinker of "cogs," but is derived from "cogito," to cogitate. All were welcome to Coger's Hall, class distinction being unknown there: but though strangers were admitted, and were allowed to speak, members had a prior claim on the chairman's discretion. There the tradesman and manufacturer jostled the mechanic, and the reporter hob-nobbed with the barrister. It may be remarked that "No. 10 Shoe-lane" was the rendezvous of the cogers, though owing to the incessant re-numbering of London streets, this, as in many other places, has been changed.

Coming out into Fleet street again, a little fur

TOM STEELE.

ther on, at the house known as "No 134," we come upon a truly historic spot. The present house stands on the site of the old " Globe Tavern," a great resort of the Irishmen of the last century—Goldsmith, Macklin, Hugh Kelly, Edmund Burke, William Cooke (of Cork) the poet, and the witty Dr. Glover, an Irishman like the rest, and very charitable withal. Dr. Johnson, the " presiding genius of Fleet-street," as Leigh Hunt calls him, was, of course, also a frequenter. Here was held the " Wednesday Club," founded by Johnson (meeting on every Wednesday), and it was at one of the weekly reunions of this club that Goldsmith read the famous epitaph on Edward Purdon, his unfortunate countryman, having composed it as he came from his lodgings in the Temple. Most of our readers have probably read this epitaph before, but as there may be some to whom it is unknown, we quote it :—

> Here lies poor Ned Purdon, from misery hurled,
> Who long was a bookseller's hack;
> He led such d———ble life in this world,
> That I don't think he'll wish to come back.

One of the most remarkable members of the club was certainly the Hugh Kelly above referred to. He is not so well known as he deserves to be, yet he is the author of two of the best and most successful comedies of the last century—" False Delicacy " and " The School for Wives." Both are original works, and are considered the foundation of the English sentimental comedy. " False Delicacy " became the rage, so to speak. It had a splendid run in London, was translated into French by Madame Riccoboni; into Portuguese by order of the famous Minister, the Marquis de Pombal ; and also into German. Kelly was a native of Roscommon, and a pungent satirist and bitter polemic.

Almost opposite 134 Fleet-street is SALISBURY COURT and SQUARE, with the " Daily Chronicle " office at the corner. At No. 12 here, now occupied by Lloyd's paper-works, lived Samuel Richardson, the printer and novelist. Here he printed his well-known works, " Pamela " and " Clarissa Harlowe," and here it was that Oliver Goldsmith acted as a printer's reader. This kind of work, however, did not suit him, and therefore he gave it up without regret after a short time.

Crossing Fleet-street again, we reach WINE-OFFICE COURT, notable also for its memories of Goldsmith. At the corner is an ancient tavern greatly modernised as far as exterior goes), called " The Old Cheshire Cheese." This used to be greatly frequented by Goldsmith and Dr. Johnson, and up to a short time ago their favourite seats were pointed out to all visitors, and may be so even now. It was from Wine Office-Court that Goldsmith wrote to Johnson the me-

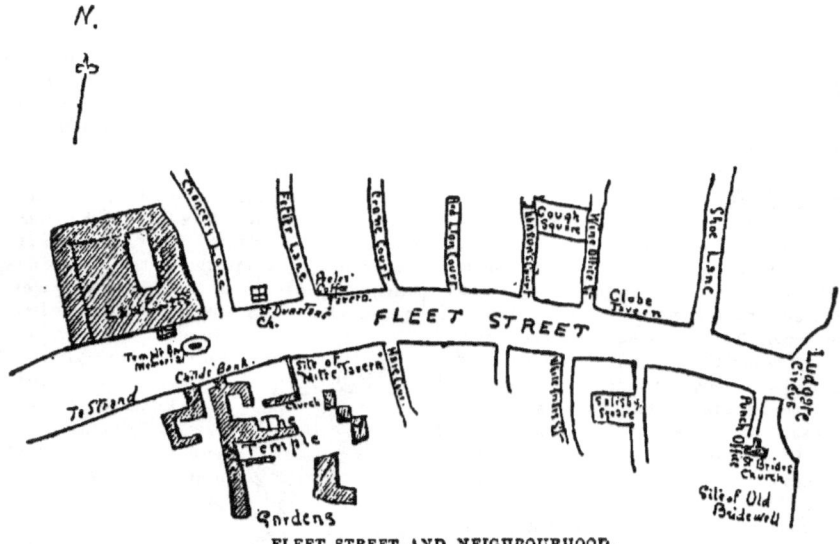

FLEET STREET AND NEIGHBOURHOOD.

morable letter, in which he mentioned that his landlady had arrested him for non-payment of rent, and implored Johnson to call on him. As every reader of Goldsmith's life knows, Johnson went, first sending a guinea. When he arrived, he found Goldsmith had already changed the guinea, and was provided with a bottle of wine, the irate landlady meanwhile threatening him with all sorts of penalties. Johnson first took

Irish painter, lived. Leading from Gough-square back to Fleet-street, is JOHNSON'S-COURT, where Goldsmith, Burke, and Arthur Murphy (the dramatist) constantly visited Dr Johnson, who lived there. Edmund Malone, the great Shakesperian scholar, was also a visitor here. Close by is RED LION-COURT, which has the unenviable notoriety of being the scene of a murderous attack on a Catholic priest on the 5th of September, 1794.

THE TEMPLE CHURCH.

away the wine, or rather put the cork back into the bottle, and then took the MS. of "The Vicar of Wakefield" (which he found in a drawer) to Newbery, the publisher, and received sixty pounds for it, with a part of which the landlady was soon satisfied.

Wine Office Court leads into GOUGH-SQUARE, where Hugh Kelly, already mentioned, died, and where George Chinnery, R.H.A., the distinguished

Father Anthony Carroll was a distinguished Jesuit, and was passing through this court on the evening of the above-mentioned day when he was knocked down and robbed. His injuries were such that he died in a few hours in St. Bartholomew's Hospital.

The next turning to Red Lion-court is Crane-court. Here, in 1749, Matthew Concanen, the poet, died. Like many other Irishmen of his time, he came to England penniless and friendless, and won name and fame as a writer. Although Pope has given him a niche in his "Dunciad," on account, it is said, of an adverse criticism, Concanen did not deserve what was intended as an indignity. His poetic abilities, though not very great, were certainly very creditable, while his political writings earned him great distinction. He became Attorney-General for Jamaica as a reward for his services to the party in power. His volume of poems, and his excellent comedy, "Wexford Wells," which contains some good songs, will indisputably preserve his name from that oblivion which has overtaken so many of his contemporaries. Crane-court is noteworthy on another account. From 1710 to 1782 the Royal Society (then, as now, the leading scientific body of England) held its meetings here. When Sir Isaac Newton died in 1727, Sir Hans Sloane became President of this famous body, and kept the post till his death in 1753. He was neither the first nor the last of its Irish Presidents, as we shall hereafter see. As we shall have occasion to recur to Sir Hans Sloane, it is only necessary to say here briefly that he was a native of county Down, and was one of the greatest scientific men of his time, distinguished alike as a physician and as a naturalist.

Exactly opposite Crane-court is HARE-PLACE or court, a spot instinct with Irish associations Its ancient name was RAM-ALLEY, and it was once the resort of the worst riff-raff in London. As such it has been immortalised by Lodowick Barry, the earliest of Irish dramatists, in his amusing and indeed famous comedy, "Ram Alley." In his time, apparently, lawyers of various kinds resided close by, for he says :—

"There's many a worthy lawyer's chamber
Buts upon Ram Alley."

All Irishmen will be interested in knowing that it was in this very court that Wolfe Tone lived for two years (1787-1788) while studying at the Temple close by. During his residence here, at No. 4, he supported himself by reviewing books for the "European Magazine." Here also he wrote a satirical novel, " Belmont Castle," in conjunction with some friends. It is needless to recall to the Irish reader the splendid record of the life of such a noble personality, whose memory is one of the greatest possessions of his admiring countrymen. A few yards past Hare-court is No. 37 Fleet-street, now the banking-house of Messrs Hoare, which stands on the site of the old "Mitre Tavern," a favourite resort of many of the Irishmen already mentioned, and others yet to be noticed. It was particularly favoured by Goldsmith and Macklin. Those who read the lives or memoirs of the distinguished Irishmen of the last century, and who remember the occasional references to the " Mitre," will be glad to know its exact locale.

OLIVER GOLDSMITH.

Nearly opposite is FETTER-LANE, where in 1798 Benjamin Binns, the United Irishman, and one or two of his friends, were arrested and taken to Newgate. Binns's brother, John, had already been captured, as well as Arthur O'Connor, and many others. In this street also lived, in 1609, the most famous of all the musicians of the Elizabethan age, John Dowland. It is extremely likely that this fine composer was an Irishman, as his latest biographer has hinted, for one of his songs is dedicated to " My loving countryman, John Foster, merchant, of Dublin." Added to this is the ignorance as to his birthplace. It, as is more than probable, Dowland is Irish, Ireland may well be proud of this latest acquisition to the ranks of her musicians. His son, Robert Dowland, was also an admirable composer. At the corner of Fetter-lane is a house which has some interest for Irishmen—Peele's Coffee-house it used to be, but it is now Peele's Family Hotel—for it is the house in which Tom Steele, O'Connell's famous lieutenant, died on the 15th June, 1848. The "Head Pacificator of all Ireland," as he was styled, became inconsolable after his great chief's death, and in one of his fits of despair tried to commit suicide by jumping into the Thames. He was rescued and taken to Peele's, the kind-hearted proprietor of which took charge of him and cared for him until he died on the date above given.

Two or three doors past Fetter-lane is St. Dunstan's-in-the-West, one of the few churches in this neighbourhood that escaped the ravages of the Great Fire, which approached to within three doors of it. It has been partly rebuilt during the century, but is still a peculiar structure. In this church several eminent persons have been buried, notably one famous Irishman, Father Peter Walsh, one of the most remarkable characters of the seventeenth century. His works are important, from the great learning displayed in them, and his life was a somewhat adventurous one, his biography occupying no less than twelve pages of T. D. M'Gee's work on the "Irish Writers of the Seventeenth Century." Father Walsh was a native of Kilkenny, and became a devoted adherent of that great Duke of Ormond whom he unsuccessfully endeavoured to convert to Catholicism, and who enters so largely into the history of his time. Not far from St. Dunstan's, and where the great campanile of the Law Courts now stands, there used to be a turning called SHIRE-LANE, facing the Temple. Here the renowned Kit-Cat Club used to meet. It was a social club, named after one Christopher Catt, a pastry-cook, at whose house its meetings were held. All the great wits of several generations patronised this club, but it had no more notable member than Sir Richard Steele, the great essayist and humourist. This most lovable of writers was born in Dublin in 1671, his father being an Englishman and his mother a native of Waterford. As his personality charmed his contemporaries it has likewise charmed the writers of succeeding generations, until Steele shares with Goldsmith and Charles Lamb the praise of being one of the most beloved of English or Irish writers. Steele is not only considered the true founder of English periodical literature, but is also regarded as the originator of the English novel, as, apart from his delightful little tales, it was his account of 'Robinson Crusoe" that led Defoe to write his famous work, the first of regular English stories. Steele was besides the first in England to write the genuine critical essay, and from his "Spectator," "Tatler," and "Guardian," many exquisite things might be quoted, all forming part of what may be fairly claimed as Irish literature.

Opposite the site of Shire-lane is Child's Bank, by the side of the Temple. Part of this bank stands on the site of the old "Devil Tavern," a great resort of the writers of Shakespeare's as of Swift's time. Swift, as well as Steele, and, at a later period, Goldsmith, were very frequent visitors, as their works no less than their biographies testify.

ST. BRIDE'S CHURCH, FLEET STREET.

Now let us enter the quaint old place known everywhere as the "Temple," and though in two parts, with two separate entrances, we may take it as a whole. It receives its name from the Knights Templar, who removed here from Holborn in 1184, and who were succeeded by the Knights Hospitallers of St. John of Jerusalem—when the estates of the former were taken over by the Pope. The armorial bearings of the Middle and Inner Temples are carved over their respective gateways. That of the first is a Lamb, of the last a Horse. A wag once chalked on one of the gates some verses satirising the lawyers, of which the following is a couplet:—

"The Lamb sets forth their innocence,
The Horse their expedition."

The Temple is one of the many relics of Catholic England that still exist in London, sometimes in all their pristine beauty. Such names as Blackfriars, Whitefriars, Austinfriars, and the like, with their obvious associations, yet linger about Fleet-street and its neighbourhood. The Temple is filled with memories of numberless eminent Irishmen of more or less affectionate memories. Its stillness contrasts startingly with the roar, bustle, and din outside in Fleet-street, and its curious old-world air is very different from the work-a-day aspect of its immediate surroundings. No wonder a legion of poets has hymned its praises, for it is impossible for anyone, let his nationality be what it may, to stroll through this relic of the Middle Ages without feeling that he treads upon what is almost holy ground. Irishmen cannot but recollect that it was here Goldsmith lived for many years, and wrote some of his most remarkable works, and that he died here, close by the spot where his grave now is. Here he used to receive from the demesne of Earl Nugent (his countryman and sole patron, and an excellent poet) a fine buck every year, the gift of which inspired one of Oliver's best poems—namely, " The Haunch of Venison," commencing :—

Thanks, my lord, for your venison, for finer or fatter
Never ranged in a forest or smoked on a platter."

It was in the Temple that Thomas Southerne, the best of Irish tragic playwrights, wrote his comedy, " Disappointment," and here also lived Tom Moore, " Pleasant" Ned Lysaght, Congreve, Sheridan, Hugh Kelly, Henry Brooke, the author of " The Fool of Quality," one of the best novels of the eighteenth century. Here also dwelt Edmund Burke, Edmund Malone, and Lord Clare of Union fame. Many and many a time have such patriots as Henry Grattan, Wolfe Tone, John Philpot Curran, William Molyneux, Peter Burrowes, Henry Flood, and Lord Cloncurry trodden its beaten paths as they proceeded to their chambers in the buildings around, while in very recent times such Irishmen as Eaton Stannard Barrett, the witty novelist and poet, Lord Cairns, Sir Joseph Napier, John D'Alton, Chief Justice Whiteside, and the lamented A. M. Sullivan, have honoured the place by residing there. The peculiar old church also has its distinct associations. This circular edifice is one of the four erected in England by the Knights Templar in 1185, one in London and three in other parts of the country. This church was no doubt frequently visited by the various Irishmen just enumerated, and its interior is as well worth a visit as its exterior and surroundings. There is a tablet here to the memory of Oliver Goldsmith, the best-loved resident of the Temple. Here, nearly 250 years ago, the learned Archbishop Ussher used to preach to the Benchers. Ussher is certainly one of the most remarkable men Ireland ever produced. His stupendous learning astonished even the most learned men of his day, and its visible outcome may be seen in his great and, indeed, monumental works. Concerning one of these a curious anecdote is related. When " The Antiquities of the British Churches," one of his greatest

ARCHBISHOP USSHER.

works, was published in 1639, the great French Minister of the period, Cardinal Richelieu, sent its author a gold medal and a congratulatory letter, in return for which Ussher sent the mighty Cardinal some Irish wolf-dogs of superior breed ! Of Ussher's learned work just referred to, an eminent Irish scholar, Dr Elrington, says :—" To panegyrise this extraordinary monument of human learning is unnecessary; to detail its contents impossible."

The Temple, its ancient church, its tranquil and narrow churchyard, and pleasant gardens overlooking the river cannot fail in meditative Irish minds to call up some reminiscence of its past glories, and the share Irish genius has taken in making it one of the most delightful and remarkable places in the metropolis. An exquisite poet, J. F. O'Donnell, in a poem worthy of the place and of himself, has described the Temple so

Ireland in London.

finely that we cannot refrain from quoting a few lines. He says :—

> I love this quiet Temple nook,
> This ancient haunt of wren and rook,
> Thick writ with legends like a book.
>
> Dark-circled in the town it lies,
> Above it loom the misty skies,
> Outside the songs of commerce rise.
>
> Ten paces from the bustling street
> Lurks the old-fashioned, quaint retreat—
> A land of murmurs low and sweet.
>
> . . . .
>
> I love those alleys deep and old,
> While all around in gusts of gold
> The autumn leaves fall manifold.

CHAPTER III.

IRISH ASSOCIATIONS OF THE CITY PROPER.—FROM LUDGATE HILL TO THE TOWER.

BEFORE proceeding westward from TEMPLE BAR, where our first walk ended, let us retrace our steps until we reach Ludgate Circus. LUDGATE-HILL, facing the end of Fleet-street, takes its name from one of the half-dozen gates that once shut in the ancient city of London. Their names still exist in various thoroughfares—Ludgate, Newgate, Aldgate, Cripplegate, Aldersgate, and Bishopsgate. LUDGATE-HILL, up which we propose to proceed, is not a long street, but about it many interesting Irish memories hover. Here stood the coffee-house kept by the father of John Leech (the famous cartoonist), who, it is not generally known, was Irish by parentage as well as in temperament. He, with other eminent Irish artists, has been among the worthiest illustrators of "Punch." As we intend to show later on, Irishmen have almost monopolised the most artistic features of that famous periodical. In STATIONERS' HALL COURT, close by, is the Stationers' Hall, where all published works are copyrighted. There is here a fine portrait of Sir Richard Steele, well worth a visit on account of its intrinsic merits. The first turning on the left in Ludgate-hill is the OLD BAILEY, where the gloomy prison of NEWGATE is situated. It has a melancholy interest for Irishmen, for many of their countrymen have been imprisoned here, but mostly either for national principles or for trivial faults such as would not now be thought deserving of punishment. Some have been executed here for small offences; a few, however richly deserved their fate. One of the most eminent inmates of Newgate in past times was Thomas Delaune, a native of Brinny, county Cork, a leading Nonconformist, and admittedly one of the most remarkable men of his time. He wrote some famous works, for the best of which --his powerful "Plea for the Nonconformists"—Daniel Defoe wrote a preface. He was imprisoned for refusing to conform to the principles of the Established Church, and died here in 1684, after fifteen months of suffering. Here were executed Governor Wall, an Irish officer, for cruelty, ending fatally, to a soldier under his command, while Governor of Goree in 1802, and James MacLane, a native of Monaghan, son of a dissenting minister, and one of the most notorious highwaymen of the last century. Having disgraced his family he took to the road, and led a reckless life before he finally fell into the hands of the law. Among the most celebrated of the trials that have taken place at Newgate have been those of James Quin and Charles Macklin the two great Irish actors. They were both tried for the same kind of offence—that of killing a brother actor, and were sentenced to be burned in the hand—a very light punishment, as in both cases the fatality was caused through their own impetuosity. Captain Macnamara, an Irish duellist, was also tried here on the charge of killing an adversary in a duel, but as the law winked at the gentleman's pastime of duelling, Macnamara was not much inconvenienced by his sentence. None of the Irish prisoners of Newgate have had a stranger career than George Barring-

WOLFE TONE.

ton, the celebrated pickpocket. His real name was Waldron, and he was born at Maynooth, in Kildare. After some very extraordinary successes as a thief, he was at length arrested in 1790, tried, and sentenced to transportation. Previously incorrigible, he seems to have become in Australia a law-abiding citizen, and at the time of his death held the post of chief constable of one of the leading colonial cities. He wrote several excellent works, and is universally known as one of the earliest of Australian poets. His famous couplet—

"True patriots we, for be it understood,
We left our country for our country's good,"

occurs in the fine prologue he wrote for a play acted by convicts in one of the Australian cities.

DOOR OF NEWGATE.

The political troubles of recent years have sent several living Irishmen to the cells of Newgate on charges of treason-felony, the most distinguished of whom is Michael Davitt. It is noteworthy that the last public execution in England took place here on the 26th May, 1868, the culprit being Michael Barrett, on suspicion of being concerned in the Clerkenwell explosion ; and here also was executed Patrick O'Donnell for shooting James Carey, the informer.

Leaving Newgate we note at the top of the Old Bailey the site of GREEN ARBOUR-COURT, destroyed about twelve years ago, where Goldsmith lived for some time in great poverty, and where he wrote several of his works. Returning to Ludgate-hill, and proceeding eastwards, we pass such highly suggestive names as AVE MARIA-LANE and CREED-LANE, with PATERNOSTER-ROW and AMEN-CORNER close by, all referring to pre-Reformation days.

At the north-western corner of St. Paul's Churchyard stood the publishing house of NEWBERY, who published Goldsmith's finest works, buying " THE VICAR OF WAKEFIELD " from Dr Johnson almost at a glance, so great was his confidence in Johnson's judgment.

Close to this spot, in ST. PAUL'S SCHOOL (now removed), a very remarkable Irishman was educated. Apart from his great attainments as a statesman, SIR PHILIP FRANCIS is likely to descend to furthest posterity as the author of the " LETTERS OF JUNIUS," that remarkable series of political attacks on the Government of the time(1796). Although it is not absolutely certain that Francis wrote these letters, the balance of probability is heavily in his favour. It is curious that the most favoured candidates for having written them were five Irishmen—namely, Edmund Burke, Colonel Barré, Hugh M'Auley Boyd, Laurence Maclaine, and Sir Philip Francis. It has been proved that neither Burke nor Boyd could have written them, and there are grave doubts as to whether Barré or Maclaine had anything to do with their production. Sir Philip Francis, on the other hand, has very strong claims to the authorship, and has by far the largest number of believers in his identity with the mysterious JUNIUS.

SIR PHILIP FRANCIS.

In a court close to St. Paul's GERALD GRIFFIN once lodged, and it was here that John Banim was startled to hear from the landlady of the poet that Griffin had, apparently, scarcely tasted anything for days, and never went out until nightfall, being, in fact, on the road to starvation.

Close by the north door of the Cathedral was buried Colonel Edward Marcus Despard, a gallant Irish soldier, and brother of an officer still more celebrated. Despard was a native of Queen's County, and after a brilliant career in the British army became a conspirator, being moved thereto by what he considered unfair treatment in return for his many services. He was arrested and imprisoned for some years, and soon after his release, showing no friendlier disposition towards the Government, was rearrested, brought to trial for high-treason, and executed in 1803, at the age of 48. He had been the friend of such dissimilar personages as Lord Nelson and Lord Cloncurry.

Merely remarking that St. Paul's Cathedral will be dealt with in our next article, we pass round it and enter CANNON-STREET. Some distance down here, on the left, and facing the railway station, is ST. SWITHIN'S CHURCH. Fixed into its outer wall, and protected by iron railings, is a curious relic of the past—LONDON STONE. Anciently it was a kind of Roman milestone, and where it formerly stood, near the Mansion House, was a terminus from which all the great Roman roads radiated over England. This stone has, however, other memories. When JACK CADE entered London in 1450, he proceeded direct to this stone, and, placing his foot upon it, proclaimed himself Lord of the City. Readers of Shakespeare's "Henry VI., Part 2," will find the scene described there. By some Jack Cade is supposed to have been really an Irish physician named Aylmer; others believe him to have merely assumed that name and profession. He was finally slain, and his head impaled on one of the gates of old London Bridge, distant only a few yards from London Stone, the memento of his former triumphs.

By the side of LONDON BRIDGE is the HALL OF THE FISHMONGERS' COMPANY, one of the wealthiest of the city guilds, owning thousands of acres in Londonderry. THOMAS DOGGETT, the famous Irish actor, was a member of this company, and being a staunch Whig, left a sum of money to purchase a coat and badge to be rowed for by six young watermen of the Thames on each succeeding 1st of August, the anniversary of the accession of George I. This boat-race has now been run 167 times, and is annually witnessed by crowds of persons, who, perhaps, have but little notion of the origin of "Doggett's Coat and Badge."

Just past London Bridge, on the right, is FISH-STREET HILL, and, at the corner of MONUMENT-YARD here, Goldsmith acted as a chemist's assistant, but only for a short time, as his position was a miserable one.

A few steps along GREAT TOWER-STREET and we are on TOWER-HILL, where so many of the noblest, and also, indeed, of the vilest of mankind were executed. The Irishmen who suffered that fate here were unimportant, and do not deserve special mention.

Opposite TOWER-HILL is the vast pile of fortifications known as the TOWER OF LONDON. No spectator can view it without interest and wonder. Its Irish associations are of a uniformly dismal character. Before entering it, however, we must refer to an interesting place quite near its gates. THE MINT, where the coinage is carried on, is on our left as we emerge from Tower-street into the open space in front of the Tower. RICHARD LALOR SHEIL was Master of the Mint from 1846 to 1850, and the following incident is related of his administration. Some new florins were issued, and startled the public by the omission of the inscription surrounding the coin, which signified that Queen Victoria was "DEFENDER OF THE FAITH," &c. The omission was attributed to Sheil's Catholicism, but he effectually repudiated sectarian motives for

RICHARD LALOR SHEIL.
(From a bust.)

his action, and showed a precedent for it.

The Tower is, perhaps, next to Westminster Abbey, the most interesting edifice in London. Its oldest part was built by William the Conqueror in 1078, other monarchs adding to it, and since then it has been by turns a fortress, a Royal palace, and a prison, and part of it is now a barracks. From the time of its erection down to the reign of Charles II., it has been frequently used as a palace, and although in modern days it has not been much utilised as a prison, many famous Irishmen have "counted the weary years" within its walls, and in some cases have been put to death in one or other of its noisome dungeons. With the Tower as a royal residence or as a fortress we have nothing to do. As a prison, however, it has many interesting Irish associations.

The JEWEL-ROOM is generally the goal of most visitors, and is certainly worth making a long journey to visit. The Crown jewels are valued at about three millions sterling, and in speaking of them a very remarkable personage recurs to every student of history. The notorious attempt to steal the Crown jewels was made on the 9th May, 1671, by Colonel Thomas Blood, a desperado born in Ireland in 1628, the son of an ironmaster residing at Farney, in Meath. After

GENERAL VIEW OF THE TOWER OF LONDON.

an adventurous career as a soldier in the Parliamentary army, he quitted it and took to more reckless courses. His attempt to hang the Duke of Ormond in the London streets terrified some of the people in power, not excepting the weak King, Charles II. By a skilful *ruse* aided by several confederates, Blood managed to worm himself into the good graces of Edwards, the old keeper of the jewels. Under the pretext of wishing to see them, Blood induced the keeper to accompany himself and his friends into the Jewelroom, and when Edwards had locked the door on

THE BEAUCHAMP TOWER.

the inside, as was the custom, he was set upon by the confederates and rendered senseless. Luckily, however, his son arrived, and while Blood and his gang were packing up, the old man recovered strength enough to call out for help.

Seizing the Crown (the most valuable part of the collection), Blood tried to escape, but was caught. Strange to say, the daring of the attempt so alarmed the King that instead of being punished Blood was not only pardoned, but actually allowed a pension of £500 a year; and, stranger still, the old keeper, instead of receiving his legitimate pension when due, was almost allowed to die of destitution. So true is the statement of a great writer that wickedness done in a brilliant manner is always more appreciated than a benefaction silently performed.

The most remarkable of the Irish prisoners of the Tower was, perhaps, THOMAS FITZGERALD, 10th Earl of Kildare, or "SILKEN THOMAS," as he was more commonly styled. His history is well known to Irish readers; suffice it here to say that he and his five uncles, for the crime of high

THE TRAITORS' GATE—TOWER OF LONDON.

treason, were imprisoned in the Tower, and afterwards hanged and quartered at Tyburn in 1537. On the walls in one of the upper rooms of the BEAUCHAMP TOWER (between the last recess and the entrance to the cells) — where "Silken Thomas" passed the sixteen months of his confinement, and was treated in a barbarous manner —may be seen his autograph, roughly cut into the stone in the following fashion:—

AS : YT : IS : TAKY . .
THOMAS FITZGera——

Another notable prisoner was Richard Creagh, Archbishop of Armagh. He escaped once from the Tower, but was recaptured, and spent eighteen years there, dying after many sufferings in 1585, aged about sixty or thereabouts. Here also

Ireland in London.

suffered Thomas Butler, 10th Earl of Ormond, and his grandson Thomas, Earl of Ossory. Among the Desmonds who also tasted the horrors of the Tower were Gerald, the 15th Earl, and his brother, Sir John Desmond, both imprisoned for six years; and here also James, the 16th Earl, and the still greater "Sugan Earl," James, nephew of the 15th Earl, died and were buried.

In ST. PETER'S CHAPEL in the Tower are buried Gerald, the 8th Earl of Kildare, (father of Silken Thomas), and his grandson, the 9th Earl.

In the Tower were also imprisoned Gerald, the 11th Earl of Kildare, and his family; Donough M'Carthy, 4th Earl of Clancarty (who escaped once and was retaken); Connor Maguire, Baron of Enniskillen, and his friend, Captain MacMahon, who were imprisoned for complicity in the rising of 1641, and who both escaped, but were again captured, and were executed at Tyburn; Niall Garv O'Donnell and his son (the former for eighteen years). Con O'Neill, son of the great Hugh, died here; and here also were imprisoned Richard Talbot, the great Duke of Tyrconnell, one of the finest soldier-statesmen Ireland ever produced, and the Irish Earls of Tyrone and Orrery.

Another great Irishman, Sir James Ware, the distinguished writer, suffered ten months' imprisonment in the Tower at the hands of the Parliamentarians for his Royalist principles. We have only to mention a few other famous Irishmen of more modern times before we take leave of the Tower's prisoners. In 1798 the noted United Irishman, Arthur O'Connor, who afterwards became an eminent French General, was brought here in company with his fellow "rebels"— John Allen, John Binns, and James O'Coigly. In the same year the Tower received Lord Cloncurry as a prisoner. He was suspected of being a United Irishman, and was arrested whilst in London studying at the Temple. The Duke of Leinster (father of Lord Edward

ARTHUR O'CONNOR
(From Madden's "Lives of United Irishmen.")

Fitzgerald), Henry Grattan, and John Philpot Curran, who happened to be visiting Lord Cloncurry, were also arrested on suspicion and conveyed to the Tower, but were almost immediately liberated.

The above list is not a complete one, but the most important of the Irishmen who have passed

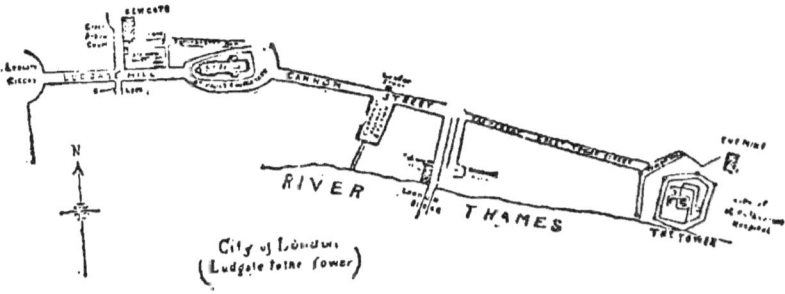

the "Traitors' Gate"—"that gate misnamed"—have been specified. They were all distinguished in some way, and their only crime appears to have been a disposition to resent tyranny

The Tower possesses few relics of peculiar importance to Irishmen, although the axes and other such instruments of death or torture have doubtless been used on many of the Irish inmates of the place. One part, the Broad-arrow Tower, was specially reserved for priests, a very significant fact. On the staircase leading to the White Tower may be seen a very interesting object—a sword shown as William Smith O'Brien's. In the Horse Armoury are some old Irish weapons, dug up near the Giant's Causeway, and here also may be seen the uniform worn by Wellington as Constable of the Tower.

Irish visitors should not fail to explore every

accessible corner of this hoary pile, and they may rest assured they will not want food for thought as their eyes wander over the dark cells, the occasional inscriptions, and the rusty and dust-covered weapons and implements, not to speak of the priceless treasures that abound here.

CHAPTER IV.

IRISH ASSOCIATIONS OF THE CITY PROPER.—ST. PAUL'S CATHEDRAL AND ITS IRISH MEMORIALS— IRISH OBJECTS IN THE GUILDHALL—IRISH ART AT THE MANSION HOUSE—THE ROYAL EXCHANGE, ETC.

ALMOST facing the rear of Newgate Prison, and lying some distance back from NEW-GATE-STREET, whence we start for our second peregrination through the city, is a splendid old building known as Christ's Hospital. In ancient times this was a monastery of Grey Friars; it is now a school for the sons of well-to-do tradesmen and others, having been diverted from its founder's intention to endow it as a charity-school for friendless boys. In the Dining-hall is a very notable picture by a distinguished painter, John Singleton Copley, R.A., depicting the narrow escape from a shark of one of the scholars (who afterwards became Lord Mayor of London). Copley was American by birth, but of purely Irish parentage, and his paintings are generally considered masterly.

Where Newgate-street ends and Cheapside begins is St. Martin's-le-Grand, on the left, with, on the right of the way, the GENERAL POST OFFICE, in connection with which it is a curious fact that, in 1603, the revenues of the Post Office were "farmed" for the sum of £21,000 by one Daniel O'Neill, whose worldly means and business enterprise must have been considerable, and whose nationality is certainly unmistakable.

The continuation of St. Martin's-le-Grand is ALDERSGATE-STREET. In Aldersgate Church there is a fine stained-glass altar-window, executed by an Irish artist, John Pearson, who became well known in the last century as a distinguished painter on glass.

Returning to CHEAPSIDE, the first turning on the left is FOSTER-LANE. Here is the Hall of the Goldsmiths' Company, which possesses two of the best works of Sir Martin Archer Shee, P.R.A.— namely, a portrait of Queen Adelaide and

DR. CROLY.

one of William IV. Shee was a very fashionable painter at the beginning of the century, and so highly esteemed by his brother-artists that his election to the Presidency of the Royal Academy was unanimous—an event of rare occurrence. He was essentially a portrait-painter, and many of his best works are to be found in various parts of London. Crossing Cheapside, from Foster-lane. we are in view of ST. PAUL'S CATHEDRAL. Before ascending the flight of steps in front, however, we cannot omit to notice the group of sculpture outside. It was executed by Francis Bird, one of the early English sculptors, and represents Queen Anne on a pedestal, surrounded by more than life-size figures of Britain, America, France, and Ireland—the last-named country being figured as a beautiful female with flowing tresses, and bearing a harp of somewhat small dimensions.

The vast Cathedral of St. Paul's, Sir Christopher Wren's noblest and greatest work, was built in the seventeenth century, the ancient edifice having been destroyed in the Great Fire. Many interesting incidents that occurred in the older Cathedral might be enumerated, but one or two will suffice. Thus: it was in St. Paul's that King John, in 1213, acknowledged the supremacy of the Pope; and it was in the same building that Cardinal Wolsey publicly burnt the Protestant Bible on Shrove Tuesday, 1527. Under the Commonwealth, the soldiers of Cromwell stabled their horses in the nave of St. Paul's, as if to show their contempt for sacred edifices. The present building is erected on the site of the ancient one. Though not nearly so crowded with tombs and monuments as Westminster Abbey, the Cathedral contains the remains of many of the greatest men these islands have produced. Irishmen, of course, form a goodly proportion of the number. Here, in the Artists' Corner, by the side of Reynolds, Wren, Lawrence, Turner, Opie, and West, lies the greatest of Irish sculptors, John Henry Foley, R.A.; while not far off rests another great Irish artist—James Barry, R A., the famous allegorical painter. And, if an eminent authority is to be believed, here also reposes the dust of Sir Martin Archer Shee, though he is commonly thought to be buried at Brighton. The great majority of the tombs and monuments of St. Paul's are those of naval and military heroes. Among the Irish soldiers commemorated here is Sir Robert Rollo Gillespie, a native of county Down, and a brilliant general. His statue, by Chantrey, is a conspicuous ornament. Here also is the statue of a still greater Irishman—Sir William Francis Napier, the famous historian, whose "History of the Peninsular War" is the best of all military histories. Napier was born near Dublin in 1785, and died in Clapham in 1860. His statue is by Adams, as is also that, close by, of his brother, "the hero of Scinde." The magnificent tomb of the Duke of Wellington, by a gifted sculptor of the modern school, is also well worth particular mention. The tracery on this tomb was executed by a clever Irish artist named Doherty, who has executed some fine works in London and elsewhere. Sir Arthur Wellesley Torrens, who fell at Inkerman in 1854, is here honoured by a bas-relief, sculptured by an eminent artist, Baron Marochetti. Among other famous Irish soldiers whose tombs or monuments are in St. Paul's are several who, if space allowed, would call for detailed notice. Sir Henry Lawrence, of Lucknow fame, was the son of an Irish soldier,

GEN. GILLESPIE.

a native of Ulster, but was born in India. As an administrator and as a soldier he ranks exceptionally high, while most of his brothers and descendants were also notable by their achievements as statesmen and soldiers. Other Irish soldiers commemorated here are Sir John Byrne Skerritt (with statue by Chantrey), General Sir W. Ponsonby, who fell at Waterloo (with a grace-

ST. PAUL'S.

ful monument by E. H. Baily, R.A.), and General Sir Edward Pakenham, whose death, at the age of 36, while leading the attack on New Orleans, January 8th, 1815, was a particularly heavy blow to the English Army. His statue, by Sir Richard Westmacott, is well worthy of that sculptor's fame. Several other Irish soldiers of lesser note have their monuments here, including one, the most recent of all, to Sir Herbert Stewart, who was of a Kerry family, and whose career in the Soudan was so brilliant and of such brief duration.

A memorial here which will attract the visitor's particular attention is that to the war correspondents killed in the Soudan, among whom two Irish names stand pre-eminent. Edmund O'Donovan and Frank Power are fitly honoured by the memorial brass to their memory and that of their colleagues being placed among the monuments of the most illustrious dead of the United Kingdom.

The fine statue to Dr. William Babington (who will be presently referred to) is a worthy recognition of the great labours in science of a distinguished Irishman.

Among the monuments in St. Paul's there are two executed by Irish artists which deserve a passing reference. One is the splendid statue to Turner, the great landscapist, by Patrick M'Dowell, R.A., one of the best of the modern sculptors of Ireland. The other work is the monument of Sir Thomas Picton, which was executed by Sebastian Gahagan, one of a family of good Irish sculptors and modellers.

Leaving St. Paul's and returning to Cheapside, we reach WOOD-STREET, on the left, and St. Michael's Church, noteworthy as being a place where Dr. Nicholas Brady, the divine and poet, frequently preached. He is chiefly known from his translation, in conjunction with Nahum Tate, of the Psalms.

A short distance past Wood-street is MILK-STREET, at the bottom of which, in the turning known as Aldermanbury, stands the Church of St. Mary the Virgin. Here is buried the Dr. Babington above mentioned. This celebrated man was a native of Portglenone, county Antrim, was born in 1756, and died in 1833. As a mineralogist, chemist, and geologist, Dr. Babington was almost unrivalled, his contributions to his favourite sciences being many and valuable.

In Cheapside are situated the Mercers' Chapel and the Hall of the Saddlers' Company. In the first-named is buried James Butler, one of the Earls of Ormond (1428), and also his wife (1430). The Saddlers' Hall possesses one of Thomas Frye's finest works, a full-length portrait of Frederick, Prince of Wales. Frye was one of the best Irish artists of the eighteenth century. He is believed to have been the first in England to paint on porcelain, while both as a mezzotint engraver and portrait-painter he is very highly praised.

Passing Bow Church, with its beautiful steeple by Wren, and its famous bells, only within the sound of which true Cockneys are born, we come to KING-STREET, on the left. At the end of this street is situated the Guildhall of London, belonging to the Corporation. This great and ancient civic hall well deserves a visit, if only on account of its magnificent library, which is perfectly free to all persons on entering their names in the visitors' book. It contains many Irish works— its most valuable possessions relating to Ireland being, perhaps, " The Annals of the Four

SIR H. LAWRENCE.

Masters," and the publications of the Irish Archæological and Ossianic Societies, and other works of a kindred nature.

Among other objects of interest in the Guildhall are several specimens of Irish art. In the Common Council Chamber are Copley's great picture, " The Siege of Gibraltar," his portrait of Lord Cornwallis, and an excellent bust of the Duke of Wellington by Peter Turnerelli. Turnerelli, an exceedingly clever sculptor, was a native of Belfast, his father being an Italian modeller, and his mother a native of the chief city of the North. Some of his works are truly admirable : he excelled in portrait-busts. He was greatly patronised by Royalty and various eminent persons, and so admired was his celebrated and life-like bust of George III. that he had to execute no fewer than eighty copies of it (one of them being in the Trinity House on Tower Hill).

In the Waiting-room are to be seen the enormous pictures by Sir Robert Ker Porter, entitled respectively, " The Siege of Acre," and " The Battle of Agincourt." The painter was very highly esteemed during the early part of the century, and it is interesting to know that the picture last named, which was finished before Porter was nineteen years of age, owed not a little of its general excellence to the fact that William Mulready, the greatest of Irish painters, then (1808) unknown, assisted him in its production. Porter was born in England, of Irish parents, his sisters being the well-known novelists, Jane and Anna Porter.

In the same room as the above pictures is a splendid folding-screen, a veritable masterpiece, said to be painted by Copley. In the Guildhall are also a grand monument to Wellington, and others equally fine to Nelson, Chatham, and Pitt, the inscriptions upon which were written by three notable Irishmen—Sheridan, Burke, and Canning respectively.

Finally, at the entrance to the library is a fine bust of Sir Andrew Lusk (a recent Lord Mayor) by H. P. M'Carthy, an Irish sculptor.

Returning to the main street, we leave Cheapside after a few paces, and enter the POULTRY, a continuation of the former thoroughfare. On the left is Grocer's Hall Court, where lived for a time in great destitution Samuel Boyse, the poet. Like many other Irish writers of his time, he seems to have been unjustly neglected by his contemporaries, for his poetical gifts were of a somewhat high order, and won the admiration of Henry Fielding, the novelist, and a few other great writers. On the right, as we emerge in view of the Mansion House, Bank of England, and Royal Exchange, is WALBROOK, a turning running by the side of the first-named building. Here is St. Stephen's Church, one of the grandest churches in England, where Dr. Croly, its celebrated rector, is buried Croly was a distinguished Irish poet and dramatist, and exquisite prose writer, and earned a solid and wide reputation as a clergyman of active industry and vivid eloquence. His monument, by J. B. Philip, R. A., is in the church, as also a fine marble bust presented to him during his lifetime by his parishioners; while several stained-glass windows have been also placed here to his memory.

The MANSION HOUSE is noteworthy as being the residence of the Lord Mayors, and as the repository of some magnificent examples of Irish art. We have already referred to the fact

MANSION HOUSE.

that even the Mayoralty had not been inaccessible to Irishmen, and gave as an instance the name of Sir William M'Arthur. But in reality there has been more than one Irish Lord Mayor, for in the reign of Henry the Seventh, in the year 1485, the Chief Magistrate of London was an Irishman named Hugh Brice or Bryce. Only recently, too, another Irishman (Sir William Lawrence) has held that once exalted position. Besides the names just mentioned, there are also others on the list of Lord Mayors which have an Irish appearance, though it is difficult to say whether the bearers were Irish or not. Thus, there have been Lord Mayors with such names as Michael Thovey in 1244 and 1248, Stephen Slany in 1595, William Gill in 1788, Sir Richard Welch in 1802, Thomas Kelly in 1833, Sir George Carroll in 1837, and also other names like Huyes, Bryan, &c., among the High Sheriffs.

Inside the Mansion House Irish art is splendidly represented by some of the finest works of Foley and M'Dowell. The former's beautiful

"Caractacus," "Egeria," and "Elder Brother in 'Comus,'"

JAMES QUIN.

rank beside the noblest of London's artistic possessions. No British sculptor, with the single exception, perhaps, of Flaxman, has produced, in modern days, such wonderful works. Foley's genius may be said to be nowhere seen to better advantage than in the Egyptian Hall of the Mansion House which contains many other fine pieces of modern sculpture. Among them is the "Leah" of Patrick M'Dowell, R.A., a Belfast man, than whom no more gifted artist could be found to worthily fill one of the niches of this hall. His works, more truly than those of other great sculptors, are genuinely poetical conceptions in themselves, altogether apart from his exceptionally fine and imaginative treatment of his subjects. His female figures are generally considered the best efforts of his genius. It is much to be regretted that the sculpture of the Mansion House is not in some easily accessible building

Exactly facing The Poultry, and standing between Cornhill and Threadneedle-street, is the ROYAL EXCHANGE, with an equestrian statue in front, by Chantrey, of the "Iron Duke." The Royal Arms in massive-relief, finely sculptured, is the work of John Edward Carew, an excellent sculptor, and a native of Waterford. He was born in 1785 or thereabouts and died somewhat recently. Much of his best work is in private collections, though there are a few examples in London public institutions. Carew was very highly esteemed as a sculptor, and the flattering opinions held of him by such artists as Sir Francis Chantrey and Sir Richard Westmacott were certainly fully deserved. On the North side of the Exchange, and overlooking Threadneedle-street, is Carew's statue of Sir Richard Whittington, 'thrice Lord Mayor of London"—the hero of famous nursery tales and rhymes. The romantic stories current of Dick Whittington are not, however, strictly true —he was not poor, as the legend goes, but the son of a wealthy knight, Sir William Whittington.

Carew's statue is excellent, but the climate or the dust and smoke of London have given it an appearance of great antiquity.

It is interesting to note that the original proprietor of the Gresham Hotel in Dublin was an *enfant trouvé* found on the steps of the Royal Exchange, and who, taking the name of Sir Thomas Gresham, the greatest city magnate of that time, rose afterwards to affluence in the Irish capital.

On the right of the Exchange is CORNHILL, which has some very interesting Irish associations. One of the most noted frequenters of the Fleece Tavern, which stood here, was James Quin, the great comedian. It was in Cornhill, at the Pope's Head Tavern (on the site of the present POPE'S HEAD ALLEY), that Quin killed his fellow-countryman and brother actor, Bowen—an excellent performer. Though of an exceedingly generous disposition, Quin could not resist uttering the many sarcastic words which frequently came to his tongue, and was, as a consequence,

THE GUILDHALL.

frequently involved in quarrels. His encounter with Bowen was owing to slight causes, and as he was furiously attacked by the latter with a sword, Quin was compelled to draw, and being an expert swordsman, gave Bowen a mortal wound. It was also in Cornhill, in 1798, that William Putman M'Cabe, the famous United Irishman, was attacked by the police, but, after a brief struggle, baffled them with his usual luck and daring, and escaped arrest. It was probably his reckless boldness and determination to fulfil his mission which led him so often to London at the risk of death, and may have helped him eventually to escape the many perils by which he was surrounded.

LEADENHALL-STREET is a continuation of Corn-

SIR W. M'ARTHUR.

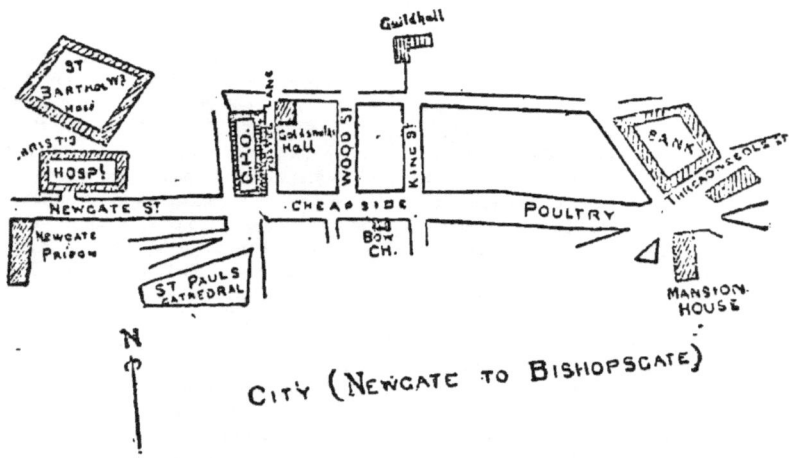

CITY (NEWGATE TO BISHOPSGATE)

hill. On the left is the Church of St. Katherine Cree, of which the most prominent rector has been the Dr. Nicholas Brady above referred to. Threadneedle-street runs from the Bank of England to Bishopsgate-street. In the Hall of the Merchant Taylors, which is in the former street, may be seen Wilkie's splendid portrait of Wellington, and among the magnificent collection of plate here are some very curious and valuable old Irish silver tankards of 1683. Off BISHOPSGATE-STREET is Gresham College (BASINGHALL-STREET), where the Royal Society was started in 1663. Its first President, Sir William Brouncker, an Irishman, and others of his countrymen who afterwards became Presidents, such as Robert Boyle, Hans Sloane, and Lord Carbery, were frequent visitors here.

In completing our survey of the City, we have only to add that not a few of its most successful business men have been Irish. As a mere list of names would be of little use or interest, it will, perhaps, be better to mention only one conspicuous instance, which will, perhaps, effectually disperse the doubts that exist in many persons' minds as to the commercial capabilities of Irishmen. The late Mr. M'Calmont, brother of Lord Cairns, was one of the richest men the City has ever produced, and worth millions when he died. And, as there have been several Irish Lord Mayors, as every Lord Mayor must necessarily be a successful city man, it is clear that M'Calmont was not the only Irishman who has acquired great wealth and great influence in the ancient and teeming City of London.

CHAPTER V.

THE STRAND AND ITS IRISH ASSOCIATIONS.—FROM TEMPLE BAR TO THE ADELPHI.

OUR first chapter on the London streets concluded with a notice of the Temple and its famous students and residents. The hideous "Griffin" memorial which marks the site of Old Temple Bar, also marks the termination of Fleet street and the commencement of the STRAND. Standing at Temple Bar and looking west, we have on our right the splendid buildings, only recently erected, known as the Law Courts, which are finely situated near the most important abodes of legal learning in London. Although the Law Courts can boast of few historical associations, many famous lawyers have been connected with them during their brief existence; and they have been the scene of some important trials. It is, strictly speaking, within their walls that Sir Charles Russell has won his great forensic triumphs, and that several other great Irish lawyers have earned distinction. One of the most successful of the advocates of the day is Mr. Gerald Geoghegan, who has acted in more than one cause celebre. This distinguished lawyer is a member of both the Irish and the English Bar, and it will interest many lovers of Irish literature to learn that he is the son of the well-known poet, Arthur Gerald Geoghegan, author of the celebrated poem, " The Monks of Kilcrea," and of many stirring bal- lads. The Law Courts being a recent addition to the architectural beauties of London, there are few direct or personal Irish associations to be recorded in connection with them. We will leave them, therefore, with the remark that when the "Parnell Commission," now sitting there, is at an end, and the chief actors in the momentous trial shall have passed away, the Law Courts will, in years to come, be indisputably a spot instinct with Irish memories.

Opposite the central doorway of the Law Courts is a small turning or alley, called DEVEREUX COURT. A few yards down this court, on the right hand side, stood at one time the famous *Grecian Coffee-house*. Its place is now occupied by a tavern, and its site marked by the bust, placed some height from the ground, of Robert Devereux, Earl of Essex. The "Grecian" had many Irish frequenters, and it was especially notable as the resort of the great Irishmen residing or studying in The Temple. The first number of *The Spectator*—that mine of delightful thought and lofty teaching, and the foundation of English periodical literature—was addressed from this coffee-house by *The Spectator* himself—Sir Richard Steele, the gentle essayist and dramatist. To the "Grecian" frequently came Goldsmith, to play whist ; and here he often delighted the assembled company by his performances on the flute. The pleasure he caused, and the applause he evoked, were doubtless gratifying to the simple-hearted poet, but the remembrance of his previous wanderings on foot through France and Italy, with his flute, in search of a livelihood, must often have been present to his mind. Finally, it was from the "Grecian" that John O'Keeffe, the inimitable farce-writer and wit, sent his first piece to George Colman, the manager of the Haymarket Theatre, and had the satisfaction of finding it accepted. The career thus opened proved beneficial both to O'Keeffe himself and to the dramatic literature of the 18th century.

On the evening when Goldsmith was presented a worthy and well-to-do baker was president, whose grave and judicial aspect, and air of great importance so impressed Goldsmith that he whispered to Derrick his opinion that "the chairman must be a lord-chancellor at least." "No," returned Derrick, softly, "not exactly; he's only a *master of the rolls!*"

Facing Essex-street is the church of St. Clement Danes, one of the most prominent rectors of which was Dr. George Berkeley, the son of the great Irish philosopher and Bishop of Cloyne. In the church, or in the narrow strip of churchyard surrounding it, lies buried Charles Coffey, an

NEW LAW COURTS.

A few paces beyond Devereux-court is Essex-Street, with the office of the *Freeman's Journal* at the corner. As the chief London office of the oldest and greatest of Irish newspapers, it has necessarily had many interesting Irish associations, which, however, it is needless to particularise here. Essex-street is well known to readers of the lives of Burke, Goldsmith, and Johnson. Here were held the meetings of the Robin Hood Debating Society, of which the above writers, as well as Arthur Murphy and other Irishmen of note, were members. A humorous anecdote is related of Goldsmith's first visit to the society. He was introduced by Samuel Derrick, an Irish wit and poet,

cellent Irish farce writer, and author of one of the most amusing pieces ever written, "The Devil to Pay," which has held the stage for more than a hundred years. St. Clements was the favourite place of worship of Dr Johnson, and the inscription on the tablet erected to his memory over the pew he used to occupy, was, it is interesting to note, written by Dr. George Croly, the well known poet.

Arundel-street is but a few yards farther on, on the left, and on entering it we come upon some very interesting facts. In a house which stood on the site of the Temple Club, the Catholic Association used to meet during the struggle for

Emancipation. O'Connell was, of course, a frequent visitor, and the rooms very often resounded with the echoes of his splendid accents. Richard Lalor Sheil, Lord Cloncurry, and other distinguished Irishmen also spoke here occasionally. In the Crown and Anchor Tavern, which occupied the site of the present Courts of Justice Hotel, O'Connell often pleaded his country's cause and denounced her enemies. On the 21st of January, 1838, he was entertained here at a banquet, the chairman being a distinguished Irish soldier, General Sir De Lacy Evans, a native of

O'CONNELL.

Limerick, and M.P. at the time for Westminster. The speech of The Liberator on this occasion, in which he accused the members of the Parliamentary Committees of perjury, drew down upon him the wasted censure of the House of Commons.

In May, 1841, a great Repeal meeting was held here, when O'Connell spoke lengthily and eloquently on the burning question of the hour. At the "Crown and Anchor" used also to meet a club, under the title of "The King of Clubs," among the habitués of which was John Philpot Curran, with whose life, oratory, and wit everyone is more or less familiar.

In SURREY-STREET, a little further on the left, died, in 1729, the great dramatist, William Congreve. There is great doubt as to his birthplace. Several writers, notably Charles Anderson Read, in his comprehensive "Cabinet of Irish Literature," and Mr. Halliday Sparling, in his "Irish Minstrelsy," most emphatically deny that he was born in England, but that he allowed his biographer to place his birth in Yorkshire. On the other hand, it seems pretty clear, from the baptismal entry in the parish church of Bardsey, in that county, that he was born there, while the same town is given as his natal place in the books of Trinity College, Dublin, whither he was sent on leaving school. But wheresoever born it is certain he was educated in Ireland, first at Kilkenny School and afterwards at Trinity College, and his superior classical knowledge, as compared with that of most of his contemporaries, was certainly due, as Lord Macaulay candidly admits, to his Irish education. Apart from his eminence as a writer, and his supposed Irish birth, he does not deserve the kindly remembrance of Irishmen, for his character was a contemptible one. He was, if recorded statements be true, as much ashamed of his profession as he was of his country, and wished to be known only as "an English gentleman." When Voltaire was in London and visited Congreve, for whose plays he entertained high admiration, the latter particularly impressed upon the French wit the necessity of not referring to his productions, because he wished to be considered as "a gentleman," and not as a great dramatist. This miserable plea called forth from Voltaire the obvious retort that if he had known that Congreve was merely "a gentleman" he should not have taken the trouble to call upon him.

Just past Surrey-street, and still on the left, is the STRAND THEATRE. It is notable as being the spot on which the first panorama was exhibited. Its inventor, Robert Barker, a distinguished Irish artist, was a native of Kells, county Meath. He was born in 1739, and died in 1806. The first thought of his invention occurred to him whilst sitting on Calton Hill, in Edinburgh, and he carried it out most successfully, exhibiting it, when completed, at 169 Strand, now the Strand Theatre.

STEELE.

KING'S COLLEGE, still on the left, is only noticeable as possessing Peter Turnerelli's fine statuette of George III.

The splendid building close by, on the same side of the way, known as SOMERSET HOUSE, is interesting to Irishmen for several reasons. In the old palace of Charles II., which stood on its site, the body of the great Archbishop Ussher lay in state, previous to burial in Westminster Abbey. In the

Ireland in London.

quadrangle of the present building are six colossal statues, each 7ft 6in in height, emblematical of the principal cities and towns in the United Kingdom. Two of them represent Dublin and Belfast. In Somerset House may be seen the wills of many famous Irishmen, including Burke and Wellington, and Richard Cantillon, the father of political economy, whose Irish origin is not sufficiently well known.

Facing Somerset House, and by the side of the church of St. Mary-le-Strand, is DRURY-LANE. This dingy and gloomy thoroughfare, which is at present, with its outlying narrow courts and alleys, the resort of the poorest Irish in London, was once a fashionable place of residence, especially in the reign of Elizabeth. It received its name from the town house, which stood there, of Sir William Drury, Lord Deputy of Ireland, in the 16th century. It has had few well-known Irish residents, perhaps the most celebrated of them being Walter, the eleventh Earl of Ormond, a distinguished soldier, who lived here in 1625; and Connor Maguire, Baron of Enniskillen, and his friend Captain M'Mahon. The two last escaped from the Tower on the 18th of August, 1643, and lay hid in a house in Drury-lane until the 20th of October, on which day one of them happening to call out after an oysterman in the street, his voice was recognised by some of his enemies, and the fugitives were soon after recaptured and executed.

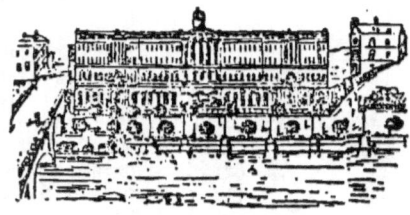

SOMERSET HOUSE.

Off Drury-lane, at the northern corner of Vere-street, in October, 1869, a man was thrown out of a cab and severely injured, and, on the police asking his name, feebly replied "Kelly." The police, at the time eagerly on the look-out for Colonel Kelly, one of the Fenians rescued from the prison van in Manchester, immediately concluded that they had effected a magnificent capture, and roughly hauled off the injured man to prison, instead of to hospital, with the result that his death shortly ensued. Evidence was given at the inquest on his remains that he had gone by name of Edward Martin. The Irish of London, however, partly to draw the authorities off the scent of the Fenian leader, and partly to show their resentment at the conduct of the police, organised a monster funeral, and on the 10th October, an orderly procession of some 20,000 respectably-clad Irishmen and women, augmented by contingents along the way, conveyed the remains of the deceased from Lincoln's Inn, through the principal streets, to Stratford Churchyard. Nearly opposite Drury-

BARRY.

lane, and just past Somerset House, is a tailor's shop with the words " Formerly Holyland's " on the name-board outside. This is very probably the house where O'Connell was arrested on the morning of the 19th September, 1815, just previous to starting off for Calais in order to fight a duel with Sir Robert Peel, whom he had challenged. He was taken before the magistrates and bound over in very heavy sums to keep the peace.

On the right, in WELLINGTON-STREET, is the LYCEUM THEATRE. For some years this theatre was managed by an excellent Irish actor, dramatist, and poet named John Brougham, who was born in Dublin in 1814, and died in 1880. His connection with the "Lyceum" began in 1840. He is supposed to have been the original of Lever's "Harry Lorrequer," and, whether the supposition be correct or not, he certainly resembled Lever's creation in many respects. His excellent comedies and farces, notably " Playing with Fire," are likely to endure on the stage for a long time.

The "Lyceum" is noteworthy on another account. Behind its stage used to be held the meetings of the famous BEEFSTEAK CLUB, among the earliest members of which were the Duke of Leinster and Richard Brinsley Sheridan. The latter's name will occur so frequently and prominently henceforward in these articles that we may safely say he was, perhaps, of all Irishmen the most intimately connected with London. There are few leading thoroughfares that do not possess some remembrance of this greatest of Irish dramatists, this brilliant orator, sparkling wit, and graceful poet.

Other famous Irishmen and women were connected with the Beefsteak Club. Among them were Arthur Murphy, the dramatist, and Mrs. Jordan, the great actress, a native of Waterford, and the "finest Rosalind that ever trod the stage." Lacy Ryan and Jack Johnstone (known as "Irish Johnstone"), two inimitable Irish comedians, were also among its members.

SHERIDAN.

John Binns, the United Irishman, who in after life became one of the greatest of American journalists, had a lecture-room in the Strand, which was a great resort of his fellow-countrymen and brother Nationalists during the '98 movement. Its exact position is nowhere stated. Binns was only 26 years of age when arrested and taken to the Tower on a charge of high treason.

Passing SOUTHAMPTON-STREET on the right, where Congreve lived for some time, we reach BEDFORD-STREET, near the Adelphi and Vaudeville Theatres. In this street lived James Quin and Thomas Sheridan, the two great actors. Quin, who resided here from 1749 to 1752, is universally admitted to have been the greatest of all impersonators of Falstaff, and he was also a good tragic actor. We shall deal with the histrionic triumphs of these and other Irish actors in future articles; at present it is sufficient to say of Sheridan that, though his innovations in acting and elocution were ridiculed in their day, as all innovations are, they are now considered excellent, and their author is accounted one of the truly great actors of the 18th century. It may be added that he was a native of the county Cavan.

Opposite the Adelphi Theatre is Adam-street, leading to ADELPHI-TERRACE. The Greek word "Adelphi," meaning "brothers," has reference to four brothers, Scotch architects, of the surname of Adam, who built, on a series of arches, the principal streets about here, on the south side of the Strand. The fine Adelphi-terrace, fronting the river, is justly considered an ornament of architecture. Part of this neighbourhood is built on the site of Durham House, the ancient residence of the Bishops of Durham. DURHAM-STREET occupies the site of what was known as the New Exchange, one of those covered thoroughfares, or "arcades," so common in Paris. It was simply a row of shops, kept chiefly by milliners; and here a clever Irish poet of the 17th century, Thomas Duffett, had a shop for the sale of millinery. His poems are now little known, though his "Come all you pale lovers," and "Since Celia's my foe," are excellent songs, and bear a favourable comparison with the poetical productions of his day. Nothing is known of Duffett's early life or of his later years. In the New Exchange, also, after the fall of James II., and the consequent decline of her family fortunes, the widow of Talbot, the great Duke of Tyrconnell, acted as a seamstress, wearing a white mask, so that she might not be recognised by friends or enemies. She was eventually discovered, however, and taken care of by her friends.

In JOHN-STREET, Adelphi, are the rooms of the Society of Arts, where the greatest works of James Barry, R.A., the painter, are to be seen. All the best authorities admit that although his treatment of his subjects is at times a little grotesque, and even ludicrously absurd, his conceptions are in general grand, and occasionally sublime. His paintings are so important and his eccentricities so strange that we may be pardoned for dealing with his life and works at some length. Were it not for his hot temper, carelessness, and irritability, he might have ended his days in luxury, surrounded by "troops of friends," and all that "should accompany old age" and genius, instead of dying, as he did, poor and neglected. He was born in Cork on the 11th of October, 1741. After some success in Dublin as a painter, he was taken under the patronage of Edmund Burke, who first brought him to England, and afterwards sent him to Rome at his expense. Barry became a member of several famous bodies, both in England and Italy, and in 1772 became A.R.A.—an Associate of the Royal Academy. In the following year he was elected a full R.A. Such speedy recognition by fellow academicians has very rarely occurred; Mulready being another of the few so highly honoured. Barry exhibited at the Royal Academy for the first time in 1770. In 1782 he was appointed professor of painting at the academy. but he was so quarrelsome and independent that he was finally expelled from that body in 1799. The Society of Arts, wishing to have their great room decorated by the principal artists of the day, approached eight of them for that purpose, Barry among the rest. The result was a refusal on the part of Sir Joshua Reynolds, and the others followed his example. However, three years after (in 1777), Barry offered to do the work by himself, gratuitously, on condition that the society should pay for colours, frames. and other materials. His models cost £30, and this Barry offered to pay out o. his own pocket. Before learning the name of the artist the committe accepted this magnanimous and disinterested offer. It will hardly be credited that when he commenced the work Barry only possessed sixteen shilings, having been unable to raise a loan. During the six years he was engaged

are portraits of Edmund Burke and Keane Fitzgerald. In the sixth picture, as Barry himself says, are "brought together those great and good men of all ages and nations who have acted as the cultivators of mankind." Among the great number of persons, ancient and modern, represented are William Molyneux, the patriot, holding in his hand his gieat work, the " Case for Ireland Stated ;" Robert Boyle, the famous chemist; Ossian, Swift, Sterne, and Goldsmith Barry himself is represented in the third picture, seated at the base of the statue of Hercules. In a corner of the sixth picture, where the famous poets, painters, and sages are congregated, is represented Tartarus, where (to again quote the painter's description) " two large hands are seen. one of them holding a fire-fork, the other pulling down a number of figures hound together by serpents, representing War, Gluttony, Extravagance, Detraction, Parsimony, and Ambition; and, floating

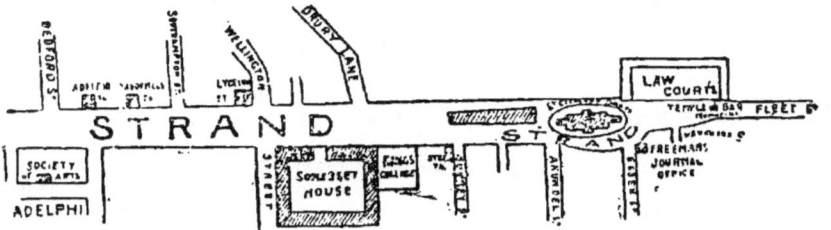

n painting the six great pictures he supported himself by etching.

The pictures when exhibited were greatly appreciated. The two largest are each 42it long ; the others are smaller in size. Their subjects— representing the growth or evolution of Happiness—are as follows : —I. " Man in the Savage State ;" II. " A Grecian Harvest Home ;" III. " The Victor at Olympia ;" IV. " Navigation ; or, the Triumphs of the Thames :" V. " The Distribution of the Society's Rewards." and, VI. " Elysium ; or, The State of Final Retribution." Three of these pictures are poetical in subject ; the other three may be called historical. Barry made the supreme mistake of introducing portraits of living celebrities into strange places in his pictures. Thus, in the fourth picture, his friend, Dr. Burney, the musician, is represented as a sea nymph(!)—a kind of personification of Harmony. In the fifth picture, Arthur Young, the friend of Ireland and a famous writer on agricultural matters, is represented as a farmer carrying specimens of various seeds. In the same picture

down the fiery gulph are Tyranny, Hypocrisy, and Cruelty, with their proper attributes." The greatest of German art critics, De Waagen, has spoken in high terms of the sublimity of conception and the frequent beauty of expression displayed in these paintings. Canova, the great Italian sculptor, when in London, said of the " Victors at Olympia "that if he had known of the existence of such a work while in Italy he would have come to England specially to see it. Besides his greatest works, there are here many of Barry'se tchings, and also his portrait and that of his mother, both painted by himself. A bust of the great artist is also to be seen in the rooms. In conclusion, it should be mentioned that before its burial in St. Paul's Cathedral his body lay in state in the great room here, among his magnificent works.

Altogether the collection forms one of the most interesting sights of London ; and as it is perfectly free and open every day of the week, Irishmen should make it a point to see these masterpieces of Irish artistic genius.

CHAPTER VI.

THE STRAND AND ITS IRISH ASSOCIATIONS.—FROM THE ADELPHI TO ST. GILES'S.

CLOSE to ADELPHI-TERRACE, and on the same side of the Strand, is CECIL-STREET, where a once famous Irish orator and politician died, on the 8th of August, 1837. "Honest" John Lawless, as he was called on account of his invincible probity, was born in or about 1772, and became a prominent journalist and politician. He was greatly admired by the majority of his contemporaries, but having believed O'Connell wrong on the question of enfranchising the "forty shilling freeholders" he opposed him, and consequently incurred his enmity. Besides his qualifications as an orator, which were unquestionably important, Lawless wrote a clever "History of Ireland," or rather a pamphlet on the history of Ireland; a work which excited the admiration of Shelley the poet, but which is not now considered of much value as an authority.

Opposite ADAM-STREET is the ADELPHI THEATRE, the "home of melodrama," a building associated in latter days with the successful production of some of Dion Boucicault's Irish dramas. Among other notable Irish dramatists whose plays have also succeeded here are Mrs. S. C. Hall, the well-known novelist, whose "Groves of Blarney" had a lengthened run here in 1838; and Joseph Stirling Coyne, a native of Birr, one of the founders of "Punch," and an excellent writer, who has given to the stage no less than 90 pieces, the best of which have been produced at the Adelphi.

Proceeding on our course we soon reach BUCKINGHAM-STREET, notable as being the street in which John Henderson, the great tragedian, died. Born in London, of Irish parentage, in February, 1746, he became distinguished as an engraver, and executed some admirable works in that capacity. He afterwards joined the dramatic profession, and soon became known both as a fine actor of tragic parts and as an excellent comedian. The popularity of Cowper's famous ballad, "John Gilpin," was greatly due to his inimitable rendering of it at various places in London. He is buried amongst the illustrious dead of Westminster Abbey.

Buckingham street leads to the VICTORIA EMBANKMENT, one of the greatest of modern engineering feats, and built chiefly of granite from Dalkey, county Dublin.

In the northern public garden on the Embankment, overlooking the river, is Foley's statue of the great political economist, John Stuart Mill. This statue, like everything from Foley's chisel, is a fine work of art, suggestive of its clever creator in its artistic pose and fidelity as a likeness, and is palpably superior to the other statues on the Embankment.

In VILLIERS-STREET, leading back to the Strand, is YORK-PLACE, formerly York Buildings, where Sir Richard Steele lived from 1721 to 1724, and where he wrote his clever comedy, "The Conscious Lovers." This narrow turning or court seems to be still narrower than it really is, owing to the great height of its houses, most of which are more than 150 years old, the place having undergone little change since Steele's time. From references in the letters of the great philosopher, Bishop Berkeley, it seems clear that it was here he visited his fellow-countryman, Steele. He was certainly very intimate with the great essayist, having sought him out and been warmly welcomed by him on his first visit to London.

BOYLE.

At the corner of Villiers street, in the Strand, is the Charing Cross Hotel and Railway Station, built by E. M. Barry, R.A., the distinguished architect. The peculiar structure in front, resembling a fountain, is an exact fac-simile of the ancient Cross of Charing, and was also executed by Barry. Just past the Hotel and Railway Station is CRAVEN-STREET, where Sir Martin Archer Shee lived in 1789. Having only recently come to London, he was little known, but his genius soon displayed itself; and, as his reputation and income increased, he moved to more fashionable quarters. Shee was born in Dublin on the 20th of December, 1769, and in course of time became not only a distinguished painter but also a clever poet and dramatist. Byron, in his

"English Bards and Scotch Reviewers" (1811), attacked nearly every one of his contemporaries, but the following lines show his high appreciation of Shee's powers:—

> And here let Shee and Genius find a place,
> Whose pen and pencil yield an equal grace:
> To guide whose hand the sister arts combine
> And trace the poet's or the painter's line;
> Whose magic touch can bid the canvas glow,
> Or pour the easy rhyme's harmonious flow;
> While honours, doubly merited, attend
> The poet's rival, but the painter's friend.

Shee died at Brighton on the 19th of August, 1850, deeply regretted by his fellow-artists and others who were acquainted with him. It was partly through his exertions that the Royal Hibernian Academy received its charter, and, in short, his life was one long record of good works.

It was at his lodgings in Craven-street, in 1798, that Roger O'Connor was arrested for treasonable conspiracy about the same time that his brother Arthur was committed to the Tower.

The next turning on the left is NORTHUMBERLAND STREET, which has a more than ordinary interest, as being the home of the "Museum Club," which counted among its members the well-known Francis Sylvester Mahony ("Father Prout"). This famous Corcagian's writings are familiar to most lovers of Irish literature, and therefore need only a passing reference here. He was by no means so genial a man as one might suppose from his works, and was certainly not such a lovable writer as his more eminent townsman and friend, William Maginn. Neither should it be forgotten that he was not the sole author of the famous "Reliques"—for not a few of the best of them, notably the Greek versions, were written by his collaborator and countryman, Francis Stack Murphy, a sergeant-at-law and an inimitable scholar. Dr. Maginn also had a hand in the production of the "Padre's" writings. Prout was not greatly liked by his contemporaries—his bitterness and occasional unscrupulousness having made him enemies. His feelings against O'Connell and the National Party generally were intensely bitter, and led him to write some very discreditable things—witness, his "Lay of Lazarus," which appeared in the "Times," and had reference to the Repeal "rent." The "Museum Club," of which he was an ornament, was very short lived, although it numbered some of the best wits of the day, including Douglas Jerrold, among its members.

A few paces past Northumberland-street and we are on "the finest site in Europe"—TRAFALGAR-SQUARE. On our right, at one corner of ST. MARTIN'S-LANE, is ST. MARTIN'S-IN-THE-FIELD, a fine church built by Gibbs, the eminent Scotch architect. At the opposite corner is the NATIONAL GALLERY, where the national treasures of art are enshrined, and which was partly rebuilt by E. M. Barry, R.A. TRAFALGAR-SQUARE itself was planned by Sir Charles Barry, R.A., and the fountains here were designed by him. It is built on the site of the Royal Mews of several monarchs. The keeper of the Royal stables was for some time Owen M'Swiney, the Irish dramatist and theatrical manager, who died in 1754, leaving his wealth to Peg Woffington, the Irish actress. The Nelson Monument or Pillar, facing Whitehall, deserves notice here for one reason only. On the side facing Whitehall is an immense alto-relievo in bronze representing "The Battle of Trafalgar." It is an exceedingly fine work of art, and was executed by John Edward Carew, the Irish sculptor, who has been previously

HENDERSON.

mentioned. Close to the pillar is the statue of the eminent soldier, Sir Charles James Napier, who, though not born in Ireland like his brother, had Irish blood in his veins.

THE CHURCH OF ST. MARTIN'S-IN-THE-FIELDS (a strange misnomer at the present day) has some very interesting Irish memories. Here, in 1811, Thomas Moore was married to Miss Bessie Dyke, his faithful wife, who survived the poet some years, living down to 1865. It is, of course, unnecessary to discuss anew the life or works of this greatest of Irish song-writers—"the poet of all circles and the idol of his own," as Byron happily termed him. St. Martin's is highly interesting for other reasons, for within its precincts were buried two celebrated Irishmen, each almost unrivalled in his own particular sphere. George Farquhar, a native of Londonderry, born in 1678, was one of the most eminent dramatists of his age. His works still endure, and are counted among the English classics. Unfortunately for literature, Farquhar died at the early age of 29, and he was buried here in 1717. He was a clever actor as well as a distinguished dramatist; but it is by his plays, particularly his "Beaux' Stratagem," "Recruiting Officer," and "Inconstant," that he will be known to remote posterity.

Here also, in 1692, was buried a still greater Irishman—namely, Robert Boyle, the celebrated philosopher and savant, and the real founder of the science of pneumatics. He was a native of Lismore, county Waterford, where he was born on the 25th of January, 1627, and may justly be termed one of the most remarkable members of that great scientific body, the Royal Society. His funeral sermon was preached by the great divine, Bishop Burnet. The illustrious foreign savant Boerhaave said of Boyle's discoveries and investigations in science—"To him, ... the ornament of his age and country, . . . we owe the secrets of fire, air, water, animals, vegetables, fossils; so that from his works may be deduced the whole system of natural knowledge!"

ST. MARTIN'S-LANE, with its continuations, runs from Trafalgar-square to Bloomsbury. It has several interesting Irish associations, the most important of which, perhaps, centres in MAY'S BUILDINGS, a narrow turning on the right, only a few yards from St. Martin's Church. Here used to meet the celebrated club of "Eccentrics," prominent among whose members or visitors were four Irishmen—Sheil, Sheridan, Maginn, and "Prout." The careers of Sheil and Sheridan are too well known to need comment. Both as orators and dramatists they were unquestionably distinguished; but at the present day Sheil is chiefly remembered as an orator and Sheridan as a dramatist. Dr. Maginn, that truly extraordinary genius, does, however, require slight mention. Like "Prout," he was a native of Cork, where he was born in 1794. His splendid scholarship and powerful mind, no less than his abundance of wit and humour, brought him into connection with some of the foremost men of the day—not a few of whom served under him on the staff of "Frazer's Magazine," which he edited on its foundation. He is universally considered the greatest scholar and wit of his time, and many of his distinguished contemporaries did not hesitate to place him in the rank and on the same level with such masterminds of the past as Swift, Lucian, and Rabelais. His versatility has never been surpassed—it is a question whether it has been even equalled in modern times. His native city has been a veritable "birthplace of genius," and has produced writers like Sheridan Knowles, Crofton Croker, Richard Millikin, Dr. E. V. Kenealy, J. D. Murphy, Arthur O'Leary, Richard Sainthill, Richard Caulfield, Edward Dowden, and J. J. Callanan, and such artists as Barry and Maclise, the Royal Academicians, Grogan and Rogers, Skillin and Forde, Butts and Hussey, Kirk and West, Willis and Pope, Adam and Frederick Buck, and the eminent architects, Sir Thomas Deane and Sir Richard Morrison.

In ST. PETER'S-COURT, close by, was the Academy of Fine Arts, of which several of the best Irish artists of the 18th century were members. Not one of them was more justly famous than the great mezzotinto engraver, James M'Ardell, a native of Dublin, born in 1710 or thereabouts, whose engravings after Vandeyk, Rembrandt, Murillo, and others are highly praised by all authorities. He is better known, however, by his magnificent engravings of Sir Joshua Reynolds's best portraits, than which nothing can be finer. He died in London on the 2nd June, 1765, having been, with Sir Joshua Reynolds, one of the earliest members of St. Martin's Academy of Arts. One of the most distinguished masters of this school in recent times was William Linnæus Casey, who was born at Cork in 1835, and who died, still young, in 1870. His portraits are always excellent, and sometimes masterly, and fully deserve all the high praise which they have received.

A little higher up, at what is now 70 St Martin's-lane, another eminent Irish painter, Nathaniel Hone, R.A., exhibited the picture which led to his expulsion from the Royal Academy. It was intended as a satire or caricature of one of Sir Joshua Reynolds's works, and as Reynolds was then President of the Academy, and held in great esteem by artists generally, Hone was punished for daring to ridicule a great painter by being expelled from the Academy. Hone excelled in portraits, his miniatures being exceptionally fine. He was a native of Dublin, and was born in 1718. His son, Camilus Hone, who died in 1807, was also a clever painter, while his grandson, Horace Hone, A.R.A., born in Dublin about the middle of the last century, was one of the best miniature painters of his time, and became an Associate of the Royal Academy in 1799, and died in 1825.

At the upper end of St. Martin's-lane, on the left hand or west side, stood the celebrated old coffee-house known as "Old Slaughter's," a great resort of the artists of the last century. Three of its most remarkable habitues were Charles

Jervas, Luke Sullivan, and James M'Ardell. Jervas was a very fashionable painter of his time, and a great friend of Alexander Pope. He was born in Ireland in 1675, and died in 1739. His vanity was certainly excessive, if the following story is authentic. It is stated that, having copied a picture by the great painter, Titian, he was seen to glance from his own copy to the original, and heard to say " Poor little Tit, how he would stare !"

Luke Sullivan was a much greater artist, though not so good a portrait-painter as Jarvas. He was born in County Louth in 1705, and is remembered for his fine engravings, especially the " March to Finchley," after Hogarth's great picture. Sullivan was also a good landscapist and a clever miniature painter. He died in great poverty in 1771, one of the best of a remarkable group of Irish engravers who worked in London during the last century.

SLAUGHTER'S COFFEE-HOUSE.

Some distance farther up the street, and lying on the left of HIGH-STREET, BLOOMSBURY, is the Church of ST. GILES-IN-THE-FIELDS. In former times the gallows used to be erected in close proximity to the Church, and as each place in London where the gallows had ever stood was called Tyburn, so was this particular spot. He here executed many Catholics, including priests, Irishmen among others, for the crime of attending or celebrating Mass; and here, too, was executed the saintly prelate, OLIVER PLUNKET. Archbishop of Armagh, on a charge of high treason. His remains were deposited in St. Giles's Church or its churchyard, but were afterwards removed, either to Landsprung, in Germany, as is commonly stated, or, as is more likely, to Armagh Cathedral. Here also probably were executed " Silken Thomas " and his five uncles, whom we have already mentioned in connection with the Tower. In St. Giles's Church was buried in 1698 a very celebrated Irishman—Dr. Bernard O'Connor—who was born in Kerry in 1666, and who died at the early age of 32. As a physician he was highly appreciated by his contemporaries, and while quite young was appointed physician to Sobieski, King of Poland. On his return to England he wrote his " History of Poland,"

FATHER PROUT.

which even at this day is the best work on the subject according to English critical testimony. A curious incident in connection with O'Connor's works may be noticed. Two of the most remarkable of them are in the British Museum, and in both the " O " has been cut out of the title page. It is not known who did the act, but it was evidently due to a wish to destroy the Celtic character of the name. When O'Connor died he was a member of several learned bodies, including the Royal Society and the Royal College of Surgeons.

In leaving St. Giles's it is only right to mention that a considerable number of the inhabitants of this parish are, and have been since the days of Queen Elizabeth, Irish of the poorest class. Retracing our steps down St. Martin's lane, we reach again the National Gallery, two of the prominent objects in the vestibule of which are busts of Mulready and Wellington, both by Weeks. The gallery may, on the whole, be said to contain but few works of Irish, or, indeed, of English art. It is rich in examples of the foreign schools, but the artists of the United Kingdom are, with one exception, scantily represented. The exception alluded to is J. M. W. Turner, R.A., the great landscapist, many of whose finest works occupy a separate room. The only Irish artists whose works find a place here are William Mulready,

Daniel Maclise, Francis Danby, Sir M. A. Shee, and Gavin B. O'Neill. To these may be added John Singleton Copley, R.A.; William Collins, R.A.; and William Clarkson Stanfield, R.A., who were of Irish parentage, though born out of Ireland. Mulready is certainly the greatest of all those above mentioned. He was born at Ennuis, county Clare, in 1786, and died in 1863. His works are characterised by all those competent to judge art as truly wonderful. For colouring, for ideal expression, and for humour, his pictures are almost unrivalled. In the National Gallery there are six of his works—three of which are among his best. "The Last In" depicts an Irish school, with several shock-headed pupils poring over slates and books The door is slightly opened, and a scholar is creeping stealthily in, being presumably late. The withered schoolmaster, a delightful creation, with a most unmistakably Irish physiognomy,

STANFIELD.

is, however, aware of the laggard's entrance, and is making him a most profound bow, covering him with confusion. The faces of the children in this picture, as in all of Mulready's works, are exquisite in character. The landscape seen through the open window is also very beautiful, and proves, if there is any need for proof, Mulready's talent for landscape painting. Another picture close by, "Crossing the Ford," is by the same great artist, and in its refined portraiture and beauty of colouring are worthy of his fame. "Fair Time," which shows some revellers returning from the fair; "A Snow Scene," and one or two sketches make up the total of Mulready's contributions to be seen here. Maclise has three pictures here—viz., his enormous picture of the "Play Scene in Hamlet," "Mulvolio and the Countess" (from Shakespeare's "Twelfth Night"), and a portrait of Charles Dickens. The last-mentioned picture is considered an admirable likeness, and the "Play Scene" is certainly a fine work, containing some beautiful heads; but as it is admitted that Maclise succeeded better in fresco painting and in sketching than in subject painting, there is no real necessity to dwell here upon his works in the latter branch of art as his best productions are to be found elsewhere. On the staircase in the entrance hall is Sir M. A. Shee's full-length portrait of W. Lewis, the famous comedian, and in one of the rooms is a single work by Francis Danby—"The Fisherman's Home." As Danby (who was a native of Wexford, and who early received the distinction of election as A.R.A.) is considered one of the most imaginative and poetical of landscape painters, this is a rather meagre representation of his genius, but makes up in quality what it lacks in quantity, for the picture just mentioned is a veritable masterpiece, although not so grand as some of his other works in London public institutions. Danby was born in 1793, and died in 1861, leaving two sons, both of whom became distinguished painters, and only died recently.

John Singleton Copley is represented by two or three of his greatest works. One is the magnificent "Death of Chatham," an event most graphically described on canvas; and his equally fine "Death of Major Pierson, at St. Helena." The last is a genuine battle-picture, and places war before us in all its terrible aspects, therein somewhat differing from the conventional battle-pieces, which resemble more closely the stage-fight in a melodrama than "the real thing." Copley was born in Boston, in America, in 1737, his parents being poor Irish emigrants, whose real name it is

NATIONAL GALLERY.

said was Collopy. J. S. Copley died in 1815 His son became first a judge, and finally Lord Chancellor of England, with the title of Lord Lyndhurst.

There are one or two fine pictures here by William Collins, R.A., a most delightful painter of seascape. His father, the author of the "Life of George Morland," and a clever carver and modeller, was a native of Wicklow. His son, the painter now under notice, was born in London in 1788, and died in 1847. The present eminent novelist, William Wilkie Collins, is a son of the last-named, and, therefore, possesses some Irish blood in his veins.

It is not so well known that the great marine-painter, William Clarkson Stanfield, R.A., was also of Irish parentage. The fact is generally ignored by English compilers, but it is, nevertheless, a fact, and one which should not be forgotten by Irishmen. He was born in Birmingham in 1792, and died in 1867. He was one of the most intimate friends of Dickens and Maclise, and as a marine-painter had very few superiors. The

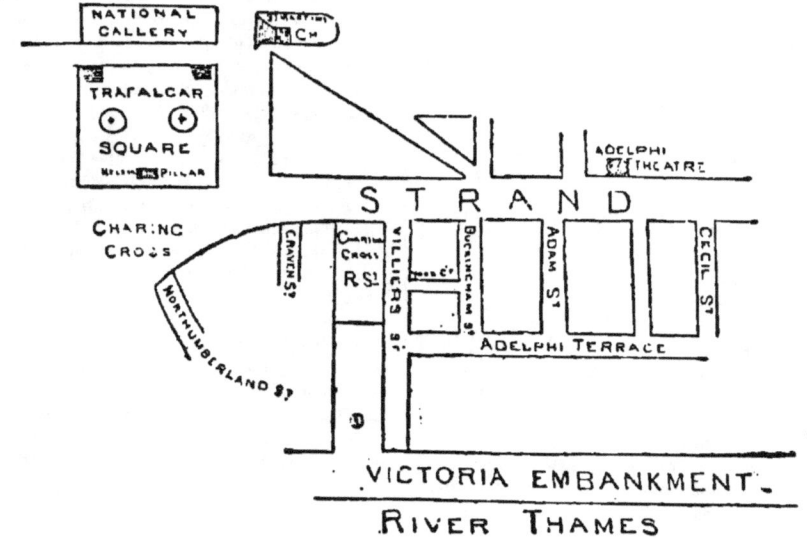

National Gallery contains about six of his works, and they are all of the utmost beauty. Nothing could be finer than his glorious view of "The Lake of Como." They are all so clear, so distinct, and so natural that one feels that their greatest merit is, perhaps, that of accuracy of description. London is full of the works of Stanfield and other Irish artists, and we shall endeavour to give a complete account of both the works and the men who have produced them as we proceed on our journey through the metropolis.

CHAPTER VII.

COVENT GARDEN AND ITS NEIGHBOURHOOD.

LEADING out of St. Martin's-lane, and on our right as we come from Charing Cross, is LONG ACRE, once a fashionable thoroughfare, but now almost wholly occupied by the shops and factories of coachbuilders. Before, however, we actually leave St. Martin's-lane we should mention that it was there, in 1770, that Henry Jones, the clever but ill-starred Irish dramatic poet, was run over, dying shortly afterwards in the parish infirmary. Long Acre runs from the street just mentioned to Drury lane, passing at its commencement the street named after Garrick, where the Garrick Club is situated. As this club contains the finest collection of theatrical portraits in existence, we shall have something to say of it later on. In Long Acre used to stand the "Sun" Tavern, a much frequented resort of the actors of the neighbouring theatres. Here Lacy Ryan, an excellent Irish comedian, was one night attacked by an old enemy of his, and, being compelled to draw for his safety, killed his adversary. Not long after, strange to say, Ryan was shot at and severely wounded almost on the same spot, dying in a short time from the effects of his injuries. In Long Acre used to meet a club founded by another well-known Irish actor, Isaac Sparkes by name, which became the haunt of the nobility and of the actors of the day.

The first turning on the right in Long Acre is JAMES-STREET, where both David Garrick and Charles Macklin lodged for a time. Garrick, though born in England, had no English blood in his veins, his father being French and his mother Irish: and there can be no question—as, indeed, Mr. Irving admitted in a recent lecture of his on "Four Great Actors"— that Garrick, by reason of his French and Irish blood, was admirably equipped for the histrionic profession. Apart from his greatness as an actor (and he is probably the greatest actor England has known). Garrick was an excellent dramatist and a clever epigrammatist. Several of his farces, notably his "Irish Widow," still keep the stage, and there are comparatively few good modern actors who have not acted in one or other of his dramatic pieces. Charles Macklin, his famous rival, whose real name was Maclaughlin, was a native of Westmeath, and born about 1700. This great actor, it should not be forgotten, was the originator of the now universally accepted method of playing Macbeth and Shylock. Previous to his time Macbeth was played in all kinds of anomalous costumes, such as that of a British soldier, and the like. Macklin was the first to brave the ridicule of the malicious by habiting the Scotch warrior in a kilt, and gave also the correct rendering of a play that had hitherto been strangely misinterpreted. Similarly Shakespeare's creation of the "immortal Jew" was before Macklin's time actually played as a comic part, and was a favourite character of Tom Doggett and other low comedians. Macklin's impersonation of Shylock was so excellent, so minutely correct in every detail, that it is stated that Pope, the poet, who

GARRICK.

was present at the first performance, uttered the well-known exclamation "This is the Jew that Shakespeare drew!" For other details of Macklin's career, the admirable account by Mr M'Donagh in "Irish Graves in England" should be consulted. In concluding our notice, we may merely mention that Macklin died in 1797, and as it is believed that he was born some years previous to 1700, he is thus supposed to have reached the patriarchal age of 106 years.

James-street leads directly into COVENT GARDEN, now the greatest fruit and vegetable market in the kingdom, which stands on the site of the ancient Convent Garden of the monks of Westminster. On the dissolution of the monasteries it was given by Edward VI. to his uncle, the Lord Protector Somerset, but it eventually fell into the hands of the Bedford family, who still hold it. The market is one of the sights of London, and is in the form of a square, part of it being known on that account as the Piazza, the Italian equivalent for square. Here in the last century Macklin kept a coffee-house, tavern, and school, and gave lessons on elocution; and here also, many years after, the Tumbler Club used to meet, counting among its visitors no less a person than Father Prout, the wit and scholar.

On our right is HART-STREET, where Macklin lived for a time, and where Hugh Primrose Dean, a well-known Irish artist of the eighteenth century, exhibited several of his best pictures. Dean was an eminent painter in his day, and was a member of the Florentine Academy of Arts. He executed some very meritorious works, mostly in Italy, however, there being very few, if any of them, in England. KING-STREET is a continuation of Hart-street, and here Jas. Quin, the great actor, was born in February, 1693, being shortly afterwards taken to Ireland by his parents. Adopting the stage as an avocation, he won for himself a prominent position among the many distinguished actors of the day, and is now considered by competent critics the greatest impersonator of Falstaff and similar characters.

MACKLIN.

On the right of the square, between Hart-street and Henrietta-street, is the ugly, barn-like ST. PAUL'S CHURCH, remarkable for the number of eminent personages buried within its precincts.

including several Irish men and women of note. Here were interred Charles Macklin, and another famous Irish actor, Robert Wilks, who succeeded admirably in genteel comedy, and who was born in 1670, at Rathfarnham, county Dublin, and died in 1732. In St. Paul's were also interred that most touching of Irish playwrights, Thomas Southern, also a native of Dublin, and the amusing comedy writer—Mrs Centlivre. Southern deserves the praise of posterity on other grounds besides that of dramatic genius, for, according to the great historian Hallum, he was the first writer in the English language to hold up to abhorrence the vice of slavery. This he did in his most pathetic play, " Oroonoko." He was born in 1660, and died in May, 1746, having made a fortune out of the success of his fine dramas. Mrs. Centlivre, whose maiden name was Freeman, was also born in Dublin, and has, by her clever comedies, especially " A Bold Stroke for a Wife," secured a conspicuous place in the ranks of dramatic writers. In this same church is also buried Michael Kelly, the well-known composer and singer, whose musical pieces, though little studied or played nowadays, prove him to have been a most talented musician. But as an operatic singer he is admittedly more worthy of notice, while his lively " Reminiscences " are valuable as a record of entertaining particulars of the great men and women of the 18th century. St. Paul's is also noteworthy as the church where the clever and handsome actor and dramatist, William O'Brien, was married to the daughter of the Earl of Ilchester. As an actor O'Brien was inimitable in certain parts ; and his most amusing farce, " Cross Purposes," is still occasionally played, and has therefore stood the test of a hundred years.

A couple of doors past St. Paul's is HENRIETTA-STREET, famous as the place of residence of Kitty Clive, the charming actress, and James M'Ardell, the great engraver, and as the scene of a duel between Richard Brinsley Sheridan and an insignificant adversary over some matter of very little importance. Kitty Clive was probably born in the North of Ireland in 1711. Her father was a lawyer, named Raftor, of Kilkenny. She became one of the most fascinating actresses on the stage, and excelled in the light and lively parts of fashionable comedies, acting the " fine lady " and the impudent lady's maid to perfection. Her forte was low comedy, and in this she was pre-eminent. In the opinion of the grim old Dr. Johnson she was the best player " he had ever seen," and as he had seen all the great actors of the epoch, this was very high praise indeed. Dramatic authorship was not unknown to her, for she wrote a bustling comedy which had some little success. Her kindness and tenderness of heart and sensitive temperament endeared her to all who knew her, while her private character was beyond reproach. She died at Twickenham in 1785, and was buried there.

KITTY CLIVE.

On the opposite, or east, side of Covent Garden is TAVISTOCK-STREET, where Macklin died at a great age. Macklin-street, close by, perpetuates his name. We have not spoken of his excellent comedy, " The Man of the World," or of his clever farce, " Love a-la-Mode," though they are destined to last as long as witty dialogue, when combined with good characterisation and striking situations, is appreciated. In the next turning, RUSSELL-STREET, stood the celebrated old coffee-houses known as " Will's," " Tom's," and Button's," so frequently mentioned in the literary annals of the last century. They have recently ceased to exist, but there is a host of memories connected with them. Their most noteable Irish habitues were Dean Swift, Sir R. Steele, Oliver Goldsmith, Arthur Murphy, John Moody, and Sir Philip Francis ; but, besides these, everybody of note in the literary, artistic, or theatrical world were accustomed to drop in for a game of whist or a bowl of coffee, or for the purpose of discussing politics, literature, or scandal, with the well-informed on such matters. Their places have been usurped by the fashionable clubs of later days; and the romance that once centered in these humble institutions, where intellectual prince and plebeian met almost as equals has been dissipated by removal to the " gilded salons" and gorgeous palaces of Pall Mall. From frequent references in the writings of Swift and Steele it would almost appear as if they lived altogether in their favourite coffee-houses. It is pretty certain that no day passed without their paying a visit to their accustomed corners to talk over the latest news. And, in days when the regular newspaper was unknown, we can scarcely estimate the importance which attached to those famous resorts.

As we enter Russell-street from Covent Garden we have Bow-STREET on our left and DRURY-LANE

THEATRE in front. This historic building, the oldest theatre in London, has, from its foundation, been distinguished for its Irish actors, managers, or dramatists. Irish musicians, like Balfe, Kelly, Carter, and Cook, have led its orchestra or sung on its stage; while among its Irish managers have been Sir Richard Steele, Thomas Doggett Robert Wilks, David Garrick, Owen M'Swiney (the dramatist), R. B. Sheridan, and his father, Thomas Sheridan, and Charles Kean. Concerning the management of R. B. Sheridan, a half-humorous, half-tragic incident is related. One night, in 1809, while Sheridan was attending to his Parliamentary duties in the House of Commons, the theatre was burnt down. On hearing the news, Sheridan at once hastened to the scene of the fire. Thousands of people were watching the progress of the flames with interest, and, perhaps, with enjoyment, and Sheridan tried to push his way to the front, but was stopped by a watchman, who wished to know where the person most interested was going. Sheridan, who even under this great financial calamity did not lose his accustomed wit, is said to have promptly replied—" What? Cannot a man warm his hands at his own fireside?"

In the vestibule of the theatre is a fine statue of Michael Balfe, by a Belgian artist, which is supposed to be a good likeness of the great musician, whose earliest and latest triumphs were obtained at " Old Drury.".-

Opposite the front entrance, in BRYDGES STREET, is a publichouse named after Sheridan Knowles, the well-known dramatist and elocutionist, who was " chancellor " of a club known as " The Owls," which used to meet here, and of which many distinguished men were members. Knowles was the most successful playwright of his time, and was very highly appreciated by his contemporaries for his amiability and geniality. In one of Charles Lamb's poems he is termed one of

" Those fine spirits, warm-souled, Ireland sends
To teach us, colder English, how a friend's
Quick pulse should beat."

It should be mentioned that he was a Cork man, and was born on the 12th of May, 1784. He died on the 1st of December, 1862, aged 78, having been in receipt of £200 a year from the Civil List for some time previously. His son also be-

BALFE.

came an eminent writer, and died not very long ago.

Another prominent member of the " Owls " was Pierce Egan, who died on the 3th July, 1880, having made a reputation as a novelist and sporting journalist. He was the son of the author of the celebrated novel, " Life in London ; or, Tom and Jerry," who died in 1849, at the age of 77.

Entering Bow-STREET, which is on the right of Russell-street as we return, we are among other Irish associations, some of them of a different nature to those of which we have just been treating. Not a few eminent Irishmen have lived in this street, once the most fashionable in all London. At what was No. 6, resided Charles Macklin, Peg Woffington, and David Garrick, at various times. Quin and Wilks also lived in Bow-street, while here also lived Robert Carver, the gifted Irish painter; and here he died in November, 1791. His paintings have always been held in high esteem, his landscapes being considered exceedingly fine. He executed some splendid scene-painting for Garrick, who had been one of his greatest friends. Carver was probably born in Dublin, and was the son of another clever painter, a native of Waterford, who painted the altarpiece of one of the churches of that city. This street was also the place of residence of Mr. Bernard O'Connor, the eminent physician, who has been referred to in Chapter VI. Bow-street Police Court is exactly opposite Covent Garden Theatre and the Floral Hall, both built by E. M. Barry, R A. It has been the scene of some important episodes. After the troubles of '98, William Putnam M'Cabe was brought up here on a charge of high treason, but was sent elsewhere to take his trial.

Another involuntary occupant of the dock here was the notorious George Barrington, previously mentioned, who was tried for stealing a gold snuff-box, valued at £30,000, the property of the Russian Prince Orloff. The box was stolen in Covent Garden Theatre; but, as Orloff declined to prosecute, Barrington was discharged Not long afterwards, however, he was charged with some other offence, and, being convicted, was transported to the colonies—a punishment which resulted most beneficially for him, as we have already shown. Here, too, O'Connell was brought before the magistrates after his arrest in the Strand, for challenging Sir Robert Peel to a duel. He was bound over in very heavy sums—himself in £5,000 and two sureties in £2,500 each.

COVENT GARDEN THEATRE having been rebuilt in 1857-58, cannot be called a very historic building, and has few and very unimportant associations of an Irish interest. But it stands on the site of the old edifice where some of the greatest triumphs of the foremost Irish actors, musicians, and dramatists have been won. Even more literally than that of Drury-lane, old Covent Garden Theatre was the scene of the successes of a multitude of Irish men and women. The best plays of Farquhar, the first piece from Sheridan's pen, and plays by Goldsmith, Macklin, O'Keeffe, Sheridan Knowles, and Sheil were first produced here, and many eminent Irish actors and actresses ing to Byron, wrote 'the best comedy ("The School for Scandal"), the best opera ("The Duenna"), the best farce ("The Critic") . . . the best address (the "Monologue" on Garrick), and, to crown all, delivered the very best oration (the great "Begum" speech) ever conceived or heard in this country.' In this street is the Freemasons' Tavern, famous for the clubs that used to meet there, and as the headquarters of Freemasonry. The Royal Society Club used to hold its meetings here, and numbered many Irishmen among its members.

On the 25th of February, 1825, a great meeting was held in this building, the Duke of Norfolk,

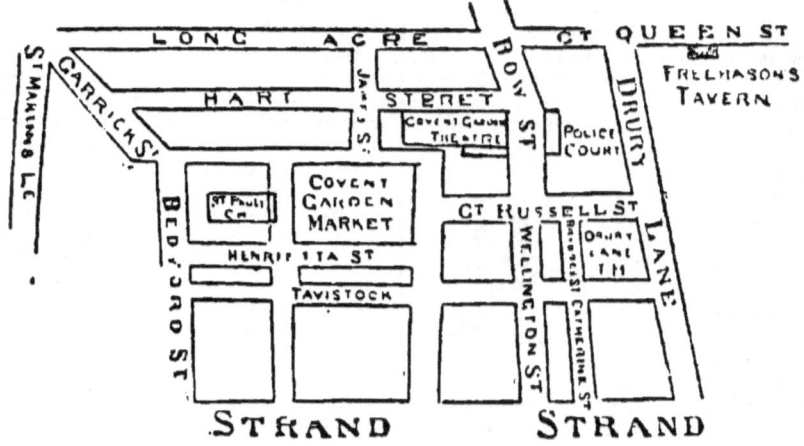

made their first bow to a London audience from its stage. But it has other memories too, for O'Connell, when in the height of his fame, was banquetted here by his London sympathisers, and afterwards attended the great meetings of the Anti-Corn Law League when they were held in this theatre.

Bow-street leads again into Long Acre, and, turning to the right and crossing Drury-lane, we reach GREAT QUEEN-STREET, which runs into LINCOLN'S INN FIELDS, as the large square sacred to lawyers and solicitors is called. In Great Queen-street lived for some time the delightful Kitty Clive, and in the same street, later on, in 1778, resided Richard Brinsley Sheridan, who, according Earl Marshal of England, taking the chair. On this occasion O'Connell delivered the speech he had intended to deliver at the bar of the House, but which he was prevented from making. Among the other speakers on this memorable evening was Richard Lalor Sheil, and among the ordinary spectators in the body of the hall was no less a person than Gerald Griffin, who has left in his letters an account of the meeting. We will conclude this chapter without entering upon the classic ground of Lincoln's Inn, reserving its many interesting spots for description in our next chapter, in which we will also introduce a notice of Gray's Inn, Holborn, Smithfield, and Clerkenwell.

CHAPTER VIII.

COVENT GARDEN AND ITS NEIGHBOURHOOD.—FROM LINCOLN'S INN TO CLERKENWELL.

ENTERING LINCOLN'S INN FIELDS, from Great Queen-street, we have on our left, at No. 13, the museum of Sir John Soane, which contains a few objects of interest to Irishmen. It was founded by Soane, an eminent architect, in the present building, which had been his own residence and property. It is chiefly remarkable as possessing the great series of pictures by Hogarth—"The Rake's Progress" and "The Election"—and also for the magnificent Egyptian sarcophagus, formed out of a single block of alabaster. This great treasure is 9ft 4in long, 3ft 8in wide, 2ft 8in deep, and 2½in thick, and is beautifully carved and inscribed. These objects alone are worth many visits, and there are also one or two admirable pictures and drawings by Irish artists. Prominent among them is F. Danby's picture, "A Scene from the Merchant of Venice;" while James Barry is represented by two excellent sketches, entitled, "The Fallen Angels" and "Adam's Detection;" and George Barrett, R.A., one of the greatest of landscapists, and a native of Dublin, has several good drawings here. On the staircase is an excellent bust of Richard Brinsley Sheridan, which is perhaps the only marble likeness of that great writer in London.

On the opposite side of the square, facing Soane's Museum, is the ROYAL COLLEGE OF SURGEONS, which was partly rebuilt by Sir Charles Barry, and contains some most interesting objects It stands upon the site of the old Duke's or Lincoln's Inn Theatre Royal, whose stage was often trodden by Macklin, Quin, and the other great actors of the past. Over the door of the room as you enter the Museum are the antlers of an Irish elk of immense size, while in the collection itself is a gigantic skeleton of the extinct red deer, found in a bog in Limerick, and measuring 8ft across the antlers, the latter being 7ft 6in in length, and the skull 7ft 6in from the ground. But by far the most interesting things here are the cast of Patrick Cotter's hand and the skeleton of Charles Byrne (commonly called O'Brien), two famous Irish "giants." Cotter was born in Kinsale, county Cork, and died in 1806, aged 46 years. He is said to have been 8 feet 7 inches in height, and such was his success as a giant that he made a fortune by exhibiting himself. He is buried in the Jesuit Chapel, Trenchard-street, Bristol. Byrne was a more famous personage, although less of a giant, than Cotter. He was born in Ireland in 1761, and died prematurely in 1783, aged 22, having reached the height of 8ft, or a little over. Before his death he sold his body to John Hunter, the great surgeon (and founder of the present College of Surgeons); but as his death approached he became morbidly afraid of his bargain, and wished to get out of it. As he could not do this, he arranged with one or two of his compatriots for a secret funeral in order to outwit Hunter, but that wily Scot proved too much for the giant's executors, and obtained possession of his body. The strange colour of the skeleton is

ABERNETHY.

due to the fact that Hunter was obliged to boil the dead giant, and the copper or boiler which was used for that purpose is still to be seen in the house of the great surgeon in West Kensington. A curious anecdote is related of Byrne's visit to Edinburgh. During the last century, before the introduction of gas, oil-lamps were used in the streets, and Byrne used occasionally to light his pipe at one of them. One night the suddenness and phenomenal singularity of the feat so frightened a watchman who had witnessed the apparition of the giant with wonder, that he fell down in a fit, fairly deprived of his senses.

Before leaving this remarkable but somewhat gruesome exhibition we must mention that in the library may be seen an excellent portrait, by Cline, of John Abernethy, the great surgeon. He is believed to have been born in London, but was unquestionably of Irish parentage. His career was equally extraordinary for the rapidity of its success and the height to which it conducted him. His deep insight into the science of physiology and anatomy showed him that much empiricism existed in the profession, and he lavished his contempt with a free tongue. He was the first to attempt the cure of a local disease through the general constitution, and to prove the practicability of operations of a bolder character than had been hitherto attempted. Original in his ideas and treatment, he was no less so in manners and appearance, and many and absurd are the stories related of his "eccentricities." His lectures, which he loved to give, were enlivened by the most lively wit and humour. An eye-witness describes his very mode of entering the lecture-room as "irresistibly droll; his hands buried deep in his breeches pockets, his body bent slouchingly forward, blowing or whistling, his eyes twinkling beneath their arches, and his lower jaw thrown considerably beneath the upper."

The first turning on the right of the College is DUKE-STREET, in which is situated the SARDINIAN CHAPEL, the oldest consecutively Catholic chapel in London. It was built in 1648, the year before the execution of Charles the First, as the chapel of the Sardinian Ambassador, and was singled out for special attack by the Gordon rioters in 1780. In their fury they partially destroyed the sacred edifice, and heaped all kinds of insult upon the devoted clergymen attached to it. Readers of Dickens's "Barnaby Rudge" will find therein a powerful and accurate description of these infamous rioters and their ravages, and of their chief instigator, the half-crazed Lord George Gordon. Many eminent singers used to perform here in the days when this chapel was the place of worship of noble Italian refugees and their foreign visitors. Among these great vocalists was the famous Luigi Lablache, who deserves to be singled out for mention in this place as the son of an Irish mother. Coming out of Duke-street we enter PORTUGAL-STREET (where Halam, the actor, was killed by Macklin), and notice on the left, behind Lincoln's Inn, New-square, where, at No. 1, Arthur Murphy lived for over twenty years. He was a native of Roscommon, and was born in December, 1730. After a long life, devoted chiefly to literature, he died in June 1805. Some of his dramas still hold the stage, and all of his dramatic works show great cleverness of construction, and evince considerable ingenuity in their plots. Murphy is also well known as a classical author and translator, and as the biographer of Dr. Johnson, his intimate friend. Just here in Portugal-street is the old shop immortalised by Dickens as the "Old Curiosity Shop," which fact is prominently advertised on its front walls. CAREY-STREET is at the end of this thoroughfare and immediately behind the Law Courts. Here lived Thurot, the well-known French privateer captain, when he was in London. All Irish readers remember his gallant and successful landing at Carrickfergus in 1760, which came to nothing owing to the failure of the people to support him in his effort to free Ireland. Thurot, it should be remembered, had some Irish blood in his veins, his mother being an O'Farrell, and daughter of an officer of the Irish Brigade. Passing through Clare Market on the left we reach WYCH-STREET, a very old street, and containing some curious ancient houses. In a garret here William Maginn wrote his "Tobias' Correspondence," which appeared in "Blackwood's Magazine" (vol. 48). At the time of writing it he was expecting arrest for debt, and may be supposed to not have been in a very comfortable frame of mind. Nevertheless, the articles are brimming over with his usual wit and learning.

Returning to Lincoln's Inn Fields, we see on our right LINCOLN'S INN, where not a few great Irishmen have studied law. It occupies the site of an ancient monastery of Black Friars, who afterwards removed to that part of London which bears their name. The land then became the property of the Earl of Lincoln, and after his death, in 1312, it became an Inn of Court. The great Archbishop Ussher was chaplain to the Benchers of Lincoln's Inn, and often preached in the splendid old chapel here, built by Inigo Jones in 1623. Lincoln's Inn was largely used by Irish law students, among those who resided here for the purpose of study being Richard Stanyhurst, an early Irish writer; Sir Richard Belling, an Irish historian of the seventeenth century; Sir John Denham, a poet of the same period; and, coming down to later times, Richard Lalor Sheil (who, during his residence in 1811 and onwards, composed his plays—"Adelaide," "Bellamira," "The Apostate," and "Evadne"); Sir James Emerson Tennant, a well-known politician and author; Lord Plunket, the great orator; the somewhat recent Lord Chancellor of Ireland, Francis Blackburne; Lord Cairns, and the present Baron Huddleston. Arthur Murphy was also a member, and resided close by, as we have seen.

Continuing our journey past Lincoln's Inn, we

reach HIGH HOLBORN, a great thoroughfare, extending from Oxford-street to Newgate. We enter Holborn from the narrow turning leading out of Lincoln's Inn Fields, known as the Great Turnstile. On our right, at a little distance up the road, is Bedford Chapel, at the corner of Bloomsbury-street. The late incumbent of this chapel

ENTRANCE TO LINCOLN'S INN FROM THE 'FIELDS.'

was J. C. M. Bellew, the famous elocutionist, who was, next to Charles Dickens, the most successful public reader of the age. He was born in England, but came of a Galway family. The present pastor of Bedford Chapel is one of the best poets and critics of the day, the Rev. Stopford A. Brooke, who is stated by some authorities to be a native of Dingle, in Kerry, but who is, we have his own authority for saying, a native of Letterkenny, in Donegal. He is admittedly one of the finest of living critics, and his poems stamp him as a poet of great power and thought, while his sermons are models of eloquence and culture, and are widley read and admired. His strong opinions on the past and present misgovernment of Ireland are well known to all Londoners, while the bitterest Tory cannot deny that he is one of the most distinguished men of the present time, and as profound a scholar as he is an enthusiastic Home Ruler.

The turning opposite leads into Great Russell-street, where that storehouse of the world's treasures, the British Museum, is situated. As we shall deal fully with this magnificent institution in a subsequent article, we must pass it by at present and come to BLOOMSBURY-SQUARE, which abuts upon Great Russell-street. This square has had some celebrated residents, among them being Sir Hans Sloane (whose splendid collections formed the nucleus of the Museum's possessions). Dr. George Croly, Sir R. Steele, and John Abernethy. Dr. Croly, the admirable poet and prose writer, died in Holborn in November, 1860, having expired in the street very suddenly.

In BEDFORD - PLACE, close by lived Richard Cumberland for some time, and there died. He was the son of an Irish bishop, was known as the author of a remarkable play, "The West Indian," and may not unjustly be termed the originator of present day melodrama. Cumberland wrote many other pieces, but the above-named play is his best-known, if not his best, work. He flourished during the last century, and was intimate with all the great writers of his time. Although born in England, he received the best part of his education in Ireland—a fact which is admittedly of importance, seeing that Ireland produced some of the best scholars of the period.

STOPFORD A BROOKE, M.A.

In TAVISTOCK-SQUARE, which is reached through Southampton-row, on the left of Holborn, died in 1880 another notable Irishman, Dr. E. V. Kenealy, a native of Cork, born in 1819, distinguished as a lawyer and as a writer. He is more popularly known from his connection with the great Tichborne case, which exhausted all his energy during the latter years of his life, and led people to forget his other claims upon the remembrance of posterity. He was an excellent poet, a vigorous political writer, and a humorist of some note. His extraordinary classical and linguistic knowledge is well exemplified by his Greek, Latin, Irish, Hebrew, Arabic, and other renderings of English verses.

TAVISTOCK CHAPEL, close by, is noteworthy on account of the Rev. William Jackson's connection with it. Jackson was in early life a popular preacher here. He afterwards adopted the principles of the United Irishmen, and became one of their most active agents. He was eventually betrayed by a treacherous friend to whom he had confided some intelligence, and was arrested and brought to trial in Dublin. On the day of his trial, April 30th, 1795, before entering the court, he contrived to swallow some poison, from the effects of which he died in the dock.

In GLOUCESTER-STREET, Queen's square, close to Tavistock-square, lived John Boyne, the clever caricaturist, and an admirable artist in every way. He was a native of the county Down, was born about 1750, and died in 1810. He kept a drawing-school here, and had among his pupils the two eminent water-colour painters, Holmes and Heaphy.

Returning to Holborn, through Southampton-row, and crossing the road, we pass SOUTHAMPTON BUILDINGS (where W. P. M'Cabe, the United Irishman, lived during one of his flying visits to England), and reach GRAY'S INN, just beyond Chancery-lane. Here Arthur Murphy lived for a time, and wrote some of his works, while a far greater Irishman, Daniel O'Connell, also studied law at Gray's Inn at the close of the last century, having previously resided at Lincoln's Inn for a short period. On the left of Holborn, a little lower down, is Gray's Inn-road, in a turning out of which, ACTON-STREET died Bartholomew Simmons, the poet, who is supposed to have written the finest poem in the English language on the subject of the great Napoleon. Just beyond Gray's Inn-road is FURNIVAL'S INN, a resident of which was Francis Stack Murphy, a clever lawyer and a fine scholar, whose contributions to "Fraser's Magazine" almost equal those by the worthy "Prout" himself—to whose "Reliques," by the way, Murphy contributed some admirable Greek and other versions. Here in the days of '98 met the United Irish Society, of which Lord Cloncurry and other prominent United Irishmen were members. Valentine Lawless (Lord Cloncurry) was not of such an unselfish and intense nature as some of the other patriots of his time, such as Tone and Lord Edward Fitzgerald, but he was unquestionably an earnest opponent

ARTHUR MURPHY

to the Act of Union, and a thoroughly estimable man.

A short distance further on, in HATTON-GARDEN, is the Italian Church, at which the great Dominican orator, Father Tom Burke, occasionally preached. In this same street lived Thomas Frye, one of the most esteemed Irish artists of the last century, and admirable alike as a mezzotint engraver and as portrait painter. Quite close to Hatton-garden is ELY-PLACE, the site of the ancient palace of the Bishops of Ely. The old chapel of St. Ethelreda's has now reverted to its original uses as a Catholic place of worship, and it is interesting as a beautiful relic of ancient Catholic times. The sculptured decorations in this church, it should be noted, are admirably executed, and are the work of the artist whom we had occasion to mention when dealing with St. Paul's—namely, M. Doherty.

A short distance further, on the left of Holborn, we reach Giltspur-street (the name of which commemorates the knightly jousts or tournaments of old times at Smithfield), which leads directly into Smithfield, a large space now partly covered with market buildings, but not so very long ago a broad, open field. It is the great cattle market of London, and is famous as the place where, in the old days, the martyrs of religion were sacrificed for refusing to renounce their religious beliefs. Many of them were burned at the stake at this very spot, so thronged at present with traffic and with people. On the right is St. Bartholomew's Hospital, which has had many Irishmen among its physicians and surgeons. There is a memorial erected here to Dr. Walter Moxon, an eminent Irishman; and here also is Sir Thomas Lawrence's fine portrait of John Abernethy, the founder of the lecture system at St. Bartholomew's.

THE CHARTERHOUSE, one of the most interesting buildings in London, is behind Smithfield. It is the remains of an old Carthusian monastery, founded in 1371 and dissolved during the reign of Henry VIII. It was formerly a school for the sons of gentlemen and tradesmen, and its name is but a corruption of the French "Chartreux." It is now a refuge for decayed tradesmen or merchants, and the school of the Merchant Tailors' Company. Among the eminent men educated here may be mentioned two Irishmen, Sir R. Steele and John Leech.

In ST. JOHN'S-STREET, hard by, is another relic of ancient London—St. John's Gate, once used as the gateway of the great monastery of the

Knights of St. John of Jerusalem (founded in the year 1100), which formerly stood here. There are rooms over the gateway, and among his tenants has been the worthy Dr. Johnson, who was here engaged in the editorial work of the "Gentleman's Magazine," a periodical numbering among its constant contributors some of the most eminent Irish writers of the time, and which was first started in this building by a publisher named Cave, in 1731. The latter fact explains

plosion occurred, making a triangular breach in the prison wall of about 20 feet wide at the base by 70 feet at the summit, utterly destroying the houses immediately opposite, partially wrecking all in the neighbourhood, killing 12 persons and injuring 40 others. The authorities had received warning of the intended attempt, and although not successful in preventing it, they had taken the precaution of removing Burke and Casey to another part of the prison, a step for which, per-

EFFECT OF CLERKENWELL EXPLOSION. SCENE FROM WITHIN PRISON.
(From a Sketch taken at time.)

the presence on the covers of the magazine of a representation of St. John's Gate. In the large room over the gateway Garrick made his first essay as an actor in the part of "The Mock Doctor," in the farce of that name.

Off Clerkenwell-green, and quite close to the memorial of bygone days just mentioned, is the House of Detention, better known as Clerkenwell Prison.

Here on the 13th December, 1867, was made a desperate attempt to rescue two Fenian prisoners, Colonel Richard Burke and Joseph Theobald Casey, resulting immediately in fatal or dangerous injuries to a number of innocent persons, and being more remotely one of the causes of events of great historical importance to Ireland.

A barrel of gunpowder was placed and ignited in an entry by the side of the prison wall opposite Corporation lane, and inside which Burke was supposed to exercise every day. A terrible ex-

haps, the prisoners had very good reason to thank them.

Six persons—Timothy and William Desmond, brothers; John O'Keefe, Michael Barrett,

ST. JOHN'S GATE.

Nicholas English, and a woman named Ann Justice—were put upon their trial for the offence.

All were acquitted except Barrett, a respectable and esteemed citizen, who, after an able and eloquent speech, was sentenced to death, and executed on the 26th May, 1868.

The explosion, occurring in the very heart of the metropolis, and so soon after the rescue of Kelly and Deasy at Manchester, created a sort of panic not alone in London but all over England. One thousand men were added to the London police, special constables were sworn in in large numbers throughout the country, and the provincial papers were filled with reports of wholesale arrests for Fenianism and of magisterial meetings to enrol defenders of law and order.

England was awakened to the "intensity of Fenianism," and we have the highest testimony as to the influence these events exercised in opening the eyes of public men to the evils of Irish misgovernment. "What happened," said Mr. Gladstone in a remarkable speech, "in the case of the Irish Church? That down to 1865 the whole question of the Irish Church was dead: nobody cared for it; nobody paid attention to it in England. . . . It was beyond the reach of practical politics. When it came to this that a great jail in the heart of the metropolis was broken open, under circumstances which drew the attention of the people of England to the Irish people, to the state of Ireland, and when a Manchester policeman was murdered in the exercise of his duty, at once the whole country became alive to the Irish question." "The ringing of the chapel bell," to which Mr. Gladstone subsequently compared these desperate deeds, rang, it is needless to add, the death knell of the Irish Church Establishment, and its echoes were heard in the Irish Land Act of 1871.

CHAPTER IX.

FROM HAMPSTEAD TO SOHO.

THE road which runs westward from Bloomsbury, and is a continuation of Holborn, is New Oxford-street, which runs into Oxford-street at the corner of Tottenham Court-road. Turning into the last-named thoroughfare, which is on our right, we reach PERCY-STREET in a few moments. In this street lived at different times two distinguished individuals—Samuel Cotes, the miniature-painter, and Master William Betty, the actor. Cotes was the brother of Francis Cotes, R.A., and although born in London was of Irish parentage. He was an excellent artist, and highly esteemed by his contemporaries. Master Betty, "the infant Roscius," as he was called, lived here with his parents, North of Ireland people, at the beginning of the century. He was born at Shrewsbury in 1791, and entered the theatrical profession at the very early age of nine or ten years, his qualification for the stage being unquestionably important. Numerous instances might be given of his extraordinary popularity, but a few will suffice here. When only eleven years old, after a successful tour in Ireland and the provinces, he appeared at Covent Garden Theatre, and night after night filled the place to overflowing, a detachment of guards being posted with a large body of constables to preserve order

MASTER BETTY
At the age of thirteen.
(From the "European Magazine.")

among the thousands who assembled before the opening of the doors. His salary was at first £50 a night, increased after three performances to £100 a night, and he cleared in his first London season the enormous sum of £17,000. He was a great favourite with many ladies of fashion and title, who competed with each other for the privilege of taking him to the parks with them in their carriages. On one occasion the House of Commons adjourned, on the motion of Pitt, in order that the members might be able to see the precocious boy act in the character of Hamlet. He acted in all the best theatres, and impersonated many leading characters, such eminent actors as Charles Young and G. F. Cooke not deeming it beneath them to play subordinate parts. Such was the remarkable ability and precocity he evinced that a grand career was prophesied for him—a prophecy that was unfulfilled, for when he grew to man's estate he lost the power to please, and at the somewhat early age of 32 he quitted the stage for ever, retiring to enjoy the handsome fortune he had accumulated.

A little farther up the road is STORE-STREET, on the right. Here the unfortunate Irish authoress, Elizabeth Ryves, died in great poverty in April, 1797. Cheated out of a small fortune by the forms of law, she devoted herself to literature, and wrote several novels, plays, and poems of more than ordinary merit. Notwithstanding vigorous struggles against the apathy of the public, she was allowed to sink into distress, and to die prematurely of neglect. In CHENIES-STREET, near here, the celebrated writer on art, Mrs Anna Jameson, lived just after her marriage in 1824. She was the daughter of G. Brownell Murphy, a painter of note, and was born in Dublin in 1797. She wrote numerous works on historical and art subjects, such as her "Lives of the Early Italian Painters," "The Poetry of Sacred and Legendary Art," "Memoirs and Essays on Art," displaying a profound acquaintance with the principles and a refined appreciation of the great examples of art. Her labours in this respect may be said to have been the precursor of that large and discriminating fine art criticism which has since sprung up in England. She devoted the later part of her life to the improvement of the position of her own sex, and in her "Lectures on the Social Employment of Women," evinces that deep sympathy with their labour which only an earnest worker could do. For some years previous to her death, which occurred on St. Patrick's Day, 1860, she was in receipt of a well-deserved pension from the Civil List, as a reward for her services to literature. In his "Noctes Ambrosianae," Professor John Wilson, the well-known Scotch critic, speaks of her as "one of the most eloquent of our female writers, full of feeling and fancy, a true enthusiast with a glowing soul."

Higher up on the left is Grafton-street, leading into Fitzroy-square, once famous as a resort of artists. In UPPER FITZROY-STREET lived from 1843 till his death, Nicholas James Crowley, the clever Irish painter. He was born in Dublin on Decem-

WILLIAM HAZLITT.
Autograph.

ber 6th, 1819, and died here on 4th of November, 1857, aged nearly 38 years. His most remarkable work, "Cup-tossing," is known and admired everywhere. In RUSSELL-PLACE, also close by, Maclise lived for a time in the earlier part of his life, and also at UPPER CHARLOTTE-STREET, within sight.

A little distance farther on, Tottenham Court-road ends and Hampstead-road begins. Running at angles to both is Euston-road, extending from Marylebone to King's Cross and Pentonville.

In PENTONVILLE PRISON were confined for a period of six months, from December, 1885, to May, 1886, sixteen of the Fenian prisoners convicted of treason-felony in Dublin a short time previously, and sentenced to various terms of penal servitude. Among them may be mentioned O'Donovan Rossa (sentenced to imprisonment for life), John O'Leary, T. C. Luby (twenty years' imprisonment), the gentle and gifted Kickham (fourteen years'), Charles O'Connell, Denis Dowling Mulcahy, James O'Connor (ten years'), and Casey, "the Galtee Boy" (five years').

In the old St. Pancras Churchyard, which is in St. Pancras-road, not far distant, were buried many famous men, and among them two notable Irishmen, Arthur O'Leary and Arthur Dillon.

EDMUND BURKE.
With his Autograph.

Dillon became a distinguished French divine, and afterwards Archbishop of Narbonne, and ultimately of Toulouse. Many Catholic Irish were buried here during the last century, including members of several noble families.

With Euston-road one or two facts of importance are connected. In STANHOPE-STREET the great actor, William C. Macready, was born on the 3rd of March, 1793. He was the son of Irish parents, his father being a well-known actor and dramatist. As is generally known, Macready reached the highest position obtainable on the stage in his day, and in some tragic parts has been unequalled. He excelled in the characters of Richard the Third and Virginius, but he did not possess the versatility of some other Irish actors. Like J. P. Kemble, he played Roman parts to perfection, and among his greatest triumphs were those won by him in plays written by such Irishmen as Gerald Griffin and J. Sheridan Knowles, notably in "Gisippus" and "Virginius." He was highly esteemed in private life.

In SEYMOUR-STREET, Euston-square, close by, Patrick Macdowell, R.A., lived and kept his studio directly after starting in life as a sculptor on his own account.

Before leaving Euston-road there are few Irish exiles in London who will not gaze with interest on Euston Station, the London terminus of the L. and N. W. Railway, and an exit to the shortest route to the old country.

Proceeding up Hampstead-road, we pass several

REV. ARTHUR O'LEARY.
Autograph.

places of interest. In AMPTHILL-SQUARE, Master Betty died in August, 1874, at an advanced age, and in ARLINGTON-STREET Edward A. Foley, an excellent sculptor, and brother of John Henry Foley, lived and worked during a great part of his too brief existence. Hard by, in ROBERT-STREET, the great Foley himself had his studio, and here he executed some of his most graceful and matured works. His residence, THE PRIORY, Hampstead, where he died at the age of 56 on the 27th of August, 1874, is not far distant. In the Hampstead-road, on the right, is the church of St. James the Less, a chapel-of-ease belonging to St James's, Piccadilly. It is probable that James M'Ardell (who was certainly buried somewhere in Hampstead) was interred here. This great artist died on 2nd of June, 1765, and not long afterwards his friend, Charles Spooner, another excellent Irish engraver, died also, and was buried by his side.

The district at the foot of HAVERSTOCK-HILL is known as CHALK FARM, and was not so very long ago all open country and a famous place for duels. Among other hostile meetings which took place here were those between Captain Macnamara and Colonel Montgomery, and Theodore O'Callaghan and Lieutenant Bailey; but the most important (to Irishmen) were the two with which Tom Moore and Charles Lever were connected.

Moore's duel with Lord Jeffrey occurred in 1806, and was caused by a stinging and just review of his juvenile effusions by the eminent Scotch reviewer. It was a farcical affair and ended in nothing, for somebody, it was found, had extracted the bullets from the pistols of the combatants. Byron, in his "English Bards and Scotch Reviewers," speaking of Jeffrey, thus satirised the event:—

> Can none remember that eventful day,
> That ever-glorious, almost fatal fray,
> When Little's leadless pistol met his eye,
> And Bow-street myrmidons stood laughing by?
> . . . .
> But Caledonia's goddess hovered o'er
> The field, and saved him from the wrath of Moore;
> From either pistol snatched the vengeful lead,
> And straight restored it to her favourite's head.

For writing this account of the duel, or attempted duel, the fiery little poet, being in a peculiarly pugnacious mood, immediately challenged Byron, who took no notice of the epistle, and afterwards, as is well known, became one of the warmest friends of Moore.

The other meeting above referred to was that in 1844 between Charles Lever and S. C. Hall, husband of Mrs. Hall. Lever at the time was editor of the "Dublin University Magazine." An article appeared in that magazine charging S. C. Hall, who had expressed some advanced views, with having been bought by the Whigs, and condemning a letter of his on Irish Temperance Societies. Lever, although not the writer of the article, accepted responsibility for it as editor, and Hall wrote him a bitter letter, in which he said—"The charge came well from one who for about fifty months has been employed in slandering his native country and its people; labouring most successfully to persuade the English public that every Irish gentleman is a blackguard and every Irish peasant a ruffian." Lever came to London at once, and challenged Hall. They met at Chalk Farm, but the matter was arranged amicably by a withdrawal of the remarks on both sides.

In this neighbourhood in March, 1824, died the eccentric nobleman, Lord Coleraine, better known as George Hanger. He had attained the rank of major-general in the army, and was well known in society as the intimate of King George IV.—" the last of the fools and oppressors called George "—and shared in that disreputable monarch's vices. Hanger published his "Life and Adventures" in 1801, and adorned it with a frontispiece, representing himself hanging from a gallows. He systematically refused to assume the title of Lord Coleraine, though it was his of right, and was in every way a most eccentric individual.

In a little house on HAVERSTOCK-HILL lived Sir Richard Steele for some time. The house has long been removed, but Steele's-road, Steele's-terrace, Steele's-studios (for artists abound here), and lastly, and not inappropriately, the "Sir Richard Steele Tavern," commemorate his residence here. The members of the Kit-Cat Club used to call on Steele at his house, so that he might accompany them to their place of meeting, which, in the summer months, was "The Upper Flask," on HAMPSTEAD HEATH. This large tract of country, the popular resort of London cits at holiday times, is interesting to Irishmen for another reason. On the green sward behind "Jack Straw's Castle" (a well-known tavern) the infamous John Sadleir, M.P., was found dead on the morning of Sunday, the 17th February, 1856. Sadleir, who was born

MRS. JAMESON
At the age of sixteen.
Autograph.

in 1814, is known to every reader of Irish history as one of the prominent members of that rotten

Parliamentary party which acquired the name of the "Pope's Brass Band" from its blatant and hollow advocacy of supposed Catholic interests, another member of the band being the notorious William Keogh, afterwards made judge as the reward of apostasy, as Sadleir himself was made a Lord of the Treasury. Sadleir's people were large bankers; and about 1845 he founded and became director of the Tipperary Joint Stock Bank, of which brother James was his manager and sole director. He was besides engaged in a number of commercial undertakings, and in large speculative purchases under the Incumbered Estates Court. In all of these concerns he perpetrated the most extensive frauds, swindling on a grand scale, and keeping up the game to the last. His defalcations in connection with the Tipperary Bank alone amounted to over £400,000, the most appalling misery being created among the unfortunate depositors, chiefly small farmers and tradesmen in the south of Ireland. Sadleir's habits and style of living were very moderate, his London residence in Gloucester-square was simply furnished, and he had little of the bearing of a dashing swindler. But little suspicion of the extent of his villainy was entertained until too late. When at last he had played his final card and detection stared him in the face, he committed suicide under circumstances of great deliberation on the spot mentioned above. By the side of his body, when found, were lying a bottle of poison (oil of almonds), a silver creamewer smelling strongly of prussic acid, and a case of razors, and in his pockets, among other things, a piece of paper on which he had written his name and address in a clear, bold hand. At the inquest held on his remains a letter was produced which had been written by the deceased the night before his death, and which, as perhaps of interest to our readers, we reproduce. It was as follows—

Saturday Night.

I cannot live—I have ruined too many—I could not live and see their agony—I have committed diabolical crimes unknown to any human being. They will now appear, bringing my family and others to distress—causing to all shame and grief that they should have known me.

I blame no one, but attribute all to my own infamous villainy, ——, ——, ——, ——, ——, and others ruined by my villainy. I could go through any torture as a punishment for my crimes. No torture could be too much for such crimes, but I cannot live to see the tortures I inflict on others.

J SADLEIR.

It is a curious fact that there existed then, and exists to this day, a widespread belief that the body found on the Heath was not that of Sadleir, and that he for many years after enjoyed the fruits of his turpitude in some secure part of America or Australia, but the evidence at the inquest seems quite clear on the point of identification.

Near the Heath is Belsize Park-road, where W. C. Stanfield, R.A., the great marine painter, died in May, 1867. From the Heath one may obtain the finest view of London to be seen anywhere, and the prospect well deserves Goldsmith's eulogy of it, to be found in one of his essays.

At the beautiful cemetery of Highgate, within a short distance of Hampstead are buried many illustrious personages, including Coleridge, George Eliot, Faraday, &c, but there are few Irishmen among the number. The most notable of them are Pierce Egan, the novelist and sporting journalist; Joseph Sterling Coyne, the wit and dramatist; and probably Bartholomew Simmons, the poet—although the latter's name, according to Mr. M'Donagh, who has investigated the matter, does not appear on the register. The three authors above mentioned have been noticed quite recently in these articles, and require no further mention. In describing this cemetery, we conclude our review of the Northern Heights of London, and return to Oxford-street, whence we proceeded up to Highgate.

On the left of OXFORD-STREET, as we proceed in a westerly direction, we reach in a moment or two, Charles-street, leading into Soho-square, once a fashionable neighbourhood, but now wholly occupied by manufacturers of various kinds. In SUTTON-STREET, to the left of the square, is one of the most remarkable Catholic chapels in London—ST. PATRICK'S. It was originally the music-room of Lord Carlisle's mansion, which stood here, and was purchased through the exertions of the famous wit, divine, and controversialist, Father Arthur O'Leary, to whose memory it contains a mural tablet bearing his likeness.

Externally it has a strange appearance, resembling one of the warehouses by which it is surrounded rather than a Catholic place of worship. Internally, however, it is not unworthy of its purpose, and possesses over the altar one of Vandyck's finest religious paintings. It is attended by numbers of the Irish and foreign residents of the district, the latter being a particularly numerous body in Soho. Here Cardinal Wiseman used occasionally to preach to crowded congregations, and as this eminent ecclesiastic, although born in Spain, was of Irish parentage, the fact is fitly mentioned here. The little chapel is hallowed by many interesting Irish memories, but indisputably the most notable personage connected with it has been the redoubtable Father Arthur O'Leary. He was born in Cork in 1729, and died in 1802. Although believed by his friends, and most people generally, to be a model of rectitude and fidelity to Ireland, it has been discovered since his death that he was in the service and pay of the Government—in short, an informer. His biographer, writing before these disclosures were made, relates that O'Leary on his deathbed uttered the exclamation —" Alas! I have betrayed my poor country."

Opposite Sutton-street, on the other side of the square, are GREEK-STREET and FRITH-STREET. In the latter died the distinguished essayist and critic, William Hazlitt, on September 18th, 1830. His father was a Unitarian clergyman, and an Irishman, and his most eminent son was born in 1778. He began life as a painter, and exhibited at the Academy once or twice, following his profession with much success. The charms of literature were, however, too attractive, and he gave up painting in order to devote himself to it. His claim to rank among the great critics can hardly be doubted, and his works fully deserve all the popularity and eulogy they have obtained. His brother John was also an artist of note.

In Greek-street lived the clever inventor of musical instruments, Charles Claggett, a native of Waterford, a sound musician and competent violinist. He kept a shop here for a time during the last century, and was visited by Haydn, the great musician, who spoke very highly of Claggett's inventions, which have proved of great value to the musical world. Another distinguished Irishman—Bryan Higgins, the chemist—was connected with this street. He started a school of practical chemistry here in July, 1774, and is considered an eminent scientist. He was a native of Sligo, was born about 1737, and died in 1820, aged 83, leaving behind him a worthy reputation.

Greek-street leads into COMPTON-STREET, which is interesting as the place where Mulready, the great painter, resided when he first came to London with his parents. Here his father carried on his occupation, that of a leather breeches maker.

Compton-street runs into WARDOUR-STREET, a place of some notoriety for its connection with various remarkable events of the last century. A few yards to the left, as we emerge from the first-named street, is ST. ANNE'S CHURCH, Soho, where William Hazlitt is buried. It was in an

eatinghouse in Wardour-street that James Barry, the painter, was taken ill, in February, 1806, dying soon after, on the 22nd of the same month. On the left or western side of Wardour-street is a pawnbroker's shop named Harrison's, which is the identical house, same name and same firm, where R. B. Sheridan, the great but improvident w.t, used to pawn his valuables when in necessity —a not infrequent event.

At No. 37 GERRARD-STREET, close by, lived Edmund Burke for many years, and a tablet on the front of the house records the fact. As a philosophical writer, and as a master of prose, Burke is pre-eminent among the writers of the English tongue. Though he had no experience of practical statesmanship, he was profoundly versed in its philosophy, and to him are due many of its most important and finest maxims and aphorisms. As an orator he was likewise supreme, while friend and foe alike joined in admiration of his gigantic intellect. Matthew Arnold, the eminent critic, declared him to be, in his opinion, the greatest prose-writer in English literature; while Sir James Mackintosh, politically opposed to him on many points, said that "Gibbon (the great historian) might have been taken out of a corner of Burke's mind and not be missed;" and even Macaulay, who seemed to detest everybody and everything Irish, is stated to have remarked, as he finished reading Burke's works— "Wonderful! Wonderful! The greatest man since Milton!" Burke's fame increases with the flight of time, and he is an object of admiration, and his works the subject of the deepest study to all the best thinkers of the age. The distinguished writer, John Morley, is one of his most loving biographers, and has written several excellent works on this greatest of Irishmen. Burke was a true and great philosopher, and no mere propounder of metaphysical theories, as so many others who usurp that name are.

In close proximity to Burke's house, and at the "Turk's Head Tavern," in Gerrard-street, the well-known Literary Club was founded by Sir Joshua Reynolds. Among its most important members and visitors were many Irishmen, including Burke, Goldsmith, Malone (the Shakesperean commentator), R. B. Sheridan, Arthur Murphy, Earl of Charlemont, and Earl Nugent— not to mention their friend, the autocratic Johnson and their critic, the wily Boswell. The power and eloquence evinced in the debates of this club, and the brilliant sayings, the concentrated wit and wisdom that emanated from a group of ...lebrities as those mentioned, may be bett... ...ed than described. Such an assembly ... ...ry giants it would be difficult, if not impo......, to equal in point of mental power; and this quiet little street in Soho, with its innumerable memories of other great men, certainly takes rank among the historic spots of the metropolis.

CHAPTER X.

FROM SOHO TO MARYLEBONE.

WARDOUR - STREET, with which we dealt in our last chapter, runs into Oxford-street, and faces NEWMAN-STREET and RATHBONE-PLACE, two turnings on the right, as we proceed towards Marylebone. In the latter street died the distinguished portrait-painter, Nathaniel Hone, R.A., in 1784, while in the former street an Irish sculptor of repute, Peter Turnerelli, died in 1839. Turnerelli was born in Belfast in 1774, and came to London when 18 years old; and soon came into repute by a fine bust of the young Princess Charlotte. He was employed as teacher of modelling by Royalty and many noble families, and in a short time chiselled a number of busts of eminent persons in Great Britain. His works are to be found in London and the provinces, and in several Continental cities, and he has executed more busts of eminent characters than any British artist of the day. Two of his best works are busts of his illustrious countrymen, Grattan and Curran, the former of which, executed in a very few hours, was declared by Canova to be the finest modern bust he had seen in this country. To Turnerelli we are principally indebted for the sensible innovation of dressing busts in the exact costume of their originals, instead of absurdly habiting them, as was universal, in the costume of Roman Senators.

MORTIMER-STREET is at the top of Newman-street, and here lived, soon after his arrival in London, that most versatile of Irish writers, Samuel Lover. He was not only, as his biographer puts it, "poet, painter, novelist, composer, and dramatist," but he succeeded in all these capacities. It was the success of his miniature of Paganini, the celebrated violinist, painted in Dublin, and exhibited in London, which led to his removing permanently to the British metropolis, where he continued to exhibit for twelve years on the walls of the Royal Academy. His varied talents, combined with great conversational powers and unfailing good humour, soon made him a favourite in London with all classes and gained him an entry into the most exclusive society. His tastes were simple and his life pure, and possessing a warm heart and a happy disposition, he was loved by all who knew him.

LOVER.

His most inimitable productions are his songs, of which he wrote nearly 300, and most of which will live as long as genuine humour is appreciated. As a miniature painter he deserved and obtained the highest praise, and if he had confined himself to that art, or to any other of which he was master, a lasting fame would be assured to him. Lover was a master of repartee, and several instances might be quoted of his ready wit. On one occasion a lady who took a great interest in Ireland and sympathised deeply with the deplorable condition of that country, said to him—"I believe I was made for an Irishwoman." "Cross over to Ireland," replied Lover, "and they will swear you were made for an Irishman!"

On the right and left of Mortimer-street is GREAT TITCHFIELD-STREET, where, in September, 1788, the great painter, William Collins, R.A., was born. His sea-pieces are exquisitely true to nature, and the best of them are everywhere known by numerous engravings. In this street it

Ireland in London.

was that James Barry, the painter, died in great poverty in 1806. He was taken ill in a French eating-house in Wardour-street, and was first conveyed to his own miserable lodgings, but the door could not be opened, owing to the mischievous conduct of some urchins in obstructing the keyhole. He was then taken to the house of a brother Academician, where he soon expired. A lamentable ending to a career wholly and unselfishly devoted to the furtherance of Art !

CASTLE-STREET, where Barry lived many years, also runs out of Mortimer-street. The house, No. 86, which he occupied, can be easily recognised, as a tablet recording the fact is placed on its front. It is stated that he once invited his great friend and benefactor, Edmund Burke, to dine with him here, and, with characteristic contempt for display of any kind, asked Burke to attend to the steak he was cooking while he hurried to the nearest publichouse for a pot of porter !

Returning to Oxford-street through Castle-street we notice BERWICK-STREET, which is on the left. Here, in 1788, died George Anne (Georgiana) Bellamy, one of the cleverest of comedy actresses, and a formidable rival to Peg Woffington and Kitty Clive. She was born at Fingal, in Ireland on the 23rd of April (St. George's Day), probably in the year 1727. In certain characters she was unapproachable, and where she found her equal it was mostly in an Irish woman, such was Ireland's pre-eminence as the birthplace of great actresses. In the next turning, POLAND-STREET, is St. James's Workhouse, where Luke Sullivan, the fine engraver, was taken after death, and in the burying-ground of which he was interred.

CARDINAL WISEMAN.

On the opposite side of the way is GREAT PORTLAND-STREET, which is noteworthy as the place of residence of Arthur O'Leary. He died here in January, 1802. W. P. M'Cabe, the well-known United Irishman, made this street one of his numerous resorts during his daring and dangerous visits to the metropolis. Here also, on the 26th of February, 1848, died Thomas Simpson Cooke, an excellent musician and vocalist,

and a still more successful teacher. He was born in Dublin in 1782, and gained a great reputation by the numerous operas and songs he composed. Among his pupils, perhaps the most famous has been Sims Reeves. On the right is MARGARET STREET, containing one of the most beautiful churches in London—All Saints. Its interior is superbly decorated, the fine painted windows being by a living Irish artist of renown—namely, John O'Connor. In this same street M'Dowell the sculptor kept a studio towards the close of his life, and at an academy here the famous critic and antiquary, Dr. John Doran, was educated. He was born in London, of parents who came from county Cavan, and was essentially Irish in feeling and sympathies. To him we owe many facts concerning Irish writers and other Irishmen of note which would doubtless have remained in obscurity if he, with his intense enthusiasm for everything Irish, had not rescued them from neglect and dwelt with full emphasis upon them. He seemed to take a great interest and much pride in quoting every fact which was creditable to the race from which he sprung, and Ireland owes him a debt of gratitude for his works on theatrical matters. His books are most fascinating to read, owing to his sprightly style and the immense number of entertaining anecdotes with which he enlivens their pages. Notably so is his "Annals of the Stage," a book which is as absorbing and diverting as one of the best novels of the day, and a splendid edition of which, with innumerable illustrations, has only recently been published.

Just past Great Portland-street the thoroughfare is crossed by REGENT-STREET, which deserves a little more notice than usual. It is certainly one of the finest streets in the world, and is interesting to Irishmen for several reasons. At No. 112 here was the publishing house, now removed, of Fraser, where the well-known magazine of that name was first published in 1830. William Maginn was its first editor, and in the room behind the shop he wrote many of his finest criticisms and wittiest poems and tales. Here also many of the learned and humorous "Reliques" of "Father Prout" were dashed off by the owner of that pseudonym. At the dinners which were frequently given here to his contributors by Fraser, a gathering of remarkable men took place. Carlyle and Dickens, Thackeray and Lockhart, Hogg and Allan Cunningham were prominent among the English and Scotch guests, while little Crofton Croker, "Father Prout," Serjennt Murphy, Daniel Maclise, and, lastly, the erudite editor himself, who graced the chair, never failed to attend these convivial meetings. But Regent-street has other memories. Among its remarkable residents, perhaps the most important (certainly so to Irishmen), was Gerald Griffin, one of the sweetest of our poets and the most popular of our novelists, who lived here in 1824, in what was then No. 76. He was at the time in somewhat affluent circumstances, his fight against poverty and the indifference of the English public being partly over.

In this street also, on the 3rd of February, 1848, died General Sir Charles Doyle, the eminent soldier, who served with great distinction in the Spanish War—one of the many Irish soldiers of that time who rose to a high position in the English army.

In WARWICK-STREET, which leads out of Regent-street, is the Bavarian Roman Catholic Chapel, containing one of J. E. Carew's finest works. It is a sculptured tablet, 14 feet high and 7 feet wide, representing the Virgin surrounded by cherubim.

Behind Regent-street, on our left as we look towards Piccadilly, lies GOLDEN-SQUARE, notable as the place where Charles Phillips, the orator and friend of O'Connell, died on the 1st of February, 1859. As a rhetorician he dazzled his contemporaries, but his speeches, full of fervent declamation and brilliant imagery as they are, no longer attract readers. At the top of Regent-street is LANGHAM-PLACE, where O'Connell lived in 1838, and beyond this is PORTLAND-PLACE, which is considered a fine thoroughfare, and was partly built by an architect named O'Neill, father of Hugh O'Neill, the eminent draughtsman and artist. Sebastian Gahagan's statue of the Duke of Kent is at the top of this street, and is one of his best works. It is of bronze, and stands 7ft. 6in. in height. The likeness is an admirable one, and in every respect the statue is a good specimen of Gahagan's powers.

DR. DORAN.

In the MARYLEBONE-ROAD, which crosses the top of Portland-place, is the New Church of Marylebone, in the burial-ground attached to which was buried George Canning, a clever poet and general author, who died in 1771, and who is now remembered chiefly as the father of the great statesman of the same name. In the same road, and within sight, is the famous wax-work show (Madame Tussaud's), which, as it contains some interesting relics of Wellington, and a great many models of illustrious and notorious Irishmen, cannot be passed by unnoticed. In MARYLEBONE-STREET, in the immediate neighbourhood, William Paulett Carey, an Irishman and a celebrated art critic, kept an art establishment or paint shop. He was one of the United Irishmen, but did not become a very prominent member of that body. Besides his works, some of which are excellent, his chief title to praise and remembrance is that he was among the first to recognise and to encourage the genius of three distinguished sculptors, John Hogan, Sir F. Chantrey, and John Gibson; and he was also one of the earliest in his recognition of the abilities of James Montgomery.

Returning to Regent-street by Portland-place, the first turning on the right in the former leads into CAVENDISH-SQUARE, the neighbourhood of which is famous for its Irish residents. No. 32 was once occupied by a good painter, of Irish parentage, named Francis Cotes, R.A., who was followed in his tenancy by Sir Martin Archer Shee, then at the height of his reputation as a portrait painter, and during the time he was President of the Royal Academy. Every street about this spot has had among its dwellers many distinguished Irish personage. Thus, in CAVENDISH-STREET, Mrs Jameson, one of the best authorities on art subjects, lived for a time; and on the opposite side of the square, in HARLEY-STREET, lived several other Irish writers of note, including Sir Philip Francis and Sir Aubrey de Vere. Here the latter wrote his "Duke of Mercia," in the winter of 1822. As a dramatic poet and sonnetur, Sir A. de Vere is widely known and highly praised by competent critics; his son, the present Aubrey de Vere, being equally distinguished in the same branches of literature. Another resident of Harley-street was Lord Strangford, also a good poet, and well known as the translator of Camoens' "Lusiad," the epic of the Portuguese. In QUEEN ANNE STREET, also in close proximity to the square, have lived at various times Edmund Burke, Edmund Malone, Sir A. de Vere, and Richard Cumberland.

One other street calls for mention here, and that is WIGMORE-STREET. No. 40 was one of the many London addresses of Thomas Moore, whose songs, according to James Hogg, the Ettrick Shepherd, will "last to a' eternity." No other songs, not even Burns's, are so popular all over the world, and whether this is due to the melodies or to Moore's words it is needless to inquire. In the majority of instances Moore's felicitous language and brilliant imagination are worthy of the entrancing old airs to which they are wedded, and no higher praise is necessary or could be given to them.

Proceeding up Oxford-street, we reach Duke-street, which leads into MANCHESTER-SQUARE, where Lady Blessington lived in 1816. This remarkable Irishwoman, whose maiden name was Margaret Power, was born in Clonmel, Tipperary, in 1789. By her powers of fascination rather than by sheer literary ability she raised herself to a very high position among the writers of her time. As for her works, they are now mostly forgotten, her best novel being, perhaps, "The Repealers," a tale of a somewhat national character, though not as the term "national" is nowadays understood.

In SPANISH-PLACE, off this square, is situated the Spanish Catholic Chapel, where, about 1830, the great wit and scholar, Rev. Francis Sylvester Mahony, afterwards known as "Father Prout," used to preach occasionally.

Quite close to this spot is PORTMAN-SQUARE, reached through Seymour-street. This was also a neighbourhood greatly favoured by Irish literary men and others. In ORCHARD-STREET, Richard Brinsley Sheridan lived in 1773, and here he wrote his admirable opera, "The Duenna," and the amusing comedy, "The Rivals." Another resident of the same street was George Barrett, R.A., whom even English critics describe as one of the most eminent of English (!) landscape-painters. YORK-PLACE here is interesting to Irishmen, for at No. 8 died one of the greatest of divines, Cardinal Nicholas Wiseman, who was filled with Irish sympathies. So precociously talented was he that at the age of 18 he published a book of some merit on the languages of the East, and attained the rank of D.D. some time before the ordination age of 23. In 1835 he came to London, and the next year delivered a course of Lenten lectures at Moorfields Chapel which created a great sensation. In 1849 he was appointed Vicar Apostolic of the London District in succession to Dr. Walsh. In 1850 commenced a stormy period of his career. The Vatican issued a Bull changing the system of Catholic Church government in England, and establishing dioceses with bishops, and created Dr. Wiseman Cardinal Archbishop of Westminster. A perfect whirlwind of indignation, difficult now to understand, burst forth from the Protestant population of England at this "Papal aggression." The most alarming and absurd rumours were circulated of an intended descent on the country by the Pope at the head of a new Armada; public meetings were held all over the country to rouse popular excitement to boiling point; there were wild and prolonged debates in Parliament, and the famous "Ecclesiastical Titles Bill" was passed, making illegal the assumption by Roman

GRATTAN.

Catholic prelates of such titles as the Pope had recently conferred on them. The excitement, however, was only temporary, the bill when passed was openly violated, without an attempt at prosecution, and was repealed some years afterwards with almost universal assent. The Cardinal, who had lost no time in endeavouring to throw oil on the troubled waters by the publication of 'An Appeal to the reason and good feeling of the English People," became, after the storm had passed away, extremely popular even in circles outside his own Church, through his genial manners, great abilities, and vast accomplishments. He lectured frequently before the most widely different audiences in London and the provinces on subjects connected with art and science. His knowledge of languages was exceptionally great, extending to almost all the Continental and many Oriental tongues. His writings are varied and voluminous, dealing with religious controversy, science, philology, and art. Perhaps his best-known works are his graphic "Recollections of the Last Four Popes," and a romance, entitled, "Fabiola," vividly depicting the Catacomb worship of the early Christians. He was born in 1802, and died on the 15th February, 1865, leaving behind him a name as one of the greatest of Cardinals, and, among the Irish Catholics of London a loving memory for active sympathy and untiring labours among them.

In SOMERSET-STREET died Sir John Doyle in August, 1834. Both as a soldier and as an administrator Sir John Doyle was very distinguished. He was Governor of Guernsey for many years, and the fine monument there erected in his honour is a testimony of the esteem in which he was held by its people. His nephew, Sir Francis Hastings Doyle, who died recently, was widely-known as a poet and critic, and was for some time Professor of Poetry at Oxford. In BAKER-STREET, which leads off Portman-square, two important events occurred. One was the death of Henry Grattan, the greatest of Irish orators and statesmen, and one of the most sterling of her patriots, which took place on the 4th of June, 1820. This event was of such great importance that we may be pardoned for dwelling upon it at a little length. Lecky, in his "Leaders of Public Opinion," says—"He lingered for a few days, retaining to the last his full consciousness and interest in public affairs. Those who gathered round his deathbed observed with emotion how fondly and how constantly his mind reverted to that Legislature which he had served so faithfully and loved so well." He wished to be buried in Ireland, but was overruled, and consented to a tomb in Westminster Abbey. Almost his last words were—"I die with a love of liberty in my heart, and this declaration (in support of the Catholic claims) in favour of my country in my hand." It is a remarkable example of the manner in which physical deficiencies are overmastered by commanding intellect and nobility of soul that this brilliant orator and statesman was as ill furnished by nature with the bodily attributes calculated to prepossess his audience as could be conceived. In person he was low-sized, his arms were of disproportionate length, his face thin, marked slightly with the smallpox, his chin remarkably long, and his action in delivery most ungraceful.

In this street, at the house of a friend named John Macnamara, Lord Cloncurry first met Pitt, towards the close of last century, and for the first time heard of the project of the contemplated Union.

Baker-street runs to REGENT'S PARK, which, when it was open fields, was a favourite place for duels in the days when such a practice was universal. Among other hostile meetings which took place here was one between Morgan O'Connell and Lord Alvanley. The cause of it was as follows:—The Liberator, on account of some provocation from the nobleman referred to, termed him in the House of Commons "a bloated buffoon," but having resolved to fight no more duels after the disastrous result of that which occurred between him and D'Esterre, refused a challenge from Alvanley. The latter brought the matter before the club (Brooke's) to which they both belonged, and sought to get O'Connell expelled. The club refused, though Alvanley's attempt was backed by twenty-four prominent members. On hearing of the affair, O'Connell's son, Morgan, challenged Alvanley, after saying in a letter containing the challenge that everybody knew his father had vowed not to fight another duel, and could therefore throw out their challenges with impunity. The meeting took place in May, 1835. After exchanging two or three shots the parties withdrew from the field, perfectly satisfied on the score of honour, if not with the result of the encounter.

CHAPTER XI.
FROM PADDINGTON TO NOTTINGHILL.

THE Marylebone-road runs into EDGWARE-ROAD, at about the centre of the latter, which reaches from Hyde Park almost to Kilburn, one of the north-western suburbs of London. As we leave Marylebone-road, Kilburn is on our right through MAIDA VALE. In this road died in 1883, a distinguished Irish novelist, known to all lovers of books of adventure as Captain Mayne Reid. He was born in Kloskilt, county Down, in 1819, and in his writings showed all the splendid vigour possessed by so many of his Northern brethren. His works are greatly superior to those of many other "purveyors" of "adventurous" literature from the fact that he had a thorough and practical acquaintance with the life he generally describes, and thrilled his readers by his evident sincerity and the forcible truth of his delineations. In common with most prolific authors he wrote much that was unworthy of his reputation, but his best work, as in "The Hunter's Feast," &c., is equal to that of J. F. Cooper, and quite entitled to rank beside it.

Of his "Scalp Hunters" alone above a million copies are said to have been sold. It is stated that in Russia he is more popular than Scott or Dickens, and most of his works have been translated into various European languages. It is pleasing to record that, unlike many Irish writers whose works lay in paths removed from politics, Captain Mayne Reid was thoroughly in sympathy with the Irish struggle for freedom, and a good later of the misgovernment of his native country.

In this neighbourhood there also died in 1868

CAPT. MAYNE REID.

another Irishman—John Doyle—whose conspicuous powers as an artist reflect great credit on his Irish art education. He was born in Ireland in 1797, and after studying for a time in Dublin, his native city, came to London, and soon astonished and delighted the town by his exceedingly clever and almost unique political caricatures or cartoons, which were always signed "H. B.," the letters being formed by his initials doubled and placed one above the other thus :— "I D." This wonderful series of drawings is now very valuable, as much for their historical importance as for their artistic merit. They came out to the number of 917, in batches at irregular intervals, from 1829 to 1851, and were considered so important as to be noticed for many years by a semi-leader in the "Times" explaining their meaning. Great pains were taken to conceal the name of their author, and to the last the secret was well preserved. They were the best cartoons that had appeared since the days of Gillray and Rowlandson, to whose works they were, besides, immensely superior in their higher sense of humour and complete freedom from coarseness and vulgarity. The chief politicians of the day became familiar to the public through these excellent sketches, which received the praise of some of the most eminent men of the time. Doyle died in CLIFTON GARDENS, here, at the age of 71, leaving two sons, both of them eminent artists. One, Henry Doyle, is now Director of the National Gallery of Ireland ; the other, Richard, made a special branch of illustration his own, and reigned supreme in it. KILBURN, though now a populous suburb of London, was until comparatively recently a country village. A very curious incident, of some interest to Irishmen, occurred here in 1829. At this time William Smith O'Brien was a Conservative and an opponent of O'Connell, and made what was practically his first appearance in politics in an address to the electors of Clare, in which he asserted that O'Connell, when they had returned to Parliament, was supported in his agitation by none of the gentry of Clare. Tom Steele, being a native of that county, attacked O'Brien violently for this statement, and was answered by a challenge to a duel The meeting took place in June, 1829, at Kilburn Meadows, Steele being accompanied by The O'Gorman Mahon, and O'Brien by a foreigner with the unmelodious name of Woronzow Greig. It is said that the "Head Pacificator" came to this combat armed as if for "a campaign," carrying a bag of bullets and a flask of powder. Both he and his second seemed quite indignant when, after the first fire, O'Brien expressed himself satisfied. "I and my friend Mr Steele," said O'Gorman Mahon, "have come to this place with great reluctance, at the invitation of Mr. O'Brien but having come upon the field our business is to fight." However, the proceedings terminated without further hostilities, although O'Brien was immediately after challenged by Mahon, who was also a Clareman. Explanations, however, followed, and a further duel was averted.

GERALD GRIFFIN.
(Autograph.)

Returning from Kilburn, we come down the Edgware-road, which in Goldsmith's time formed part of the village of Edgware, where he wrote his delightful comedy, "She Stoops to Conquer," and other works, and reach on the right Harrow-road, leading to PADDINGTON CHURCHYARD, near the old church. Two eminent artists are buried here—William Collins and George Barrett—both of Irish origin, and both Royal Academicians. It is also believed that Captain William Baillie, one of the foremost engravers of the last century, was interred here, for he died close by on the 22nd of December, 1810. He was a native of Kilbride, county Carlow, and was born on the 5th of June, 1723. His first profession was the law, which he studied at the Temple, and which proved altogether uncongenial to his tastes, and he therefore abandoned it and became a soldier, obtaining a very respectable rank in the army. Like one or two other great engravers, he was an amateur—that is, he did not follow his art as a profession or as a means of income. Some of the plates executed by him are exceptionally fine, and rank beside those of the best engravers of his time, and are, moreover, much sought after by experts and collectors. As he merely gave his leisure to such purposes, his plates are not numerous, but they are uniformly good. Paddington Churchyard likewise contained the remains of John Philpot Curran, from his death in 1817 till 1834, when they were removed to Ireland for more fitting burial amidst more appropriate surroundings.

Paddington was one of the principal places of residence chosen by Gerald Griffin during his stay in London. In PADDINGTON-STREET, hard by, he lived during 1825, afterwards removing to NORTHUMBERLAND-STREET, in the vicinity of Regent's Park, where he lodged during 1826-7. While here his brother, Dr. William Griffin, found him, when he visited London, in better circumstances than he expected, for his struggles for fame had been especially severe. Griffin was at this time writing to several papers in London, and was also preparing some of his most notable works. As a novelist he ranks amongst our foremost writers, and he was also a poet of high order. His "Collegians" is believed by many competent judges to be the best Irish novel ever written; but although there may be some difference of opinion on that point, there can be none as to the beauty and exquisite feeling of his many lyrics. Few Irish poets have written more touching verses than he did at his best, and few have been more Irish or more natural in their writings.

Proceeding down Edgware-road, BRYANSTON-SQUARE is on the left, behind the main road. At the church here Lady Blessington was married to the Earl of Blessington in 1818, her first husband, Captain Farmer, having been killed the year before in a drunken quarrel. She had plenty of ability, and wrote some fairly good works, but she is chiefly remembered only as a brilliant conversationalist and a lover of literature and the arts, and for her close connections with all the most eminent writers and artists of her time. BRYANSTON-STREET here was the place of residence of Edward Quillinan, one of the best of the rather numerous translators of Camoens, the Portuguese poet. Quillinan was born in Portugal of Irish and Catholic parents, and in his somewhat brief lifetime made some meritorious contributions to literature. He was the son-in-law and intimate friend of the great poet Wordsworth, and wrote a good many graceful and melodious lyrics, besides translating Camoens' "Lusiad," an epic poem which has attracted several other Irish scholars and poets—especially Lord Strangford and Sir Richard Francis Burton. At the foot of the Edgware-road is UXBRIDGE-ROAD, which stretches from Oxford-street to Notting-hill, skirting Hyde Park for a considerable distance. Opposite Edgware-road and quite close to the Marble Arch (as the entrance to Hyde Park is named from its fine gateway built of Carrara marble) is a red stone, almost touching the railings of the park. This is the identical Tyburn Stone, bearing the inscription—"Here Stood Tyburn Gate," which brief and simple words are pregnant with meaning to the student of history. This spot was one of those whereon the gallows stood, and where pious and holy persons as well as highwaymen and other disturbers of the peace were executed. This was probably the place where after the Restoration the bodies of Crom-

W. SMITH O'BRIEN.
(Autograph.)

well and other regicides were carted and suspended to the gallows amid the execrations of the populace.

Uxbridge-road was once infested by highwaymen, and a peculiar incident is stated to have happened here to Mulready, the great painter, in the early part of the present century. He had been frequently warned of the dangers he incurred in walking home by night instead of returning by the coach, but he laughed at the fears of his friends, being of powerful frame and, moreover, an expert boxer. One night he was suddenly stopped on this road by a man who presented a pistol and uttered the stereotyped phrase of the highwayman. Mulready, instead of tremblingly handing over his purse, made a determined attack on the surprised robber, and easily overpowered him. He bore his prisoner in triumph to his house in LINDEN-GROVE, which was not far distant, and, having given him into the charge of his father, interrogated him as to the cause of his having taken to the road. It turned out the man had been driven to rob by sheer want, and Mulready, not wishing to expose him to the death penalty, which then was attached to all such offences, released him after having given him some substantial assistance.

HYDE PARK also was at one time the haunt of highwaymen, its most notable frequenter for felonious purposes being James MacLean, the son of a Monaghan clergyman, and a worthy follower of Claude Duval and Dick Turpin. His exploits were numerous and daring, and, what is more, well authenticated, unlike the reputed deeds of the two worthies referred to. The well-known writer, Horace Walpole, in an epistle to one of his friends in 1749, records his having been waylaid and robbed here by MacLean, whose pistol going off accidentally nearly put an end to the life of the brilliant raconteur. MacLean was hung at Tyburn the following year, when the brightest eyes among ladies of high birth were in tears at his loss.

This great park is only one of many in London, but is certainly THE PARK *par excellence*, so far as fashion is concerned. During the summer its roads are alive with gorgeous equipages; the promenade known as "The Lady's Mile" is one blaze of colour, and the course termed the "Rotten Row" is black with male and female equestrians. On other occasions it presents quite another sight. Countless thousands of people congregate on its green sward in order to express their convictions or to expose their grievances, social or political. Many a great demonstration has been held here, and once or twice the "Sons of Toil" have "demonstrated" their strength to some purpose in defence of free speech. In 1866 the people of London were forbidden to use the Park for political meetings, but they assembled there on a certain eventful day in that year, and, in spite of soldiers and police, asserted their right. In the riot that ensued the railings of the Park were used with great effect as weapons against the police. Sir Richard Mayne (an Irishman), who commanded that body, was pulled from his horse and severely injured. There were many Irishmen concerned on both sides in this affair, which produced a great effect upon the Government and the "governing classes."

In October, 1862, some extraordinary riots occurred here. Meetings of the English labouring class were held in the Park to express sympathy with Garibaldi, and the violent language used by some of the speakers with reference to the Pope seems to have excited the wrath of the poorer classes of the London Irish. They assembled in large numbers and stormed the various improvised platforms, and drove the "Garibaldians" from the field. The latter, however, collected afterwards in immense crowds, and a series of determined riots ensued, in which over 60,000 persons are stated to have taken part, and in which the police, as usual, got roughly handled by the contending factions. The disturbances were eventually quelled by a strong display of police and military.

In 1868-69, and subsequent years, great Irish meetings were held here to demand the amnesty of those condemned to penal servitude for complicity in Fenianism, one of the largest with this object taking place on the 15th March, 1874, even the most hostile testimony computing the number of people present on this occasion at about 30,000. In later years some of the largest meetings held in this park have been demonstrations against coercive government in Ireland; and altogether it is in such demonstrations as those mentioned—attended by masses of Irish people, old and young, from the most distant and outlying parts of the metropolis, in the most inclement as well as the most favourable weather—that Londoners have best understood how the hearts of Irish exiles in London beat true to the old country. Hyde Park was once a famous meeting place for duellists, but there have been apparently few Irishmen of note concerned in these affairs. The Earl of Shelburne (an Irish statesman of note, and afterwards Prime Minister of England), fought a duel with a Colonel Fullarton here in 1780, and R. B. Sheridan also fought one with Matthews here during the last century. But these duels were of little moment, and are not of historical interest. Before leaving the Park we may add that it was a favourite resort of Gerald Griffin, to whom its green sward

FERGUS O'CONNOR.

and quiet, shady avenues afforded a pleasant retreat from the dust and noise and bustle of the city in which he had to struggle so hard for a living. In one of his letters to his sister he writes— "We (John Banim and himself) walked over Hyde Park together on Patrick's Day, and renewed our home recollections by gathering shamrocks and placing them in our hats even under the eye of " John Bull." As the genuine " green immortal" leaf is said not to grow out of Ireland, it is probable that our two novelists, like many of their exiled fellow-countrymen, were forced to put up with the large rough-leaved Cockney trefoil which is commonly sold outside the Catholic churches on " the 17th," and of which many a John Bull in these changed days makes a lavish display. In the BAYSWATER-ROAD, an eminent scholar and divine, Dr. Adam Clarke, died in 1832. He was born in the county of Derry in 1760, and before his death had acquired a great reputation for scholarship, especially in Biblical matters. In this road is situated the cemetery of ST. GEORGE'S, belonging to the church in Hanover-square. It is notable as the burial-place of two distinguished Irishmen—Laurence Sterne, the author of "Tristram Shandy," and Sir Henry Parnell (afterwards Lord Congleton), who wrote a couple of excellent works in favour of the Catholics, and who died in 1842, aged 65.

In the neighbourhood, at QUEENSBORO-TERRACE, opposite Porchester Gardens, died Charles Keane, the celebrated actor, on the 22nd of January, 1868. He was a native of Waterford, and a son of the great tragedian, Edmund Keane. He was a thoroughly good Shakespearean actor, and succeeded in both tragedy and comedy, and was also excellent in melodrama. For many years he was one of the leading impersonators of Shakespearean parts in London, and held his own successfully against Macready, Phelps, and other great performers and rivals. WESTBOURNE-GROVE is chiefly noteworthy as the place where George Barrett, the painter, lived and produced some of his finest works, and where he died in 1784. LINDEN GROVE, close by, was the last place of residence of Mulready, who died here on 7th of July, 1863, aged 77.

Bayswater leads direct to Notting-hill, and here at NOTTING HILL-TERRACE died the famous Chartist leader, Fergus O'Connor, in August, 1859. For some time before his death he had shown unmistakable signs of mental derangement and had to be cared for in a private lunatic asylum kept by a Dr. Tuke. O'Connor was a native of Cork, and was born in 1796. He was at first an Irish member, but opposed O'Connell on some points, though always an ardent Repealer, and was consequently obliged to seek a seat elsewhere. He ultimately became member for Nottingham and editor of a paper called the *Northern Star*, which had a tremendous influence in the politics of those days, and also an enormous circulation (for that time), sometimes reaching 60,000. His speeches were terribly bombastic in tone, but he had a large amount of ability and could at times be very eloquent and forcible. His unselfishness is indisputable and undisputed. He spent a large fortune in the Chartist movement, and underwent severe imprisonment for what he was convinced was a just and reasonable cause. His very recklessness and carelessness endeared him to a large majority of the Chartists, who hold his name and labours in affectionate remembrance, and many Chartists pay annual pilgrimages to his tomb, which is not far distant, in KENSAL-GREEN CEMETERY, where a striking monument has been erected over his grave. In person he was "huge," in manner "boisterous," and was possessed of plentiful and flaming red hair. Whatever his individual faults were, and they were many, servility or greed were not of the number. His conduct was somewhat autocratic, and he displeased some of the other Chartist leaders by attempting or aspiring to be sole chief of the movement. So far as Ireland was concerned, his patriotism was undoubted. Two of his most prominent colleagues in the agitation were Irishmen—James Bronterre O'Brien, the author of some excellent works on social and economical subjects, and Rev. Arthur O'Neill, who was intimately connected with the movement in Birmingham, and who is, we believe, still alive (1888). KENSAL-GREEN CEMETERY, which we have just referred to, is situated at the end of the LADBROKE GROVE-ROAD, Notting-hill. It may fairly be called the London Glasnevin, judging by the number of its Irish dead. It is divided into two portions, the Catholic and Protestant burial-grounds. As the last resting-place of many who have done good service to Irish art and literature, or who have helped her in her centuried struggle, this cemetery is worthy of many Irish pilgrimages. Here are buried many eminent artists, like Mulready, Stanfield, Maclise, John Leech, and John Edward Carew; and some of our best musicians, such as Balfe, Wallace, and Thomas S. Cooke. Samuel Lover, J. F. O'Donnell, and Ellen Fitzsimon (daughter of O'Connell, and author of "The Woods of Killinoe"), are among the Irish poets whose dust also reposes here. Here, too, lie Catherine Hayes, the exquisite vocalist; Sir Robert M'Clure, the great Arctic navigator; Macready, the actor; Mrs. Jameson, the well-known writer on art; Cardinal Wiseman, one of the greatest of English prelates and the first English cardinal since the Reformation; Dr. John Doran, one of the most delightful writers on theatrical and antiquarian matters; Peter Burrowes, a member of Grattan's Parliament, a sound lawyer and thorough patriot; Fergus O'Connor, the most prominent of the Chartist leaders; and Dr. Marsden, one of the most distinguished of Irish scholars and Orientalists. Besides those mentioned, there is a magnificent tomb here over the grave of a remarkable Irishman, John St. John Long, who was a native of Limerick and a clever artist, but who became notorious as a quack doctor, professing to cure anything or anybody. He was greatly believed in by many persons, and made a large fortune by his pretended powers. Several Irish physicians of note are also interred here, including Dr. Robert B. Todd, an eminent anatomist and brother of the Celtic scholar of the same name. Among other Irishmen who rest here may be noted Sir Henry Keating, a great lawyer, recently dead; Eyre Evans Crowe, the novelist and journalist; Robert Bell, a well-known critic and versatile author; and John Sydney Taylor, one of the acutest of art critics and art reformers of recent times. There are a great number of Irish men and women buried in this "city of the dead," but we have only spoken of those whose fame was very great in their lifetime or is destined to be lasting. Irishmen should take a pride in visiting the graves of many of those we have referred to, for, as has been said, a people who do not honour their illustrious dead are unworthy of possessing either freedom or a share in the intellectual triumphs of the ages.

CHAPTER XII.

PICCADILLY AND MAYFAIR.

E spoke of the Marble Arch in our last chapter, and will commence our present journey from that point. PARK-LANE runs thence to Piccadilly, and is in the neighbourhood of some very interesting places. To our left lie Mayfair and other fashionable quarters, and on our right stretches Hyde Park. In Park-lane died, a few years ago, Dr. Archibald Billing, one of the most eminent physicians Ireland has produced in modern times, who received some of the highest awards Science could bestow for his remarkable researches into and discoveries of the causes of the sounds of beats of the heart, which subject he made peculiarly his own. MOUNT-STREET, one of the first turnings on the left, is notable as the place where John Banim, the poet and novelist, lived during 1826-27, and where Gerald Griffin and other Irish writers visited him. A genuine poet and most powerful novelist, Banim was also one of the most

JOHN BANIM.

enerous friends a struggling genius ever found. The help and encouragment given by him to Griffin are remarkable, and readers of the latter's "Life" will find plenty of proofs of it. Indeed Banim seems to have taken more interest in Griffin's success than in his own, no trouble being too great or too wearisome for his unselfish nature. It is unnecessary to tell our readers anything of the career of a writer so well-known as John Banim. There are presumably few who have not read one or other of the enthralling "Tales of the O'Hara Family" (some of which were written by Banim's gifted brother, Michael), or who have not admired the touching lyric, "Soggarth Aroon," not to mention his less known but scarcely inferior poems. His native county, Kilkenny, has furnished no greater name than that of the Banims to the roll of Irish literature.

Grosvenor-street, which is just past Mount-street, leads directly into GROSVENOR-SQUARE, where Elizabeth Farren, the celebrated actress, of whom we shall have occasion to speak in our theatrical chapters, lived after her marriage with the Earl of Derby, and consequent retirement from the stage. As a comedy actress she ranks among the greatest of the last century. She was a native of Cork, born in 1759, and went on the stage at an early age. She was not very beautiful, but by her fascinating manners and engaging appearance she succeeded in storming the hearts of many eminent personages, including Charles James Fox and the Earl of Derby, both of whom were deeply smitten by her charms. She was married to the latter in 1797, and took leave of the stage about a month after her marriage. Her death took place in April, 1829, at the age of 70, deeply regretted by all whom she had delighted in her earlier years. In private life she was irreproachable, and thereby earned the esteem and affection of the majority of her country men and women.

In BROOK-STREET, which leads out of Grosvenor-square, lived Charles Lever in 1859, over a tradesman's shop. Lever is at once the most humorous, the most popular, and the most exciting of all Irish novelists, and is likely to remain so, for there are few who possess the quantity of "animal spirits" necessary to surpass him in his own peculiar sphere. In spite of the occasional unreality of some of his characters and incidents, his works are remarkable for wit, good nature, and keen observation, and fully deserve all the enthusiastic esteem they have hitherto enjoyed. He always endeavoured to hold up the Irishman to the eyes of the world as brave, magnanimous, faithful, and, above all, as humorous, and to show his best qualities in the most favourable light. If he sometimes burlesques the real character of the Irish peasant, it is not done, as in other cases, with wilful and malign intent. He depicts the humour and bravery of his countrymen most faithfully and completely, but does not as a general rule, succeed so well in the pathetic parts of his stories—at any rate not to the extent Carleton, Kickham, Banim, and others have done in their works. He

MISS. FARREN.

never maliciously defamed the Irish character, but was always charitable towards its faults and enthusiastically proud of its virtues—always good-humouredly sarcastic, or absolving when he thinks it right to admonish. He certainly does not deserve the reproaches he has received from time to time on account of his "buffoonery," for it is very rarely to be found in his pages.

Almost within sight of Brook-street is GEORGE-STREET, Hanover-square, where John Singleton Copley, the painter and Sir Michael O'Loghlin, the eminent lawyer, died—the former in 1815, and the latter on the 28th of October, 1842.

On the left of Park-lane, to which we return, is HERTFORD-STREET, situated in Mayfair, a small but very select neighbourhood. In this street lived at one time Richard Brinsley Sheridan, and also Mrs. Jordan, one of the most delightful actresses even Ireland can lay claim to. She was born in county Waterford in 1762, her maiden name being Dorothea Bland. Charles Lamb it was, we think, that termed her the "finest Rosalind that ever trod the stage," and Hazlitt's opinion is also well worth quoting:—"Her face, her tones, her manner, were irresistible; her smile had the effect of sunshine, and her laugh did one good to hear it; her voice was eloquence itself—it seemed as if her heart was always at her mouth. She was all gaiety, openness, and good nature; she rioted in her animal spirits, and gave more pleasure than any other actress, because she had the greatest spirit of enjoyment in herself." She died in 1816, in France, and is there buried.

A little farther down, Park-lane runs into Piccadilly. On the right is Apsley House and Hyde Park Corner opposite are the Green Park and St. James's Park. APSLEY HOUSE is of interest as the chief residence—indeed, almost the only one in London—occupied by the Duke of Wellington during his life. It contains some interesting relics, including the cloak worn by him at Waterloo the sword of Napoleon the First, a portrait and statuette of the Duke, a bronze bust of his brother, Marquis Wellesley; Chantrey's statue of Castlereagh, Lawrence's portrait of the eminent Irish soldier, Viscount Beresford, and one of Lord Anglesey by the same great painter, besides other portraits of various members of the Duke's family. All the latest years of his life were passed here, but he died at his country seat in September, 1852, at the age of 83. Though generally the idol of the Londoners, he was mobbed and stoned by them for his opposition to the people's rights. Apsley House, which adjoins Hyde Park Corner, was also attacked, and the Duke had iron shutters put up to the windows as a standing reminder of the fickleness of that "many-headed monster," the people. In a small, bare, and comfortless room here slept the greatest warrior of his age even in his last years; it is said that he had such a fondness for anything which he had grown accustomed to that he could hardly be prevailed upon to change it. Thus the camp-bed he used on the field of battle was the only bed he slept upon here, and he was also known as the rider of the sorriest nags in all London—nearly wearing them out in his service. Opposite the house stands a splendid statue, newly-erected in place of an absurd one which stood on a lofty arch at the top of Constitution Hill. The pedestal of the present statue has at each of its four corners a typical warrior, dressed in the military costume of the Waterloo days. One of them is an Irish dragoon, resting upon a sword, and with a truly Milesian smile broadening his countenance.

Facing Hyde Park Corner is GROSVENOR-PLACE, where Lady Dufferin, the mother of the present Marquis, lived for some years. As the author of the incomparable song, "I'm sittin' on the stile, Mary," which has no superior for pathos and delicacy in the whole range of Irish literature, and of the excellent "Terence's Farewell" and "Dublin Bay," Lady Dufferin, it is safe to presume, will never be forgotten by those who admire beauty of language wedded to intense pathos. She died in

CHARLES LEVER.

1867; and although her writings are few in number, their supreme grace and tenderness will assuredly render her fame higher and more lasting than that of many who have written volumes of inferior verse.

Proceeding up Piccadilly in an easterly direction we reach in a few moments HALF MOON-STREET, which is noteworthy for several reasons, but particluarly as the street where Mrs. Pope, the actress, died, in 1803. She was born in Waterford in or about 1777, her maiden name being Maria Campion. She married Alexander Pope, a clever painter and an excellent actor, who was a native of Cork, and they generally performed together until death parted them. In some characters she was unequalled, and may be accounted one of the best of the second-class actresses of the century. Her husband lived in Half-Moon-street, and there painted his admirable portrait of Henry Grattan, and other works. In the same street died, on 3rd of April, 1824, William Cooke, a native of Cork, well known as a poet of merit and as the biographer of Macklin and others. He was a friend of Burke and Goldsmith, and was a member of some of the celebrated clubs to which they belonged, notably the "Literary Club," of the members of which he has left us an excellent description in his "Conversation," which is considered to be his best poem.

Half-Moon-street leads into the heart of Mayfair. In CURZON-STREET here died Lord Macartney, the great diplomatist, in March, 1806, and at the chapel here an extraordinary affair occurred in February, 1752. A hurried marriage was performed one night in that month, at half-past twelve, the chief actors being Elizabeth Gunning, the popular Irish beauty, and James Duke of Hamilton and Argyll, the ceremony being performed with the aid of a curtain ring in default of a proper wedding circlet. Miss Gunning was one of three sisters, all remarkably beautiful, daughters of a Roscommon gentleman. Such was the curiosity in London with respect to two of them, Maria and Elizabeth, who both married into noble families, that they had to be guarded by soldiers from the inquisitiveness of the public, and were the objects of an equal curiosity in the drawingrooms of Royalty, where people of all stations in life clambered upon chairs and other articles of furniture in order to have a look at them. Once, it is said, 700 people waited up all night at an inn on the mere chance of seeing them pass by in their carriage in the morning.

In SEAMORE-PLACE lived Lady Blessington, and in CHESTERFIELD-STREET resided the Hon. Mrs. Norton for over thirty years. She was the sister of Lady Dufferin, and a member of that remarkably gifted family—the Sheridans. Mrs. Norton, or, as she afterwards became, Lady Stirling-Maxwell, is widely known by her numerous novels and poems. Some of the latter, as "The Blind Man's Bride" and "Bingen on the Rhine," are very pathetic, and worthy of such a highly poetical mind as their authoress possessed, and indeed such as the whole of the Sheridans seemed to possess, for a more convincing example of the force of heredity could hardly be found than the talent displayed by the descendants of the distinguished Dr. Thomas Sheridan. Another street of Mayfair is also worth mentioning. STANHOPE-STREET is the place where Colonel Isaac Barre, the distinguished Irish orator, politician, and author, died on the 20th of July, 1802. After serving with great gallantry in the army, he entered Parliament, and gained a wide renown as an orator as well as by his advanced Liberalism. His powers of invective were almost unequalled in those times, and he was recognised as a very formidable opponent of any retrogressive Government. During his life he received several very high appointments for his services to the Liberal party. He warmly espoused the cause of the Americans after their Declaration of Independence. He was a native of Dublin, was born in 1726, and reached the age of 75 or 76. Having been wounded severely in the cheek at the siege of Quebec, his face presented a rather savage appearance. His political writings are so vigorous and incisive that he has been believed by many to have been the author of the famous "Letters of Junius."

Ireland in London.

BERKELEY-STREET, opposite Half-Moon-street, leads into BERKELEY-SQUARE, where Lansdowne House, the residence of the Lansdowne or Fitzmaurice family is situated. Here lived the first Marquis, better known as the Earl of Shelburne, who became Prime Minister of England towards the

GEORGE CANNING.

end of the last century. He was born in Dublin, and, apart from his fame as a statesman, is entitled to remembrance as the donor of the valuable collection in the British Museum known as the Lansdowne MSS. The house contains some very valuable treasures of art, among those possessing a peculiar interest for Irishmen being Charles Jervas's portrait of Pope, the poet, and Sir Joshua Reynolds's fine portraits of David Garrick and Laurence Sterne.

The next turning to Berkeley-street in Piccadilly is Dover-street, and facing this is the BATH HOTEL, where John Banim occasionally resided and was frequently visited by Gerald Griffin. ALBEMARLE-STREET has several interesting associations. Here resided the well-known statesman and Viceroy of India, the Marquis of Wellesley, and here also Lord Charlemont was a frequent visitor of the Duc de Nivernois, the French Ambassador of Charlemont's time, who lived here. This same street has a very sad story connected with it too, for here, on the 14th of May, 1734, Richard Cantillon, the "father of Political Economy," was robbed and murdered by his cook, who had set fire to the house. Cantillon was an Irishman, and may be justly termed one of the most original thinkers of his time, as to him the so-called "dismal science" owes a great many of its propositions.

Opposite Albemarle-street is ST. JAMES-STREET, a principal part of the region known as "Clubland." So many interesting facts are connected

with it that space will only allow us to touch upon them slightly. Among its best-known residents have been Sir William Brouncker (First Viscount Castlelyons, and a native of Cork), the eminent mathematician and first President of the Royal Society, and James Gillray, the great caricaturist, who also died here on the 1st of June, 1815. He had become deranged during his last years, and endeavoured to commit suicide by jumping from his window into the street. He was born in 1757 and was the son of an Irish pensioner (of Chelsea) who had fought at Fontenoy. His very first caricature was entitled, "Paddy on Horseback," being a satire on the Irish fortune-hunter. Besides his famous works in this direction, which stamp him, according to most people, as the greatest of English caricaturists, he also executed some excellent engravings, several of his subjects being drawn from Goldsmith's "Deserted Village." Some of his works are savage in spirit, but of course that does not detract from their merit historically or intrinsically.

In this same street lived, in splendid style, the famous highwayman, James M'Lean, and here

JAMES MACLEAN, HIGHWAYMAN.
From the Chronicles of Newgate.
(Rare Portrait.)

also stood many old taverns and coffee-houses of great historical interest. Thus, on the site of the present "Conservative Club" was situated the "Thatched House Tavern," a popular resort of literary men and politicians, especially of Moore and Brinsley Sheridan; while here also the Dilettanti Society used to meet, among its most prominent members being Lord Charlemont and Sir M. A. Shee. "St. James's Coffee-house" stood at the bottom of the street, facing the Palace, and was greatly used by Swift, Steele, Goldsmith, and Garrick, to mention but one or two of its frequenters. Garrick used to "chaff" Oliver so mercilessly that he vowed to be revenged, and at their next meeting here produced his celebrated poem, "Retaliation," which ranks among his happiest and most humorous efforts. On the site of No. 64 stood the "Cocoa Tree Tavern," another famous meeting-place for the wits, including Sir Philip Francis, and, previous to him, Swift and Steele.

'Brooks's Club', also here, deserves mention if only on account of its eminent or notorious Irish members, among them having been "Fighting" Fitzgerald, Daniel O'Connell, R. B. Sheridan, Sir P. Francis, and General Fitzpatrick, a well-known *dilettante* of the last century.

St. James's-street was likewise the scene of one of Colonel Blood's reckless exploits. The Duke of Ormond, surnamed "The Great," had, while Lord Lieutenant of Ireland, so severely treated some of Blood's friends that he declared he would be revenged on the Duke, threatening to waylay him in the public streets, carry him to Tyburn, and there hang him with his own hands. On the evening of the 6th of December 1670, Blood, accompanied by several desperate allies, attacked his carriage, and after putting the footman to flight, dragged out the famous soldier (who was then 60 years of age), and had carried him as far as the corner of Berkeley-street when, being pursued, he was reluctantly obliged to relinquish his project. A reward of £1,000 was offered for the apprehension of those who committed the outrage, but it was not then known that Blood had anything to do with it.

CLEVELAND-ROW is on the right, nearly at the end, and here died Charles Jervas, a very clever but excessively vain portrait-painter, and friend of Pope and Swift. In Stafford House here is one of Danby's grandest pictures, a veritable masterpiece, entitled "The Passage of the Red Sea," universally admitted to be a really sublime production, befitting the subject. On the right, higher up, is also ST. JAMES'S-PLACE, where lived Thomas Parnell, the poet, and author of "The Hermit," one of the most harmonious and finished poems in English literature.

On the left is JERMYN-STREET, where Henry Grattan resided in 1788, and Sir M. A. Shee in 1791 ; and where Thomas Colley Grattan, the novelist, died on the 4th July, 1864. His novels are still popular, but his best work is, perhaps, his "Highways and Bye-ways," a series of entertaining sketches. In this street is also situated the GEOLOGICAL MUSEUM, which is well worth a visit for its fine collection of Irish marbles and granites from Galway, Limerick, Dublin, Donegal, and King's County.

DUKE-STREET, which runs across Jermyn-street into Piccadilly, is notable as the place of residence of Edmund Burke in 1795, and of Moore in 1833. BURY-STREET, close by, is still more remarkable for its Irish residents, for at different times Swift, Steele, Mrs. Pilkington, Moore, Lord Strangford, and O'Connell have lived in it. Swift, in his "Journal to Stella," thus describes his lodgings here—"I have the first floor, a diningroom and bedchamber, at eight shillings a week —plaguy dear!"

Reaching Piccadilly through St. James's-street

MRS. NORTON.
(Autograph.)

we have BOND-STREET almost opposite us. Laurence Sterne, the author of "Tristram Shandy," lived and died here, over a cheesemonger's shop, now occupied by Agnew's Picture Gallery. In this street also died Henry Tresham, R.A., a distinguished Irish painter of the last century, some of whose allegorical pictures are excellent. The first turning on the right leads past London University into SAVILE-ROW, where two eminent Irishmen died in the earlier part of the century —Sheridan, the dramatist and orator (at No. 14, where a tablet is placed to that effect), and the Right Hon. George Tierney, the well-known statesman. The exterior of the University is decorated with twenty-four statues, all finely carved, of great savants, philosophers, and scientists. Of these, the three occupying niches to the right of the entrance are by Patrick

M'Dowell, R.J.., whose works we have more than once referred to in the course of these chapters. The three philosophers represented by M'Dowell are Cuvier, Leibnitz, and Linnæus.

BRUTON-STREET, which is on the left of Bond-street, was another place of residence of the ever-moving R. B. Sheridan, whose creditors pressed him so hard while here that provisions had to be secretly conveyed over the area railings to the watchful prisoner, lest the duns should see him. Mrs. Jameson also resided here for a time. Opposite BRUTON-STREET is CONDUIT-STREET, where the last-mentioned writer died, and where such distinguished Irishmen as Michael Balfe and George Canning have lived. The house, No. 37, occupied by Canning, still exists, and bears a tablet recording the residence of the great statesman. Some people do not consider Canning as an Irishman, because he was born in London, but he himself always called himself one, and when claimed as an Englishman used it is said, the phrase erroneously attributed to Wellington when claimed as an Irishman—"Is one a horse because he is born in a stable?" Besides, in a letter written by Canning to Sir Walter Scott, when the latter was visiting Ireland, he expressed himself pleased that his "countrymen" had received him well, and adds—"Though born in London, I consider myself an Irishman." This letter proves that Canning was not ashamed of his Irish origin, and may be well contrasted with the miserable pleas put forward by some unworthy Irishmen for the purpose of denying their race. Whatever may have been his other faults, Canning was not "that meanest thing on earth," the anti-Irish Irishman. As one of the greatest of England's Prime Ministers, a fine orator, and a gifted writer to boot, he reflects credit on Irish genius, apart altogether from his deficiencies in patriotism towards Ireland and Irish wrongs as Irishmen of the present day understand them. Opposite Bond-street is the EGYPTIAN HALL, which has two peculiar colossal figures sculptured over the entrance.

These were executed by L. Gahagan, brother of Sebastian Gahagan, and are meant to represent the Egyptian gods Isis and Osiris. They have been unfortunately daubed with paint, and deprived of any artistic merit they possessed. Just past Bond-street is BURLINGTON HOUSE, the home of the Royal Academy, Royal Society, and other bodies, which is so interesting that we reserve it for separate treatment. It was partly built by Barry, and stands on the site of a house occupied by Sir John Denham, a native of Dublin and a poet of the 17th century. The "Albany," a famous set of chambers, is just past here. George Canning lived in this house, and here Lord Byron wrote his "Lara." The place is immortalised in the well-known novel, "The Bachelor of the Albany," written by a clever Irish novelist named Marmion Savage. Almost opposite is the Institute of Painters in Water Colours, held at the PRINCE'S HALL. Among the busts over the front of the building is one of George Barrett, one of the founders of the water-colour school of artists, an excellent painter, and son of the R.A. of the same name.

A little further on is ST. JAMES'S HALL, which has resounded to the brilliant oratory of Father Tom Burke, and which has been the scene of many remarkable Irish political demonstrations. It faces ST. JAMES'S CHURCH, one of Sir Christopher Wren's works, wherein is buried the eminent Irish physician, Sir John Macnamara Hayes, a native of Limerick, who died in 1809, to whose memory a mural monument has been erected under the gallery in the church. Here, or in the ground attached, was also interred the brilliant writer, Mrs. Margaret Delany, wife of Dr. Patrick Delany, the friend of Dean Swift. Though a witty and clever woman, Mrs. Delany was not Irish, but lived a good deal in Ireland and admired the country and its people greatly. In the ground behind the church was also buried James Gillray, whom we have already referred to.

CHAPTER XIII.

THROUGH PALL MALL TO WESTMINSTER.

PALL MALL begins at the bottom of St. James's-street, and though once a popular and fashionable place of residence is now largely given up to palatial clubs. On the right as we proceed eastward is the WAR OFFICE, with one of Foley's finest statues in front. This statue—of Sidney, Lord Herbert—is splendidly carved, the bas-reliefs round the pedestal, depicting scenes in the eminent statesman's life, being also very delicately and gracefully executed. It is acknowledged to be one of the best examples of modern sculpture that London possesses.

In the last century Pall Mall was noted for its distinguished residents, not a few Irishmen being among them. Here lived Hugh Douglas Hamilton, an exceedingly good portrait painter, and a member of the Royal Hibernian Academy. Royalty sat to him at his lodgings here, so widespread was his reputation as a painter. Two other

CASTLEREAGH.

Irish artists of note lived here. One, the eminent engraver, William Nelson Gardiner, kept a bookshop in this street; while the other, Hugh Howard, also a fashionable painter, died here on the 17th of March, 1787. In Pall Mall, on the 15th of July, 1847, died also The O'Conor Don, father of the politician of that name now living, and a well-known character himself. Among other Irish residents of this street were Laurence Sterne, Dean Swift, and Robert Boyle (on the right or south side), and Mrs Pilkington, the friend of Swift, and a poetess and dramatist of merit, who kept a small shop here for the sale of pamphlets.

On the left, one or two turnings lead us into ST. JAMES'S-SQUARE, always a very exclusive neighbourhood. Here lived Lady Blessington in magnificent style after her marriage with the Earl of Blessington; and here also resided Sir Philip Francis (in a house occupying the site of the present East Indian Service Club), and in the 17th century the Duke of Ormonde, one of the greatest soldiers and statesmen of his age. At what was No. 16, at the north corner of King-street, lived for some years the notorious Castlereagh, who first cut his country's throat and then his own. The house referred to was not, however, the scene of the latter exploit, which took place at his country house at Crayford, in Kent. There is a tradition (doubtless incorrect) that Castlereagh bought a knife, in order to carry out his happy idea, at a small cutler's in Bloomsbury, and after some haggling, got a shilling knife for tenpence-halfpenny. No person living at his time was more execrated than Castlereagh, and Byron's powerful and oft-quoted lines in "The Irish Avatar," accurately express the popular feeling towards the worst enemy Ireland ever had. This same house was, after the death of Castlereagh, occupied by the well-known author, Irish politician, and diplomatist, Sir James Emerson Tennent.

LITCHFIELD HOUSE, the scene of a famous historical event, stood on part of the site of the present London Library. O'Connell's agreement with the Whigs, known as the Litchfield House compact, was fraught with danger to Ireland and Irish interests. O'Connell met the leaders of the party at this house, and agreed to help them to oust the Tories from office, which, with O'Connell's aid, they succeeded in doing, when the Whigs, having gained their object, became, after some bombastic resolutions and deceptive promises, as bitterly inimical to Irish prosperity as even the Tories had been.

On the right of Pall Mall is situated the REFORM CLUB, which has had many prominent Irish members, one of them being O'Connell, whose portrait, by J. P. Haverty, a Limerick man, and an excellent artist, is to be seen here. Haverty was the brother of another clever Irishman—namely, Martin Haverty, the historian. The work of art just referred to is one of the best portraits of O'Connell extant, and is rightly considered a valuable acquisition to the club. The building itself was erected from the designs of Sir Charles Barry, as was also the TRAVELLERS' CLUB, close by. Both are fine edifices, and well worthy of the genius of that great architect. Here also is the UNITED SERVICE CLUB, which contains "The Battle of Trafalgar," one of W. C. Stanfield's finest sea-pieces.

SOUTHERN.

In CARLTON-TERRACE, which is between the Reform and Athenæum Clubs, is an excellent statue of Lord Lawrence, one of the greatest of the many Irish Viceroys of India. The ATHENÆUM, which is at the corner, has always had a creditable percentage of Irishmen among its distinguished members, including the Earl of Mayo, Maclise, and J. W. Croker among past members, and Professor Tyndall and Mr. Lecky among the living.

At the end of Pall Mall, just at the entrance to Trafalgar-square, is a massive building adorned with fine pillars. The ROYAL COLLEGE OF PHYSICIANS is interesting to Irishmen for several reasons. Ireland has at all times been noted as the birth-place of great medical men, and the "roll" of the most eminent members of this famous body emphasises the fact anew. It has had one Irish President, Sir Hans Sloane, and another of Irish parentage, Dr. Thomas Lawrence; and among its many famous Irish members have been the patriots, Dr. Charles Lucas and Dr. W. J. M'Nevin, and many celebrated physicians, including Dr. Bernard O'Connor, Dr. Adair Crawford, Sir John M'Namara Hayes, Sir Matthew John Tierney, Sir David Barry, Sir Edward Barry, Sir George Magrath, Dr. Archibald Billing, Dr. W. H. Fittor, Dr. James Johnson, Dr. W. Babington, Sir Joseph de Courcey Laffan, Dr. William Mushet, Dr. Christopher Nugent, Sir Arthur Brooke Faulkner, Dr. James Curry, Sir Robert Alexander Churnside, and a great many others—all Irish-born and of great reputation. Among the interesting objects possessed by the College are Behne's bust of Dr. Babington; Murray's portrait of Sir Hans Sloane; a portrait of Sir Gilbert Blane, by Sir Martin Archer Shee; Jervas's portrait of Dr. Arburthnot; and a fine bust of Dr. John Conolly, an eminent physician of Irish parentage.

The HAYMARKET is almost opposite, and deserves a slight mention, for some of the streets leading out of it have had their well-known residents. For example, in PANTON-STREET, on the right, lived Dean Swift at one period, and at SUFFOLK-STREET, on the same side, lived his celebrated friend, "Vanessa"—Miss Hester Vanhomrigh—to whom some of his best poems were addressed; and also Michael Kelly, the Irish musical composer and singer. In CHARLES-STREET, on the right, lived Burke. At an hotel here, close by Her Majesty's Theatre, when that building was the operatic centre of London, two very eminent Irishmen stayed for a short time in the stormy period of '48. They were none other than Sir Charles Gavan Duffy and Thomas Francis Meagher, who were paying a brief visit to London.

In Pall Mall, close by this theatre also, probably under the colonnade itself, Michael Kelly kept a shop, while he conducted the orchestra of the theatre. The shop was used for the sale of wine that Kelly imported, and of music that he composed. It was in allusion to this double occupation that Sheridan, with more wit than strict justice, suggested to Kelly as a suitable sign for his establishment the following legend—"Michael Kelly, IMPORTER of MUSIC and COMPOSER of WINE." Kelly's "Recollections," the book in which this anecdote is given, was edited by Theodore Hook, and is not only fascinating reading, but is also one of the most valuable records of 18th century life and manners of which English literature can boast. In fact Kelly is chiefly remembered by this work rather than by his numerous operas and songs. The latter are excellent, and are modelled a good deal after the Italian methods, but though at one time very popular, are rarely heard now-a-days. As a singer, Kelly was among the foremost of his day, and was a thoroughly good musical director of several theatres. To this need only be added the facts that he was born in Dublin in or about 1764, studied in Italy, and died at Margate in October, 1826.

Facing the bottom of the Haymarket is the commencement of COCKSPUR-STREET, where is situated the UNION CLUB, which possesses some excellent pictures by Stanfield. In this thoroughfare died Charles Byrne, the giant, at an early age, in 1783. George Canning lived in a turning called SPRING GARDENS, which runs out of this street into St. James's Park. In BUCKINGHAM-COURT, which is in Spring Gardens, died Mrs. Centlivre on 1st December, 1723. This accomplished dramatist was born in Dublin about 1667, and by her own great gifts and unaided energy raised herself to a high position among the comedy-writers of the last century.

MICHAEL KELLY.

Some of her plays still hold the stage, notably "A Bold Stroke for a Wife" and "The Busybody." Several of them have been translated into French and German.

WHITEHALL, on the right of COCKSPUR-STREET, is a fine thoroughfare, leading from Trafalgar-square almost to the Houses of Parliament. On the left of it, a little way down, is SCOTLAND-YARD (now the chief London Police Office), taking its name from an ancient palace of the Scottish Kings which stood on its site. There is a museum of curiosities here, among its contents being the rifles taken from some Fenians arrested in Clerkenwell, and a large assortment of infernal machines found in connection with certain explosions. The first Chief Commissioner of Police was an Irishman, Sir Charles Cowan, who was born in Antrim. He held the post from 1829 to 1850. Adjoining Scotland-yard was the residence of Sir John Denham, a distinguished Irishman of the 17th century, and one of the poets whose purity of style assisted largely in the formation of the English language, a distinction which is now his chief credit. Denham died here in 1668.

At the old PALACE OF WHITEHALL (of which the Chapel Royal, formerly the banquetting room of the Palace, is the only remaining part), Shane O'Neill visited Queen Elizabeth on the 6th of January, 1562, with his followers, causing great sensation by their wild appearance and curious attire. According to Froude, "O'Neill stalked in, his saffron mantle sweeping round and about him, his hair curling on his back and clipped short below the eyes, which gleamed from under it with a grey lustre, frowning, fierce, and cruel. Behind him followed his gallowglasses, bareheaded and fair-haired, with shirts of mail which reached beneath their knees, a wolf-skin flung across their shoulders, and short, broad battle-axes in their hands."

Opposite Whitehall Palace lived Archbishop Ussher, in a house lent him by Lady Peterboro', which stood on the site of the present Horse Guards. From the roof of his house Ussher beheld the unfortunate King Charles I. led out to execution, and fainted at the sight. The ADMIRALTY, which is near the Chapel Royal, exhibited at one time on its roof the signal known as the *Semaphore*, invented by an Irish soldier named Sir Home Riggs Popham. It was afterwards replaced by the shuttle telegraph, the invention of another Irishman, Richard Lovell Edgeworth, whose daughter Maria was one of the earliest and best of Irish writers of fiction. Edgeworth's invention was in turn superseded by the electric telegraph.

Behind the Chapel Royal is the UNITED SERVICE INSTITUTION, a very interesting museum of naval and military curiosities. Among other interesting objects, such as relics of Captain Cook, of the Crimea, of the Arctic Expeditions, of the Siege of Quebec, and of Nelson, is one weapon which, as it wielded a great influence in Irish affairs, cannot be looked upon without deep interest, being nothing less than the sword worn by Cromwell at the siege of Drogheda and elsewhere.

Between the Treasury and Home Office buildings, on the opposite side of Whitehall, is DOWNING-STREET, named after an Irish soldier and politician of the 16th century, Sir George Downing, whose grandson afterwards founded Downing College, Cambridge. The INDIA OFFICE here is decorated by many memorials of eminent Anglo-Indian officials and others, including a bust of Lord Laurence, statues of the Marquis Wellesley and the Marquis of Hastings (formerly Lord Moira), three great Irish Viceroys of India; and one of Sir Eyre Coote, an eminent Irish soldier who did not a little towards the conquest of India.

In Downing-street lived John Boyle, one of the Earls of Cork and Orrery, a tolerably good poet and dramatist, considering the age in which he lived.

In the narrow little thoroughfare of KING-STREET, between Whitehall and Parliament-square, two very distinguished personages once lived. They were Oliver Cromwell and Edmund Spenser. The former started from his house here in July, 1649, on his "mission" to conquer Ireland, or, failing

A. HAMILTON ROWAN.
(Autograph.)

that, to devastate it. How successfully he carried out the latter alternative no Irish reader needs to be informed. Spenser lived here on his return from Ireland, where his castle had been attacked and burned down by the wronged insurgents of the South. His great poem, "The Faery Queen," was doubtless written in Ireland, and its scenery and characters are partly Irish. Thus, Una and Queen Mab (who is thought to be the Irish Queen Maeve) are doubtless embodiments of some of Spenser's Irish memories; and

"The strains sweet foreign Spenser sung
    By Mulla's shore "

were literally inspired by the scenes he saw in the lovely South of Ireland.

Charles-street, to the south of the Home Office, leads into ST. JAMES'S PARK, where one or two events happened that call for brief notice. While crossing the Park, Charles Connor, one of the best actors and impersonators of Irish character in his day, died suddenly of heart disease on the 7th of October, 1826. He was a worthy successor of Jack Johnstone in certain parts, and very creditably filled the interval that elapsed between Johnstone's leaving the stage and Tyrone Power's most favourable introduction to it.

In this same Park, O'Connell had a narrow escape from death. While studying law at Gray's Inn in 1795 he came to St. James's in order to see the King's return from the House of Lords. He saw the Royal carriage, which was surrounded by an angry and excited mob, one of whom broke the glass of one of the doors. They were charged instantly by the dragoons in attendance, and as O'Connell leaned forward to get a glimpse of the King, a dragoon made a wild slash at him with his sword, just missing his head, and making a deep cut in a tree beside him, about an inch above.

BUCKINGHAM PALACE, which is at the western side of the Park, is only interesting to Irishmen in that the summer-house or pavilion in its grounds contains two fine frescoes by Maclise and Stanfield—the subject being taken from Milton's "Comus."

Reaching PARLIAMENT-SQUARE from the Park, through Great George's-street, we have to the left of Parliament-street, a row of houses and shops called BRIDGE-STREET, where Dr Patrick Duigenan, the celebrated controversialist, and a powerful and vigorous writer, died on April 11th, 1816. He was a master of invective and raillery, and, being of a most unscrupulous and grovelling nature, was paid by the Government to assail O'Connell or any other patriot who dared to say a word in behalf of his countrymen. In PALACE CHAMBERS here was for some seven years the central office of the Irish Land League and National League of Great Britain. In Parliament-square is Westmacott's colossal statue of George Canning, which is probably the identical one which caused the death of the brother of Sebastian Gahagan, the sculptor, who assisted Westmacott, for he is stated to have been crushed to death by the falling on him of a statue of Canning on which he had been engaged.

Between the Abbey and the Houses of Parliament, which will be dealt with in subsequent articles, is Poet's Corner, and in one of the houses here, in a small upper room, was the earliest London office of the Home Rule Confederation of Great Britain, when that association was still in its infancy.

Passing round to the other side of the Abbey we reach WESTMINSTER HOSPITAL, which stands on the site of a house once occupied by Edmund Burke. The hospital, which has had some eminent Irish physicians connected with it, particularly Sir John Macnamara Hayes, is quite near TOTHILL-STREET, which has at its corner the WESTMINSTER PALACE HOTEL, where Mr. Parnell inaugurated the Irish Land League of Great Britain, and which is a favourite resort of the Irish members during the sessions of Parliament. In this street died, on the 26th of May, 1746, at the age of 85, one of the best of the tragic dramatists of Ireland, Thos. Southern.

He was a native of Dublin, and devoted himself to literature in preference to the law, which he had studied in the Temple. He is the author of "Isabella"

MRS. CENTLIVRE.

and "Oroonoko," two of the most pathetic tragedies written since Shakespeare's time, and immortalised by the acting of many great actors and actresses in their leading parts.

Opposite the hotel just referred to is GREAT SMITH-STREET, and where Sir R. Steele and Southern once lived, and where (at No. 26, facing the Westminster Public Library), the offices of the National League of Great Britain are at present situated. It leads up towards BOWLING-STREET, Tufton-street, where Colonel Blood, the notorious adventurer, lived and died. He was probably buried in the neighbouring church, in the BROADWAY, though it is believed by some that he was buried in St. Margaret's Church, by the side of the Abbey.

At the corner of Great Smith-street is WESTMINSTER SCHOOL, which has had several notable Irishmen amongst its scholars. Thomas Sheridan, the great actor and elocutionist, and father of R. B. Sheridan, was educated here; as also John Boyle (Earl of Cork and Orrery), Temple Henry Croker, an Irishman, and a clever translator of Ariosto, &c.; and last, but not least, Archibald Hamilton Rowan, one of the most prominent of the United Irishmen. He was born in London of Irish parents on May the 12th, 1757. He went to Ireland in 1784, and soon became involved in the National movement, joining the Volunteers first and the United Irishmen afterwards. He was tried in January, 1794, for complicity in treasonable practices, and, after a magnificent speech from Curran, his counsel, was sentenced to two years' imprisonment, and also fined £500. Knowing that the Government, after his trial, had discovered certain facts which might bring him to the gallows, Rowan determined to escape from Newgate Prison, Dublin, which he did in May, 1794. He reached France, after some difficulty, and after staying there a while, proceeded to America, where he remained some years. He petitioned the Government to let him return to Ireland, and expressed in his memorial his great satisfaction and delight at the "happy Union" which had been effected (in the most unscrupulous manner). His prayer was granted, and he returned to his paternal estate, where he lived during the remainder of his life, dying on November 18th, 1834, aged 77. It is only right to add that the French Revolution, with its attendant horrors, of which he had been a witness, caused the great change in his mind which we have described.

Turning down by Wood-street and proceeding along by Grosvenor-road to the River Thames, and skirting its brown current, we soon come within view of MILLBANK PRISON or Penitentiary. This prison held within its walls for various periods during the years 1866-7-8 a famous batch of Fenian "penitents,"

EDWARD DUFFY.

notable among them being Mulcahy, Rossa, Costello, Richard Burke, John Devoy, Stephen Joseph Meaney, Edward Duffy, and Xavier O'Brien.

O'Donovan Rossa, who was imprisoned here for twelve months and two days, gives in his "Irish Rebels in English Prisons" a graphic account of his prison life and of the treatment to which he was subjected—treatment which goes far to explain his subsequent notorious and virulent animosity against England and all things English. He was subjected, without chance of redress, to the most persistent and mean annoyances at the hands of warders, was gradually deprived of every ordinary privilege, stripped naked and submitted to an ignominious search several times a day, for weeks together, punished for not obeying contradictory orders, for doing his work too soon, or for resenting insolence; and persecuted, in fact, in every way possible. Although he came to Millbank from Portland Prison a mere skeleton, with the flesh rotting off his hands, he was put on starvation diet for petty breaches of discipline. He was the last thirty-two days in Millbank on bread and water (one of these days being Christmas Day), and 158 days on penal class diet in a darkened cell. Perhaps the most degrading punishment inflicted on him in this prison (for he was destined to receive worse later on at Chatham) was his being immured two days and nights in an underground cell, destitute of means of light or ventilation, where, his hands being manacled, he was necessitated to go down on all fours and lap up his dish of thick stirabout like a dog.

The most ingenious devices were resorted to by Rossa and the other Fenian prisoners confined here to communicate with each other and with the outside world. By a system of tapping on the walls Rossa conversed with Burke, Costello, Devoy, and others, and by this means, as well as by hurried words from motionless lips at exercise time, interjected remarks during the responses to the Litany at chapel, the establishment of a "post office" or hiding-place in the closet wall, he contrived not alone to obtain the fullest information as to the course of events without the prison gates, but also to secure writing materials, and even loaves of bread to eke out his famine fare and keep soul and body together.

Rossa was more successful in this last achievement than his young friend, poor Edward Duffy, who succumbed here to harsh treatment on the 17th of January, 1868, aged 28, and on whose death, the rumour of which was conveyed to him through the bars of his cell by a passing prisoner, Rossa wrote a touching poem, of which we give the following stanzas:—

The world is growing darker to me—darker day by day.
The stars that shone upon life's path are vanishing away;
Some setting and some shifting, only one that changes never.
'Tis the guiding star of liberty, that blazes bright as ever.

. . . .

The news of death is saddening even in the festive hall,
But when 'tis heard through prison bars 'tis saddest then of all,
When there is none to share the sorrow in the solitary cell,
In the prison within prison, a blacker hell in hell.

That whisper through the grating has thrilled through all my veins—
"Duffy is dead?" A noble soul has slipt the tyrant's chains,
And whatever wounds they gave him their lying lips will show
How they very kindly treated him, more like a friend than foe.

For these are Christian Pharisees, the hypocrites of creeds,
With the Bible on their lips and the devil in their deeds,
Too merciful in public gaze to take our lives away,
Too anxious here to plant in us the seeds of life's decay.

. . . .

But sad and lone your death, Ned, 'mid the jailors of your race,
With none to press the cold, white hand; with none to smooth the face;
With none to take the dying wish to homeland friend or brother;
To kindred mind, to promised bride, or to the sorrowing mother.

Among the other Fenian prisoners who were seriously injured by their treatment in Millbank were Burke, M. H. Carey, and Thomas Ahern, who were driven temporarily insane, and Daniel Reddin, who completely lost the use of his limbs.

A later and more important Irishman who was incarcerated within these walls was Michael Davitt, who was imprisoned here for ten months. His published "Prison Life" describes his little cell, ten feet long by eight feet wide, with stone floor, no table, chair, or fire, with a three-plank bedstead raised only a few inches above the floor, and his only seat a covered bucket holding the washing water, and on which he worked ten hours a day, picking oakum with his one hand, aided by his teeth. The most dismal sound to him in his cell was the regular quarter-hour chiming of "Big Ben," the great clock in the Parliament Tower close by—a sound which ever since reminds him of his dreary days and nights in Millbank Prison.

It would no doubt have solaced those lonely hours could he have foreseen that in a comparatively few years, as the lives of nations are reckoned, the efforts of himself and other bygone and living sufferers in the Irish cause would have been crowned in the very walls of that Parliament House itself by the initiation of a measure to have the way for the restoration of the long-lost liberty of Ireland.

CHAPTER XIV.

FROM HYDE PARK CORNER TO FULHAM AND CHELSEA.

PROCEEDING westward from Hyde Park Corner, we reach in a few moments a street which has more than usual interest, for at a house still standing (No. 11) died that remarkable Irishwoman, Lady Morgan, on the 13th of April, 1859. WILLIAM-STREET had been her chief place of residence during her long life in London, but her literary career was practically over before she came here. Whatever may be now thought of her numerous works, there can be no question of their former great popularity. An especial favourite was "The Wild Irish Girl," which had the rare good fortune to run through seven editions in less than two years, and of which we are told that it was the last book read by William Pitt in the illness which preceded his death. Ac-

LADY MORGAN.

cording to Mr. W. J. Fitzpatrick, her excellent biographer (than whom no better authority exists), she was born not in Dublin, as is generally stated, but at sea, in the year 1778, a date which is very probably correct, though there will always exist some doubt as to the exact year. Her cleverness in evading questions as to her age, no matter how subtly put, was quite astonishing; her dislike to give any particulars on the subject being abnormally great, but she always wished it to be thought that she was born about the beginning of the century.

Her father, Robert Owenson, whose real name was M'Owen, was an admirable actor and musician, and his two daughters, Sydney and Olivia, were possessed of talent of a high order. They both wrote good verse, but Olivia (afterwards Lady Clarke) never acquired the fame of her gifted and very shrewd sister. Lady Morgan was of diminutive size, and showed that restless energy said to be universal among small people. Like her equally diminutive countrymen, Crofton Croker and Moore, her intellect was unusually keen and brilliant.

A little farther on we reach SLOANE-STREET, which, like the various other thoroughfares of the same name about here, derives its name from Sir Hans Sloane, the eminent Irish naturalist and physician. In this street died Eyre Evans Crowe, the novelist and journalist, and here was born his son, Eyre Crowe, A.R.A., an artist of great power. Another son of the former, Joseph Archer Crowe, is ranked among the first art-critics and art-historians of the time.

CADOGAN-PLACE, on the left, is notable as one of the residences of Mrs. Jordan, the celebrated actress, while HANS-PLACE, which is reached through Hans-street, on the right, has several points of interest connected with it. At a house here, No. 22, now rebuilt, lived at different times several distinguished women, including two English and two Irish women. The former were Letitia Landon, the poetess (better known as "L. E. L."), and Mary Russell Mitford, the novelist; the latter were Mrs. S. C. Hall, one of the most popular of Irish female novelists, and Lady Bulwer-Lytton, mother of the present Earl and wife of the "literary fop" and prolific novelist, who ill-treated her shamefully. She was a native of Limerick, named Rosina Wheeler, and was a greatly and variously-gifted woman. Once she married the author of "The Last Days of Pompeii" her happiness ceased. She wrote several clever works, and doubtless helped Lytton in some of his numerous productions. Another resident of Hans-place deserves mention, though not an

Irishman, and that is the great poet, Percy Bysshe Shelley, whose sympathy with Irish grievances is well-known. At one end of the place or square (for such it is) is a graceful fountain erected to the memory of a gallant Irish soldier, Sir Herbert Stewart, who once lived here, within sight of it, and who is also remembered in the name of Herbert-crescent, close by. The fountain bears in front a good likeness of the eminent soldier, the whole structure being surmounted by a broken pillar or column, having reference presumably to Scott's fine lines—

"Now is the stately column broke," etc.

Sir Herbert Stewart, it will be remembered,

ALBERT HALL.

was fatally wounded while leading his troops in one of the engagements of the Soudan expedition for the relief of General Gordon.

At the bottom of Sloane-street, to the left, are situated some very fashionable squares, forming part of Belgravia. One or two of them require slight mention. Passing EATON-TERRACE, formerly Coleshill-street, where at No. 37 Francis Danby, the great Irish painter, lived in 1842, we reach EATON-SQUARE, where died, in 1886, the eminent scholar, poet, and divine, R. C. Trench, Archbishop of Dublin, some of whose works are now ranked among the English classics. ECCLESTON-SQUARE, almost adjoining, is interesting as the place where, in 1869, Sir James Emerson Tennent, the well-known author and politician, died suddenly. In EBURY-STREET, close to Eccleston-square, lived William Smith O'Brien for a time during the 1848 movement.

Returning to the top of Sloane-street, we find that the main road, after a few yards, branches into two directions, one towards Kensington and Hammersmith, and the other towards Chelsea and Fulham. Taking the former road first, we enter what is called the HIGH-STREET, and a little way up, on the left, pass the residence (at the corner of Hill-street) of one of the famous past editors of the "Times," Edward Sterling, and his son,

the poet, John Sterling, who will be more particularly noticed in subsequent chapters.

Just past Hill-street is KINGSTON HOUSE, where the eminent statesman, the Marquis of Wellesley, brother of Wellington, died in September, 1842, at the ripe age of 82.

On the left, a little higher up, is the ALBERT HALL, one of the most curious buildings in London, and the largest concert hall of which the metropolis can boast. It is a handsome circular edifice, and is undoubtedly an ornament to the neighbourhood. It was designed by an excellent architect, Captain Francis Fowke, a native of Belfast, who is well known also as an engineer and an inventor. He was born in 1823, and after a life devoted to his adopted profession, died on the 3rd December, 1865, aged about 42.

Opposite the Albert Hall, and just inside the railings of Hyde Park, is one of the finest monuments in Europe—the ALBERT MEMORIAL, erected in honour of the late Prince Consort. It is in the shape of a canopy, in the pointed Gothic style of architecture, and has been most gorgeously decorated by the best artists in the kingdom. It is reached by wide flights of granite steps formed out of grey Irish granite. Round the base of the monument are sculptured portraits of the greatest men of all nations (except Ireland), including poets, painters, philosophers, musicians, &c. At each corner of the structure is a group emblematical of some industry, one of them, and by no means the least meritorious, that of "Engineering," being the work of an Irish sculptor of note named John Lawlor, who acquired a worthy reputation in his profession, and died not long ago. At the four corners of the flights of steps are the corner-groups of the whole monument, representing Asia, Africa, America, and Europe. The first and last of these are by two of the greatest sculptors Ireland has produced. Patrick M'Dowell has executed the group typifying "Europe," and has completed it in a masterly manner. The central figure, a bull, is not thought to be a great success, but there can be no question of the beauty of the rest of the work. The female figures representing Power, Commerce, Fine Arts, and Learning, are, as was to be expected from such a sculptor, all imaginative, and are withal natural in conception and treatment.

"Asia" is the work of that greatest of modern sculptors, John Henry Foley. Neither pen nor pencil could adequately describe this magnificent group. It is the admiration and wonder of all visitors to this noble memorial. The vast Continent of Asia is represented by a kneeling elephant, bearing on its back a half-veiled figure, and having around it, in different attitudes, the Hindoo, the Chinaman, the Persian, and the Tartar. Each of the faces of these human figures is so full of expression that they actually seem to live and move, and each face is characteristic of its nationality. The elephant, too, is splendidly carved, and altogether the group is immeasurably superior to most public sculpture in England. It is impossible, in presence of this sublime work, to do more than admire in silence. Few of the multitude of visitors who gaze at this work every day in the year know that its sculptor was one of the priceless gifts Ireland has bestowed on England, and that he has helped to refute the charge so often made in the past

LADY BLESSINGTON.

by Continental nations, that Britain produces few good artists. Under the canopy of the central structure is the seated figure of the late Prince Consort. This work is also by Foley, the commission to execute the work being given to him when the first sculptor failed to send in a good design. The artist whom Foley succeeded was the eminent Italian, Baron Marochetti, who has executed other works which are highly esteemed. The statue, which is of immense size, is said to be life-like in its resemblance to its subject, but, sad to say, this fine work of Foley has been spoilt through the superlatively bad taste of those "in high places," the beautiful white marble being covered over with gold paint from head to foot! This outrageous act of vandalism has been universally condemned, but it was apparently the wish of the perpetrator to make the whole affair as gorgeous and as "loud" as possible. Luckily for the sculptor's peace of mind, he died before this barbarism was carried out, and one of the most conscientious artists that ever lived was thus spared a measureless indignity. It only remains to be stated that the marble used in the formation of the monument came chiefly from Down and Armagh.

Almost the first feeling in the mind after an examination of this work of art is one of regret that such a magnificent monument has been wasted on a prince who, apart from his position, was a most insignificant personage. The Albert Memorial cost about £100,000, and one cannot help wondering whether a day will ever come, when either Government or the moneyed men of the kingdom will give one-hundredth part of the amount towards statues of Shakespeare or Burke, or any other of the great minds of the past.

Partly on the site of the Albert Hall stood formerly GORE HOUSE, the residence of Lady Blessington, where she assembled all the illustrious men and women of her time at her levees and drawingrooms. The assemblies of this brilliant and fascinating woman were attended by a greater number of literati than most Royal presences could boast of, and to mention the foremost of whom would be to mention everybody of note in those days. After the death of her husband her resources became very much strained, and the income from her Irish estates being considerably reduced through failure of the potato crop, she was obliged to pawn her jewellery and fly to the Continent, leaving debts to the amount of £100,000. To meet some of the demands of her creditors, Gore House, with all its artistic treasures, was put up for sale, and attracted a crowd of as many as twenty thousand people. It realised the comparatively trifling sum of £10,000.

A little up the road, almost facing Kensington Palace, stood KENSINGTON HOUSE, where, at a school once kept there by Huguenot priests, Richard Lalor Sheil was educated. Passing through High-street, we reach in a short time, on the right, HOLLAND HOUSE, one of the most historic houses in England. Those who may be interested in the subject cannot do better than read the splendid essay by Macaulay on this famous residence, which has had among its most prominent frequenters such Irishmen as Moore, Curran, Croker, Sheridan, Lord Moira, Lord Lansdowne, and the witty poet, Henry Luttrell. Among its valued art treasures is Sir M. A.

HOUSE IN WHICH ARTHUR MURPHY DIED.

Shee's finest work, his portrait of Moore, who, as Byron truly said, "dearly loved a lord," and is here in congenial company.

ADDISON-ROAD, which commences near here, was once the place of residence of Annie Keary, the author of "Castle Daly" and other popular novels. It runs to HAMMERSMITH, where (at the TERRACE, overlooking the river) lived Arthur Murphy, his burial-place being the parish church in QUEEN-STREET, not far distant.

CHISWICK, one of the prettiest of London suburbs, is close to Hammersmith, and as it has been the place of residence of several celebrated Irishmen, we may briefly deal with it here. Here lived Fergus O'Connor, who for a time was confined in a private lunatic asylum in Chiswick, kept by a Dr. Tuke; and in this village also lived O'Connell (at Walpole House) in 1795, while studying law at one of the Inns of Court. Hither, in 1827, for change of air, came George Canning, and here he died; while another Irishman, Thomas Keightley, the eminent historian and novelist, died here in 1872. CHISWICK CHURCH is noteworthy as the place where Lord Macartney, the famous Ambassador and traveller, was buried.

Returning now to the top of Sloane-street, whence we branched off, and keeping to the left along BROMPTON-ROAD, we suddenly come upon a very interesting house. It is partly a tobacconist's and partly a dyer's, and is the identical house in which Arthur Murphy, the dramatist, died in 1805.

Some distance lower down the road, near the present Montpelier-street, stood until comparatively late years a line of houses known as BROMPTON ROW, where Arthur Murphy also lived for a time; while opposite, on a site now occupied by a grocer's shop, next to "The Grapes" publichouse, stood a house (demolished in 1844) where John Banim, the famous novelist, lived from May, 1822, to October, 1824, being immediately followed as a tenant by Gerald Griffin, who took up his lodgings here in 1825. EGERTON MANSIONS, adjoining, are built on the site of Michael's Palace, where, at No. 8, lived Dr. Croly, the eminent poet and divine.

Facing Egerton Mansions is BROMPTON-SQUARE, which has had at all times a great number of eminent residents. The most important among those of Irish birth was undoubtedly Henry Luttrell, whose witty poems, though rarely read nowadays, are not the less a valuable contribution to English and Irish literature. Luttrell, who died here on the 19th of December, 1851, was a native of Dublin, and was born about the beginning of the century. He is known as the author of some of the best "vers de société" ever written. One stanza of his composition is likely to be immortal, for most biographers of Moore quote it and emphasise it. Alluding to the immense popularity of "Lalla Rookh" in the East, Luttrell wrote (or rather sang)—

> I'm told, dear Moore, your lays are sung
> (Can it be true, you lucky man?)
> By moonlight, in the Persian tongue,
> Along the streets of Ispahan.

A little further past the Brompton Oratory, one of the most important Catholic churches in London, and greatly frequented by the Irish of West London, is the South Kensington Museum, which is so full of Irish art and objects of interest to Irishmen that we will reserve it for special and separate treatment in a future article. Further on, in CROMWELL-ROAD, is the NATURAL HISTORY MUSEUM, which not only possesses a fine collection of specimens of the animal, vegetable, and mineral worlds, but is architecturally also one of the most remarkable buildings in London. Among its unrivalled collection of minerals are many found in Ireland, including precious stones of nearly every description. The Irish crystals, agates, &c, are exceptionally fine, as are also some specimens of different coloured marbles. There are also several of the basaltic pillars of that "world's wonder," The Giant's Causeway; but the most remarkable objects in the

Museum, so far as Irishmen are concerned, are the skeletons of the extinct quadrupeds, the elk and red deer. There are three fine skeletons of the latter animal, all of magnificent size, and two specimens of the gigantic elk, male and female. It would be impossible to enumerate the thousand-

CURRAN.

and one curiosities among the sea-shells, animals, and minerals brought hither from Ireland, and which, as indeed the whole vast collection deposited here, are well worth seeing, and of absorbing interest.

FULHAM-ROAD is a very long thoroughfare, running from Brompton to Putney, but, though its points of interest are few and far between, they are of too great importance to be passed over altogether. On the right, as we enter the road, is ALEXANDER-SQUARE, where the eminent novelist, Captain William Nugent Glascock, "the Irish Marryat," lived for a long time. His naval stories are so excellent in plot and so vivid and lifelike in narrative, that he is fully entitled to rank beside Captain Marryat and Michael Scott, the English and Scotch naval storytellers. Glascock died in 1847, and, like Mayne Reid and Maxwell, his countrymen, is widely read by the youthful lovers of adventure in these islands.

Some distance further on, close to the "Admiral Keppel" publichouse, and beginning immediately beyond it, is a row of houses, on the left, once forming AMELIA-PLACE, but now bearing no distinctive title. From the opposite side of the way can be seen the original houses, now almost hidden behind the shops built on their front gardens, and in the lowest house of the row, once No. 7, died the famous orator and patriot, John Philpot Curran, on the 14th of October, 1817. His never-failing wit was present even during his last illness, if the following anecdote is to be believed. His doctor, noticing his racking cough, remarked—"Your cough has not improved, I see, Mr. Curran." To which the latter promptly replied—"That's odd, for I have been practising all the evening."

After Curran's death, John Banim came to England, and one of his first actions was to make a pilgrimage to the house where his great countryman had died. Finding lodgings were "to let" in the house, he immediately took them, in order, as he himself said, "that he might dream of his country with the halo of Curran's memory around him." In MARLBOROUGH-STREET, close by Amelia-place, died on January 7th, 1841, James A. O'Connor, an exquisite landscape painter, in the 49th year of his age.

PELHAM CRESCENT, opposite, has had some distinguished residents, including the eminent Frenchman, Ledru Rollin, a particularly warm friend of Ireland, and one who did his best to get the French Government, in 1848, to lend her assistance in her fight for freedom.

In SYDNEY-STREET, on the left, lower down, is St. Luke's Church, the first rector of which was Dr. Gerard V. Wellesley, brother of the Duke of Wellington. In the burial ground attached to it was buried in 1826 Charles Connor, one of the cleverest Irish actors of his time.

YORK-PLACE (now York Mews), still on the left of Fulham-road, was once the place of residence of

MUNSTER HOUSE.

Moore, and at No. 7 FINBOROUGH-ROAD, some distance on the right, died the great artist, Richard Doyle, on the 11th of December, 1883. Doyle is best known by his most inimitable drawings for "Punch," with which he was for a long time connected. But he also painted some delightful pictures, all conceived in a genuinely humorous spirit, and worthily executed. The cover of

Ireland in London.

"Punch," with its innumerable elves, all excellently drawn, is known far and wide as the characteristic work of Doyle. He left "Punch" for reasons wholly creditable to himself and equally discreditable to that journal. As a sincere Catholic he could not tolerate its blatant and oft-repeated attacks on the Pope, and therefore resigned his position on the staff, a step which, it is certain, "Punch" little relished. Thenceforth Doyle devoted himself to book illustration, in which he excelled, and produced some of his finest work, now considered invaluable.

BROMPTON CEMETERY, just past here, contains the graves of some notable Irishmen and women. Lady Morgan's fine monument, by S. Westmacott, is just inside the entrance, but has been most wantonly despoiled of some of its decorations, including an Irish harp carved in marble. A plain stone, at the other end of the ground, records the death of Thomas Crofton Croker, the antiquary and folk-lorist, and his wife and father-in-law. Here also reposes the dust of an eminent Irish musician, William Michael Rorke (O'Rourke), the instructor of Balfe, and a composer of great merit; General Sir John Lysaght Pennefather, a "gallant Tipperaryman," and a soldier of brilliant achievements, is likewise buried here, as is also Captain Francis Fowke, the architect and engineer.

In THISTLE GROVE, on the right of the road, lived John Burke, the genealogist, whose two sons, Sir Bernard and Peter Burke, have both achieved distinction in literature, the latter as a biographer and novelist, and the former in the "science" of genealogy. Burke's "Peerage" and similar works are among the most valuable works of reference in existence.

Keeping to the left as the road winds in that direction, we pass on the right a former residence of John Wilson Croker, called "Munster House," which received the nickname of "Monster" House, owing, it is said, to the fact that two hideous composition lions adorned each gateway; but we may be allowed to refer its name to its unprincipled owner, who, though a writer of immense vigour and ability, was a treacherous friend and an intensely bitter opponent of his country and countrymen. His famous edition of Boswell's "Johnson" is the only work of his which is likely to live, though its author wrote with great versatility on many subjects and in many styles. He wrote a great deal of poetry, which is now somewhat unjustly forgotten, a natural retribution for one who destroyed, or endeavoured to destroy, the reputations of many of the great poets of the time he lived in. His house is in exactly the same condition as when he left it, and appears not to have had a tenant for

T. CROFTON CROKER.

many years. Croker was a Galway man, but was not proud of the fact, boasting rather of his English descent.

In PARSON'S GREEN LANE is a small house called Audley Lodge, which was the famous "Rosamond's Bower" of T. Crofton Croker, who lived there for about nine years, and there collected his treasures and regaled his various friends and countrymen. The main road leads over the Thames to PUTNEY, where John Toland, an eminent Irish philosophical and controversial writer of the latter half of the 17th century, died and was buried in 1722, aged 51. He was a native of Donegal, and whatever may be thought of his inferences and deductions regarding Christianity, his great learning and genius are unquestionable.

Retracing our steps for a good distance along the Fulham-road, we reach CHURCH-STREET, Chelsea, on the right. In this street both Steele and Swift resided, Chelsea being then as now, a favourite place of residence of literary men. At the bottom is CHEYNE WALK, by the river side, a street hallowed by innumerable historical associations. At old CHELSEA CHURCH here, where Dr. Nicholas Brady, the well-known translator of the Psalms, used to occasionally preach, were buried two great Irishmen, Sir Hans Sloane and Henry Mossop, the tragedian. Both have fine tombs, the first outside, the second inside the church. Mossop died in destitution close by, and, as in the case of Sheridan, his friends resolved to give him, whom when living they neglected, a grand funeral, which they accordingly did, thereby proving the old saying, "He asked for bread, and they gave him a stone," once more applicable to genius in difficulties. Mossop was a great actor, but he possessed a violent and overbearing nature, which led him into many troubles. Like other eminent men of his profession, he was frequently in a chronic state of impecuniosity, and when he died was the possessor of one small coin of the realm— a halfpenny—and no more. Sir Hans Sloane was the physician of Queen Anne, and attended her on her death-bed. He was created a baronet by George I., and was the first physician who ever received that distinction. The BOTANIC GARDEN, which is almost opposite the church, was given by Sloane to Chelsea, in return for which valuable present his statue was erected in the garden, and may be seen there to this day.

In CHEYNE-ROW, near the church, lived Thomas Carlyle for many years, and at his house, which is easily identified, John Mitchel and Sir Charles Gavan Duffy were occasional visitors. The grim "Sage of Chelsea" had a sincere regard for both of these distinguished Irishmen, and said of the former—"Poor Mitchel! I told him he would probably be hanged, but I also told him they could not hang the immortal part of him!"

Sir Hans Sloane lived in Cheyne Walk, at MANOR HOUSE; and at No. 4 here died Maclise, the great painter, in April, 1870, at the age of 59.

QUEEN'S-ROAD (formerly Paradise-row) was the place of residence of Lord Carbery, the eminent scientist and President of the Royal Society, and in the same street died Samuel Cotes, the clever miniature painter, and brother of a still more notable painter. Any of the turnings on the left lead into King's-road, where two interesting places may be pointed out, ARGYLL HOUSE, at the corner of Oakley-street, wherein Richard Curran, eldest son of J. P. Curran, died on the 11th of December, 1846, and the DUKE OF YORK'S SCHOOL, which stands on the site of a house occupied in the 17th century by Lord Ossory, the celebrated soldier and courtier.

But the most interesting building in Chelsea has yet to be noticed. The ROYAL CHELSEA HOSPITAL, which lies between Queen's-road and the river Thames, is to the Army what Greenwich Hospital is to the Navy—an asylum for wounded and aged warriors. It is a magnificent building, built by Sir Christopher Wren, the architect of St. Paul's, and its gardens are the most beautifully laid out of any public grounds in London. A great number—the majority, we should think—of the "old pensioners" are, and have always been, Irish, and some of the oldest of them are lavishly adorned with hard-won medals and decorations. On a monument in the grounds, which was erected in honour of the soldiers who fell at the battle of Chillianwallah (during the Indian Mutiny) a great number of the names inscribed are of a decidedly Celtic character, the O's and the Mac's forming a very large proportion of the total number. The hospital has had among its governors no less than three eminent Irish soldiers—Sir Andrew Barnard (a native of Donegal), Sir Edward Blakeney, and Sir J. L. Pennefather. Its chaplain during a part of the last century was the Rev. Philip Francis, the well-known translator of Horace, and father of the supposed author of "Junius's Letters." Among other famous Irishmen connected with this historic pile was George Barrett, R.A., the landscape painter, appointed master painter to the Hospital through the influence of Burke, who was ever ready to befriend a countryman of his, or anybody else in need of aid. It should be also mentioned that after Wellington's death his body lay in state here for a few days in presence of many of the veterans who had shared in his battles if not in his distinctions.

Inside the Hospital are many interesting objects, especially the tattered flags of many famous regiments, and the eagles captured from time to time from the French by Irish and other regiments. In the cloister is a monument to Sir Arthur Wellesley Torrens, who fell at Inkerman, in 1854.

In the burial-ground attached to the hospital are many interesting tombstones and many Irish graves. Two Irish centenarians are buried here, one Peter Dowling, aged 102; and another, aged 111, who fought at the Boyne, and died a great many years after that great battle. Here also were buried Sir Andrew Barnard and Sir Edward Blakeney (Governors of the Hospital), and the Right Hon. James O'Hara, Baron of Tirawley, who died in July, 1773. But the most remarkable grave here is that of Christian Kavanagh (afterwards Davies), one of the most remarkable of female soldiers. She was born in Dublin in 1667, and entered the British army disguised as a man. She fought at the battles of Blenheim, Landen, Ramilies, etc., and was wounded several times, her sex being finally discovered. She received a pension in 1712, and married a soldier named Davies, and it was whilst visiting him here that she died in 1739. She was buried with full military honours, in the churchyard.

CHAPTER XV.

SOUTH LONDON AND THE SOUTH-WESTERN ENVIRONS.

CROSSING Westminster Bridge, ST. THOMAS'S HOSPITAL is on our right. One of its most distinguished physicians in the past has been Dr. Adair Crawford, the chemist, a native of Ulster, who was born in 1748, and died in 1795. The chief surgeon at present connected with this hospital is Sir William M'Cormac, a native of Belfast, and one of the greatest practitioners of the day. The hospital has a fine river frontage, at its end being situated LAMBETH PALACE, the residence of the Archbishops of Canterbury, and one of the oldest buildings in London. This picturesque-looking edifice has not many objects of peculiar interest to Irishmen, but although few, they are of relatively great importance. Here is Shee's excellent portrait of Archbishop Howley, whose name seems to betoken his Irish origin though he was born in England. The portrait of Bishop Berkeley, the great Irish philosopher, who was the first Bishop of an American See, is also here. Berkeley was a native of Kilkenny, and one of the greatest of Irish Protestant Bishops.

In a glass-case in the Library are the finely-illuminated "Gospels of MacDurnan," the work of an Irish scribe of that name of the ninth century. It comprises the four Gospels of the Evangelists, exquisitely written and magnificently illuminated, and ranks in value with some of the most unique Irish manuscripts in Dublin, Oxford, and the British Museums. This priceless treasure once belonged to Athelstan, King of the West Saxons and English in the tenth century, who gave it to the city of Canterbury; hence its presence in the archiepiscopal residence. The illumination of manuscripts in these islands in the early ages was almost exclusively confined to Irish monks, whose unremitting labours were given to the dissemination of useful and necessary knowledge, and the preservation and production of most beautifully-executed art objects, the admiration and envy of succeeding ages.

There are also in the Library the Carew Manuscripts, in 42 volumes, compiled by Sir George Carew while Lord Deputy of Ireland under Elizabeth, for the purpose of a History of Ireland, and a digest of which was published in 1633, under the title of "Pacata Hibernia," or "Ireland Appeased"—that is to say, after the plunderings and slaughters committed by the Elizabethan generals. These volumes, which contain curious illustrations of the old castles, cities, and fortifications that withstood the campaigns of the time, contain an immense fund of original historical matter, and are said to be the most largely-read books

HENRY BROOKE, WITH AUTOGRAPH.

in the Lambeth collection. The Library is open to the public on Mondays, Wednesdays, and Fridays, from 10 to 3.

In LAMBETH CHURCH, close by the Palace, was

buried Robert Barker, the distinguished artist, and inventor of the Panorama, who was born in Kells, county Meath, in 1739, and died in 1806.

Returning to Westminster Bridge, and proceeding a little way through it, we reach Oakley-street on the left, where Colonel Despard, with 32 other persons, were arrested in November, 1802, on a charge of high treason, when, being found guilty, Despard and seven of his associates were subsequently executed on the top of Horsemonger-lane Jail, off the Borough, Southwark.

Proceeding further, we come to ST. GEORGE'S-ROAD. Here is situated St. George's Cathedral, a fine specimen of the work of Pugin, the great architect. It is built on the precise spot where, in 1780, Lord George Gordon assembled his rabble in order to march to Parliament to oppose any concessions being offered to Catholics. The cathedral was dedicated on July 4th, 1848, High Mass being sung by Dr. Wiseman, the first English Cardinal since the Reformation. He was here for two years after being installed as Archbishop of Westminster, and preached here his famous sermons on the re-establishment of the Hierarchy. One of the most prominent founders and chief divines of St. George's Cathedral was the Rev. Dr. Thomas Doyle, an Irish priest, in whose honour a memorial has been erected in the Cathedral. His exertions in getting together the funds necessary to build it were as great and untiring as his efforts on behalf of the Irish of South London, by whom he has been always venerated. There is another point in connection with St. George's Cathedral which should not be forgotten. One of the most munificent donors to its funds was the Earl of Shrewsbury, the same nobleman to whom O'Connell addressed his famous letter, after he had been attacked by that nobleman in which he declared himself "the hired servant of Ireland, and glorying in his servitude." Lord Shrewsbury had accused O'Connell of living upon the bounty of the poorest of his countrymen, and this splendid and well-known letter, the most vigorous piece of writing we possess from O'Connell's pen, was his sufficient answer.

At the end of Westminster Bridge-road are BLACKFRIARS-ROAD (on the right of which, at No. 155, opposite the Surrey Theatre, was started the first London branch of the Home Rule organisation) and LONDON-ROAD, where is situated the Southwark Irish Literary Club. This body, which meets in BATH-STREET HALL, has now been established some years, and may fairly claim to be the only purely literary and Irish society in London. Though its "lease of life" has not been very long, its main objects—the spread of a knowledge of Irish literature and the cultivation of Irish literary talent—have been so far most successfully carried out; the result being chiefly due to the individual labours of its members, though its work has been materially assisted by the various eminent Irish litterateurs who have honoured it by their presence, including such well-known and gifted Irishmen as Sir C. Gavan Duffy, T. D. Sullivan, Justin M'Carthy, Richard Dowling, Edmund Downey, J. A. O'Shea, Daniel Crilly, W. B. Yeats, and J. F. Molloy, some of whom are honorary members of the society. A little past Bath-street is a music-hall, which oc-

SAINT GEORGE'S CATHOLIC CHURCH, SOUTHWARK.

cupies the site of the former Roman Catholic Church of Southwark, which was opened on 17th of March, 1793, the sermon being preached by the redoubtable Father Arthur O'Leary.

At the top of this road, to the left, is the Borough, a thoroughfare leading to London Bridge. Here, a few yards beyond Horsemonger-lane Jail, is situated the Church of ST. GEORGE THE MARTYR, where two celebrated Irish personages were buried. One was Nahum Tate, the Irish poet of the 17th century, and the only Irishman of note who was made Poet Laureate of England. In spite of the abuse that has been showered upon him by various English critics, Tate was by no means so bad a poet as they would wish us to believe. Looked at from the present-day point of view, his poetry may be called dull, but he was certainly equal, and, indeed, superior, to some of the English poets (so-called) of his time, and his productions compare very favourably with those of Settle, Shadwell, Cibber, Pye, and other English Laureates. He wrote a good many lines of "Absalom and Achitophel," Dryden's masterpiece; and although they do not equal the parts written by that master of satire and pungent verse, he must be a very prejudiced critic who will not admit them to be exceedingly creditable and above the average of satirical verse. Tate, who was born in Dublin in 1652, died in the Mint, or debtor's prison, which stood close by here, in 1715.

Mrs. Glover, the admirable Irish actress, who is also buried in St. George the Martyr's, was a native of Newry, county Down, where she was born in 1781. As an impersonator of old-women characters, especially Mrs. Malaprop, in Sheridan's "Rivals," she has been almost unrivalled, and was in every respect a comedy actress of the highest order. She died on July 16th, 1850, leaving a son, William Howard Glover, who was an accomplished musician and a composer of great merit.

At the end of London-road is the Elephant and Castle, and directly opposite is New Kent-road, leading direct to Greenwich, where one of the many interesting sights of London is situated.

GREENWICH HOSPITAL is the asylum of the naval pensioners, and though not quite so many Irish memories cluster around it as in the case of Chelsea Hospital, it is nevertheless a place of absorbing interest. It was in former days a palace of Henry VIII., or rather stands on the site of his palace, for it has been much altered. Part of its fine river front is the work of an Irishman —namely, Sir John Denham, the poet and architect.

It was from the old Palace of Greenwich that Henry VIII., in 1536 (the same year in which he grabbed the spoils of the monasteries) wrote a famous letter, still extant, to the people of Galway, ordering them to shave their lips, allow their hair to grow over their ears, and wear English caps. They were also to wear gowns and hose of English fashion, and by no means to appear in garments of saffron dye. And hither, in 1541, came Con (Bacach) O'Neill, father of Shane the Proud, to make humble submission to Henry and be created Earl of Tyrone, "the first of his race who had received a title." The following year saw other Irish renegade chieftains—O'Brien, Ulick MacWilliam, and O'Donnell—received at the Royal Palace with lavish ceremonials, "the Queen's apartments being gaily hung with arras and strewn with rushes." And here, after Mass, the King sat in state surrounded by his nobles, and the three chiefs came forward, and having given up their tribal lands, to which they had no title whatever, and accepted a royal patent of proprietorship for the same, and a fair promise of the share of the plundered Church property his Majesty dubbed them respectively, Earls of Thomond, Clanricarde, and Tyrconnell, and girt swords upon them, and put gold collars upon their necks; and after some right merry feasting the new-fledged peers returned home to experience a right lively reception from their disgusted and revolted clansmen.

There have been several Irish governors of Greenwich Hospital, particularly two—Sir John Colpoys, and Matthew, Lord Aylmer, whose portraits, with those of other notable Irish Admirals, including Sir Thomas Graves, Sir Francis Beaufort, Sir H. Blackwood, Sir Robert Stopford, and Sir Hugh Palliser, are to be seen in the Painted Hall. There have been at all times a large number of Irish Admirals, as of Irish soldiers, in the British service, even in early days—when Sir Peter Warren and Sir Richard Tyrrell distinguished themselves—as in more modern times, when such celebrated Admirals as Sir J. Rowley, Sir Robert M'Clure, Sir M. O'Reilly, and Sir F. L. M'Clintock (still living) have upheld the fame of their race for dashing exploits. M'Clintock and M'Clure are, however, better known as two of the greatest of Arctic discoverers, a more honourable title than that of successful warriors.

There are two excellent examples of Irish art at Greenwich Hospital which reflect immense credit on the artists who produced them. One is the magnificent bronze equestrian statue of Lord Exmouth, by Patrick M'Dowell, R.A., one of the most vigorous conceptions of that artist; and the other is the admirable marble statue of Admiral Sir Sydney Smith, by Thomas Kirk, R.H.A., a native of Cork, and a graceful artist. Kirk was born in 1784, and died in 1845, the present Irish sculptor, J. R. Kirk, R.H.A., presumably his son, following worthily the same profession. Thomas Kirk's finest works are in Ireland, and are all excellent.

Here also, in the Painted Hall, is the full-length portrait of Lord Hawke, the great Admiral, by Francis Cotes, R.A., an eminent portrait painter, and the son of a Mayor of Galway, who came to London about 1720, and lived at Cork-street, behind Regent-street. His son Francis, who was born there in 1726, died in 1770, aged 45, one of the best portrait painters of the time.

The Hospital also contains a bust of Sir Joseph Banks, the great naturalist, executed by Peter Turnerelli, and Copley's portrait of Admiral Sir E. Berry.

In GREENWICH CHURCH, close by, was buried General Wolfe, the great soldier, in 1759, who was of Irish descent; and it also contains the dust of Lord Aylmer. In LEWISHAM CHURCHYARD, not far off, was buried, in 1802, the luckless poet, Thomas Dermody, whose poems, though intrinsically worth little, gave evidence of remarkable precocity of genius. He was born in Co. Clare, and through neglect or other causes became unfortunately addicted to drink at an early age. This besetting sin proved his ruin, as he died prematurely in great poverty. He was over and over again rescued from improvidence and dissipation, only to repay kindness with the basest ingratitude, and to fall back into his evil ways. His wretched life was, if we may believe his biographer, redeemed by scarcely a single generous or worthy act, and ended, as it began, in misery. Some of his poems were written while quite a child, and, considered as mere juvenile efforts, are certainly wonderful. His maturest productions are very vigorous, but they do not entitle him to rank with the celebrated poets with whom he has been often inaptly compared. He never had a good word to say of his country or countrymen, and does not deserve their respect or their praise; he did not consider it wrong, apparently, to libel Ireland in order to curry favour with his English patrons.

We may now return to London-road, and, turning to the left, proceed towards Clapham. On the left, some distance down the main road, is KENNINGTON PARK, known in history as Kennington Common, where the great Chartist meetings, presided over by Fergus O'Connor, used to be held in the revolutionary times of '48. In that year the great assembly that was to frighten the Government into submission was announced to be held, O'Connor vowing that he would bring an unlimited number of armed men to the meeting-place. The Government were certainly alarmed, and prepared themselves, enrolling an extraordinary number of special constables (Louis Napoleon, subsequently Emperor of the French, vaingloriously including himself amongst them), and amassing their horse and artillery; but comparatively few Chartists answered their leader's expectations, and the meeting was practically a fiasco.

By the side of Kennington Park is a Hall called "The Horns," where Mr. Parnell addressed what was probably his first public meeting in London. The road by the side of Kennington Park runs through Brixton to STREATHAM, where is the MAGDALEN HOSPITAL, which has had many eminent Irish physicians connected with it, and which possesses one of the best portraits—a full-length one—of the distinguished Irish painter, Thomas Hickey, a native of Dublin, and an admirable artist, who flourished during the last century. His brother, Noah Hickey, who died in 1795, aged 39, was one of the most notable sculptors of the time.

CLAPHAM COMMON, at the end of Clapham-road, is chiefly remarkable in that the eminent scholar and divine, Dr. John Jebb, Bishop of Limerick, is buried at the church of the Holy Trinity there, a tasteful monument by Baily being erected to his memory. On the right of the Common, from Clapham-road, is MACAULAY-ROAD, where, at Kenley Lodge, lived for some years the lamented A. M. Sullivan, M.P. Both as author, orator, and politician, his reputation was equally great, and his death caused universal sorrow, as he was respected by all parties. Although his works have received very high praise from the best authorities, especially his invaluable "New Ireland," it is doubtful whether they have been

W. F. NAPIER.

fully and adequately valued. The latter work is a particularly fine one, some of its chapters being most dramatic and thrilling in their intensity, and remarkable for their historical completeness and impartiality. His descriptions of the stormy scenes of '67 and of landlord extermination of tenantry are so powerful and enthralling that his readers are carried away by the rush of the narrative.

On the opposite side of the Common is situated the district known as CLAPHAM PARK, where, at "Scinde House," Sir William Francis Napier died in 1860. He was born in county Dublin in December, 1785, and, entering the army, achieved remarkable distinction, especially in the Peninsular War. Great as is his reputation as a soldier, it has been probably eclipsed by his fame as an historian. His "History of the Peninsular War" ranks among the first of military histories, and its vigorous style shows that its author could wield the pen as well as he could the sword. He pays the highest tributes to the valour of his countrymen in that great work, and there are other evidences of the fact that he was proud of his native land. He deeply sympathised with her wrongs, having in his youth witnessed the horrible excesses of the Orange Yeomanry, the memory of which remained with him for the rest of his life. When Smith O'Brien and the other patriots were tried at Clonmel, Napier attended, having with him an important letter, which he believed would prove serviceable to the case of O'Brien, whose nobility of character he highly appreciated. This letter proved that the Whigs themselves, who were now so horrified at the idea of disturbing "law and order," had at one time thought of civil war as an alternative to the defeat of the Reform Bill of 1832—for they asked Sir W. F. Napier to take command of the Birmingham men, who were to march on London in the event of a Whig defeat. Almost needless to say, his evidence was declared inadmissible, and the '48 men received their barbarous sentences. Throughout his correspondence there are frequent proofs of Napier's attention to Irish affairs and profound sympathy with the sufferings of his countrymen. An extract from one of his letters to Lady Hester Stanhope (quoted by Duffy in his brilliant book, "Four Years of Irish History") conclusively proves that he was not, as has been thought and stated, a Scotchman in feeling. He says: "Curse on the cowardly calumniators who have told you that Irishmen are cowards. They are equal to the English in bravery, superior to them in hardihood of sufferance and devotion to their friends in the hour of trouble; and they are superior to the Scotch in everything. And yet there are good soldiers among the Scotch; I like them not, but I will not belie them." He died at the house above-mentioned on the 12th of February, and was buried in NORWOOD CEMETERY, in the neighbouring suburb of Norwood.

Battersea lies to the north of Clapham, and adjoins it. In Battersea Fields, now BATTERSEA PARK, the Duke of Wellington fought a duel with the Earl of Winchelsea in 1829, one of the very few duels fought by that grim warrior. It is noteworthy as one of the very latest duels that occurred in London.

Close to the Park, in Victoria-road, is situated the ALBERT PALACE, which deserves mention, as it was built out of the material of the last Dublin Exhibition, forming one of the largest buildings in or near the metropolis, and as having been used for the purpose of several large Irish political demonstrations.

At SYDENHAM, to the west of Clapham, died Catherine Hayes, the great vocalist, in 1861, at an early age. Here also, at Perry Vale, died Dermody, the poet, in destitution, and in the same suburb died and was buried Ann Kelly, the actress, on March 15th, 1852, aged 103, who, though married twice, never had occasion to change her maiden name of Kelly, as both her husbands bore the same name.

The Crystal Palace, on Sydenham Hill, contains some excellent specimens of Irish art. There are statues or busts of Moore, Burke, Sir Michael O'Loghlen, Curran, Father Mathew, Cardinal Wiseman, and Mulready, by Christopher Moore, of Dublin; a medallion of Sir F. Chantrey, by Heffernan; statues or busts of William Dargan, O'Connell, and Sir Henry Pottinger (an Irish soldier), by John E. Jones, of Dublin; several excellent pieces of sculpture by John Lawlor, also of Dublin, including his graceful "Emigrant;" and several of the works of Thomas Crawford, an Irish-American, who has been considered one of the best of American sculptors. There are also statues or busts here, by other than Irish hands, of Macready, J. C. Calhoun (an Irish-American statesman), Lord Monteagle, Oliver Goldsmith, Canning, Wellington, and Anglesey. In an obscure corner, under one of the staircases, may be discovered plaster casts of two of the famous crosses of Monasterboice and Clonmacnoise; and in a portion of the grounds devoted to the exhibition of ancient geological specimens may be seen plaster casts of a male and female Irish elk.

The Palace, as the annual meeting-place of the "League of the Cross," has often been the scene of Irish gatherings, when light-hearted exiles find solace for hard toil in the social converse, the old songs and merry jigs and reels that restore to them, for a time, "a little bit of Ireland."

Adjoining Clapham is WANDSWORTH, where Bishop Jebb died and John Eugene O'Cavanagh, the Celtic scholar, lived.

Wandsworth leads to WIMBLEDON COMMON, formerly a famous place for duels, three of which are of some interest to Irishmen. Here, owing to some misunderstanding, afterwards cleared up, George Canning and the notorious Castlereagh had a hostile meeting in September, 1809, when

Canning was slightly wounded in the thigh. Here also, in June, 1839, Lord Londonderry, the half-brother of Castlereagh, came to answer for applying, in the House of Lords, the words "base" and "infamous" to the conduct of Mr. Henry Grattan (son of the great Irish patriot) in making a remark attributed to him by O'Connell—namely, "that the Queen's life would not be safe if the Tories got into power." Mr. Grattan repudiated the expression, and, not being satisfied with the explanation given, a duel was the result, when Grattan, after receiving his opponent's fire, discharged his pistol into the air, and so the affair ended "in smoke."

The third encounter took place on the 27th May, 1798, between William Pitt, then Prime Minister, and George Tierney, the eminent statesman, and was due to an angry altercation in the Commons. After exchanging two shots each, honour was declared satisfied.

Close by Wimbledon is RICHMOND, where Dr. Nicholas Brady, one of the translators of the Psalms and a well-known preacher of the 17th century, was for some time a curate, and in the parish church of which he is buried.

In Richmond were also buried Hugh Howard, the Irish portrait painter, and also Joseph F. Ellis, one of the best marine painters of his day, who, born in Ireland, died here on the 28th May, 1848.

At EAST SHEEN, Richmond, Swift lived for two years, and here Lord and Lady Castlereagh occupied a villa in 1805; and at MORTLAKE is buried Sir Philip Francis, the reputed author of "Junius's Letters."

The celebrated song, "The Lass of Richmond Hill," is stated by Sir Jonah Barrington, in his "Personal Sketches," to have been written by Leonard M'Nally, a distinguished Irish barrister, who defended the United Irishmen in '98, and is the author of several works; but Mr. Jesse, the well-known authority on the history of London, states that M'Nally, although he married the daughter of a gentleman who resided on Richmond Hill, had nothing to do with the authorship of the song, which was written by a Mr. Upton, and has, moreover, reference not to Richmond, Surrey, but to the village of that name in Yorkshire.

At TWICKENHAM, close by, lived at one time Robert Boyle, the philosopher, and also Henry Brooke, the novelist and dramatist, whose masterpiece, "The Fool of Quality," has won the admiration of some of the greatest of modern critics, including Charles Kingsley. Here, too, in a villa bought for her by Horace Walpole, called "Little Strawberry Hill," lived and died Kitty Clive, the inimitable actress, the neighbouring parish church being her last resting-place. Walpole's famous villa became a few years ago the property of Chichester Fortescue (Lord Carlingford), who has been prominently identified with the misgovernment of Ireland.

With this account of South London and the southern suburbs, our chapters on those London streets and houses which are of interest to Irishmen come to an end; and, commencing with the British Museum, we shall proceed to describe some of the famous London institutions, which, by their associations, or the literary, scientific, or artistic treasures they contain, throw light on the history of Ireland or bear witness to Irish intellect and genius.

CHAPTER XVI.

THE BRITISH MUSEUM.

It should be a matter of pride for Irishmen to reflect that the British Museum—the finest collection of national treasures in the world—owes its foundation to the intelligence and munificence of an Irishman.

Sir Hans Sloane was born in Killileagh, county Down, in 1660. Coming to London at the age of nineteen, he studied medicine, and became early distinguished for his zeal and industry in scientific research, and for his skill in medicine. When 27 years old he was appointed physician to the Governor of Jamaica, and on his return home a year later brought with him a collection of rare and valuable natural objects, which afterwards became the nucleus of the British Museum treasures. He again practised in London, and continued actively engaged in his profession until his 80th year. He was appointed physician to George I., and on the death of Sir Isaac Newton was elected President of the Royal Society. Remarkable for his care for the poor, he formed the plan of dispensaries for the gratuitous distribution of medicine to them, and he is said to have been no less estimable for his private than for his public virtues. He continued to add to the treasures brought with him from Jamaica until his death in 1753, and directed in his will that they should be offered to the nation on condition that a sum of £20,000 should be paid to his family. The offer was accepted, and an Act of Parliament passed for their purchase, the necessary funds being raised by the then common method of a lottery.

SIR HANS SLOANE.

Lest the bequest of the Sloane collection on the condition mentioned may be considered an act of as doubtful generosity as that of the individual who

"—— Out of his bounty
Built a bridge at the expense of the county,"

we hasten to state that, apart altogether from the extreme rarity of most of his collection, and the labour and time involved in its acquisition, Sloane had actually expended on its purchase the sum of £50,000, and had at one time been offered £60,000 for it, together with some honorary mark of Royal favour, by the then reigning King of France. Some idea of its nature, extent, and importance may be gathered when we mention that it contained, among other objects of worth and interest, 50,000 volumes of rare and valuable books, 3,516 scarce manuscripts, 32,000 coins, medals, precious stones, and gems of all kinds (the medals alone being valued, if sold merely by weight as bullion, at £7,000), 1,500 of the most exquisite cameos, 542 vessels of agate, jasper, &c.; besides a collection of 8,186 skeletons of animals, 1,172 of birds, 1,555 of fishes, and 5,439 of insects, all of the strangest character.

The Sloane Collection, together with others purchased or bequeathed about the same time, was placed in Montagu House, Russell-street, Bloomsbury, which was replaced by the present Museum, on the same site, in 1850, the former building proving inadequate for the increasing store of treasures, as indeed the present structure has since become, necessitating the removal of the whole of the Natural History collection to a separate splendid edifice in Cromwell-road South Kensington.

Among the various persons from whom additions to the Museum collections have been since acquired four Irishmen are noticeable.

A valuable store of manuscripts was bought from William Petty Fitzmaurice, First Marquis of Lansdowne, a statesman of considerable political knowledge and detailed acquaintance with foreign affairs, who was born in 1737, and died in 1805, and who employed the later years of his life in purchasing the libraries and MSS. of various persons. The sum of £4,925 paid for the "Lansdowne MSS." is noteworthy as the first grant made by Parliament for the improvement of the national collection of books in the Museum.

In 1832 the nucleus of the stock of Irish MSS. was acquired by purchase from James Hardiman, author of the "History of Galway," editor of the well-known "Hardiman's Minstrelsy," and one of the most prominent members of the Royal Irish Academy in his day; and an addition to this collection was made in 1858 from the library of

BRITISH MUSEUM,

Henry Monck Mason, LL.D., an Irish barrister, author of a learned volume on the Irish Parliament and a Grammar of the Irish Language, who died in that year. A splendid cabinet of Oriental coins was bequeathed to the Museum in 1836 by Dr. William Marsden, a Dublin man, who had been nearly all his life in the East India Company's service, and is noted for his great work on the Malay language, but most for his numismatic knowledge.

The external appearance of the British Museum, with its splendid columns and noble front, formed of 800 stones from five to nine tons in weight each, is impressive, and indeed, except on rare days of London sunshine, oppressive in the extreme, a feeling which is scarcely removed by the grand yet sombre aspect of the interior of the building.

THE READING-ROOM.

Facing the entrance is the Reading-room, a circular building, 110 feet in diameter by 106 feet high, the dome of which is the largest in the world, with the single exception of that of the Pantheon at Rome. Admission to view the room is readily granted, but permission to read requires the slight formality of a personal application, supported by the recommendation of a householder. Chance Irish visitors to London, with but limited stay, should know that even this formality is waived where admission is required for purposes of study or reference. The number of printed books in the Reading-room and adjacent galleries is, of course, immense, reaching to over a million and a half, and ranking next in amount to that possessed by the National Library of France, which is said to be the largest in the world.

The Museum is empowered by law to claim a copy of every book printed in the British Empire,

SHRINE OF BELL OF ST. CULANUS.

and hence its stock of books is yearly increasing at a rate that bids fair to monopolise all the available space in the building. It will be safe for the Irish student to assume that he will find here a copy of nearly every Irish book that has ever been published either in the English or Irish language, and of every English and many foreign printed works which treat in any way of Ireland, her history, people, resources, &c. There are, of course, exceptions (and not a few remarkable ones), especially in the case of obscure or minute books and pamphlets, although the number of even these to be found, chiefly gathered together in large miscellaneous folio volumes, is extraordinary. But until he is intimately acquainted with the mysteries of the many and bewildering catalogues, and has exhausted the patience of the obliging and much suffering attendants, the Irish reader should not despair of finding even the rarest and least known work dealing with his country.

Of the rare and curious Irish volumes a few deserve special mention. One of these is the first book ever printed in the Irish language and character. It is a tiny volume, called "O'Kearney's

Irish Catechism," printed at Dublin in 1571, from type presented by Queen Elizabeth (no less!), "with a view to instruct the native Irish." Then there are the New Testament in Irish (Dublin, 1602), being the first portion of the Bible ever printed in Irish, and a translation of the Church Prayer Book into Irish (1608)—all early attempts at proselytism: the first Irish dictionary, "O'Clery's Glossary" (Louvain, 1643), the first Irish Grammar, "O'Molloy's" (Rome, 1677); together with a number of rare Irish imprints of the 18th century. Of some of these books there is no other copy extant. Among later printed works of great value or interest are the Royal Irish Academy's facsimile reproductions of the ancient Irish books, the "Leabhar na-h-Uidhre," the "Leabhar Breac," the "Book of Leinster," and "the Book of Ballymote;" the late Lord Dunraven's book on Irish architecture—two very large volumes, containing magnificent photographs, with descriptive letterpress; Dr Petrie's two great quarto volumes on "Christian Inscriptions in the Irish Language;" O'Donovan's "Annals of the Four Masters," in seven quarto volumes; Gilbert's "Facsimiles of National Manuscripts;" the "Transactions of the Royal Irish Academy," and the Ossianic, Celtic, and other Irish learned societies, &c.

Irish newspapers were regularly added to the Library about 1850. Besides files of current Irish papers and magazines to the number of 140, including the "Nation" from its commencement, with the exception of its famous first number and a few others, the Library possesses copies of most of the thousand and one ephemeral prints which have appeared in Ireland from time to time, rising proudly, and soon failing miserably through various causes, such as Lawless's "Ulster Register" (1816-7), Francis Davis's "Belfast Man's Journal," the entertaining "Penny Journal," the "Satirist," "Spy," "Kottabos," "Salmagundi," "Zozimus," "Zoz," "Hibernia," "Harp," "Celt," "Citizen," and Duffy's excellent "Fireside" and "Hibernian Magazines." Here also may be had the sixteen numbers of Mitchel's "United Irishman," and the five issues of its successor, "The Irish Felon," edited by John Martin, and the "Irishman," from its first number to its last. There are also some curiosities of Irish periodical literature to be met with, the most notable being the single number of the "Irish Monthly Mercury," a small quarto sheet of eight pages, published in Cork in 1649, containing an account of the movements of the Cromwellian army in the South of Ireland, and which, if it can be called a newspaper, is one of the earliest newspapers published in these islands.

Before leaving the Reading-room, it should be mentioned that among its most celebrated frequenters may be enumerated some of the greatest Irish literati from John O'Donovan and Eugene O'Curry, in the past, to Lecky and Justin M'Carthy, in the present. Not a few of the Young Ireland party, during their visits to London, came here to avail themselves of its vast treasures of Irish literary material. Duffy, in his "Four Years of Irish History," relates how D'Arcy M'Gee was sent by him "as special correspondent to London during the session of Parliament, but his political letters were a little wild and speculative. . . It was plain from certain voluntary contributions which he sent to the 'Nation' that he had plunged into the British Museum, and was more absorbed in the achievements of Luke Wadding and Art Kavanagh than in those of Sir Robert Peel and Lord John Russell." And so M'Gee was soon relieved of his uncongenial "Parliamentary penny-a-lining," and has left us in his "Art MacMurrough" and "Irish Writers of the 17th Century," splendid testimonies to the use made by him of his time in London.

Several of the prominent officials of the Museum have also been natives of Ireland; among them was Arthur O'Shaughnessy, the well-known poet. He entered the institution as a transcriber at the

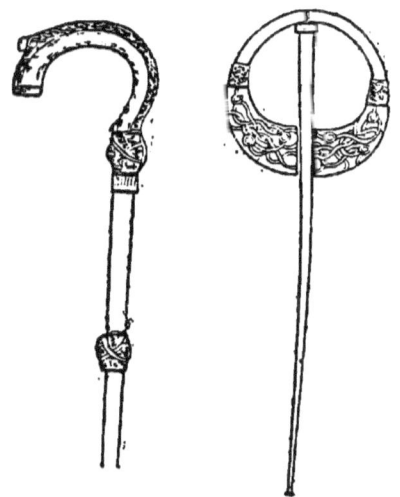

CROZIER OF MAELFINNIA.   BROOCH.

age of 20, through the influence of Lord Lytton, nd was afterwards promoted to the Natural History Department, where he remained until his death in 1881. His contributions to zoological science are considered of great value. Sir Frederick Madden, the eminent antiqary, who was Chief of the MSS. Department for about 40 years, was also of Irish descent ; and George Bullen, the distinguished scholar, who has been Head of the Printed Book Department since 1838, and Louis Fagan, Assistant Keeper of the Print Room, a well-known author and artist, whose lectures on the contents of the Museum are so highly popular, are of Irish parentage.

THE MANUSCRIPTS.

More prized than the printed books is the Museum collection of Manuscripts, declared by competent judges to be the finest, without exception, in the world, and of the extent of which no man has made himself master. They amount to over 50,000 volumes on every conceivable subject. Those relating to Ireland are very numerous and important, dealing with history, topography, politics, genealogies, literature, &c—a practically inexhaustible fund of original unpublished material for our future historians and writers. Most of these volumes are naturally of the highest interest. Here may be seen a variety of original letters from many of the eminent men and women of Ireland, contemporary accounts of important historical events, original drafts of many famous Irish works, besides a mass of those dry-as-dust documents into which genius breathes the breath of life and makes entrancing. There are contemporary copies of all the works of the historian, Sir James Ware, of Spencer's "View of Ireland," of Keating's "History," and the production of other old writers. Here are—the first Anglo-Irish composition in English verse, being a satire by a Kildare friar of the 14th century; a contemporary account of the great defeat of the English at the Blackwater in 1598; and copies of the debates in the Irish Parliament for a number of years. And some of the MSS. are of the utmost beauty and elegance, notably one written by a French officer in the Court of Richard I., giving an account of that monarch's ill-starred campaign in Ireland in 1399, with many curious illustrations in gold and silver, one of them depicting the meeting of Art MacMurrough and the Earl of Gloucester, and another the arrival of ships at Waterford, bringing food to the famished soldiers of Richard, who rush into the sea in their eagerness to receive it.

There are also a number of most curious maps of Ireland, or parts of Ireland, dating from the time of Henry VIII., downwards, which well repay inspection, and tell in a graphic way the story of the gradual tightening of the grip of England on the country.

The MS. collection in the Irish language is the third largest known, numbering 170 volumes, the Royal Irish Academy being first with over 600 volumes, and Trinity College, Dublin, second with over 290. The Museum collection, the greater part of which originally belonged to James Hardiman, contains much valuable matter dealing chiefly with the history, literature, romances, and poetry of Ireland, and was catalogued for the trustees in 1849 by the celebrated Irish scholar, Eugene O'Curry, a copy of whose catalogue may be consulted in the Reading-room. Most of the MSS. are not very old, being merely transcripts made in the 17th or 18th century of earlier works, but there are a few both old and interesting. The most notable is a 12th century copy of the famous Brehon Laws—the "Seanchus Mor," or "Great Law Digest," compiled in 439 by St. Patrick, two bishops, three kings, and three sages—the oldest body of laws in Europe, and a code by which the Irish people were governed for 2,000 years. Then there are the "Leabhar Breac," or Speckled Book of MacEgan, of the 12th century; the "Leabhar MacPartholain," and Leabhar Ua Caemnaigh" of the 15th century; the only copy now extant of the "Tripartite Life of St. Patrick," the identity of which was discovered by O'Curry himself on his very first visit to the Museum; besides several tracts of the 13th and 14th centuries.

Of the marvellously written and illuminated books, the work of the scribes of the early Irish Church, of which the Book of Kells in Trinity College is a world-renowned specimen, the Museum possesses two examples which are exhibited to the public, as will be mentioned further on. One of these is an ancient Psalter written in Latin, probably in the 8th or 9th century; the other and more remarkable one is the Four Gospels, written in Latin, by Maelbrigte Ua Maeluanaigh, a splendid illuminated specimen of minute writing, in the Irish hand, of the 12th century. At the foot of a small slip the transcriber, pardonably proud of his exquisite penmanship, has written in exceedingly small Irish characters—"If I wished I could do the whole like this."

A large number of the so-called Anglo-Saxon manuscripts, both here and in other English libraries, are stated by the best authorities to be undoubtedly the work of some of the many Irish monks who established monasteries in Britain in the early Christian period, and Miss Stokes is of opinion that to this origin is due the Gospels of St. Cuthbert of Lindisfarne (7th century), one of the priceless treasures of the Museum. Of the immense number of autograph letters, manuscripts, charters, and other documents, a selection interesting but necessarily limited is exhibited to the public in labelled cases in the Department of Manuscripts and the King's Library, to the right of the entrance hall. Here are shown autograph letters of Dean Swift, Sterne, Garrick, Wellington, and others; an agreement in Goldsmith's handwriting, and a dedication in "Junius's" handwriting of the famous Letters. There is a letter from Sir Richard Steele to Henry Pelham (May, 1720), inquiring whether the Duke of Newcastle will recall the order of silence imposed on Drury-lane Theatre, and threatening to petition the judges, the Parliament, and the King before he would allow his lordship to send his children a-starving. Of great interest is one from Charles James Fox (October, 1798), to the Duchess of Leinster, relative to the bill of attainder of her son, Lord Edward Fitzgerald, concluding with the words—"Nor can anything make me have, I will not say a friendly, but even a patient feeling towards the Government of this country till his poor children are reinstated in their rights." The most interesting, however, to Irishmen must certainly be a letter which they might reasonably expect to find written in letters of blood, being from Oliver Cromwell in the high tide of his butchery at Wexford, and dated there the 15th of October, 1649, in which the sanctimonious slaughterer announces thus to Lord Fairfax his capture of the town—"The Lord shewes us great mercye here; indeed Hee, Hee only gave this stronge towne of Wexford into our handes."

The early Irish MS. treasures of the Museum are but sparsely, although finely, represented in these rooms by the Gospels of Maelnanaigh and the copy of the Psalter already mentioned, but the slightest glance at the so-called Anglo-Saxon illuminated books, which lie by the side of these, will show how large a share Irish hands had also in the production of the latter volumes.

PRINTS AND DRAWINGS.

Among the greatest treasures of the Museum are the prints and drawings. They are kept in the PRINT ROOM, which is reserved for students, but excellent specimens of the best masters are shown on the walls of several galleries devoted to that purpose.

The Print Room contains specimens of the work of every Irish engraver of note, besides sketches and drawings by Barry, Barrett, Tresham, Collins, Mulready, Maclise, F. Cotes, Copley, Chinnery, J. J. Barralet, Danby, Donaldson, Hickey, Sir R. K. Porter, Alexander Pope, Charles Robertson, William Sherlock, and other admirable Irish painters. These are all well represented—in some cases by masterly drawings. But few things in this department are more valuable than the examples of the work of James Gillray, John Doyle, and Richard Doyle. Of Gillray there are some powerful caricatures, and indeed the greater part of his maturest work. His drawings are often coarse and savage in spirit, sometimes exceedingly so, but historically they are of exceptional value, inasmuch as they depict, with his customary exaggeration, the manners and habits of his contemporaries, and English life of the last century. John Doyle's inimitable caricatures are no less valuable as a pictorial record of the political life of the first half of this century. Of his drawings there are over six hundred here, the collection of his works being, in fact, almost complete, and including besides his lithographs, numerous miscellaneous sketches and drafts of future drawings. The delightful sketches of Richard Doyle are also well represented. Apart from his ever-varying and charming designs for books and periodicals, there are in the Print Room other productions of his. One treasure is very highly valued, and may be said to exceed in interest his more careful works. This is his marvellous early note-book or Diary, which, though finished when he was only 15 or 16 years old, is of astonishing excellence. The beauty of the figures, the fertility and freshness of the designs in this book are as delicious in their way as the charm and exquisite tastefulness of his latest works, and of itself the volume is sufficient to entitle him to the name of a great artist. Austin Dobson, who has so well treated of Doyle's work, that of a kindred soul, and who avers that in the dominions of King Oberon, Doyle would have been made Court-painter, refers to the "brilliancy" of this "unique effort," with its "elves and fays and gnomes and pixies" crowding every page; and all those best able to judge have unanimously concurred in his praise. Nor must the perennial and laughter-moving sketches of John Leech be passed over. His drawings afford endless amusement, and are never either vulgar or bigoted. The foibles of the English middle-class and the vagaries of men in power are the constant yet ever fresh themes of his pencil.

All the leading Irish mezzotint engravers are represented in the Print Room, besides other artists working in various other styles and belonging to different schools. The Irish school of engraving, which has not had many equals, and of which James McArdell, Thomas Frye, Richard Houston, John Murphy, James Watson, John Dixon, Richard Purcell, and others of the same calibre may be taken as representatives, may be seen here to advantage in specimens of all of their works, as well as those of William Humphrey, John Brooks (who taught Frye, McArdell, and other fine artists), Captain William Baillie (of whose 107 plates 102 are here), and Luke Sullivan, last but not least of a splendid group of men who made Irish art of worldwide celebrity. In the same and other styles may be mentioned Thomas Burke, Nicholas Blakey, Thomas Chambers, A.R.A., Thomas Beard, William N. Gardiner, James Egan, Caroline Watson, and William J. Cooke, all of whom are in evidence in the Print Room. Most of these were Dublin artists, who came to London in the last or at the beginning of this century, in order to get that larger audience and increase of remuneration which they thought impossible in Ireland. Nor must we forget the designs of such excellent architectural draughtsmen as John Carter and Hugh O'Neill, both of whom are here well and largely represented.

Among the specimens of Irish art exhibited on the walls of the galleries above referred to are some magnificent works. McArdell takes first place with his five plates after Reynolds, Murillo, Hogarth, &c, all executed in his clearest and most finished style; Captain Baillie's two remarkable prints after Salvator Rosa and Franz Hals being little inferior. John Murphy's "Abraham and Isaac" (after Rembrandt) is a masterly plate, and will rivet attention to the exclusion of surrounding works; while Thomas Burke's three etchings of allegorical pictures by Angelica Kauffmann suggest more peaceful and pleasing reflections. Houston's four plates, the "Four Elements," after Mercier, are, like all his work, exceptionally careful and accurate; and Purcell's two plates—one of them a fine portrait after Reynolds—have been well chosen as representing the power of the artist at its highest and most attractive point. For those who appreciate steel engravings and work of a similar character nothing more pleasing

RICHARD DOYLE, WITH AUTOGRAPH.

"WOOD'S HALFPENCE."

can be imagined than a visit to these masterpieces; the subjects are excellent, the treatment more than worthy, and the artists themselves Irish, and a credit to their country.

COINS AND MEDALS.

The numismatic collection in the Museum is the finest known, and is formed in very large part from the collections of Sloane and Marsden. A large number of the coins exhibited in cases in Room VII. are of Irish interest. There may be seen six coins of Sitric, Danish King of Dublin, a farthing of Prince John (Lord of Ireland), and many well-executed specimens from the mints of Dublin, Drogheda, and Waterford, of coins of English monarchs from Henry III. downwards, noticeable among them being Charles the Second's "Money of Necessity," and the celebrated "Wood's Halfpence," whose alleged baseness* was utilised by Swift in his famous "Drapier Letters" in a manner familiar to every student of Irish history.

The next apartment (Room VIII.) contains a goodly number of gold and silver medals, illustrative of English history. Among those which have any association with Irish affairs are one of Ireton, as Deputy in 1650, one of the Duke of Ormond in 1682, and one relating to the French in Bantry Bay, 1798; but the most remarkable have to do with the campaigns of William of Orange in Ireland, every step of whose progress has been commemorated by the execution of a medal of more or less artistic design, as may be seen by the subjects of a few specimens:—Departure of William for Ireland—Battle of the Boyne—Flight of James—Entry of William into Dublin—Amnesty to the Irish "Rebels"—Battle of Aughrim—"Pacification" of Ireland.

The artistic work of Irish hands may be seen here in several medals executed by William Mossop, sen. (1751-1804), whose productions, though few, are of the highest excellence, and whose son, William Stephen Mossop, R.H.A., followed his father's profession, and produced some fine work.

ANTIQUITIES.

In the room immediately at the top of the grand staircase will be found a collection of British and Irish antiquities. The Irish assortment includes a number of curious bronze objects—bridles, bits, sickles, bowls, collars, and helmets, iron swords and spear-heads, and some very pretty and peculiar glass beads and enamelled ornaments. A more valuable and interesting collection, however, is to be found placed, strangely enough, in the "Anglo-Saxon" Room, next door. They comprise a number of bronze bells and croziers, pins, brooches, and specimens of bookbinding of the early Christian period in Ireland. There are 22 of those artistic brooches so dear to the hearts of our antiquaries, including a remark-

ARTHUR O'SHAUGHNESSY, WITH AUTOGRAPH.

able bronze specimen from Drogheda, with rings four inches in diameter, and a pin nearly a foot long; a large number of beautiful pins, many of them harp-shaped, from Westmeath and Galway; a figure from a shrine, found buried near St. John's Abbey, Thomas-street, Dublin; and the top of a processional cross, finely decorated

There are also seven bells of great antiquity, those of Saints Commin and Caimin (King's County), St. Conaill of Inishkeel (Donegal), St. Molua (Queen's County), St. Senan of Iniscattery, St. Ruadhan of Lorrha (county Tipperary), and several others. Most of these bells were in the hereditary keeping of particular Irish families, and have an authentic history. Thus, the Breslins had charge of St. Conaill's Bell, and the Keanes of Clare that of St. Senan, called the Clogh Oir, or Golden Bell: the former bell was

---

* We say "*alleged* baseness," because Sir Isaac Newton is stated to have assayed the coins in England, and found them genuine.

sold in 1835 by Connell O'Breslin, a poor man, but the oldest representative of the family, and so came into possession of the Museum.

One of the most interesting of these bells is certainly that of Ruadhan, as it is supposed, on high authority, to be the identical bell which that saint rang as he made his circuit of the Hill of Tara in the 6th century, and, in punishment for the forcible carrying off of a kinsman of the saint's, by King Diarmaid of Tara, cursed that ancient residence of the Irish monarchs, after which it was deserted for evermore.

For the better preservation of these relics it was the peculiar custom of the Irish Church to enclose them in cases or shrines, highly ornamented, and adorned with gold, silver, enamels, and gems. A beautiful example of one of these shrines is to be seen here, being that of the Bearnan Cualaun or gapped bell of St. Cualaun, brother of Cormac, King of Cashel in the 9th century. The design and tracery on this shrine are of the highest type of Irish art of the 12th century. There are also five croziers, or parts of croziers, the best preserved of which is that of Maelfinnia, an Irish ecclesiastic of Kells, A.D. 907, which is remarkable as being the oldest one extant, exhibiting in its work three periods in the history of Christian art in Ireland. First, there is the oaken staff or walking-stick of Maelfinnia, the founder of the church to which it belonged; secondly, a covering of delicate and beautiful design of the best period of Irish art; and, thirdly, an outer case of 14th century workmanship, into the panels of which exquisite filigree golden traceries, taken from the older cover beneath, are fitted. It bears an inscription in Irish which may be translated—"Pray for Maelfinnia and Cudulig."

But older and stranger than bell, bead, or crozier are the four upright Ogham Stones—blocks of red sandstone from five to nine feet in length, and inscribed on their edges with mystic Ogham characters—which, presented by Colonel A. Lane Fox, and brought over from Roovesmor Fort, Aglish, county Cork, may be seen in the first room to the left of the entrance hall, in company with a number of antique Greek and Roman busts; and after an examination of which we may take our leave of the British Museum.

CHAPTER XVII.

SOUTH KENSINGTON MUSEUM.

HIS Museum may be said with truth to contain the finest collection of modern Irish art in the world. All the greatest of our artists are represented here by fine works—some of them by numberless examples. Nowhere, for instance, can Mulready and Maclise be seen to such advantage as here, and in no other place is there such a miscellaneous collection of Irish art. No more pleasurable task can be conceived than a visit to the picture-galleries of the Museum, and a study of the many masterpieces, the products of Irish genius, hanging on the walls. Not only are all the most renowned artists of Ireland in evidence here, but almost every English painter of modern times is also represented by one or more pictures. The collections are essentially modern, nearly all the painters belonging to the present or the latter half of the last century.

The building itself, which is a series of magnificent courts and galleries, was designed by the gifted Irish architect, Capt. F. Fowke, and partly erected under his supervision. The principal entrance, however, has a very mean and sordid appearance,

SOUTH KENSINGTON MUSEUM.

and gives little or no idea of the beauty within. The Museum, in fact, was never finished, and the exterior, from the entrance, looks very prosaic, straggling, and unworthy of its purpose and its designer, having the appearance rather of a succession of warehouses, with an outhouse for entrance, than of what it really is—a fine edifice exquisitely adapted to its uses. These remarks do not apply to that portion of the Museum which abuts on Exhibition Road, for it has there a palatial exterior, proving that had the eminent architect lived to finish it, it would have been, externally as well as internally, one of the finest buildings in London.

Entering the Museum, and passing through the first court, which is devoted to replicas of various remarkable monuments, we reach several light and spacious courts, in which some of the most magnificent treasures of the country are stored, including jewellery of all kinds and of all countries, works of vertu, delicate glasswork, and other priceless art objects, some of them of a minute but beautiful character. At the end here are several cases full of medals and decorations, a gift to the Museum from Surgeon-Major J. W. Fleming, of the 4th Royal Irish Dragoon Guards. The collection is very valuable, and amongst its most interesting objects are several fine gold and silver medals executed by William Stephen Mossop, R.H.A., having for their subject the Siege of Derry, and the famous defender of the city, Rev. George Walker. Almost all kinds of English medals and decorations are here, as well as many foreign ones, one of the most curious of the latter being that awarded to an Irish soldier by the Emperor of China. A goodly number of the medals were issued in celebration of the victories of the two great soldiers, Wellington and Viscount Beresford, both, it is needless to say, of Irish birth.

In a wall-case, quite close to the medal collection, are a number of reproductions of the finest of the ancient Irish brooches. They are the work of eminent Irish goldsmiths, and as they resemble, as closely as modern art and modern ingenuity allow, the magnificent works of early Irish art, they should be seen by every Irishman who visits the Museum. The replica of the famous Tara Brooch, though it cannot equal in beauty that unique piece of workmanship, is well worthy of the closest attention, and will excite the admiration of every lover of perfection in art, mingled with wonder that such remarkable beauty of design should be found in a production manifestly due to what are strangely called the "dark" ages.

To the left of the court is the corridor where the sculpture is located. Just near the entrance to this corridor are numerous specimens of musical instruments, among them being three fine Irish harps, one a fac-simile of the celebrated harp of Brian Boroihme now in the Royal Irish Academy. The other two are very valuable instruments, but possess no historical or extrinsic interest.

The Sculpture Corridor contains, with other works of art, three notable specimens of Patrick

P. MAC DOWELL, WITH AUTOGRAPH.

M'Dowell's powers. One of these is a full-size figure of "Eve," another a marble statuette of the same, and the third is a finely carved marble bust of Sir Joshua Jebb, an eminent English administrator. The two representations of "Eve" are of characteristic excellence, and as M'Dowell surpassed nearly all modern sculptors in his treatment of the female figure, the standard of that excellence is very high. Other objects of interest among the sculptures are the busts of Wellington, S. C. Hall, Lady Morgan, and Captain Fowke, the last being placed here as a memorial to that eminent architect.

Turning to the right at the bottom of this corridor, and proceeding through a lengthy compartment filled with mediæval furniture, we come within sight of an interesting historical treasure. This is nothing less than the state-carriage of the notorious John Fitzgibbon, Earl of Clare, and Lord Chancellor of Ireland, who materially assisted in the formation of the Union. This carriage, which is gorgeously carved and decorated, and the panels of which were painted by William Hamilton, R.A., was bought at a sacrifice for £4,000 at a sale. The trappings, which are finely trimmed, are in glass cases hard by, and the whole carriage and its appurtenances are richly adorned with carvings and other sumptuous decorations.

The staircase at the end of the Sculpture Corridor leads to the Picture Galleries, which we at once proceed to visit, though not before directing our attention to the many fine samples of Irish laces and poplins which are to be found in the courts devoted to the various soft materials; and as Ireland has at all times held her own against the world in the production of those exquisite fabrics and embroideries, Irish people cannot help observing these exhibits with a feeling of pride.

The several rooms devoted to the water-colour paintings first come under notice. There is here a series, almost historically complete, of the works of the finest painters in that medium since the foundation of the art, which is almost peculiarly an English one—using the word English in the widest sense of the word, in order to admit the Irish and other artists into the compass.

CAPTAIN FOWKE.

Though a large proportion of the art here was produced by Irishmen, little of it is Irish in subject, the best part of that which is having been, strange to say, produced by Englishmen. Foremost among those (not Irish painters) who have depicted Irish scenery and character, or Irish history, comes F. W. Topham, with his deliciously coloured "Galway Peasants" and "Irish Peasant Girl at the Foot of a Cross," both good in landscape and in figure, but especially so in colouring. Francis Wheatley is also represented here by his "Irish Volunteers on College Green, 1782," which is of great historical importance; and his sketches of scenes at Kildare and Howth. Here are also Pars's "View of Londonderry," Serres' "Exchange at Waterford," Malton's "Capel-street, Dublin," Sasse's "Castle on the Liffey" and "Powerscourt Waterfall," and other scenes by the same and other artists.

The Irish pictures painted by Irishmen are not many, but they are all of high excellence. Dr. George Petrie's "Glendalough and the Seven Churches" is one of the best of them, and is an altogether admirable work, picturing that gloomy spot in a fittingly sombre manner. Other excellent works by Irish artists to be seen here are Albert Hartland's "Last Ray of Evening, Shannon Shore;" W. H. Stopford's "Study of Rocks, Co. Cork;" "St. John's Abbey, Kilkenny," by Thomas S. Roberts, R.H.A.; and George Grattan's "South View of Christ Church, Dublin;" each of them by distinguished Irish artists, and in the case of Hartland, by living ones.

A good many of the works entered under the head of "water-colours" are not pictures proper, but drawings, chalk, crayon, pen-and-ink, &c. Among these may be particularly noticed the architectural drawings by the two eminent Irish draughtsmen, Hugh O'Neill and John Carter,

F.S.A., and the many exquisite sketches in pencil and in ink by Mulready, including some of his earliest and latest work, his designs in the Academy schools, and the drafts of many of his most famous pictures. We must also mention the clever allegorical picture by Henry Tresham, R.A., a Dublin man and an eminent painter of the last century ; Matthew W. Peters' fine crayon sketch of "Falstaff, Mrs. Ford, and Mrs. Page" (a scene from the "Merry Wives of Windsor"), the production of a gifted artist, who, though not born in Ireland, was of Irish parentage, and who became first an R.A., and afterwards a clergyman of the English Church; the several excellent drawings and sketches by J. S. Copley and Francis Danby, both admittedly great painters; and the humorous "Meeting of Connoisseurs," by John Boyne, the well-known satirical draughtsman ; and "Now, then, Lazy," by J. Mahony, the clever illustrator of some of Dickens's best works.

Nor must we overlook the fruit pieces of Anna Frances Byrne, and the two vivid landscapes by John Byrne, both children of the distinguished engraver, William Byrne; nor the several delightful studies of French life and scenery by the clever Cork artist, William Linnæus Casey who died in 1870, at the too early age of 35.

Besides these works, there are several brilliant sketches and small pictures, mostly of coast scenery, by William Collins, R.A.;

WILLIAM COLLINS, WITH AUTOGRAPH.

"The Dead Stork," a study of animal life, by Eyre Crowe, A.R.A.; Jonathan Fisher's "Lymington River," the work of a self-taught and very clever Dublin artist ; several exquisite landscapes by Thomas Leeson Rowbotham and his son (who bears the same name); four characteristic drawings by W. Clarkson Stanfield, R.A.; and two landscapes by Thomas (? John) Walmsley, a Dublin man, like many of the foregoing, one of whose works here, that entitled "Moonlight," being really of great beauty.

But the gems of the water-colour collection have

not yet been mentioned, and consist of a number of Leech's most humorous drawings, three delightful pictures by Richard Doyle, some landscapes by the two Barretts, and other works to be presently referred to.

George Barrett, R.A., the great landscapist, is represented by several of his best and clearest works, none of them of very large dimensions; the works of his son George, one of a family of clever artists, amounting to even more than those of his famous father. Of the nine or ten paintings by the younger Barrett, that entitled "Weary Trampers" is perhaps the best, though in this there is room for difference of opinion. It is a most exquisite work, and highly worthy of that extremely gifted artist. He excelled in woodland and rural scenery, and his pictures are greatly sought after at the present day. He was one of the principal founders of the Water-Colour Society, one of its most respected and admired members, and died in 1842, nearly 60 years after his father, whose brilliant example he so worthily emulated.

Two other Irish painters deserve special reference here—George Chinnery and J. M. Barralet. The coast scene by the former is in every way worthy of his great reputation, and the "View on a River" by Barralet, who, like his brother, J. J. Barralet, was born in Ireland of French parents, is no less admirable.

But the works which perhaps will most delight the beholder are the exquisite sketches by Richard Doyle. Two are entitled "The Witch's Home," each having a second title; the first, "Broom Waiting; Coming out," representing the "steed" of the uncanny tenant of the "home;" the second, "She's Off," showing the hag sailing through the air over a wild and desolate country. Both of these drawings are placed on a screen, together with his inimitable "Manners and Customs of Monkeys," which is more mirth-provoking than the other works. It illustrates the African mode of catching monkeys by leaving strong drink in their way, of which these "ancestors" of man are tempted to taste; and as they imbibe large quantities of the "fire-water" they soon become helplessly intoxicated. Then the natives approach a group of them, and catch hold of their hands; and each monkey in turn grasping his nearest neighbour, a string of reeling monkeys is formed, and thus led into captivity. The picture represents the monkeys in various stages of inebriety—the comatose, the morose, and the lachrymose, led along in the manner described. Some of the belated animals are shown in the funniest of attitudes, and look not unlike the superior race in the same predicament—maudlin, quarrelsome, recklessly staggering about, or dimly conscious. To overlook this picture would be to deprive the visitor of some pleasurable moments. No artist was ever more fitted, as his works prove, than Doyle to describe with his facile pencil the humorous side of human nature, being as unapproachable in that respect as he was in depicting the whimsicalities of the denizens of the outer world.

There is a screen here occupied by some inimitable drawings by John Leech, mostly designs for "Punch," and nearly all good-natured satires on the follies of the wealthy "parvenu," or humorously illustrative of the idiosyncracies of the London street Arab, who was thoroughly understood and duly appreciated by the genial satirist.

The Chantrey Bequest Room contains a fine collection of modern and, indeed, recent pictures, bought out of the funds left by Sir Francis Chantrey for the purpose of purchasing the works, and thereby encouraging the genius, of gifted young painters, and preserving such works in a separate gallery. Here is a picture which at once commands and fixes the attention of the visitor. This is William Small's "Last Match." An Irish

MULREADY.

peasant and his daughter are crossing a bog, with the wind at its highest. The old man, who is leading a small pig by a "sugan," stops to light his pipe. Screened by his hat and by the shawl of his companion, he is in a fair way for a good "shough;" but the pig sees his opportunity in his owner's difficulty and makes a desperate dash for liberty. The exceedingly anxious look on the expressive face of the man is very naturally rendered; the terrible seriousness of the "expression" of the pig, straining every nerve in his desire for freedom, being equally well portrayed. Altogether it is a notable picture, and worthy of the eminent painter of so many excellent studies of Irish life, to which subject he seems to be exclusively devoted.

Before leaving the water-colour paintings mention must be made of the miniatures, of which there are some interesting specimens. Several are in the room occupied by the Jones collection, and include a brilliant portrait of the beautiful Contesse de Grammont (nee Hamilton), one of the 1st Duke of Ormond, and one of the Iron Duke; one, by the clever Irish artist, Horace Hone, A.R.A., is in a case in the Forster collection; but the best and most interesting are in the cases placed in the Sheepshanks Gallery. Among them are two fine miniatures of Thomas Moore, one being from the masterly hand of William Essex; another of Garrick, and several specimens of the art of the well-known miniaturists, Chinnery, Comerford, and Sherlock. John Comerford's "Naval Officer" and "An Aged Man" are equal to his great reputation, while George Chinnery's "Lady Tuite" and William Sherlock's "Sir John A. Stevenson" (the composer) make one regret that the beautiful art of which these ivory portraits are the outcome should have been eclipsed and superseded by photography, as has been the case. It is certainly a gain in cheapness, and also in faithfulness, but it is a loss to art, more especially to Irish art, for Irishmen were ever in the front rank of miniature painters.

Perhaps the most valuable pictures in the Museum are those in oils, most modern painters of note being amongst those represented in the various rooms devoted to their exhibition. The Sheepshanks Gallery is the most interesting to Irishmen, on account of the large amount of Irish art it contains. It is appropriately graced by a fine marble bust of the donor of the collection, John Sheepshanks, executed by J. H. Foley, R.A. In the swinging portfolios at each end of the room are numerous drawings by Mulready, including some very fine portraits, bits of landscape, and studies of still-life and of character. His powers as a draughtsman were and are almost unrivalled, and the perfection of his smallest sketches here is an evidence of his extreme care and finish, he evidently believing in the maxim that what is worth doing at all is worth doing well. On the walls is the finest collection of Mulready's pictures extant, numbering over thirty. Some of these priceless works are landscapes, and, like all the artist's productions, are considered to be very fine. Several of his greatest masterpieces are on these walls, and are the chief attractions of the galleries to many visitors.

Mulready was born (probably on the 30th of April, 1786), at Ennis, county Clare. He came to London at a very early age with his father, who carried on his trade in Soho, where Mulready was educated at a Catholic school in the neighbourhood. He became a student of the Royal Academy at the age of 14, and was most successful in his studies. Before he had painted many pictures his great abilities were recognised, and in November, 1815, he became A.R.A., and in three months (February, 1816), probably the shortest time on record, he was elected an R.A. From this time forward it need only be said that his life (so far, at any rate, as art is concerned) was eminently successful, as his fame grew more widespread.

JONATHAN SWIFT.

At length, after a long career devoted to his art, he died on July 7th, 1863, at a very advanced age, deeply regretted by all his contemporaries, but especially by those who had the honour of his acquaintance. In person he was tall and of giant frame, was a born athlete, and in his early days had been a devotee of "the noble art." It is said that when he had acquired fame and fortune he met one day his old professor of boxing, a noted pugilist, who asked him how "he was getting on," and what he was doing for a livelihood. Mulready told him that he was a painter of pictures. "Ah!" sighed the pugilist dolefully, as if commiserating Mulready's hard lot, "well, I suppose we must all do something!"

Of his marvellous and inimitable works, what can be said that has not been iterated and reiterated by every writer on art and every admirer of naturalness and beauty? By universal acknowledgment he has been placed beside Hogarth and Wilkie, superior to them in colouring, in blended truth and idealism, unerring in draughtsmanship, and though not gifted with their peculiar humour, yet possessing a graceful and delicate humour of his own not approachable by those two great painters. In so far as he is more ideal in conception, he is less true to nature, rarely touching the vices or passions of mankind, but always treating his subjects in the most favourable light and the most refined manner. Like his countryman Goldsmith, he touched nothing that he did not improve, and his wonderful versatility is proved by his landscapes, his admirable studies of animal life, and his exquisite sketches of plants, trees, and leaves, to be seen amongst his drawings in the portfolios above-mentioned. Just as Wilkie's "Blind Fiddler" is unsurpassable for humour and fidelity to nature, so, in different ways, is Mulready's best work.

It would be impossible to describe, *seriatim*, the many masterpieces of Mulready that adorn the walls of the Museum. We can only take several of his best works as representative of his various styles. The largest of his paintings here is "The Seven Ages"—several groups of figures typifying the different stages of life, the colouring of which is exceedingly fine; his smallest is "The Toy-Seller," which, apart from its intrinsic merit, is noteworthy as the last picture Mulready finished, and which, though done in his old age, shows not the slightest falling-off in power. It is an unpretentious picture, but is nevertheless most suggestive—the toy-seller, who is a negro, offering some toys to a child in its mother's arms, who shrinks back affrighted at the poor vendor. "The Sailing Match," "The Sonnet," "First Love,' and "The Intercepted Billet" are all fine, and in short, characteristic; but those works which are of a humorous tendency are the ones most generally and universally appreciated. "The Fight Interrupted" is perhaps the best of these. Two school-boys have been fighting, and are interrupted by the advent of the master, who catches the smallest combatant by the ear, while two boys explain matters to him. In the background the biggest boy, "the bully," is surrounded by his friends, and, putting his fingers to his mouth, shows them the blood he has lost. In contrast to the bully's crestfallen and faltering appearance, which proves that the interruption was not unwelcome to him, we have the determined look of the smaller boy, and the evident willingness to renew hostilities when opportunity is afforded, the varying expressions on the different faces being finely depicted.

Equally fine is the "Giving a Bite," close by, where the alarm of the boy who possesses the apple and is giving a friend a bite, at the large amount of surface which the mouth of the latter is covering, and the corresponding size of the morsel he is detaching, is extremely well expressed on the canvas. Then there are Mulready's "Choosing a Wedding Gown" (a scene from the "Vicar of Wakefield)," and by many considered the artist's masterpiece); "Open your Mouth and Shut your Eyes" and "The Butt: Shooting a Cherry," all of them of the highest beauty.

Near at hand are two excellent little pictures by William Mulready, jun., entitled respectively, "An Interior" and "Teal" (two fish lying on a stone slab). This clever artist was born in 1805, and won a good reputation by his small and careful works. Before leaving (for the present) the name of Mulready, it should be stated (what is not generally known) that Duncan Gray in Sir D. Wilkie's "Refusal" (a subject taken from Burns's song, "Duncan Gray") is a good portrait of Mulready. It is in the next room to the Mulready collection. Also, it is well to note that among the portraits of the great artists of ancient and modern times which decorate the great courts, and were executed here in mosaic by the eminent Welsh artist, Owen Jones, is a fine one of Mulready. It is a characteristic likeness, and may be easily seen from the gallery where Phillipoteaux' "Battle of Fontenoy" is placed—the latter picture, by the way, leading an unsophisticated observer to suppose that there were no Irish troops present at the memorable struggle it represents.

In the Sheepshanks Gallery are three very fine pictures by Francis Danby—namely, his "Disappointed Love," "Scene in Norway," and "Calypso," the last being of transcendent beauty, a most poetically-conceived landscape, with splendid effects of sunset, and Calypso wandering along the sea-shore, grieving for the loss of Ulysses. In the neighbouring room is the same painter's terribly gloomy "Upas Tree of Java," a most depressing picture—sad in subject, and hung, like others of Danby's, in a rather poor light.

In this and the adjoining rooms may be also seen other fine productions of Irish art, especially James Barry's portrait of himself, and his "Adam and Eve," and the two excellent paintings by Richard Rothwell, R.H.A., one, "Noviciate Mendicants," a charming study of two children. Rothwell was a native of Roscommon, and an artist of really great power, Sir Thomas Lawrence, the great portrait painter, especially admiring some of his works. There are also here some magnificent paintings by W. C. Stanfield and William Collins, both of them Academicians, of Irish parentage, and excelling in lake and coast scenery. Collins has likewise painted some exquisite rural scenes, some of which may be seen here; and, without particularising Stanfield's lovely Italian and Rhine views, we may briefly say that they stamp the artist as one of the greatest of the century.

Two or three of the exquisite gems of painting by that fine artist, J. A. O'Connor, are also to be found here. One, a view of "Clew Bay, Westport, Co. Mayo," is a truly glorious work, and thoroughly explains the admiration of all connoisseurs for his pictures, and the eagerness to obtain them. To many writers O'Connor's life has been a mystery, for it would seem that very few know anything about him. We are in a position to be able to give an account of his life. He was the son of an engraver who lived at Aston's-quay, Dublin, and was born in 1792. He was first taught engraving, but took to painting in preference, and early came to London with his friend Danby, returning after a while to Dublin. He made a second visit to London in 1822, and stayed for some time, making several journeys abroad—to Brussels and elsewhere, in company with his wife. In spite of his powers he was neglected by his contemporaries, and finally died poor and unfriended in humble lodgings in Chelsea (see Chapter XIV) on January 7th, 1841, nearly 49 years of age. A sum of money was collected for the benefit of his wife and family, who had been left unprovided for. His landscapes are wonderfully clear and vivid, and give him a right to a place amongst the most conscientious artists of the century.

On the staircase adjoining the Sheepshanks Gallery are several portraits of interest. One is by J. Catterson Smith, late President of the Royal Hibernian Academy, and a clever painter, whose son survives him, and almost equals him in his work; another by Thomas Clement Thomson, R.H.A., a well-known Irish portrait painter of a generation or two ago; and two full-length, life-size portraits of Viscount and Viscountess Dungannon, the former picture having been presented to the Viscountess by her husband's admiring tenantry.

The Jones Collection also contains several Irish pictures of importance, particularly Mulready's "Convalescent from Waterloo," and Collins's "Fishwomen of Boulogne"—both works of uncommon merit, and in some respects equal to the artist's best work. A splendid portrait of the enchanting Irish actress, Peg Woffington, is also here, and is certainly one of the best likenesses of her extant.

The magnificent collection of books, MSS, and pictures left by John Forster (the biographer of Dickens and Goldsmith) is of absorbing interest to Irishmen. In glass cases are displayed various autograph letters of Moore, Goldsmith, Swift, Burke, Maclise, Wellington, Macready, and many other great Irishmen. Here, too, are several relics of Goldsmith, such as his chair, writing-desk, and walking-stick, and in the different cases are autograph copies of the works of Sterne, Steele, Swift, and others of equal renown. Forster wrote the lives of the two latter Irishmen, and naturally took a great interest in their works, and obtained first editions of their most famous writings. Thus, there is here a copy of "Gulliver's Travels," with many MS. alterations and corrections by Swift, some of the variations being very curious. Among other remarkable relics of the great satirist are his diaries, his "Private Expenses" book, portraits of Stella, &c. The "Private Expenses" book is so curious and interesting, and so indicative of the habits and tastes of Swift's time, that we are tempted to extract a page from it, giving the items in the original spelling:—

From March 1st to 8th.

	£	s	D
1st. Veal, 1s 7d; Washing, 5s 5d; Coffee, 0s 7d	0	7	7
2nd. Suger, 0s 10d; Cream, 0s 2d; Coffeu, 0s 3d	0	1	3
3rd. Bread, 0s 4d; Coffee, 0s 7d; Cream, 0s 1d	0	1	0
4th. Sprouts, &c, 0s 2d; Fish, 1s 4 1⁄2; Flower, &c, 0s 2d	0	1	8
5th. Nutmeg, 0s 2d; Oranges, 0s 6d; Viniger, 0s 2d	0	0	10
6th. Ale, 0s 6d; Salt, 0s 1d; Barly, 0s 2d; S. lmon, 1s 0d...	0	1	9
7th. Coals, 5s 6d; Veal, 2s 3d; Mutton, 1s 1 1⁄2d; Oranges, 0s 3d	0	9	2 1⁄2
8th. Wheat, 0s 2d; Butter, 0s 7 1⁄2d; Ale, 0s 4d; Milk, 0s 1d	0	1	2 1⁄2
	1	4	6

In movable portfolios at each end of the Forster Room are hundreds of Maclise's drawings, some of them of the utmost beauty and precision; others mere rough sketches. The original drawings for the "Fraserian" Portraits are in these portfolios, or are hung in frames on the walls around, besides numberless other portraits not to be found elsewhere, from the same skilful pencil. In the portfolios are the portraits of James Roche, Dr. Lardner, Mrs. S. C. Hall, T. C. Croker, O'Connell and Sheil, Sir Egerton Brydges, and other notables; while the walls are adorned by lifelike presentiments of "Father Prout," Eyre Evans Crowe, Thomas Moore, and other contributors, English and Scotch, to "Fraser's Magazine" in its heyday. Here also may be seen some of Maclise's exquisite designs for "Moore's Melodies," Hall's "Ireland," and other works which he illustrated, and first drafts and sketches of his celebrated pictures. There are, besides, a number of clever sketches of Irish scenery, character, and incident, which were probably intended for use in future pictures. One or two of these, notably "Donnybrook Fair" and "The Irish Piper," are really fine, and had they been embodied in some large painting, would certainly have increased his immense reputation. The portraits of the "Fraserians" are exceptionally valuable; Maclise had the gift (more than any other artist, perhaps, of modern times) of dashing off a most startlingly lifelike portrait, and several great authorities have not hesitated to express the opinion that he is at his best in these rapid sketches, for there he is unapproachable.

On the walls are also some fine oil paintings by Maclise, as "Macready in 'Werner,'" "Scene from Ben Jonson's 'Every Man in his Humour'" (with John Forster as Kitely), and "A Girl at a Waterfall," the last named being the most pleasing of all. But the best things, perhaps, among the pictures are six exquisite little landscapes by James A. O'Connor, already referred to. The two largest of these pictures, "Night" and "Morning," are beyond praise. Few artists painted moonlight or the aspects of morning better than O'Connor, and, knowing his superiority in that respect, he frequently chose such subjects as themes for his brush. There are likewise a number of excellent sketches by W. C. Stanfield, another of Forster's great friends and intimates, and a most beautiful painting entitled, "Ancona and the Arch of Trajan," also by that great master of landscape and seascape. Nor should the characteristic and evidently faithful portrait of Swift, by an unknown artist, be forgotten in reviewing the contents of this room. The Forster Library, adjoining, contains numerous Irish works, and not a few curiosities. Among the latter may be mentioned Hayes's "Ballads of Ireland," inscribed to "John Forster, Esq., with the best regards of C. Gavan Duffy, May, 1865." This work, in two volumes, contains a few MS. notes by Duffy, some of them explaining several mysterious "noms-de-plume" of the early "Nation."

In the Dyce Collection are many autograph copies of the works of famous Irishmen, and perhaps the finest collection of the Irish dramatists in existence, some works here not being in the British Museum. Among the miniatures, too, in this collection is an excellent portrait of Sir Richard Steele.

The Art Library, which is on the ground floor of the Museum, contains a great many valuable works relating to Irish art, but no very rare Irish books.

The reader will not fail to have noticed that the Museum is particularly rich in the works of Irish landscapists and subject-painters, but possesses very few portraits by or of Irishmen. The National Portrait Gallery at Bethnal-green, in East London, on the other hand, contains many fine examples of Irish portrait painters, and numerous portraits of celebrated Irishmen; and our next chapter will be devoted to a description of its most interesting treasures.

CHAPTER XVIII.

BETHNAL GREEN MUSEUM.

ETHNAL GREEN MUSEUM is situated at the end of Bethnal Green road, in that portion of London denominated the 'East End.' It is a modest-looking building, more unpretentious externally than its rare and valuable contents deserve. Apart from those treasures to which it has a perpetual right, it is at present the temporary home of the magnificent collection of national portraits removed here some years ago from South Kensington until such time as a worthy repository could be erected for their keeping. Red-tapeism, however, is as rampant as ever, and the future home of these interesting series of portraits is not only not yet built, but the site is hardly yet decided upon.

To the ordinary visitor this collection possesses many attractions. The majority of the great personages of English history are here depicted by leading painters. To the Irish visitor who is familiar with the marvellous record of the achievements of his countrymen, the interest of the collection is deeper still. Not merely are the Irishmen who fill so large a portion of modern history represented here, but the best portrait painters of Ireland are also seen to advantage here.

Some of them bear English names, a fact easily explained when we consider that in the last century Dublin was a real art centre, many English artists settling there; and their sons, being born there and following their fathers' art, are naturally considered Irish. At the present day several eminent English painters bear most characteristically Irish names, showing their Irish descent, though they are always considered as Englishmen.

Many of the painters in the National Portrait Gallery are of foreign extraction, but only the portraits of those men and women who were born in these islands and played some prominent part in their history are considered worthy of a place on the walls. We may first deal with the products of Irish art, and afterwards proceed to indicate the remaining portraits which have any interest of a peculiar kind to Irishmen.

JAMES GILLRAY.

The total number of portraits is between 700 and 800—a number, be it remarked, rapidly increasing.

One of the earliest Irish artists represented here is one called "E. Lutterel," who can be no other than the eminent artist of the 17th century, *Henry* Luttrell, who executed some inimitable crayon drawings, and was besides one of the very earliest of the engravers who flourished in England. Of Luttrell (who was a native of Dublin) there are no less than three excellent specimens—one being a portrait of "Samuel Butler," the luckless author of the humorous epic, "Hudibras." Two of Luttrell's portraits are in crayon, the medium in which he best succeeded. Another Irish artist of the 17th century was G. Murphy, whose curious and apparently lifelike portrait of the saintly "Archbishop Plunket" is one of the most important of the acquisitions of the Gallery; Francis Bindon, a clever artist of the same period, and a native of Limerick, being represented by his portrait of "Archbishop Boulter," of Armagh. Bindon was also an architect of great merit, but his portraits are his most enduring works, those which he executed of the great Irishmen of his day being in every way admirable. Of 18th century artists there are a great number here. The much-abused Charles Jervas, who was born in Dublin about 1675, and who died in 1739, is here

represented by four excellent works, all of large size. Chief among them is his portrait of "Swift," which completely refutes the depreciatory estimates of the artist's powers, that used to be very commonly formed, but are now repented of by certain critics. Though by no means a great painter, Jervas has left a fine series of portraits of contemporary notabilities, well drawn and well painted. His vanity was excessive, but that is hardly sufficient reason for decrying his talents, which were far above mediocrity. His other portraits require no particular comment, being likenesses of English royal and other personages of his time.

Thomas Frye's fine portrait of "Jeremy Bentham" worthily sustains that great artist's reputation. As we have already said in a foregoing chapter, Frye was one of the best engravers and one of the most versatile artists of the last century. James Barry's portrait of himself attracts and deserves attention, both on account of its intrinsic merit as a work of art, the singular physiognomy of the artist, and, we may add, the misfortunes of his stormy career, which are delineated in his strongly-marked features. The face is thoroughly Celtic in type, resembling in that respect the portrait at South Kensington Museum, though differing altogether from it in colour.

The small miniature of "James Gillray," executed by himself, is one of the very few extant portraits of that vigorous satirist of the pencil, and one of the few attempts of the artist at portraiture pure and simple. His chalk-drawing of "William Pitt," also here, is another good example of the same gift. Of the two fine portraits by J. S. Copley, R.A., that of "Lord Mansfield"

JOHN SINGLETON COPLEY.
(After a portrait by himself.)

is certainly the most pleasing, though the other, of an old warrior with blood-red countenance, may be more lifelike, and better in other respects.

That extremely fine artist, Nathaniel Hone, R.A., has three portraits here, that of himself being remarkably clear and of more interest than the other two. The latter are respectively "Horace Walpole," the bitter critic, and "Rev. John Wesley," founder of the well-known sect which bears his name, and are both admirable paintings. But Hone probably succeeded better in miniature painting, those portraits of his which come into that category being universally considered his best, and estimated at great value. Thomas Lawrenson's portrait of John O'Keeffe, the fertile dramatist, is another valuable work of Irish art to be found in this Gallery. Lawrenson, who flourished during the last century, did some very good work as a portrait painter, and left a son, William Lawrenson, who became equally eminent in the same branch of art. Greater than either, however, was Hugh Douglas Hamilton, R.H.A, whose portrait of "Lady Temple" is worthy of all admiration. Hamilton's works are much sought after now, as they are rightly considered of superior excellence.

Of the Irish painters of this century Sir Martin Archer Shee is the best represented, there being no fewer than five of his works here, respectively entitled "Thomas Morton" (the dramatist), "Sir Thomas Picton" (the soldier), "Lord Denman," and "Lord Kenyon" (judges), and "Sir Francis Burdett" (the well-known politician). Each portrait has its fault, as well as its beauties. This much may be said of Shee's powers as an artist, that when he is at his best he is hard to equal, but owing to his popularity in private life—a popularity due to his gift of painting good likenesses, he painted too much for his reputation. His portraits are comparatively numerous, and necessarily obtain less attention than they sometimes deserve. They are as common as Reynolds's, but not so good. And in spite of the derogatory manner in which Shee is almost habitually referred to by modern critics, it may be safely asserted that not only was he an excellent painter, but that Reynolds was occasionally a very bad one. Both produced so much that some of it was necessarily unworthy of their respective reputations; and the same thing may be said of most eminent artists. Unfortunately, the majority of those who rail at Shee and Jervas, as at other Irish painters, and who, in fact, make Irish genius their scapegoat, will not allow that Reynolds or any other of their favourite artists ever failed in power or ever descended to mediocrity—a fact, however,

NATHANIEL HONE.

vouched for by other critics of equal importance. The critics alluded to will never admit, what is patent to the unprejudiced eye, that Turner is sometimes ludicrously inferior to other landscapists, and though never commonplace, is often grotesque and fantastic; but they never have the slightest hesitation in saying, or admit the least reason for doubting, that some Irish artists are beneath contempt.

Richard Rothwell is another eminent Irish portrait painter who has never received his due from English critics. His portraits of the famous Irish soldier, "Viscount Beresford," and of the "Right Hon. William Huskisson," the statesman, prove his great skill as a portrait painter, and show that he well deserved the high praise given to him by Sir Thomas Lawrence, one of the greatest of portrait painters.

William Hazlitt, the excellent critic, and John Hazlitt, his brother, are both represented here, the first by his portrait of "Charles Lamb" and the other by a portrait of "Joseph Lancaster," both works being admirably executed. The essayist's portrait of the "Gentle Elia" is an evidence of what he could have done in art if he had chosen to keep to that profession; as for John Hazlitt, he has always had the reputation of a clever and careful artist, and there is therefore no need to insist upon his merit. The fine portrait of "Father Mathew" by Edward Daniel Leahy is the work of another excellent Irish artist, who is supposed to have been born in London, though that is doubtful. He was clearly of Irish origin, and it is not unlikely that he was a Corkman; but no indication of his Irish extraction is given in any English work. He practised, we believe, both in London and Dublin, and we find, after a slight investigation, that he contributed to the first exhibition of the Royal Hibernian Academy in 1826. He died in 1875, aged 77, at Brighton, and is generally recognised as a very good artist. His portrait of the great Apostle of Temperance is very well executed, although Leahy was not properly a portrait painter, the majority

LUKE OF ORMOND.

of his works being landscapes or subject pictures.

The exquisite miniature of "Daniel O'Connell" (which is of more than ordinary size) was the work of Bernard Mulrenin, R.H A., and it is certainly one of the best things of the kind in the collection. The gifted artist who executed it need not fear comparison with the majority of the artists whose works surround it. It is an exquisite production, and renders to the life the familiar smiling and genial features of the "Liberator."

The last of the pictures by Irish artists is the splendid portrait of "George Eliot" by Sir Frederick W. Burton, the present Director of the National Gallery, who was born in Ireland (probably in Limerick) in 1816, and who executed some exquisite drawings of the leading Young Irelanders. Excellent specimens of his characteristically fine works may be seen in the National Gallery of Ireland, the present portrait of "George Eliot" being the only one of his pictures in any London public institution. One of his finest works was burned at a disastrous fire some years ago at a warehouse where it had been temporarily deposited, and the rest of his productions are comparatively few and far between. Of the lifelike character of this drawing of the great novelist there can be very little doubt.

There are two admirable busts here by Irish sculptors. That of "Samuel Lover," by Edward A. Foley, brother of the great Foley, is splendidly carved, and appears to be a faithful presentment of the famous humorist; while the inimitable bust of "Thomas Moore," by Christopher Moore, the well-known sculptor, represents the artist at his best. C. Moore was born in Dublin in 1790, and died about 1862. He excelled in portrait busts, all those of his execution being lifelike, as his power of seizing a likeness was remarkable. His statues are by no means so good as his busts, the pose being considered ungraceful and the figures badly executed. The finely engraved portrait of "Lord Hardwicke" here, by William Nelson Gardiner, the Irish engraver, is a credit to that distinguished artist, and worthily concludes the list of Irish works of art in the National Portrait Gallery.

We now come to the many portraits of Irishmen and women which were executed by others than Irish painters, and which commemorate, by their presence here, the services rendered by the former to either England or Ireland. Some of them have been already mentioned in our account of the Irish art contained here, and do not therefore require further mention. The remainder may be very briefly dealt with, as they are of less interest than the foregoing. As so many Irishmen and women played a very conspicuous part in the history of this country, or contributed very largely to its literature or to its amusements, their portraits naturally occupy a proportionately large space. Irish soldiers are well represented by the excellent portraits of Lord William Cadogan, a native of Dublin and a brilliant soldier,

COLONEL BLOOD.

who was the chief lieutenant of Marlborough at Blenheim and other battles; Sir Eyre Coote, the famous Anglo-Indian conqueror; Sir Henry Lawrence, who did as much as any soldier in establishing English rule in India; Thomas Butler, Earl of Ossory, the great admiral and general of the 17th century; James Butler, the second Duke of Ormond, another eminent soldier of the same period; General Wolfe, the victor of Quebec (of whom there are three portraits); the invincible Wellington (of whom there are four portraits); and lastly, Sir Charles J. Napier, the conqueror of Scinde.

There are a number of Irish statesmen, diplomatists, and orators also, whose portraits occupy a prominent position on the walls, among them being that great statesman and soldier, James Butler, first Duke of Ormond, who was so prominent in the history of his time; R. B. Sheridan, Edmund Burke, J. P. Curran, the first and third Marquises of Lansdowne (the former a Prime Minister of England during the latter half of the 18th century), George Canning (a bust), George Tierney (another bust), Lord Charlemont, J. W. Croker, Sir Philip Francis, Lord Macartney, and Sir George L. Staunton, the great traveller and scholar. The learned Archbishop Ussher and Bishop Berkeley, the eminent philosopher, fitly represent the long series of Irish Protestant divines, while such dramatists as Congreve, Cumberland, and Arthur Murphy, and such distinguished writers as Steele and Edmund Malone, the last of whom has done so much for early English literature, and particularly for the works of Shakespeare, by his investigations and researches, are very properly placed in this gallery of great men. The reckless desperado, Colonel Blood, whose savage appearance at once arrests attention, as an historical character of renown, and Sir Hans Sloare, as one of the greatest scientific men of the past, are naturally included in the collection, which is one of the finest of its kind to be found anywhere.

There are, besides the works we have mentioned, several gifted and famous Irishwomen whose portraits are also to be seen here. The most noteworthy of them is that of "La Belle Hamilton," the beautiful Countess of Grammont, the two portraits of Peg Woffington, the portrait of Miss O'Neill, another great actress, and the fine bust of Mrs. Jameson, the well-known authority on art subjects. Nor should we omit to mention that there is a fine portrait of James Barry besides the one already referred to, and an equally fine one of Daniel Maclise.

LORD CHARLEMONT.

The two immense paintings of the "Anti-Slavery Convention, 1863," and "The House of Commons, 1833," contain many portraits of famous Irishmen, including, of course, some of those we have already mentioned. Finally, the Gallery possesses some interesting autographs of Wellington, Moore, Charlemont (a letter of his to Flood), James Barry, Lansdowne, and J. W. Croker, and others of equal note, all of them exhibited in open cases.

In the Dixon collection, downstairs, there are some very beautiful specimens of Irish art. Apart from the excellent landscapes of George Barrett, R.A., there are several exquisite river scenes by Thomas and James F. Danby, the gifted sons of the great landscapist of the same name, both of them possessing the poetic imagination and power as colourists which rendered their father so celebrated. F. Nowlan's clever picture, "A Lady with a Fan," is a little gem of the collection, and the "Dunluce Castle" of an English artist, is of really superior excellence. But the best things to be seen here, so far as Irish art is concerned, are the two small works by Richard Doyle and Edwin Hayes, R.H.A. The picture of the former is entitled "Wood Elves," and depicts, in a manner that defies imitation or even adequate description, some really genuine fairies gambolling in the woods—executed only as Doyle could do it, and showing all the accustomed humour, skill, and insight of that most accomplished and genial artist. Edwin Hayes's "View of St. Malo" is a masterly work by one of the greatest marine painters of the age. As a painter of the sea in all its moods, but especially in storm, Mr. Hayes has no living superior, and it is doubtful whether any English painter even equals him. His son, Claude Hayes, is also a distinguished artist, generally choosing landscape for his subjects, who is destined to reflect as much honour on Irish genius and art as his distinguished father has done. Before leaving the Museum, the work by the eminent water-colour painter of the day, Frank Dillon, which has for its subject a scene of Japanese life, should not be unmentioned; and a glance at the fine collection of Irish poplins enshrined in one of the cases here concludes the list of objects of peculiar interest to Irishmen which may be seen in this institution the whole forming one of the most suggestive collections in London.

CHAPTER XIX.

BURLINGTON HOUSE, GARRICK CLUB, AND WESTMINSTER ABBEY.

Burlington House.

MUCH might be written of this interesting building, for its Irish associations are innumerable. It is the home of the chief artistic and scientific bodies of England, and consequently is the centre of a great deal of that intellectual life of the country, with which Irishmen have at all times been closely identified. As the Royal Academy has only been situated here for a comparatively few years, its Irish memories are by no means complete, except indirectly. Of the numberless Irish artists who have exhibited in this building it would be impossible, and even futile, to speak with any degree of fulness. But we may do what has never yet been done—namely, give a list (a perfectly complete one, we think) of all the members and associates of the Academy who have been Irish by birth or descent. This cannot but be of great interest and suggestiveness, as the names may be taken as fairly representative of the spirit of Irish achievement in art. Among its first, or foundation members, were George Barrett, the eminent landscapist, and Nathaniel

Hone, the famous portrait painter, both natives of Dublin; and Francis Cotes, of Irish parentage, a distinguished painter of portraits. Following them were Henry Tresham, Edmund Garvey, and James Barry, all of Irish birth; and Matthew W. Peters and J. S. Copley, who were born out of Ireland. In rapid succession came Sir Martin Archer Shee, who became President; William Mulready, Daniel Maclise, Patrick Macdowell, Alfred Elmore, and J. H. Foley, stretching from the close of last century to the middle of this, all eminent artists, and each of Irish birth; and William Collins, William Clarkson Stanfield, Sir Charles Barry, and Edward M. Barry, who were of Irish descent or parentage only. So much for the notable list of Irish R.A.s. The earliest A.R.A.s of Irish birth were Horace Hone in the last century and Francis Danby in this; and of those of Irish parentage were Thomas Chambers (a clever engraver of the latter half of the 18th century), and, more recently, Henry O'Neil and Eyre Crowe, the latter of whom is still living.

There has been one Irish President (Sir M. A. Shee), and there would have been a second if Daniel Maclise had accepted that honourable distinction. Though we cannot help admiring his modesty in refusing the exalted position, yet it is to be regretted he did not accept it, as it would have been an additional proof that Irishmen, in spite of the serious disadvantages they labour under, as compared with Englishmen and Scotchmen, can still win their way to the most inaccessible posts in the world of Art, as to those of the world of Literature, Science, and Politics. The list we have given above, highly flattering as it is to Irishmen, does not imply so much as it might, seeing that many admirable Irish artists have met with little or no encouragement from the Academy; and it is needless to say that the R.A.s and A.R.A.s of a period are not the greatest artists of their time, for some of the most remarkable painters, engravers, &c., of the English as of the Irish school, from Hogarth downwards, have never been connected with the Academy in any way.

The Royal Society, which also has its dwelling here, has also had a remarkable contingent of Irishmen among its greatest lights. There have been almost as many Irish Presidents as there have been English Presidents, and more Irish than Scotch ones—a really important fact, which effectually refutes the general belief and frequent assertion that Irishmen are mere romancers, and not so solidly intellectual as other races—too volatile for long application and perseverance, and too imaginative to pay any attention to facts. The first President of the Society was the distinguished mathematician, Sir William Brouncker (Viscount Castlelyons), a native of Cork, who was succeeded by Sir Isaac Newton, who, in turn, was followed by Sir Hans Sloane, the great naturalist and physician. Robert Boyle, the eminent philosopher, was offered in 1680 the post of President, but declined it on conscientious grounds. It will thus be seen that Irishmen almost monopolised the presidency of this famous body for a number of years after its foundation. During the present century the post has been held by no less than three different Irishmen, all of the highest reputation and ability. Earl Rosse, the eminent astronomer, occupied the position for many years, and after him came Sir Edward Sabine, the famous electrician and a native of Dublin, who was President for about twenty years. Finally, the present occupant of the chair is Professor George Gabriel Stokes, a native of Sligo, and one of the most cele-

EDWARD M. BARRY, AND AUTOGRAPH.

brated physicists of the age, whose remarkable discoveries in the science of Light entitle him to a foremost place among the great Irishmen of any period. He is not the greatest of living Irish scientists, that honour belonging either to Professor Tyndall, a native of Co. Carlow, or to Sir William Thomson, a native of Belfast, whose startling discoveries in natural philosophy have earned for them the admiration of the whole scientific world.

Burlington House itself was partly rebuilt by E. M. Barry, R.A., having been originally designed and erected for the most part by Sir John Denham. It was in bygone times the seat of the Earls of Cork and Orrery, and the connection is commemorated in Cork-street, which is at the rear of the building. It contains some truly fine works of Irish art, and some other objects of almost equal interest. In the rooms of the Royal Society are many interesting portraits, including portraits of Sir William Brouncker and

Robert Boyle, by the famous Court painter, Sir Peter Lely, the last-named work having been bequeathed to the society by Sir Isaac Newton; another portrait of Boyle by another foreign painter; an excellent portrait of Sir Hans Sloane; and Jervas's admirable portrait of Sir Isaac Newton, a work which has won unqualified approval from eminent judges, and which is strong evidence of the Irish artist's great power as a painter of portraits. In the Council Room of the Society is Shee's portrait of William IV.

But it is the Diploma Gallery which contains the most interesting collection of art in this building. It was acquired in this way: Each artist on his election as R.A. is required to deposit in the Academy an example of his work within six months after the date of the election. This diploma work is retained by the Academy, and is publicly exhibited in special rooms here. The gallery is filled with admirable and mature works by most of the R.A.s, from the earliest time down to the present. Several are missing, but the series is nearly complete. The rooms are open free daily, almost throughout the year. There are some splendid works in these rooms, among the finest being John Singleton Copley's "Tribute Money," a really grand work; Foley's statue of "The Younger Brother" (in Milton's "Comus"); Maclise's "Woodranger," one of the best pictures he ever painted; Mulready's "Village Buffoon," a work slightly different from his better-known works, and more in the manner, as regards colouring, of Wilkie; Macdowell's graceful statue of "A Nymph" Alfred Elmore's exquisitely painted "Scene from 'The Two Gentlemen of Verona,'" the production of one of the most gifted of modern Irish painters, and a native of Clonakilty, county Cork; an excellent "Landscape" by Garvey; a delightful work by William Collins, entitled "The Young Anglers," depicting two urchins absorbed in piscatorial occupations at a stream; and Stanfeld's glorious view "On the Scheldt," one of the most remarkable works by that great master. Besides these there are M. W. Peters's "Children," a clever study of child-life; Tresham's "Death of Virginia," executed in his most brilliant manner; "Belisarius," by Shee, in a style rarely attempted by that painter, and in which the blind king and a little child are very ably portrayed; a splendid "Portrait" by Cotes, one of the best things in the room; a characteristic portrait by an admirable painter, Nathaniel Hone, of himself; and several masterly drawings and plans by Sir Charles and E. M. Barry, the great architects.

In an inner room are several other objects of more than ordinary interest to Irishmen. Apart from the fine easel, a work of art, which belonged to Sir Joshua Reynolds, by him given to Lady Inchiquin (afterwards Marchioness of Thomond), and bought at the sale of her effects, after her death, there are two productions of Maclise's pencil which are deserving of no less an epithet than "magnificent." One is the beautiful design for the Turner gold medal, a small but exquisite work; the other is the cartoon for the artist's great fresco of "The Meeting of Wellington and Blucher at Waterloo." This marvellous work, which has entranced all who have seen it, would of itself suffice for the reputation of a great artist. The extraordinary draughtsmanship displayed in the work, and the lifelike nature of the scene, are vividly impressed upon the beholder. Altogether, it is a triumph of Irish art, and should be seen by all those who visit the annual exhibitions of the Royal Academy. In fact, the whole collection here, in the Diploma Gallery and the adjoining rooms, is more interesting and more creditable to Irish genius than many other and better known exhibitions.

The Garrick Club.

This famous club, which is situated in Garrick-street (as mentioned in Chap. V.), contains the finest collection of theatrical portraits to be found anywhere. The club was founded about the close of last century, and was then called "The School of Garrick Club," numbering among its earliest members such clever Irish actors as Andrew Cherry, John Moody, James and Francis Aicken and Michael Kelly, the well-known composer and singer. The portraits number at present about 500, and were partly bequeathed to the club and partly bought. The general belief is that Charles Mathews, the celebrated comedian, left the majority to the club, but that is a mistake. He offered his collection to it for a certain sum, but the club could not afford to buy them; they were ultimately purchased by a

MRS. ROBINSON.
("Perdita.")

wealthy tradesman, who finally bequeathed them to the club. Additional purchases and gifts have made the collection what it is—a remarkable one, historically as well as artistically.

Irish art is not largely represented here, but the amount and the quality are nevertheless creditable. Among the portraits, Shee's "Jack Johnstone" as Sir Callaghan O'Brallaghan, in "Love-a-la-mode," his "Alexander Pope," "Mrs. Pope," "Munden," and other similar portraits, are perhaps the best portraits by Irishmen in the collection. But there are likewise Thomas Hickey's excellent likeness of "Mrs. Abingdon," and Henry O'Neil's "Robert Keeley," which are very good works, and reflect credit on the eminent artists that produced them. The best works of Irish art here are, however, Stanfield's exquisite "Lugger coming out of Monniken dam," and his view of "Ancona;" Leech's inimitable drawings, of which there are a goodly number, and Maclise's fine sketch of W. M. Thackeray. The Irish portraits are so numerous that we cannot hope to do more than give an idea of the extent of the collection. Thus of Garrick there are over a dozen portraits and two busts; of George Frederick Cooke, another eminent actor, who was born in a Dublin barracks, there are no fewer than seven portraits; charming Peg Woffington is here depicted by four different painters; and there are several portraits of Macklin, two of Quin, one of Kitty Clive, several of John Henderson, two of Andrew Cherry, several of Mr. and Mrs. Pope (besides those mentioned as by Shee), several of Macready, several of the sprightly Mrs. Robinson (known as "Perdita," and whose maiden name was Darby, not M'Dermott, as has been stated), two portraits of Miss O'Neill, the great tragic actress, one of them representing her with her Irish harp; and numerous other portraits of the following Irish actors and actresses, among others—Master Betty, Thomas Sheridan, Thomas Doggett, Charles Kean, Mrs. Glover, Miss Farren, Mrs. Bellamy, Mrs. Partley (née O'Shaughnessy), Mrs. Edwin (née Richards), Mrs. Jordan, and Miss Fanny Kelly, and lastly, a very fine portrait of John Moody, the famous comedian, and a Cork man, as Teague in "The Committee," one of his favourite and best

MISS O'NEILL.

MOODY, AS TEAGUE.

parts. Curiously enough, the Teague of this play, which was written by a Sir Robert Howard, is the first Irish character, properly so-called, ever presented on the English stage, as Shakespeare's ridiculous Captain Macshane can hardly be dignified with the name of a character. Howard's Teague is, of course, a mere caricature, but it is one of the most popular and important parts in his old-fashioned play. We give a rare illustration of Moody in the character of this early "stage Irishman." There are other portraits of Irish actors and actresses of note, by the greatest painters of succeeding generations, but we have mentioned the most important of them. The club, or rather its interior, is somewhat inaccessible to the general public, but the trouble of getting admission is amply compensated by the absorbing interest of the art treasures within.

CHAPTER XX.
WESTMINSTER ABBEY.

AN account of the historic and interesting buildings of London without a reference to the Abbey would be as defective as the representation of the play of "Hamlet" without the leading character. The Abbey is so important historically and so interesting to visit that it deserves and requires a chapter to itself. But even in that space there is only room enough for a brief reference to the graves and memorials of Irish men and women, and a slight description of several of the most elaborate works of art erected in honour of various notabilities in the Abbey.

The visitor's first impression on entering the edifice is sure to be one of disappointment at the meagre appearance of the interior, and surprise

WESTMINSTER ABBEY.

at the inordinate number of ridiculous tombs that have been allowed to accumulate in the various aisles, preventing a full and uninterrupted view of the noble proportions of the Abbey. One cannot help feeling indignation at the action of the different Deans of Westminster in allowing elaborate and, in most cases, inartistic monuments to block up the many magnificent arches of the building. If these monuments were only erected in honour of real genius, or were fine works of art, the complaint would lose half its force. But the greater part of the tombs and memorials in the Abbey are those of insignificant persons. In the earlier days they were allowed plenty of space, with the result that the Abbey contained long since quite as many tombs, &c, as it could conveniently hold, and therefore many of the great minds of the last few generations are commemorated simply by a bust or a tablet, or their grave is represented merely by a flag-stone half hidden under pews and kneeling-boards. At one time many of the nobility were buried here, dead geniuses being relegated to some out-of-the-way parish churchyard. But, as space became more limited, there was necessarily some choosing of those who were to be "honoured" by burial in the Abbey, and in that way a few statesmen, poets, actors, and dramatists received a small share of the space set apart for interments, and previously wholly monopolised by soldiers, courtiers, and sycophants of various reigning monarchs. At present the abbey appears more like a sculptor's workshop than a sacred edifice—most of its numberless tombs and monuments commemorating the virtues of perfectly worthless but notorious personages, or testifying to the fame and prowess of worthy individuals who were never very notable and whose names and deeds are buried in the deepest oblivion.

There have been only two Irish Deans of Westminster so far as we have been able to discover. The first was William Markham, who afterwards became Archbishop of York, and who is buried in the cloisters here. He was born in Ireland, and was a very distinguished English prelate. More recently there has been Dr. R. C. Trench, the late Archbishop of Dublin, who was Dean for some years, and who introduced some welcome and much-needed innovations.

It is difficult nowadays for anybody, but especially so for Irishmen, to see what "honour" is conferred upon a great writer or any great personage by the mere fact of being buried in the

Abbey. When we consider that so many plain Smiths and Browns are buried along with the Grattans and Sheridans and Cannings, we perceive that, after all, the Abbey is like any other burial-place—that, in fact, it contains not many more

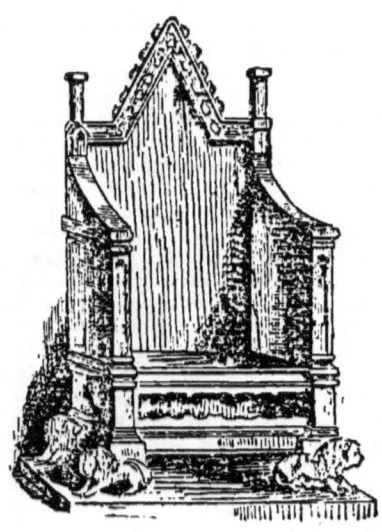

CORONATION CHAIR, WESTMINSTER ABBEY.

distinguished persons than are laid in Kensal-green or other cemeteries. And it is a mistake to suppose that only truly great men and women are buried in the Abbey at the present day. Apart from those who may have filled important positions and occupied some share of public attention, but whose greatness may nevertheless be strongly called in question, there can be no doubt that many persons, merely because they are relatives of the Dean of the moment, are interred in this great edifice.

The principle which is supposed to regulate the admissions of monuments, &c., has been at times strangely perverted. At no time have Irishmen been particularly warmly welcomed; the refusal of one Dean to allow a memorial to Balfe, the distinguished composer, to be placed in the Abbey, is only equalled by, and may be contrasted with, the unseemly willingness of another in allowing the suicide Castlereagh to rest in the same plot of ground as the patriot Grattan—an insult to the latter's great and valued memory. Irish visitors to the Abbey now glance with feelings akin to disgust to the narrow strip of ground separating the graves of the saviour and the destroyer of Irish liberty. The shameful manner, too, in which Grattan's grave is hidden under the kneeling-boards of the pews in the North Transept looks not unlike a premeditated insult, while the conspicuous statue of "cut-throat Castlereagh" arrests everybody's attention.

Room could not be found for a bust of Balfe by Dean Stanley, but he easily found space for a grave

MEMORIAL TO BALFE.

(and a memorial) for Darwin, whose remains were welcomed to the Valhalla to which those of Byron were refused admittance. Of Irish art there is not much in the Abbey, but the small quantity includes such a masterpiece as Foley's fine statue of Earl Canning, which almost touches those of his father, George Canning, and his relative, Stratford Canning. There are, besides Foley's work, such creditable productions of Irish art as the admired monument to Sir George Hope, by Peter Turnerelli, the clever sculptor (whose somewhat rare portrait we are enabled to give), and Sebastian Gahagan's bust of Dr. Charles Burney, the eminent musician. Turnerelli's work is at the west end of the nave, and Gahagan's in the south aisle, in what is known as the Musicians' Corner.

The number of Irish men and women who have been thought worthy of a place in this national Pantheon is very great, in spite of all prejudices. Even several Catholics have been interred here since the Reformation, such as Lord Stafford (1719), and some of his family, and De Castro, the Portuguese Envoy (1720), all in St. Edmund's Chapel.

Altogether, about three thousand persons have been buried in or immediately around the Abbey. The principal reason, it would seem, why so many of these are nonentities was the largeness of the fees, which precluded almost all but rich people from interment in the Abbey. Goldsmith makes his Chinese Philosopher, in his "Citizen of the World," denounce the Deans and other officials as "the sordid priests, who are guilty, for a superior reward, of taking down the names of good men to make room for others of equivocal character, or of giving other than true merit a place in that awful sanctuary."

FOLEY'S STATUE OF EARL CANNING.

There are many Irish soldiers buried here, among the earliest being Sir Richard Bingham, whose inscription is in the South Aisle, and who died in 1598; Lord William Blakeney, an eminent soldier of the 18th century, the whereabouts of whose tomb we have not been able to find; Lord William Cadogan (Henry VIII.'s Chapel), the great soldier of Queen Anne's time, one of the best staff-officers the British army ever possessed; and, lastly, Field-Marshal Lord Ligonier, who has a bust, and an elaborate monument, representing History holding a scroll, upon which are inscribed the following battles:—Schellenberg, Blenheim, Ramillies, Oudenarde, Taniere, Malplaquet, Dettingen, Fontenoy, Rocoux, and Laffeldt. Ligonier, who was an Irish peer, died on the 28th of April, 1770, aged 92. The tomb is in the Chapel of St. Michael. Ligonier was a fine soldier, and commanded in many of the wars of Anne, George I., and George II., and it is related of him that when the last-named monarch reviewed his (Ligonier's) regiment on one occasion, and remarked that the men looked good soldiers but that the horses were wretched, Ligonier replied—"Yes, the men are Irish, the horses are English." Other Irish soldiers buried here are General James Johnston, a Governor of Quebec (Middle Aisle), who died in December, 1797, aged

76; several of the Ormond or Butler family, including the great Duke, James Butler, who died in 1688, and was interred in the vaults of Henry VII.'s Chapel; and Sir Charles M'Carthy, another distinguished soldier, whose precise burial-place is apparently undiscoverable. There are other warriors of Irish birth or parentage, who, though not buried here, are commemorated in various ways. Thus, there is a decorated tablet in the North Transept to the memory of Sir Richard Kane, a native of Down, and a Governor of Minorca, who died in 1736; a very elaborate and well-executed monument to Sir Eyre Coote (same place), representing on the one side a weeping Mahratta captive, and on the other Victory hanging Coote's portrait on a palm tree, the elephant in the front of the monument

MEMORIAL TO LORD LAWRENCE.

showing the locality of the scene depicted; another large monument, tastelessly executed, to General Wolfe, in the Chapel of St. John the Baptist; and also one in the North Aisle to General Stringer Lawrence, erected by the East India Company, and representing the genius of the Company pointing to a bust of Lawrence, while Fame is telling of his exploits, and holding a shield bearing a suitable inscription.

Of Irish Admirals there are three buried and commemorated here—namely, Sir Peter Warren (North Transept), Sir Richard Tyrrell (South Aisle), and Sir Henry Blackwood (North Transept). The first two sailors belonged to the early part of the 18th century, and distinguished themselves greatly against the French. Blackwood, who died in 1832, has a sculptured tablet to his memory, setting forth his private virtues rather than his public services. Sir Peter Warren's monument is not a bad one, though the sculptor, evidently determined to execute a faithful likeness, has actually made the features of the bust pock-marked. Hercules is placing the bust of the eminent Admiral on its pedestal, the figure of Navigation being on the opposite side, holding a laurel wreath in her hand and gazing at the bust with an expression of mingled admiration and sadness. The monument to Sir Richard Tyrrell was at one time considered a very grand affair, but it has been discredited by this time, as it deserved. Still, it is in conception a very curious monument and an improvement upon the usual weeping angels and crying babies generally executed in the sculptors' best wooden manner. In this particular monument Tyrrell is represented rising from the waves (presumably at the Resurrection); three figures, History, Navigation, and Hibernia are shown amongst the rocks, the whole bearing this inscription, cut on a piece of rock—"The sea shall give up her dead, and everyone shall be rewarded according to his works," having reference to Tyrrell's burial at sea.

Several eminent Irish actors and actresses were buried in the Abbey, such as Spranger Barry, John Henderson, David Garrick, and Maria and Elizabeth Pope—the two wives of Alexander Pope, the Irish actor and painter. The two actresses just mentioned are both buried in the West Cloister. Maria Pope was a native of Waterford, her maiden name being Campion ; Elizabeth Young, the other Mrs. Pope, being probably of Irish birth also. She died in 1797, aged 52; Maria Pope dying in 1803, aged 28 (according to the Registers of the Abbey). They were both excellent actresses, and as there has been a considerable amount of confusion between the two, we are able thus satisfactorily to clear it up. Spranger Barry was buried in the North Cloister, and has no monument; Henderson lies in the South Cross, his grave being marked merely by a flat stone. Garrick's grave is at the foot of Shakespeare's monument in Poets' Corner, his statue showing him in a dramatic attitude, throwing back a curtain, "unveiling the beauties of Shakespeare," Charles Lamb and others have found fault with this work as too theatrical for such a place as the Abbey. Garrick's funeral was a grand one, and attended by many notabilities of the day. Covent Garden and Drury Lane each sent twelve actors to represent them on the occasion.

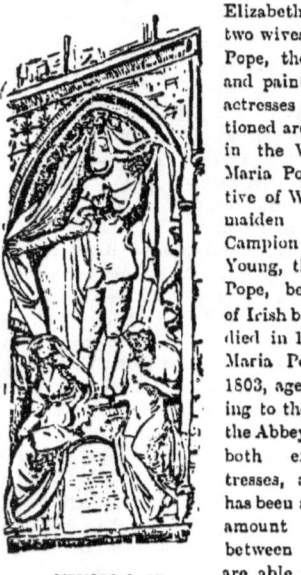

MEMORIAL OF DAVID GARRICK.

Close to Shakespeare's statue lies Richard Brinsley Sheridan, to whom there is no memorial of any kind in the Abbey. Sheridan died in deep distress, and the hollow friendship that failed him in his last hours mocked his remains with a magnificent funeral, calling forth the apt comment of a French journal on the event—"France is the place for a man of letters to live in, and England the place for him to die in."

As for the Irish poets, they are not strongly represented here. Only three who had any connection with Ireland have been buried in this famous spot—to which, it is interesting to learn, Goldsmith first gave its familiar name of Poet's

GOLDSMITH'S MEMORIAL.

Corner. The three poets referred to are William Congreve, Wentworth Dillon, Earl of Roscommon, and Sir John Denham, the latter with no memorial, the former having a bust mounted on a pedestal decorated with carvings emblematic of figures relating to the Drama. Goldsmith's bust and tablet are over the south doorway, in the South Transept (a position selected for it by Sir Joshua Reynolds), and is an admirable piece of work, executed by the eminent sculptor, Joseph Nollekens, R.A. The inscription is in Latin, Johnson, who wrote it, having refused to (as he said) "disgrace the walls of Westminster Abbey with an English inscription," and this in spite of an unanimous appeal from his own and the poet's friends. It is in this inscription that the well-known lines occur, so descriptive of Goldsmith's genius:—"Nihil tetegit quod non ornavit" ("He touched nothing that he did not adorn").

Three Irish Archbishops are buried here—namely, Ussher, Boulter, and Agar. Ussher was buried in St. Paul's Chapel by Oliver Cromwell's orders and at his expense—a remarkable fact, considering that that grim fanatic had issued a severe edict against all Episcopal ministers. The cost of the funeral was £200, and was a very grand affair. So tremendous was the crowd that a number of soldiers had to be on guard to keep order and to keep the road clear. This was the only funeral during the Commonwealth of Oliver and his merry men at which the Liturgical Service of the English Church was heard in the Abbey. The funeral sermon was preached from the very appropriate text—"And Samuel died, and all Israel was gathered together."

Hugh Boulter was an Englishman who was elevated to the See of Armagh, and is buried in the North Transept. His bust is a somewhat striking object; the inscription setting forth that he was "translated to the See of Armagh, and thence to Heaven," which is almost as good an epitaph as that of Purcell (the famous musician, whose name has an Irish appearance, and who is buried here in the Musicians' Corner), which says —"Here lies Henry Purcell, who left this life and is gone to that blessed place where only his harmony can be exceeded." The tomb of Charles Agar, Archbishop of Dublin and Earl of Normanton, who was an Irishman by birth, is in the North Aisle, and has upon it a representation of the Cathedral of Cashel, which he erected at the foot of the famous Rock. In the same grave with this eminent prelate is his relative, Welbore Ellis (Baron Mendip), an Irishman and a distinguished statesman, born in Kildare. In the North Aisle is also buried Sir George Leonard Staunton, a native of Galway, who is known as one of the greatest of the scholars of his day, and who died in 1801, aged 62. His monument is by Chantrey, and shows him expounding the law to a native Indian, a tiger being represented at the east end of the tomb.

In the centre of the nave is a memorial brass to Sir Charles Barry, who is buried there; in the Musicians' Corner is a sculptured tablet to Michael Balfe; and in the South Aisle of the Nave is a bust of Lord Lawrence, the great Indian Viceroy.

In that part of the North Transept which is known as the Statesmen's Aisle, and which is immediately within the ordinary entrance to the Abbey, were buried several very eminent and one or two notorious Irishmen. Here lie, almost side by side, Grattan, Tierney, George Canning, his son, Earl Canning, and his cousin, Sir Stratford Canning, and Castlereagh. The statues of the three Cannings are all well done, the one in the centre being by Foley, that of George Canning being by Chantrey. Nearly opposite is the statue of Castlereagh. At the funeral of the latter a remarkable scene was beheld. Dense crowds lined the streets from his house to the Abbey, and when the door of the sacred edifice was reached, and the coffin was taken out of the hearse, loud execrations burst from the assembled thousands, and the mourners had "to literally fight their way through the masses of people." The jeers and curses on the unpopular statesman resounded through the Abbey, and amid a silence within and loud tumult outside, the cordially-hated Castlereagh was buried.

Grattan's funeral was also a notable one; at his obsequies the children of the Catholic Charities were ranged at the west entrance of the Abbey, the Irish children being dressed in green. Most of the principal personages of the day attended, and yet no steps were taken to raise any monument to his memory. The following lines, quoted in the preface to his "Speeches," may be given here; they are eloquent, but hardly as severe as the occasion required:—

> Here, near yon walls, so often shook
> By the stern weight of his rebuke,
> While bigotry with blanching brow
> Heard him and blushed, but would not bow,
> Here, where his ashes may fulfil
> His country's cherished mission still,
> There let him point his last appeal
> Where statesmen and where kings will kneel:
> His bones will warn them to be just,
> Still pleading even from the dust.

Finally, we have to speak of the Coronation Chair in Edward the Confessor's Chapel, in which all the Sovereigns of England have been crowned since the days of Edward I. Under the seat of this chair is fixed the famous "Coronation Stone," 26 inches long, 16¾ inches wide, and 10½ inches thick, respecting which so many learned disputes have arisen.

It is asserted to be the identical "Lia Fail," or "Stone of Destiny," brought to Ireland from the East by the Milesians, on which the Irish monarchs were crowned at Tara from time immemorial, and which had the mystic property of ringing or moaning whenever the true king was crowned on it, and of carrying with it the power of the Scotic race. The stone is stated to have been borrowed and carried to Scotland by Fergus, first King of Scotland, and brother of the reigning Irish monarch, and the kings of Scotland continued certainly to be crowned upon this stone until 1296, when Edward I. defeated King Baliol of Scotland, and carried the relic to Westminster. The best Irish antiquaries, on the other hand, contend that this stone (which is composed of Scotch red sandstone) is not the "Lia Fail," which, they say, never left Ireland, and may still be seen, an upright block of limestone, on the side of Tara Hill, and now serving as a monument of the graves of the insurgents of '98.

However it be, the Irish visitor to the Abbey cannot help gazing with interest on this stone beneath the Coronation Chair, and wondering if it ever rang, except, indeed, for shame, beneath the succession of Royal tyrants, libertines, and imbeciles who have grasped the sceptre above it since its removal to its present position.

CHAPTER XXI.
THE HOUSES OF PARLIAMENT.

THERE is, perhaps, no building in London which has greater attractions for the average Irish visitor than the Houses of Parliament. Let his politics be of what colour they may, ranging from orange to the ultra-green, whose motto is Mercutio's—"A plague o' both your houses"—it is safe to assert that one of his earliest trips will be to this historic spot, in which so many Irish interests are centered, and which is not alone replete with so many memories of Irish eloquence and patriotism, but contains so much that reflects credit on the genius of Irishmen.

The Houses of Parliament form a magnificent pile of buildings, stretching along the Thames at Westminster. It is the largest Gothic edifice in the world, covering an area of nine acres, with an unequalled front to the river of nearly 1,000 feet, and contains 14 halls and between 500 and

INTERIOR OF THE HOUSE OF COMMONS,
Showing the Speaker's Chair, the front Ministerial Bench, and the principal Opposition Benches.

Ireland in London. 119

600 different apartments. It is quite a modern edifice, the old Houses of Parliament which stood here on the site of the old Palace of Westminster, where the great O'Neill was knighted by Henry VIII., in 1511, having been destroyed by fire in 1834, with the exception of Westminster Hall and the crypt under the chapel of St. Stephen.

CHARLES BARRY, WITH AUTOGRAPH.

Of the 97 designs sent in for the proposed new buildings that of Sir Charles Barry was selected; the building was commenced in 1840, and was ready for use in 1850, the Legislature meeting during the years 1834-50 in a temporary structure erected for the purpose. The "New Palace of Westminster," as it was originally styled, is indeed a splendid monument to the genius of its gifted designer, with its unrivalled river front, its three grand towers and innumerable turrets, and its niches filled with statues, presenting, especially in the early morning or beneath clear moonlight, an appearance fully warranting the poetical description of the late Russian Emperor Nicholas—"A dream in stone!"

Barry, who was knighted shortly after the completion of the work, appears to have been very much hampered during its progress by conflicting opinions, professional jealousy, and official interference; and one of his biographers considers that "had he not been of the toughest fibre, and of almost superhuman industry," he could never have carried out the work.

It may be added that a splendid statue of him, by John Henry Foley, is to be found within the building at the foot of the stairs leading to the Committee Rooms; and that the completion of the Queen's Robing Room, the Central and Royal Staircase, and the restoration of St. Stephen's Crypt (unfinished at his death, was entrusted to his son, Edward M. Barry. Nor should we omit to state that the unequal appearance of the land or western side of the edifice is due to deviation from the original plan of the architect, who proposed to enclose Palace Yard by a wall, and make it open by a fine gateway direct on Whitehall.

Seeking out St. Stephen's Porch (which faces Henry VIII.'s Chapel in Westminster Abbey), and giving the policeman at the door the name of any M.P. the visitor wishes to see, the visitor enters the building, and finds on his left Westminster Hall, which strangers have not been permitted to enter since the dynamite explosion that occurred here, near the Crypt entrance, in January, 1885.

This magnificent Hall, 239 feet long, 68 feet broad, and 92 feet high, was built by William Rufus in 1099, and enlarged by Rufus II. in 1394-9. Its immense timber roof, one of the finest examples of scientific construction in carpentry in the world, is formed of Irish oak, procured from the site of St. Michan's Church, Dublin, the records of which contain the following curious entry respecting it:—

> The fair greene or commune, now called Ostomondtowne-greene, was all wood, and hee that diggeth at this day to any depth shall find the grounde full of great roots. From thence, anno 1098, King William Rufus, by licence of Murchard, had that frame of timber, which made up the roofes of Westminster Hall "where no English spider webbeth or breedeth to this day."

In this Hall Parliament used at one time to assemble. Here the Law Courts were held for nearly eight centuries, and here took place the Coronation feasts and great State Trials of English history. Famous among these last was the seven years' trial of Warren Hastings, the first Governor-General of India, impeached by the Commons in 1787, for tyranny and extortion practised by him during his administration. The leader of the impeachment was the great statesman, Edmund Burke, who

JOHN HENRY FOLEY.

(with Sir Philip Francis), from no other motives than those of hatred of injustice and compassion for suffering, had roused the Legislature step by step to the arraignment of Hastings, and whose remarkable speech on this occasion, lasting four days, crowned for ever his fame as a brilliant and unequalled orator. One of his supporters was Richard Brinsley Sheridan, of whose address Macaulay writes:—"The curiosity of the public to hear him was unbounded. His sparkling and highly-finished declamation lasted two days; but the Hall was crowded to suffocation during the whole time. It was said that fifty guineas had been paid for a single ticket. Sheridan, when he concluded, contrived, with a knowledge of stage effect which his father might have envied, to sink back, as if exhausted, into the arms of Burke, who hugged him with the energy of generous admiration."

The later Irish associations of Westminster Hall are connected with Samuel Lover the poet, and the London Irish Volunteers, one of the many volunteer corps formed in England in 1859 on the rumour of a projected French invasion. Lover, though 62 years of age, joined the corps, worked actively on the Finance Committee, wrote several ultra-loyal songs for them, and attended their drills in the Hall here, at one of which the curious movements of the awkward squad of that day drew forth from him the remark—"Begorra, if Boney could only see us now he'd think twice before invading us!" Before leaving the Hall, it should be mentioned that in the reign of Charles II., when, in revenge for the execution of his father, the bodies of Cromwell, Ireton, and Bradshaw were disinterred and executed with every mark of opprobrium at Tyburn, their heads were placed on the roof of this Hall. The head of Cromwell, which had been embalmed, remained there exposed to the atmosphere for 25 years! when, one stormy night, it was blown down and picked up and hidden by a sentry, and was in 1874 in the possession of a Mr. Wilkinson, living at Seven Oaks, in Kent.

The visitor next enters ST. STEPHEN'S HALL, which stands on the site of St. Stephen's Chapel, where the House of Commons met from the days of Edward VI. down to the fire of 1834. It is to this old House of Commons (of which no vestige remains) that the earliest Irish memories of the British Parliament cling. Here originated the atrocious measures which have constituted the main features of English legislation in Ireland for so many centuries, and here were pulled the wires which moved the puppets in Dublin Castle and the "unfree" Irish Parliament to so many deeds of wrong and outrage. Here in later days rang the eloquent accents of Sheridan, one of the most popular orators in Parliament, almost whose last words in the house were—"Be just to Ireland as you value your own honour, as you value your own peace." Here Canning "called a new world into existence to redress the balance of the old;" and Burke, "in amplitude of comprehension and richness of imagination superior to every orator, ancient or modern," revelled in the full exercise of his wondrous powers; and here occurred the melodramatic scene in which, in his excessive horror of the French revolutionists, he flung a dagger on the floor of the House as a specimen of the presents which French fraternity and equality was preparing for Englishmen. Hither, like some Satanic spirit, came Castlereagh, exulting in the ruin of his country, and here thronged the venal crowd of Irish post-Union members, heedless of their self-inflicted degradation

Here, faithful among the faithless, was raised the voice of immortal Grattan, pleading for the rights of his Catholic fellow-countrymen. Hither in 1825 came an important deputation from the Catholic Association, headed by O'Connell and Sheil, to be heard against the Algerine Bill, intended to suppress that Association, O'Connell's demeanour for the first time in the British Parliament showing (says Sheil) "a perfect carelessness of manner," though "it was easy to see that he was full of restlessness and inquietude under an easy surface."

A more memorable scene occurred on the 15th May, 1829, when, in a house crowded to excess, O'Connell, having won Emancipation through dread of civil war, appeared to claim his seat as member for Clare county, and refused to take the degrading oaths imposed upon Catholics returned to Parliament. The further Irish memories of the Old House are connected with his fight, almost single-handed, against the Government of the day, his matchless voice being raised night after night

DANIEL MACLISE, WITH AUTOGRAPH.

in his country's cause, now throwing down the gage of battle to "scorpion Stanley," now ridiculing the "shave-beggars' of the Irish Government, now pouring the vials of his wrath against the "brutal and bloody Whigs" with "brains of lead, hearts of stone, and fangs of iron."

It was not here, however, but in the temporary structure erected after the fire, that the powerful accents of the great Tribune (now aged, ill, and sad at heart) were softened into touching appeals, not for alms, but for restitutory help for his poor eople stricken down by famine. "She (Ireland) is in your hands," were his last words, "she is in your power. If you do not save her, she cannot save herself; and I solemnly call upon you to recollect that I predict, with the sincerest conviction, that one-fourth of her population will perish unless you come to her relief."

It was in that temporary building, too, that Smith O'Brien declined to serve on a Parliamentary Committee on an English question. He was imprisoned for 25 days (while the Committee lasted) in a room called the cellar of the House, and was there visited by a deputation from the '82 Club, consisting of Captain Bryan, John Mitchel, T. F. Meagher, R. O'Gorman, and T. B. M'Manus, whose green and gold club uniforms created no small sensation at Westminster.

As memorials of the old house St. Stephen's Hall is decorated by ten excellent statues of eminent statesmen. To the right and left of the entrance door are statues of two Irishmen—Henry Grattan, by the Irish sculptor, J. E. Carew, and Edmund Burke, by Theed, an Englishman. The former is an excellent figure, representing the great orator in the height of debate, the face full of animation, the body bent forward, and expressive of energy. The left arm is extended across the body, as if about to sweep from right to left. This, it is said, was not the position first designed for the arm by the artist, who was requested to alter it as it now is by the Prince Consort, who was, or assumed to be, a great authority on art matters. The sculptor reluctantly complied, but left a memorial of his displeasure in the absence of his name from the usual place at the base of the statue. Four other beautiful statues in this Hall are by Irishmen—those of Chatham and Pitt, by MacDowell, and those of Selden and Hampden, by Foley. The last-named is the finest statue in the Hall, and perhaps one of the noblest specimens of Foley's creative genius. The high birth, wide knowledge, and gentleness, yet inflexibility, of the original—at once statesman, soldier, and orator—are there produced in cold marble in a manner that must strike the most careless beholder.

Passing through the swinging doors into the Central Lobby, we will suppose that the visitor gains admission to the Strangers' or Speaker's Gallery of the House of Commons by means of the proper order obtained through an M.P. On the floor of the House, directly opposite the gallery, is the Speaker's chair, in which no Irishman has, we believe, ever sat, with the worthy exception of the irrepressible Dr. Tanner, to relieve the monotony of a dull Committee hour in his own frolicsome way. Before the Speaker sit the Clerks of the House; to his right the Government, to his left the Opposition, the Ministers or "Big Guns" of each party occupying the front benches. Below the gangway, on the opposite side, sit the Irish Nationalist members, no longer shifting sides, as at one time, according as a Liberal Government was "in" or "out," but, since the proposition to that effect made by Mr. A. M. Sullivan, fixed in permanent opposition. The Irish visitor obtains from the gallery an exasperatingly small view of them. Most of them occupy various seats at different times, but a few favour certain places. Mr. Parnell usually sits on the second or third seat of the third bench (the same, we understand, once favoured by Sir Charles Gavan Duffy), and is generally flanked to his right and left by Mr. Dillon and Mr. Sexton respectively. Mr. William O'Brien always speaks from the second bench, Mr. Healy from the corner seat of that bench and Mr. Biggar from the second or third seat, generally below his leader.

How many Irish memories throng round this Chamber since its opening in February, 1852! The Irish visitor looks down upon the spot where that corrupt knot of representatives, the Pope's Brass Band, headed by Keogh and Sadleir, made Parliamentary action to stink in the nostrils of all true men; where Duffy, John Blake Dillon, and others, stemmed in vain the tide of corruption around them; where, year after year, their tentative efforts on behalf of their country were contemptuously defeated, and, year after year, fresh links forged in the long and heavy chain of coercive enactments, until, the struggle extending beyond the walls of Parliament, a master mind arose that saw in the "intensity of Fenianism" the nature of the oppression from which Ireland suffered, and strove to allay it by the disestablishment of an alien Church and the curbing of landlord despotism. Then, approaching our own day, memories needless to dwell upon come faster and more vivid. The cry of "Home Rule" becomes the watchword of a party, with some few honest men—Butt, Sullivan, Martin, &c; but made up of a rank and file whose venality bade fair to again wreck constitutional action, when, aided by an unparalleled uprising of the Irish people, a change of tactics within Parliament and a weeding-out of "nominal" patriots, an almost lost cause was snatched from destruction by Parnell and his men of to-day, and raised, through combined caution, boldness, and self-sacrifice, into a position where victory already seems to shine upon it.

Directly opposite the Strangers' Gallery is the Reporters' Gallery, where, among others, are representatives from the chief papers of Dublin,

O'CONNELL AND SHEIL IN THE HOUSE.
(After Maclise.)

Belfast, and Cork. From the earliest days of Parliamentary reporting the majority of the reporters have been Irishmen. In Sheridan's time it was especially so—most of them, according to an English authority, having been brought by him from across the Channel because of their superior qualifications for the task. He always defended them on critical occasions, and spoke most highly of their abilities, and they showed their gratitude by always faithfully reporting him when the utterances of others missed record.

Among those who fell foul of the Pressmen was no less a person than O'Connell, who, in July, 1833, drew the attention of the House to the unfairness of the London Press, at that time excelling itself in hostility to Ireland. He complained that they represented him as invariably worsted in debate, and charged their reporters with inserting reports designedly false. The reporters resolved in a body to insert no more of his speeches until he apologised. He retorted by "spying strangers," thus obliging all but members to leave the House. This went on for eight or ten nights, when the public, hungry for the news of proceedings in Parliament, grew clamorous for a settlement. A compromise is said to have been effected, but the victory apparently rested with O'Connell, who was thenceforward fully reported.

The Irish Pressmen in those early days seemed to have had among them some humorists of the first water. One of these was Mark Supple, who enlivened a dead-and-alive debate by calling in stentorian tones for "A song from Mr. Speaker." While the surprised House went into roars of laughter, the Sergeant-at-Arms rushed wrathful into the Strangers' Gallery to arrest the offender, when Mark, of whom he inquired (the reporters sat in these days in the Strangers' Gallery), pointed out an innocent Quaker in a corner as the culprit. The astonished Obadiah was hauled off in spite of his protestations, and only released next day on the discovery of the real offender, and payment of a heavy fine for Sergeant's fees.

Peter Finnerty, known best perhaps to Irishmen by Curran's speech in his defence in a libel action, was another Yorick of the Gallery. He it was who made Sullivan, a fellow-Pressman fresh from the green sod, believe that Wilberforce, the great opponent of the slave trade, had delivered himself of a great speech on the merits of the potato, winding up with these remarkable words—"Had I been reared upon that root, Mr. Speaker, I would not be the poor, stunted creature that now you see me." We may conceive the amusement of the reading public next day, and the amazement of Wilberforce himself, whose needless repudiation of such sentiments in the House subsequently was drowned in uproarious merriment.

But the Reporters' Gallery has had something more to boast of than practical jokers. Many of the most eminent literary men of the three kingdoms served here their literary "apprenticeship." Sir James Mackintosh, Dickens, Hazlitt, and Collier may be named among those hailing from Great Britain; while the list of Irish reporters includes names no less famous—Gerald Griffin, Edward Michael Whitty, Joseph O'Leary, D'Arcy M'Gee, Henry Dunphy (Parliamentary editor of the "Morning Post," with which journal he was connected for forty years), Joseph Sheehan, Michael Nugent (the best and earliest of the Parliamentary reporters of the "Times"), William Bernard M'Cabe (the well-known journalist), S. C Hall, Joseph Arthur Crowe (the great art critic) William Henry Russell (the famous "Times' correspondent), and last, but not least, Justin M'Carthy, the talented historian of our own times. It may be added that those indispensable works of reference, "Dodd's Peerage" and "Dodd's Parliamentary Companion," owe their origin to an Irishman, Charles R. P. Dodd, who was for many years Superintendent of the Parliamentary staff of the "Times."

Over the Reporters' Gallery is the Ladies' Gallery, admission to which is by Speaker's order, obtained through an M.P. The seats are generally ballotted for a week ahead, the space being very restricted, but (we may remark) not so much so as in the old House of Commons, where the ladies could only get a peep at hon. members through an opening in the roof.

Admission to the House of Lords is obtained on a Peer's order or through introduction by an M.P. With this "Upper Chamber"—the most richly decorated apartment in the world—few Irish memories are associated save one of unvary-

WELLINGTON IN THE HOUSE.
(After a Sketch by John Doyle.)

ing hostility to popular demands. Within its four walls have crystallised all the scorn, bigotry, and prejudice with which the aristocracy of this country have regarded the just claims of our people. We only linger in it to ask our readers to examine the two magnificent specimens of Irish art which are immediately over the Strangers' Gallery—Maclise's frescoes, "The Spirit of Chivalry" and "The Spirit of Justice," subjects chosen as if in satire of their lordships' peculiar attributes.

These pictures were the first fruits of the competition held in Westminster Hall in 1845 for paintings to decorate the newly-erected building. All the great artists of the day competed, Maclise among them, his choice being the subjects mentioned, which were finally approved of. They are both admirable paintings, placed, unfortunately, in a position so effectually out of sight that the visitors who pass through these apartments every Saturday are generally unaware of their existence.

The principal figure in "The Spirit of Chivalry" is a beautiful female representing Chivalry, while around her are a king clothed in armour, representing War; an archbishop as the representative of Religion, and a statesman representing Civil Government. Beneath kneels a young knight vowing himself to chivalric service, surrounded by figures—artists, a man of science, a bard, a mother with her babe, a painter, and a poet—indicative of the range and intensity of the chivalric feeling. The "Spirit of Justice" is typified by a majestic female, her eyes not blindfolded (a Pagan idea), but lifted up to Heaven. At her side stands the Avenging Angel, to her left the Angel of Mercy, in front of whom are seated the judges, lay and ecclesiastical. At the foot, to the right, stands the guilty one held by his accuser, and to the left a widow and orphans protected by an armed champion. In front kneels a negro liberated from his fetters, and next him a free citizen unrolling a charter of liberty.

It may be well to add that an Irishwoman, the Hon. Mrs. Norton, posed for the figure of "Astrea" in this picture, while portraits of Macready and other celebrities are preserved in the accompanying group

On the completion of these pictures Maclise was commissioned to reproduce in fresco in the Painted Chamber his celebrated picture, "The Marriage of Eva and Strongbow," which he had just exhibited at the Royal Academy. Maclise however, found the room so unsuited, and the proposed payment so inadequate, that he was, at his own request, released from his engagement, and was entrusted instead with the herculean labour of decorating the two large and sixteen smaller compartments of the Royal Gallery, admission to view which, as well as the other rooms in the building, is permitted on all Saturdays on which the House does not sit. The first of the larger pictures executed is that depicting "The Meeting of Wellington and Blucher after Waterloo," a painting 40 feet long by 12 feet high, containing 105 human figures life-size or larger, and 50 smaller, and 17 life-size figures of horses, and 30 smaller. The second painting on the opposite wall is of the same size, and no less elaborate. It depicts "The Death of Nelson at Trafalgar." To these gigantic works, whose wealth of detail defies description in our limited space, Maclise devoted over eight years of his life. A truly conscientious artist, he spared no pains to secure correctness, and the authenticated accuracy of every one of the thousand details in these pictures is truly wonderful. Nothing was painted without authority, from Nelson's uniform and the forage cap worn by Blucher to the smallest regimental button. The vastness of the space enabled him to reproduce to exact scale a large portion of the deck of the "Victory" where Nelson fell. As to the artistic merits of these pictures we need only quote Ford Madox-Brown, one of the greatest fresco-painters of the day, who says that "in no modern school" could "such sumptuous magnificence of design, carried out with such faultless execution of colour and expression, be seen" as in these paintings "Could I compass it," he continues, "every schoolboy in England should have a chance of looking more than once at those splendid works;" and he compares their author to "Michael Angelo, Phidias, Titian, Giotto, Raphael, and Hogarth.

It only remains for us to state how unjustly Maclise was treated with regard to these works. He undertook to paint these two large pictures for £7,000, and the sixteen intended for the smaller compartments of this gallery for £1,000 each. The time and labour involved were far in excess of the calculations made, and the £7,000 was voluntarily raised by the Fine Arts Commissioners to £10,000. Half of this additional money was, however, never paid him. The Commissioners, besides, abandoned the project of decorating the sixteen smaller compartments, and although he had executed designs for three of them he never received a penny for them, although other artists employed on the paintings in the buildings were fully compensated.

Added to this, his contemporaries, instead of being justly proud of his great productions, assailed them for the most part with carping criticism, while the long hours of constant application in the damp atmosphere of the Gallery permanently injured his health; and, all combined, the work which should have been his glory was a source to him of monetary loss, disappointment, and keen physical and mental suffering.

CHAPTER XXII.

IRISH DRAMATISTS AND ACTORS IN LONDON.

FROM the time of Shakespeare to this day London has always been able to boast of its numerous Irish dramatists, actors, and others connected with "that mirror of life"—the Stage.

It is needless to dilate at length upon the great, and, in some respects, unparalleled, success of Irish men and women in representing on the Stage the humour and pathos of human life in all its completeness and reality. In this respect we have more than held our own with England; and it is quite probable this superiority is largely due to the fact that Irishmen feel their parts more than the calmer and less impressionable English. There has lately been some discussion upon this question; to our mind there can be no doubt that they who enter most fully into the parts they play or the characters they represent make the truest and finest actors—that, in fact, as Churchill says:—

In spite of all the criticising elves,
Those who would make us feel, must feel themselves.

The earliest Irishman connected with the English Stage, so far as present knowledge extends, was Lodowick Barry, who wrote, published, and produced "Ram Alley," an admirable comedy, in 1611, five years before Shakespeare's death. This work is full of humour and spirit, and has received the commendation of such a discerning critic as Charles Lamb; but little worth mentioning seems to be known of the author, except that he was born in Ireland, and was a gentleman of fortune.

The Irish dramatists immediately following Barry were Sir John Denham, whose excellent tragedy, "The Sophey," was produced with great success in 1642; Roger Boyle, Earl of Cork, who wrote plays of all kinds, ranging from bloodiest tragedy to screaming farce, and from sentimental comedy to outrageous burlesque; Richard Flecknoe, the victim of Dryden's merciless satire; and Thomas Duffett, author of some exceedingly clever plays and burlesques, his "Spanish Rogue," produced in 1674, being a particularly entertaining work. Of Flecknoe, a few more words are necessary. He is remembered chiefly as the butt of that prince of satirists, John Dryden; but despite the vigorous lines so often quoted against him, Flecknoe was nevertheless a clever writer. His best play, "Love's Kingdom" (altered from a former play of his, entitled "Love's Dominion"), was brought out about the middle of the 17th century. To it was prefixed an admirable sketch of the English Stage, which Dryden, though he "chaffed" the author unmercifully, did not hesitate to lay under contribution for his "Essay on Dramatic Poesy." In the preface to the above-named play Flecknoe says, somewhat vaingloriously—"For the plot, it is neat and handsome, and the language soft and gentle, suitable to the persons who speak it; neither on the ground nor in the clouds; but just like the stage, somewhat elevated above the common."

Passing over John Dancer, or Danncy, who came to England in 1670, and similarly endowed dramatists, we come to Thomas Southerne, whose first play was acted in 1682, when its author was only 21 years of age. Once embarked on the career of a dramatic author, his success was conspicuous, and in those days unique. He made more money by his dramas than the Drydens, Congreves, and Wycherleys of the time, and lived to a great age on the proceeds of his genius and not less of his business-like habits. His famous tragedies, "Isabella" and "Oronooko," are likely to live for ages to come by virtue of their penetrating pathos and their lofty sentiments. His other plays are dead beyond all hopes of resuscitation, but the two plays mentioned have been, and will doubtless continue to be, favourites with the great tragic actors and actresses. In "Oronooko" he warmly denounced the system of slavery or slave-holding, whether in the East or West, and has the distinction, admitted and claimed for him by Hallam, the great historian, of being the first writer in the English language who protested against that infamous institution.

The 17th century produced many eminent actors and actresses, but few of them, comparatively speaking, were Irish. John Lacy, the favourite comedian of Charles II. and one of the best actors of the Restoration period, may have been of Irish descent but was born in England. He died in 1681, and had been the original Teague in Sir Robert Howard's "Committee; or, The Faithful Irishman" (brought out in the year 1665), a part which he acted to perfection. The idea of the character is said to have been taken from Howard's own Irish servant, and the play certainly merits reference here as being the first real attempt at depicting Irish character. It is fairly amusing even to Irishmen, and became a favourite

JAMES LACY.

role of all the leading Irish comedians for the next hundred years or so, two of its finest performers being John Moody and John Barrington, portraits of both in that character being among the treasured possessions of the Garrick Club. This same character also gave a name to most succeeding Irish characters. Thus Shadwell, the preposterous poet Laureate of a later period, atrociously caricatured the Irish priest in his "Teague O'Divelly, the Irish Priest" (1681) and "The Amorous Bigot" (1690). As Dryden was a Catholic, though a rather lukewarm one, it must be confessed his scorching satire of Shadwell's poetic attempts may have been a little influenced by the latter's blatant No-Popery shrieks. Farquhar and Mrs. Centlivre followed with Irish characters named Teague, the first in his "Twin Rivals" (1706), and not in his "Recruiting Officer," as stated by Professor A. W. Ward; the latter in her comedy, "A Wife Well Managed."

To return to the actors and actresses of the century. The greatest actress was probably Elizabeth Barry, the daughter of Edward Barry, a Bristol barrister. She was born in 1658, and died on November 7th, 1713. During her lifetime she rose to the highest pitch of tragic excellence, and ranks with such queens of tragedy as Mrs Pritchard, Mrs Siddons, and Miss O'Neill. According to Colley Cibber, the Stage chronicler of that time, "in characters of greatness she had a presence of elevated dignity, her voice full, clear, and strong, so that no violence of passion could be too much for her; when distress or tenderness possessed her, she subsided into the most affecting melody and softness." She was the first tragic actress of the period, and during the 37 years (1673-1700) she was on the stage, she originated no fewer than 112 characters. Cibber also says:—"In scenes of anger, defiance, of resentment, while she was impetuous and terrible, she poured out the sentiment with an enchanting harmony. As 'Isabella,' in Southerne's play of that name, she acted magnificently, and the same might be said of all her tragic impersonations; while she also excelled in comedy parts. She was buried in Acton Church, where a tablet is erected to her memory. It may be noted, as a curious fact, that she was the first performer who ever received a benefit, that occasionally much-abused custom being the outcome of her great popularity. Previously, benefits had been given only to authors.

The most notable, perhaps, of the low comedians of the 17th century was Thomas Doggett,

ELIZABETH BARRY.

who was born in Dublin about 1660. His first appearance on the London stage took place in 1691, and his success was rapid. His mastery of the art of "making-up" was a continual source of wonder to his contemporaries. He could represent almost any age up to ninety, in the most inimitable manner. One of his most popular characters was that of Shylock, in "improved" versions of "The Merchant of Venice"—a part which he played as a low comedy one, amidst roars of laughter. Endowed with great independence of character, he gave much offence to some managers who were accustomed to use all kinds of threats and menaces, and to exercise various small tyrannies towards their actors, by his determination not to submit to harsh treatment in any shape. He was not only an actor of great merit, but he also wrote "The Country Wake," a comedy which was performed in 1696 with some success, and which, when changed to a farce under the name of "Flora; or, Hob in the Well," was very popular. Probably his highest distinction was won in several of Congreve's plays, comic characters in which were written specially for him by the witty

and licentious author. Doggett died on September 22nd, 1721, and was buried at Eltham, a little way out of London. Contemporaneous with his arrival in England (1691) was the advent of another Irish actor, named Bowen, a clever low comedy actor, but inferior to Doggett. He was very capable, and might have occupied a very commanding position on the English Stage if his career had not been cut short by a quarrel with

THOMAS DOGGETT.
(From a rare contemporary print.)

Quin, in which he was killed—a fatal result due more to his ungovernable temper than to any wilful intention of Quin. The latter great actor, though born in 1693, belongs properly to the 18th century, and will be presently referred to. But there is one eminent actor yet unmentioned—Robert Wilks—who, born in 1670, went on the stage before the close of the century, and may be placed among the best of Irish performers. As an impersonator of the lover, the fine gentleman, and the gallant, he had in his own sphere no equal during one period of his career, and few superiors at any time. The gay sparks of Congreve, Farquhar, and

WILKS.

Cibber's comedies were his most popular parts. But it would seem as though he particularly excelled as Sir Harry Wildair, Archer, Captain Plume, Young Mirabel, and the other leading "gentlemen" of his friend Farquhar's plays. His handsome presence, dashing style, and invariable good humour and good nature all combined to make him an immense favourite with the public and with everybody. He assisted Farquhar in many ways, and was his best and most intimate friend, and after their father had prematurely died, cared for his orphan children. His death occurred in 1632, at the age of 62, deeply regretted by the public he had so well and faithfully served, but especially by his bosom friends.

Farquhar's first comedy, "Love in a Bottle," appeared in 1699, and was followed in quick succession by such masterpieces of comic drama as "The Constant Couple," "Sir Harry Wildair," "The Inconstant," "The Recruiting Officer," "The Twin Rivals," and "The Beaux' Stratagem" (the last being, in the opinion of most critics, his best work), this splendid intellectual display culminating in one of the most remarkable comedies in the English language. His powers had reached their highest point of development in 1707, when his last work was produced, and there is no question that he could have surpassed his previous efforts, but that, unfortunately for Irish and English dramatic literature, he died in April of the same year, a month after his "Beaux' Stratagem" had been brought out, and at the early age of 29. He was a native of Derry, and was born in 1678, and made a reputation, and a creditable one, as an actor before his great success as a dramatist. His plays abound with wit and humour, but they are also very coarse in parts; still, compared with the gross productions of some of his contemporaries, they are pure. His best characters are finely portrayed, the situations highly diverting and dramatic, and the dialogue of great force and cleverness, and bristling with good points. It is clear, from passages in "The Rape of the Lock" and others of his works, that Pope studied his Farquhar. The most celebrated female playwright of the century, or indeed of any century, was Mrs. Centlivre, who was born about 1667, and who, before she died in 1723, married three husbands, the last of whom gave her the name by which she is known to fame. She wrote 19 plays, and of these three are of the highest excellence. One of the characters in her "Busybody" (the first play printed under the name of Centlivre, the others having been signed "S. Carroll," from her second husband's name), is a masterly specimen of her powers of delineating character. Marplot is the busybody of the play, and a most amusing personage. It is, and has been, one of the most favourite parts of many great comedy actors. Her first piece came out in 1700 at Drury Lane, at which theatre most of her plays were first performed, as Farquhar's had been at Covent Garden. Her second best comedy is probably "The Wonder; or, A Woman Keeps a Secret" (1714), the scene of which is Spain, the land of intrigue. It is a very bustling and amusing piece, but not free from the taint of the age. Its clever characterisation and ambiguous wit made it a great favourite, both with actors and audience. But her "Bold Stroke for a Wife" is her best-known comedy, and ranks very high among the comedies of the 18th century. It was produced in 1718, and she claims for it absolute originality—a claim which, though not strictly accurate, must be allowed. Her works were collected in three volumes, and some of the best of them were translated into various languages. One character in the last-mentioned comedy, Simon Pure, from the confusion that arises about him, has given a phrase to the English language —"the real Simon Pure."

SPRANGER BARRY.

Before leaving the dramatists of the century we must give a few words to some of the minor writers, such as Dr. Brady, Nahum Tate, Dr. Sheridan, Owen M'Swiney, Dr. Madden, and John Leigh. Brady was born in 1659, in county Cork, He wrote one play, which was acted with success, but the title and subject, as much as the treatment, preclude any further reference to it. His name is remembered chiefly on account of his translation, in conjunction with Tate, of the Psalms. Tate was born in Dublin in 1652, and died in 1715; he wrote about half a dozen plays, and altered or adapted (or, as it was then called, "improved") several of Shakespeare's masterpieces. Strange to say, his adaptation of "King Lear" kept the stage for a century and a half, to the exclusion of the genuine article. It was the "Lear" of Tate's version that was acted by Betterton, Booth, Quin, Garrick, Barry, Henderson, Kemble, and Young; it was not until Macready's advent that the original masterpiece was performed by a great actor. Tate's own plays were not remarkably successful, and are not of a very high order of merit.

Owen M'Swiney was born in Ireland towards

the close of the century, and wrote four plays, which appeared in the years 1705-6-9-45 respectively. M'Swiney was one of the most successful managers of his time, and made a large fortune by his ventures. He died in 1754, very wealthy, having been keeper of the Royal Mews for some years. His plays are clever and witty, but are now buried in oblivion. Dr. Samuel Madden's "Themistocles," acted in 1729, is a good tragedy, judged by the standard of the times he lived in, but would prove dull reading to the present generation. It was acted with success, and was extensively quoted as a specimen of poetic feeling and tragic intensity. Dr. Sheridan, father of the eminent actor, and grandfather of the great dramatist and orator, wrote, or rather translated from the Greek, one play; although it was never acted, it is interesting to record the fact, as it adds to the numerous proofs that his remarkable family afford of devotion to the Drama. The Sheridan we are referring to was an eminent divine, an intimate friend of Swift, and was born at Quilca, in county Cavan, in 1686. John Leigh, one of the best minor actors of his time, was born in Ireland about 1690, came to England about 1714, and was very successful in secondary parts. His two plays were clever, and became fairly popular; but he died in 1726, aged 36, before his full opportunities had properly arrived.

MASSOP.

Sir Richard Steele's first play was "The Funeral; or, Grief a-la-Mode," which was produced (as were all his others) at Drury Lane in 1701. It was a great success, and, though of a moral didactic nature, is very entertaining. One of his best points is well worth quoting. Sable, the undertaker, in giving directions to his mutes notices one who does not look so dismal as the circumstances require. His employer protests against the unseemly air of comfort and enjoyment visible in the mute, and reminds him that he has raised his salary several times with a result the very opposite to what he expected—"Why the more I give you the gladder you are!"

The genial author's next play was "The Lying Lover" (1704), but it did not succeed, owing to its sermonising and its too frequent iteration of moral teachings. In fact, as Steele aptly and humorously put it, "it was damned for its piety." "The Tender Husband" appeared in 1705, and was a failure; but his fourth and last piece, "The Conscious Lovers," which did not come out till 1722, was a complete success. It is not surprising that so great a humorist should have failed (comparatively) as a dramatist, seeing that his quiet and subtle style was unsuitable for the stage of that day. His plays were the purest of the age, and that was, at the time, no recommendation. His delicate and airy wit was not appreciated as soon as spoken, and the wonder is that such audiences as his plays were presented to tolerated them for one night. Steele is, perhaps, the legitimate founder of the sentimental comedy school. He was, in short, nothing if not an innovator, and a welcome one—that is one of his greatest distinctions.

Towards the close of the 17th, and not long after the opening, of the 18th century, several of the greatest actors of any period were born. The versatile James Quin, Lacy Ryan, Charles Macklin, and Spranger Barry, who were at home in either tragedy or comedy, and the tragic Thomas Sheridan and Henry Mossop. The same generation also saw the birth of the inimitable Kitty Clive, Mrs. Bellamy, and others of almost equal note. These actors, some of them greatest among the great, though necessarily at a disadvantage when compared with English performers, won their way to the very topmost point of their profession. According to Churchill's estimate of his countrymen, which is not without a certain amount of truth,

Those who would gain the votes of British tribes,
Must add to force of merit, force of bribes.

and this statement refers to audiences and their reception of actors. But, as the majority of Irish actors came into England poor and unfriended, and surrounded by all kinds of prejudices, it is manifest that they owed their advancement more to their merit than to anything else—a difficult and creditable feat.

CHAPTER XXIII.

IRISH DRAMATISTS AND ACTORS IN LONDON.

O peculiar were the customs of the early days of the Drama that a reference to some of them is almost essential, and will prove instructive. Thus, Wilks was so great a favourite in Dublin at one time that the Duke of Ormond, then Lord Lieutenant, actually issued a decree forbidding him to leave that city. Wilks's immense popularity was not unnatural if some testimonies to his acting powers may be believed. It is said by one admirer that, even in his old age, when afflicted with various infirmities, he acted the sprightly gallants—his favourite parts—with as much apparent ease and finish as in his best days, and that people who saw the decrepit old man out-of-doors would never believe him to be the dashing actor of youthful characters.

One of the most pernicious customs of the 17th and early part of the 18th centuries was that of the invasion of the stage by wealthy patrons. The beaux and well-to-do idlers of the period considered

QUIN AS CORIOLANUS.
(From a rare portrait.)

they had a perfect right to intrude into every corner of the theatre, before or behind the stage. The consequence was that the players had sometimes practically to force their way to the footlights, so great was the crowd surging on the stage. All stage illusion was lost, and it speaks volumes for the great powers of the actors when they enthralled the house in the midst of such drawbacks and disadvantages. On benefit nights, occasionally, the strange scene was witnessed of ostentatious and pleased spectators pressing round the recipients of the benefits and thrusting money into their hands—in other cases speaking to them and, at times, embracing them. As an instance of the want of reality of the scenes, and as a proof of the absence of probability in the incidents of a play, it is mentioned that Juliet, supposed to die alone in the tomb of the Capulets, expired in the presence of two or three hundred spectators, who thronged the stage. This custom became intolerable at last, and in 1704 a decree was promulgated forbidding any but those connected with the play upon the stage during performance. This rule was not strictly carried out, as the "swells" strongly resisted any attempt to deprive them of what they considered their privileges. Finally, things reached such a pass that the climax occurred. On a night in 1721, at Lincoln's Inn-fields Theatre, during an important scene in "Macbeth," a drunken nobleman, an earl, crossed or reeled over the stage to speak with another loafing toper who was lolling against the opposite wings. He was remonstrated with by the manager, whom he immediately struck. The latter returned the blow; in a moment the friends of the intruder were rushing about with drawn swords threatening to kill the manager—a menace they would have certainly carried out if Quin, Ryan, and others had not rushed upon them, also armed with swords, and driven them from the stage into the street. While this was being done other friends of the ignoble earl were destroying the hangings and furniture of the house, and had, in fact, commenced to "fire" the theatre, when Quin and the others attacked them and carried some of them before the magistrates, by whom they were fined. After this event soldiers were placed upon the stage to prevent any further intrusion. James Quin, who was born in London in 1693, went upon the stage in 1714, and remained on it till 1753. His success was soon ensured, and till the end of his life he maintained his reputation almost at its highest. He suffered a temporary decline when Garrick came to the front, and was excelled in some of his favourite parts by his great rival. But as Falstaff, Henry VIII., Bajazet, Hotspur, Brutus, or Sir John Brute, he was unequalled by any one of his contemporaries. As Churchill, in "The Rosciad," says—

GARRICK AS MACBETH.
(From a rare print.)

As Brute he shone unequalled; all agree
Garrick's not half as great a Brute as he.

Quin's principal defect was an absence of that mobility of features which is so essential to a good actor. The satirist of the stage just quoted, after telling us that—

His words bore sterling weight, nervous and strong,
In manly tides of sens · they rolled along;
Happy in art, he chiefly had pretence
To keep up numbers, yet not forfeit sense.
No actor ever greater heights could reach
In all the laboured artifice of speech;

and admitting that his elocution and what has been called his "grand emphasis" were worthy of a great actor, says, notwithstanding this—

Nature, in spite of all his skill, crept in :
Horatio, Dorax, Falstaff—still 'twas Quin.

Though of a very sarcastic disposition, Quin was really a generous and warm-hearted man. Many instances of his benevolence are cited, such as his visit to Thomson, the poet of "The Seasons," in jail, where he had been lodged for debt, and his present to him of a cheque for £100, on the ground that that was a fair price for the pleasure his works had afforded him. His kindness to his fellow-actor, Ryan, was also a good trait in his character, when we remember the jealousies of actors in those days. Even after he had retired from the stage he came up from Bath every year to act Falstaff for his friend's benefit. But, having lost his front teeth, he would not, as he put it, go on the stage "to whistle Falstaff." However, in answer to Ryan's request, he replied that though he could not attend his benefit, he was leaving him £1,000 in his will, and if he wanted money he could have that sum in advance. He had many enemies on account of his sharp tongue and the difficulty he felt in restraining the bitter remarks that occasionally came to his mind. His voice, like Macklin's, was somewhat unpleasant. Churchill speaks of his "deep-mouthed bass" as unsuitable to some of the parts he played. While not a very jealous actor, he was occasionally piqued at the preference shown by his manager to other players, and in one of these moments he withdrew to Bath, expecting, doubtless, that he would be sent for. But Rich, his manager, took no notice of him; so, after a while,

MRS. JORDAN.

Quin wrote the brief note—"I am at Bath. Yours, James Quin," to which he received the equally laconic and more expressive reply, "Stay there, and be d—d. Yours, J Rich."

His friend, Lacy Ryan, was probably born in London in 1694. He was the son of a tailor named Daniel Ryan, who gave him an excellent education, and intended him to study the law; but this did not suit the future actor. Consequently, in 1710, he joined the Haymarket Company, and soon became a favourite. He may be accounted one of the most careful actors of the 18th century, though he never, of course, reached the heights that Garrick and others did. In 1729 he produced a small comic opera, which had some success, but not sufficient to induce him to continue to write. As an actor he ranks just below the greatest of his time. Hamlet and Lothario were among his best parts, Quin acting the Ghost to the former part. In opposition to Garrick, Ryan acted some of Garrick's finest impersonations, and it is no small credit to Ryan that in one or two of them he excelled Garrick, whose stunted figure was against him in a few special characters.

Charles Macklin first appeared on the stage in 1716, or thereabouts, at Bristol. For a large number of years he acted subordinate parts, and met with little encouragement, though his greatest merit was his carefulness and attention to the smallest details. But at length, on the 14th of February, 1741, his conspicuous ability and his originality were fully recognised. On this night he played Shylock. It had always been played as a comic character, and Macklin, who was the first actor to carry out Shakespeare's meaning, feared to show in rehearsal the manner in which he was going to play the part, lest the manager should prohibit it, and insist upon the time-honoured custom. When Macklin appeared he observed that the house was crowded and that the first two rows of the pit were occupied by notabilities. He involuntarily exclaimed—"Good; I shall be tried to-night by a special jury." Instead of wearing fanciful costumes, he had studied the exact dress worn by the Jews in Venice, even to the small red hat which they wore to distinguish themselves from the Christians.

During the first few scenes in which Shylock takes part, the house was amazed and silent; but it gradually began to dawn upon them that this, after all, was the correct interpretation of the author, and the pleased audience broke into expressions of delight and admiration. This was the turning-point of Macklin's career. Shylock and Macbeth were perhaps his greatest assumptions of Shakesperean parts. In 1780 he wrote and produced his amusing comedy, "The Man of the World," and in 1793 his farce, "Love-a-la-Mode." It should be noted that when he wrote these pieces he was of great age, even assuming that he was born in 1700 (for there is still a possibility of his having been born in 1690), and it is a remarkable testimony to his powers that he should have played the leading parts himself on their production, and thus have given the cue to all succeeding Sir Pertinax M'Sycophants, Sir Archy M'Sarcasms, and Sir Callaghan O'Brallaghans. These two plays still live; his others, numbering half a dozen, are now forgotten.

In private life he was irreproachable, but he was feared rather than loved by his colleagues and associates on account of his brusque and, at times, almost savage manner. His elocutionary powers were magnificent ; more than any actor of his time he knew where to lay the stress and the emphasis in subtle passages, and was thereby fitted, with his other admirable qualifications, as a performer of Shakesperean characters. With the exception of a rather brief interval, he acted almost till his last day. His friends and contemporaries were surprised that he showed no failing of his powers. Finally, however, the crash came. He had previously given a half-hint that his memory was deserting him. On his benefit night, May 7th, 1789, he appeared on the stage for the last time. He was playing Shylock, and it was clear he would not go through the performance unless by some miracle, and an understudy, in the person of Thomas Ryder, was in readiness to finish the part. Just before going on the stage Macklin asked the excellent actress who was to play Portia whether she was going to act that night. On her reminding him that she was dressed for Portia, he replied vacantly—"I had forgotten; who plays Shylock?" He went on the stage, tried to go through the part, but broke down, and was led from the stage for the last time, amidst the pained silence of the house, after he had mournfully asked the pardon of the audience. He died in 1797, leaving a daughter, Miss Macklin, who had become a very capable actress under her father's tuition.

Two other excellent actors of this period were Denis Delane and William Havard. The former was winning his way to the highest rank as an actor when his career was cut short by drink. It appears that he suffered from certain peculiarities of speech and action, and Garrick so mercilessly ridiculed them that the sensitive actor, who had played leading parts with the greatest performers of his time, took to drink, and died in poverty in 1750, twenty-two years after his first appearance. If we may judge by the comments on this sad event, Garrick's action roused bitter feelings against him. Havard was born in 1709 in Ireland, and died on the 20th of February, 1778, aged 68. Both as actor and dramatist he deserves high praise. His four plays are cleverly written, though never acted nowadays. The tragedies of those days were generally very turgid productions, ending in most cases by the indiscriminate slaughter of the leading characters, to which Dryden's pithy words refer—"The dagger and the bowl are always at hand to butcher a hero when a poet wants the brains to save him." Havard's tragedies contain good verse, have good plots, and were very successful when they were produced. His success as an actor was equally great. Fielding, the novelist, passed a very high eulogium upon him when he said—"Except Mr. Garrick, I do not know that he hath any superior in tragedy at Covent Garden Theatre." He further speaks of him as a "sensible, modest, and good-natured man." These words were written in 1752, when Covent Garden and Drury Lane possessed an unequalled array of fine actors and actresses. Havard's epitaph was written by Garrick, and runs as follows:—

> Havard from sorrow sleeps beneath this stone;
> An honest man, beloved as soon as known;
> Howe'er defective in the mimic art,
> In real life he justly played his part;
> The noblest character he acted well,
> And Heaven applauded when the curtain fell.

Unquestionably the most comic actress of the 18th century was Kitty Clive. She was born in 1711 of Irish parents, but whether in London or Ireland is doubtful. Her first appearance was at Drury Lane as a boy, on 2nd January, 1729. She merely sang a song on this occasion, but immediately became a great favourite. Strangely enough, her first appearance was in tragedy; but before long an opportunity of showing her great comedy powers was afforded her, when she at once became an object of general popularity. There is no difference of opinion whatever as to her remarkable merit as a comedy actress. She was the original Nell in "The Devil to Pay," and in this part enchanted all her audiences. Even Dr. Johnson could not resist her charms or withhold his praise. He said of her—"Mrs. Clive was the best player I ever saw." Dr. Doran says—"She was the one true comic genius, and none could withstand her." And Churchill, who had a good word for scarcely any of the great actors of his time, thus characterises her:—

> First giggling, plotting chambermaids arrive,
> Hoydens and romps, led on by General Clive.
> In spite of outward blemishe she shone
> For humour famed, and humour all her own.
>
> No comic actress ever yet could raise
> On humour's base more merit or more praise.

Kitty Clive was, besides, an authoress. Several of her pieces were acted, the title of one of the best of them being "The Faithful Irishwoman."

One of her most successful rivals was Mrs. Bellamy, who first appeared at Covent Garden on November 22nd, 1744, in a tragic character. She acted pathetic parts most exquisitely, some of Shakespeare's heroines being among her best assumptions. As Juliet, she has had few rivals. After delighting the town for some years, her extravagance and general carelessness exiled her from the stage, and in course of time she died in poverty and loneliness. Her right to a place among the

MRS. BELLAMY.

great actresses of the last century is universally admitted, and it is to be regretted she did not pursue her profession with the assiduity and care of the many actresses inferior to her in grace, dignity, natural ability, and other attributes of the art of acting.

First and foremost among the actors of the period was David Garrick. As we have said before, he was of Irish descent on the maternal side, a fact which evidently had some influence on his future career. His success as an actor was almost immediate, although it was some time before he could leave the second-class theatre where he was engaged. His first important appearance in London was on October 19th, 1741, when he played the part of Richard III. From this time his popularity was assured. His versatility was marvellous. Nothing came amiss to his extraordinary genius; and he played almost every character to perfection. He was probably the finest actor of the century; and as a further proof of his abilities, his dramatic pieces may be mentioned. Some of these are inimitable—one, "The Irish Widow," deserving the title of one of the best farces in English literature. His career is so familiar that it needs no recapitulation—his private character, however, calls for one word. He has been accused, and not without some reason, of bitter jealousy of his brother actors; and his niggardliness has been the theme of many a theatrical critic. With respect to the first charge, it may be remarked in extenuation that once his position was secured he gathered round him at Drury Lane a magnificent company, including such Irish men and women as Barry, Macklin, Delane, Havard, Barrington, Sparks, Peg Woffington, and Kitty Clive. His love of money was notorious. When Kitty Clive took leave of the stage in 1769, Garrick said to her—"I am grieved to lose you," to which the lively actress replied, "Not you, Davy; you'd light up for joy only the candles would cost you sixpence."

Of his rivals, Thomas Sheridan was one of the most important. The year 1744 saw the rise of this "bright theatric star," and Covent Garden was the scene of the event. In spite of his excellence in tragic parts, Sheridan did not receive the recognition he deserved, and it has been reserved for critics of more recent times to pay him his full due. But there was at least one keen critic who saw his splendid powers, and that was Churchill, as the following lines testify. Their author never paid a higher compliment to anyone when he said:—

Just his conceptions, natural and great;
His feelings strong, his words enforced with weight.

And then, referring to some of his faults, he continues—

But, spite of all defects, his glories rise,
And Art, by judgment formed, with Nature vies,
View the whole scene, with critic judgment scan,
And then deny him merit if you can;
Where he falls short 'tis Nature's fault alone;
Where he succeeds the merit's all his own.

Like most of his fellow-actors, Sheridan was an author; but none of his plays have survived, though written with more than ordinary taste and ability. His celebrated son's productions have completely dwarfed those of the actor and teacher of elocution.

A more formidable opponent of Garrick was Spranger Barry, the handsomest actor of his age. His fine presence (he was over six feet in height) and a voice of melting tenderness were powerful aids to his natural ability. He won the hearts and applause of the fair portion of his audiences, from his first appearance in 1746 to his farewell of the stage, thirty years after. His personal appearance "drew admiring eyes" wherever he went, and in the theatre—

None more could flood each eye,
None better formed to make the ladies sigh.

No greater Romeo has ever trod the English stage; according to Garrick, he was "the most exquisite lover that had ever been seen on the stage;" and a lady who saw Garrick and Barry act Romeo expressed the difference between them in this way —"Had I been Juliet to Garrick's Romeo, so impassioned was he that I should have expected him to come up to me in the balcony; but had I been Juliet to Barry's Romeo, so tender and seductive was he, I should certainly have jumped down to him."

Very curious stories are related of him, and of the magic of his harmonious voice. It is said that once when a bailiff came to seize his furniture for debt, another bailiff, who had come upon a precisely similar errand, was so entranced by his "silver tongue" that he paid the debt of the other officer, and left Barry with the assurance that everything was settled. But this has an apocryphal air, and may only be taken as an exaggerated popular estimate of his powers of persuasion.

Henry Mossop, the other rival of Garrick, and the emulator of his proud position, was by no means so dangerous as those already mentioned. His great tragic powers were undeniable, and as the tyrant King John, in Shakespeare's play of that name, he was unapproachable. But Mossop's excessive pride ruined him, and his career on the stage was brief, though brilliant. When he could not always obtain leading parts or "first business," he refused to accept "seconds," and finally died, primarily of poverty, but in some degree of a broken heart.

There were other clever actors of this period, who may be placed in the second-class. Such were —Samuel Reddish, whose Edgar in "King Lear" and Posthumous in "Cymbeline" were finely rendered; Luke and Isaac Sparks, excellent comedy actors; John Barrington, the Irish comedian; John Brereton, who ended by playing Orlando and other leading parts with Mrs. Siddons; Middleton (whose real name was Magann), a good imitator of Barry, whose extravagance drove him to ruin; and Crawford, first a barrister, then a very capable actor, who succumbed, like the preceding, after reckless courses, and lived in a state of chronic impecuniosity. Of the minor dramatists who either preceded or were contemporary with Sheridan and Goldsmith a few may be here dealt with.

One of the most prominent of these was Charles Coffey, whose famous farce, "The Devil to Pay," has been a great favourite with the low comedians of the last hundred years, affording them as it does, by its wit and liveliness, considerable scope for the display of their powers; John Kelly, a barrister, and author of some very clever plays;

Charles Molloy, another excellent dramatist; Dr. Michael Clancy, who by reason of one good play received a pension from George I.; M'Namara Morgan, the Rev. Philip Francis, Samuel Derrick, Mrs. Sheridan and Miss Sheridan (the mother and sister of R. B. Sheridan), Henry Brooke, Mrs. Pilkington, Frederick Pilon, Francis Gentleman, and others too numerous to mention. Matthew Concanen, by his exceptionally clever piece, "Wexford Wells," and Captain Robert Jephson and Henry Jones, by their admirable tragedies, deserve a place apart, for they were unquestionably among the first of the minor Irish dramatists of the century.

CHAPTER XXIV.

IRISH DRAMATISTS AND ACTORS ON THE LONDON STAGE.

DURING the latter half of the 18th century Irish actors and actresses were more numerous than ever, and this period also saw the fruition of the genius of such famous dramatists as Sheridan, Goldsmith, O'Keeffe, and others. The first piece Goldsmith produced was his "Good-natured Man" (in January, 1768, at Covent Garden), and though the audience were somewhat captious, and objected to one of the best scenes in the play—the scene between Honeywood and the bailiffs—it was a success, and brought more money to Goldsmith than he had ever previously handled.

JOHN O'KEEFFE.

Five years elapsed before his next play appeared; but on the 15th of March, 1773, Covent Garden had the honour of witnessing the first performance of the author's masterpiece, "She Stoops to Conquer." A good many friends of the author, with strong lungs and horny hands, were in the house, and Dr. Johnson was conspicuous in a box, giving the cue, by his smiles and laughter, to the merriment of the rest of the audience. Goldsmith was terribly nervous, but had no cause for alarm till the beginning of the fifth act, when a solitary hiss was heard, said to emanate from Richard Cumberland. "What's that? what's that?" asked Goldsmith, hurriedly; to which Colman replied—"Pshaw! my dear doctor, of what consequence is a squib, when we have been sitting for two hours on a barrel of gunpowder." The play was a remarkable success, and gave Goldsmith the means of extravagance, and enabled him to charitably disburse his earnings. The wit of these two plays is akin to that of Steele, but is occasionally of a more pronounced kind. There are not in Steele's plays such humorous characters as Tony Lumpkin, Jack Lofty, or Croaker, though the type of each is not absent from his essays. Some of Goldsmith's characters border on the farcical, it must be admitted, as, for instance, the drunken butler, but their general humour is unquestionable. It is not so well known that Goldsmith wrote (or rather revised) another play, but such is the case. It was entitled, "The Grumbler," and was played at a benefit in Covent Garden on May 8th, 1773, but was never printed.

There were a large number of contemporary Irish dramatists, some of whom cannot be passed over by reason of their popularity in this or in other branches of literature. Such were Paul Hefferman (1719-1777), the author of several plays—one, "The Lady's Choice," having been a success at Covent Garden; G. E. Howard, who wrote one or two very fair tragedies; Elizabeth Griffith (died January, 1793), who was first an actress at Covent Garden, and whose several pieces are all creditable, notably two, "The Double Mistake" and "The School for Rakes," which were well received at Covent Garden and Drury Lane respectively; John Cunningham (1729-1773), the well-known poet, author of the excellent farce, "Love in a Mist;" Henry Boyd, the translator of Dante, and author of several good tragedies; Isaac Jackman, whose "All the World's a Stage," "The Milesian," and "The Divorce," particularly the last-named piece (a musical farce), were warmly appreciated at Drury Lane on their production; and, lastly, Francis Gentleman, who, besides being a capable actor at the Haymarket in 1770 and onwards, wrote a number of plays, including "The Modish Wife," which was acted "with universal applause" at the same theatre in 1774. To the above may be added William Cooke, the poet, whose "Capricious Lady" was occasionally acted; Joseph Atkinson (1743-1818), whose "Tit-for-Tat" was successful at the Haymarket in 1786; Eliza Ryves, T. L. O'Beirne, an Irish bishop; John Simons,

William Preston, Denis O'Bryer, W. C. Oulton, Charles Hamilton, Hall Hartson, Francis Dobbs, James Field Stanfield, father of the great marine painter of the same surname; and, finally, William Macready, who, after a short career as an upholsterer in his native city, Dublin, went on the stage, and also wrote for it his popular "Irishman in London" and "The Village Lawyer," and whose son was William Charles Macready, one of the greatest of modern actors.

While those we have thus briefly mentioned are more or less honourably connected with the English Stage and English dramatic literature, there were others whose claim to a prominent rank among the dramatists of the century cannot be disputed. Among those whose works were of immense popularity, and the lightness of whose productions was one of the chief reasons, perhaps, that helped them to float down the stream of time, were four men who are rightly considered the founders and chief supporters of English comic opera and burlesque—Kane O'Hara, Isaac Bickerstaff, Leonard M'Nally, and John O'Keeffe.

O'Hara, in his "Midas," "Tom Thumb," and "The Golden Pippin," ridiculed in a most inimitable manner the Italian opera of his time. "Midas" made great fun of the gods of ancient Greece, satirising the preposterous way in which mythology was treated in some operas; "Tom Thumb" amusingly burlesqued the tragedies then in vogue, with their accumulated horrors. Of the author of these clever parodies little is known. His life is almost a mystery, but it is certain he was a musician living in Dublin, and was probably born about the commencement of the 18th century, dying in 1782 at a ripe old age. He was the true founder of English burlesque, as at present understood, though not the first author who burlesqued serious productions.

Leonard M'Nally (1752-1820), who became notorious as a Government spy, was the author of several excellent comic operas and other dramatic pieces (such as "Robin Hood"), which are likely to live as literature, though never played. He was a clever barrister, and joined the United Irishmen, apparently of set purpose to betray them. But while his political treachery exposes him to the just contempt of every honest Irishman, his literary ability is worthy of all recognition, and as one of the precursors of the modern school of writers of comic opera his works are also of historical interest. Concerning his counterpart, Bickerstaffe, little that is creditable is known. His conduct was so bad as an officer in the army that he was obliged to seek refuge abroad.

The exact date of his birth is unknown, but it was probably about 1760. He was a page to Lord Chesterfield while the latter was Lord Lieutenant of Ireland. It is a curious circumstance that long before Bickerstaffe was born, Swift had used the very same name as a pseudonym. It would seem, therefore, that either Swift was acquainted with a person of that name, and consequently used a genuine name as a cloak for his identity, or Isaac Bickerstaffe was not the dramatist's real name. If neither of these suppositions be correct, the accidental similarity of the names constitutes a strange coincidence. Steele also used the name of "Isaac Bickerstaffe," having used it in the "Tatler," borrowing it from Swift. This exceedingly amusing and prolific dramatist was still living in 1816. As the author of some of the most entertaining pieces of the last century, his name is "writ" prominently in the volume of English (or Irish) dramatic literature. His "Love in a Village," "Lionel and Clarissa," "The Maid of the Mill," and other operas were immensely popular, and are characterised by clever plots and bright dialogue, while the scraps of verse scattered throughout them are very apt and sometimes witty. Originality was not Bickerstaffe's strong point, and he borrowed from almost every body, as many more famous authors have done. But his plays, mosaics though they be, are highly diverting, and pleased the audiences of former days, some of them, in fact, still "holding the field." In "Love in a Village" occurs the well-known song, "The Miller of the Dee," which, as given by Bickerstaffe, runs as follows:—

> There was a jolly miller once
> Lived on the River Dee;
> He worked and sang from morn till night,
> No lark so blithe as he;
> And this the burden of his song
> For ever used to be—
> I care for nobody, no, not I,
> If nobody cares for me!

More lasting, perhaps, than his operas and burlettas will be his adaptation of Molière's "Tartuffe"—"The Hypocrite." To the original cast of characters he added one, Maw-worm, which has been an especial favourite with all the principal low comedians since the date of its production. This adaptation of Bickerstaffe's has quite superseded that of Colley Cibber, and holds undisputed possession of the stage.

The greatest of the four comic writers classed together above was undoubtedly John O'Keeffe. He was born on June 24th, 1747, in Dublin, his father hailing from King's County and his mother from Wexford. His education was entrusted to the distinguished Jesuit, Father John Austin;

and after this was completed he began to study art. But though he painted some good portraits, he grew tired of the profession of a painter, and went on the stage in Dublin, and remained thereon for twelve years, his brother Daniel meanwhile becoming proficient as a miniature painter. John O'Keeffe wrote his earliest piece while an actor at Smock Alley Theatre, and it was produced, but without much success. Fired with ambition, he journeyed to London, and having written another play entitled "Tony Lumpkin in Town," sent it anonymously to George Colman the elder, then manager of the Haymarket Theatre. It was gladly accepted, and was produced shortly after, on July 2nd, 1778, with success, and from that moment O'Keeffe's future career was decided. He wrote

MRS. ELIZABETH POPE.

an immense number of pieces for the stage, not a few of them being of a trivial and slight character, but there are several which will bear comparison with all but the best plays of the last century for combined humour, plot, characterisation, and well-devised situations. Such are his "Wild Oats," a comedy; "The Agreeable Surprise," a comic opera; and "The Castle of Andalusia," an opera; and some others. With regard to one of his farces, "The Man-Milliner," a disturbance occurred. The haberdashers of the town, guessing they were to be ridiculed, assembled in force at the theatre, and damned the play without hearing it.

A point of importance in connection with O'Keeffe's life must be recorded here. He just missed being made Poet Laureate. On Whitehead's death he applied for the appointment, but was informed by the then Lord Salisbury that it had "unfortunately" been promised to a Mr. Thomas Warton, otherwise he should certainly have had it. In 1826 O'Keeffe published his entertaining and valuable "Recollections," a trustworthy record of the theatrical affairs of the previous half-century. He died in 1833, aged 85, having some years previously lost his sight, and thus having been compelled to dictate his writings to his daughter. In his own sphere he was perfectly unequalled, and though he had some enemies, he was very highly esteemed by his contemporaries. Sir Walter Scott, in his "St. Ronan's Well," used the phrase "from Shakespeare down to O'Keeffe." On the latter having his attention called to this remark, he said—"I see. From the top to the bottom of the ladder. He might have put me a few rungs up." O'Keeffe's operas are no longer played, doubtless owing to the old-fashioned style of the music to which they are wedded, but his "Wild Oats" is one of the best of the English stock comedies, affording perennial delight and enjoyment to every class of audience. Two other dramatists, of a more serious, less farcical vein than O'Keeffe, and who received a not inconsiderable share of the attention of their contemporaries, were Hugh Kelly (1739-1777) and Arthur Murphy (1730-1805). Kelly, a native of Killarney, is known to fame as a clever dramatist and dramatic innovator, and as a biting political and social satirist. His personal appearance was one of his principal defects, apparently, though beyond a reference to his "belly fair and round" by an anonymous poetical critic, no details are given. Goldsmith has immortalised him in his "Retaliation," and he was abused by most of the writers of the day on account of his outspokenness or of his unfair attacks The exasperating Hugh's "False Delicacy" and "School for Wives" are excellent comedies, conspicuous for clever points, and showing his powers of character-drawing. They are comedies of the "tearful" order, belonging to what in France would be called "comedie larmoyante" Kelly was, as we have hinted, cordially hated by many of his contemporaries, and his death, at the early age of 38, may not have been greatly regretted by them, but he died too soon for the world of literature. So great was the enmity aroused by some of Kelly's political writings and his capacity for hitting hard that some of his plays had to be produced under an assumed name, as though by an unknown author, and by this ruse they were successful.

His fellow-dramatist, Arthur Murphy, lived longer, and produced some excellent work; but his works lack the point and brilliancy of Kelly's plays. As a scholar, he was greatly esteemed by the best judges of his time, and as a dramatist, his "Three Weeks after Marriage," "All in the Wrong," and "The Way to Keep Him," to mention only one or two of his busiest pieces, entitle him to a foremost place among the second-class dramatists of the period in which he lived. According to Churchill, Murphy was—

> In person tall, a figure formed to please,
> If symmetry could charm deprived of ease.

The handsomest actor on the stage at this period was William O'Brien, an inimitable comedian in special parts, and author of one of the best farces of the century. As an instance of the way in which he identified himself with his part it is stated that one night, while playing Sir Andrew Ague-cheek in Shakespeare's "Tempest" he was so richly humorous that one of the soldiers guarding the stage fell down in an uncontrollable fit of laughter, and rolled over and over on the stage, to the increased gratification of the audience. Churchill, even Churchill, that severe stage censor, pays him an unconscious compliment when he admits, after saying that O'Brien was a "shadow" of Woodward, that O'Brien had imitators—

> Strange to relate, but wonderfully true,
> That even shadows have their shadows too!

O'Brien's farce, "Cross Purposes," was produced in 1772, and became a great success. Another piece, "The Duel," also by O'Brien, produced at another theatre on the same night, was a failure, although it is quite as good as the successful farce. Both as actor and dramatist, O'Brien's name is honourably associated with the Theatre. As to the year of his birth, it is not known; but as his first appearance took place at Drury Lane in 1758, it may be conjectured that he was born about 1740. After a triumphant career on the boards, he married in 1764 Lady Diana Strangeways, daughter of the Earl of Ilchester, and retired from the theatre. He was still living in 1816 in Dorsetshire, a receiver-general and a J.P.

Among other promising dramatists of this time was John Tobin (1770-1804), who, though born in England, was undoubtedly of Irish origin. His famous comedy, "The Honeymoon," appeared posthumously in 1805, and is rightly considered one of the masterpieces of modern English comedy. Tobin died young at Cork, where he lies buried. Unlike Andrew Cherry (1762-1812), he was not both actor and dramatist. Cherry is known to fame principally as the author of one play, "The Soldier's Daughter," and of several songs, such as "The Dear Little Shamrock," "Tom Moody," and "The Bay of Biscay O;" his reputation as an actor was equally great and well-deserved. He hailed from Limerick, and played many leading parts in all the leading theatres of England and Ireland.

But nearly all the dramatists previously mentioned sink into insignificance before Richard Brinsley Sheridan (1751-1816). A member of one of the most gifted of families, almost wholly connected, in one way or another, with the Drama, he was destined to shed still greater glory upon it. His plays are few in number, but they are of unusual excellence. He may, without exaggeration, be ranked next to the "Swan of Avon," notwithstanding the dissimilarity between them. There have been greater *poets*, but not greater *dramatists*. No dramatist, not even the Immortal Bard himself, has ever been more *popular*; and his polished wit and strokes of satire and humour are as eagerly waited for and listened to by audiences as the aphoristic gems and grand soliloquies of Shakespeare. His "Duenna" is perhaps the wittiest opera extant; his "Critic" is an inimitable burlesque; while his "School for Scandal" and "The Rivals" are almost unapproachable either for keen wit or graceful satire.

ANDREW CHERRY.

So much for the Irish dramatists of the 18th century. A glance at the actors and actresses of the same period will demonstrate with equal force that Ireland's share in the history of the English Stage is enormous. Of Irish comedians proper, John Moody (1728-1813) heads the list in point of time, and perhaps in point of merit. He was a native of Cork, his real name, it is said, being Cochrane. He was known in theatrical circles as "the Irish gentleman," partly on account of his success in depicting that character, and partly because of his irreproachable character. It is said by all critics that as Major O'Flaherty in "The West Indian," as Teague in "The Committee," as Sir Callaghan O'Bralaghan in "Love-a-la-Mode," and as Sir Patrick O'Neal in "The Irish Widow," he was without an equal. He was the original Major O'Flaherty, and played the part inimitably, a formidable rival appearing afterwards in Jack Johnstone. The anonymous critic already once or twice quoted thus expresses the general chorus of praise on Moody's performances:—

> Moody we praise, with all the warmth we can
> When he depicts the Irish gentleman ;
> Nor stop we here, since he possesses sense,
> To keep from those attempts might give offence;
> May just reward his real merit crown
> Who well deserves the favour of the town.

And Churchill, departing from his usual method, warmly eulogises his powers:—

> Long from a nation ever hardly used,
> At random censured, wantonly abused,
> Have Britons drawn their sport with partial view,
> Formed general notions from the rascal few ;
> Condemned a people, as for vices known,
> Which from their country banished, seek our own ;
> At length, howe'er, the slavish chain is broke,
> And Sense awakened, scorns her ancient yoke ;
> Taught by thee, Moody, we now learn to raise
> Mirth from their foibles : from their virtues praise

Jack Johnstone was a native of Tipperary, and was born in 1750. His reputation as an impersonator of Irish characters was made in Ireland, and was thoroughly endorsed in England. He was gifted with a fine presence, a splendid voice, and was an ideal Irish comedian. The fact that so many of the plays of the last century have their Irish characters is owing to the necessity of finding a suitable part for one or other of the Irish comedians of the time. Johnstone retired from the stage after a long connection with it, and died on December 26th, 1828. He created a large number of original parts, and excelled in others created by Moody and others. Several of his Irish contemporaries, though not peculiarly Irish comedians, won their way to general recognition. Such were Alexander Pope, who was born about the middle of the last century, and died in 1835, equally eminent as painter and actor; and Francis and James Aickin, both excellent actors, the former excelling in tragedy, the latter in pathetic melodramatic parts, and possessing a fine voice. Of James Aikin, it is said—

JACK JOHNSTONE AS MAJOR O'FLAHERTY.

> Aikin, the younger, has some gifts to please,
> Just sensibility and modest ease ;
> His shins not there where Nature cannot reach,
> But lets her guide his gesture and his speech.

The elder brother died in 1805, the younger in 1803. Robert Owenson, a member of Garrick's company, and father of Lady Morgan, must also be mentioned.

Distinguished Irish actresses were less numerous towards the latter part of the century. Margaret Woffington properly belongs to the first part of the century, but did not really reach the height of her reputation till the fifties. She went upon the Dublin stage in early life, having been born in 1720 or thereabouts, and in 1740 made her first appearance in London at Covent Garden as Sylvia to Ryan's Plume, in Farquhar's "Recruiting Officer." After a while she assumed male parts, and particularly shone as Sir Harry Wildair, in another of the same dramatist's works. Though in every respect a comedy actress, Peg Woffington has the distinction of having been the original Lady Randolph (to Barry's Norval) in England. This part has always been a favourite with the best tragic actresses, as it affords plenty of scope for pathos. Her impersonations of high-born ladies were as popular as her gay sparks, though like several other great actors, she triumphed in spite of a harsh and grating voice. Everybody was fascinated by her good looks and her charming manner; yet she could be a virago at times, witness her jealousy of and quarrels with Mrs. Bellamy, Mrs. Cibber, and Kitty Clive. And though beautiful in feature and figure, she could act old women parts finely, assuming wrinkles and sourness as easily as dimples and smiles. In private life she was extremely generous, and ended her days honourably and well. Her sister, Mary Woffington, was far inferior as an actress, but she succeeded better in life, and became the wife of an earl's son. The Woffingtons were Catholics, but Margaret apostatised in order to come into an estate which had been left to her.

PEG WOFFINGTON.

There were, towards the close of the century, three actresses of the very highest reputation—namely, Mrs. Robinson, Mrs. Elizabeth Pope, and Mrs. Maria Pope. The former was notable as a performer of Shakespeare's heroines, the name of "Perdita" being given to her because of her fine rendering of the heroine of Shakespeare's "Winter's Tale." Her connection with the Stage was very brief, and calls for no particular mention. The same thing may be said of the two wives of

Alexander Pope. They excelled in second-rate parts; Maria Pope, who died young, being a great loss to the Stage, for she would undoubtedly have developed into a great actress.

A few great actors and actresses must be referred to rather briefly, as their connection with Ireland was very slight and somewhat accidental. Thus, George Frederick Cooke, according to his own account (afterwards contradicted by himself), was born in Dublin, and this is almost certainly true; but it is denied and disputed, and we must content ourselves with the mere statement that he was one of the greatest of tragedians, and was probably of Irish birth. With regard to the Kembles, that marvellously gifted family, it may be remarked that the mother of J. P. Kemble and Mrs. Siddons, and their brothers and sisters, Charles, Stephen, Elizabeth, and Fanny (the four last admirable performers) was an Irish woman, a native of Clonmel, named Ward.

GEORGE FREDERICK COOKE.

Among the great actors of this time we must not overlook John Henderson. In former chapters we have given some information respecting him, and will therefore only say here that, notwithstanding personal disadvantages, such as smallness of stature and a weak voice, he rivalled, as Macbeth, Shylock, and Hamlet, previous great tragedians, and died prematurely at the age of 38.

In conclusion, a word of cordial recognition is necessary to the labours of such a great dramatic critic as Edmund Malone, and to such ardent commentators as Ambrose Eccles and John Monck Mason, as well as to the distinguished musicians, like Michael Kelly, Thomas Carter, and Thomas Cooke, who led the orchestras, sang on the stages and composed operas for the leading London theatres.

CHAPTER XXV.

IRISH DRAMATISTS AND ACTORS IN LONDON.

THE two most celebrated comedy actresses of the closing years of the 18th century were Elizabeth Farren and Mrs. Jordan. The first-named was born at Cork in 1759, and went on the stage in very early life, making her first appearance at Liverpool. On June 9th, 1777, she came out at the Haymarket Theatre in London as Miss Hardcastle in "She Stoops to Conquer," and won the favour of her audience. Her general success in the provinces had prepared Londoners for a clever actress, but they did not altogether expect to see a really great one as Miss Farren unquestionably proved herself. In the leading female characters of high-class comedy, but especially as Beatrice, Miss Hardcastle, and Lady Teazle, she knew no rival. Mrs. Jordan excelled her in some parts, but was inferior in the characters we have mentioned. Miss Farren remained on the stage twenty years, her farewell to the theatre taking place on March 14th, 1797 (according to Dr. Doran). A month afterwards she married the Earl of Derby, who had long been fascinated by her charms.

Superior to her as Rosalind, Viola, and similar Shakesperean characters, Mrs. Jordan made her first bow to a London audience in 1785, and at once sprang into popular favour. Her irresistible beauty, grace, and her many delightful ways in some of her characters endeared her to Londoners, and as the "wayward, wilful" Rosalind and such like parts she took the town by storm. She was a native of Waterford, her real name being Dorothea Bland, and was born in 1762. She is admittedly the "finest Rosalind that ever trod the stage," and as John Bannister said: "no woman ever uttered comedy like her." Her fine ladies were less admired than Miss Farren's, but her coquettes and hoydens were unsurpassable.

W. V. WALLACE.

Next to Mrs. Siddons, Miss O'Neil was perhaps the greatest of tragic actresses that modern England has seen. Some have even preferred her to Mrs. Siddons, and it may be said that she excelled that tragedy-queen in several parts. Mrs.

Siddons doubtless played the Lady Macbeths and similar characters magnificently, and struck terror into her audiences, but Miss O'Neill was more suited to the more gentle and pathetic parts, the Juliets, Ophelias, and Desdemonas. She was born at Drogheda in 1791, and made her debut early in Dublin. On October 6th, 1814, after a most triumphant career in the provinces, the stage of Covent Garden had the honour of being the scene of her first London exploit. She played Juliet, and her fame from that night forward was assured. Nothing could exceed the tumultuous applause which greeted her every performance. Even Mrs. Siddons was declared to be eclipsed. Her stay on the stage, however, was of brief duration, for in 1818 she married an Iiish baronet, Sir William Becher, and retired from the stage the same year. She was the chief mainstay of R. L. Sheil's plays, which were produced during the last few years of Miss O'Neill's theatrical career. In "Adelaide," "Evadne," "The Apostate," "Bellamira," &c., she showed marvellous powers, and was the cause of the success of the plays. That Sheil possessed the imaginative and poetical faculty is certain, but his plays were too high-flown to be genuinely popular; they were, in short, too diffuse and too oratorical in tone, and he was by no means a master of stage effect. Several other eminent actresses of this period would deserve detailed mention if space allowed, particularly the three Misses Kelly. Frances Maria Kelly (1790-1882) was especially famous in some parts, and her namesakes Ann Kelly (1749-1852) and Frances Kelly (born in 1805) were almost equally clever. But we wish to speak particularly of several actresses who distinguished themselves even more, and yet are not so well known to modern readers. Mrs. Bartley was one of the best of these Irish actresses, and her gifts as a tragic actress have been fully recognised by the most competent critics. Her father was an O'Shaughnessy, and her mother, it is said, a daughter of General Dillon, of Galway. She was born, it is believed, in 1783, but her birthplace is not known. Her first appearance on the stage was made while she was a mere infant. After playing at many provincial theatres she was noticed by Harris, of Covent Garden, who at once saw her powers, and engaged her for his theatre, where she made her London debut on October 2nd, 1805, in a comedy part, much against her will, for her tastes leant to tragedy. She was allowed, however, to recite Collins's "Ode on the Passions," which brought down the house and atoned for the coldness of her reception in the play. She began to play tragedy, but was so overshadowed and dwarfed by Mrs. Siddons, then in the height of her great reputation, that she left London and went to Dublin, where she caused a furore. Drury Lane was the scene of her next triumph, and as Mrs. Siddons retired in 1812, Mrs. Bartley was without a formidable rival, until the rise of Miss O'Neill diminished her deservedly great popularity. After delighting the Americans for a time, and making a further success in England as Lady Macbeth, she retired from the stage with a competence, and survived until

MACREADY, WITH AUTOGRAPH.

January 14th, 1850. Various critics have eulogised her, and Leigh Hunt evidently considered her a clever comedy actress, for he says she possessed "a strong and singuar originality, a genius for the two extremes of histrionic talent, lofty tragedy and low comedy." Another critic says she had "a noble and expressive face, a full, strong, and melodious voice, capable of any intonation, and an original conception of her author." On the other hand, Macready did not care for her, and declared she did not possess "the soul" of a great artist.

Among several other excellent actresses of whom little seems to be known were Mary Chambers (Mrs. Edmund Kean), Mrs. Edwin, Mary Ann Duff, and Mrs. Warner. Mary Chambers was a native of Waterford, and was born towards the close of last century. She met the great tragedian, Edmund Kean, in that city, and was married to him there, their son, Charles Kean, being also born there during their stay. Mrs. Kean went on the stage with her husband, and played with him throughout the United Kingdom in various leading characters,

CHARLES KEAN.

and was acknowledged everywhere as an admirable actress. She survived her famous husband some years, and died on March 30th, 1849. Her contemporary, Elizabeth Richards (afterwards Edwin), was probably born in Dublin, where her father and mother were acting, and it was in that city her first successes were gained as a child-actress She came to Covent Garden in 1789, and was cordially received, her style being modelled after Mrs. Jordan's, whose principal parts she assumed and made her own. Though she did not equal that great actress, she was almost the only performer of her time who was able satisfactorily to fill the gap caused by Mrs. Jordan's retirement. In 1791 she had married John Edwin the younger, a celebrated comedian, and after his death, which occurred at a comparatively early age, she exerted herself to gain sufficient in order to allow her to leave the stage. In 1818, having acquired a handsome fortune, she retired, but was obliged to return to the boards in 1821, having been robbed of some thousands of pounds by a dishonest stockbroker who had been entrusted with the money to buy her an annuity. In 1821 she finally left the stage, and lived in comfort till her death, on the 3rd of August, 1854.

Mary Ann Duff was a sister-in-law of Thomas Moore, and was born in Dublin at the end of last century; her maiden name was Dyke. Her chief triumphs were gained in America, where she played with great success with her husband, John Duff, also a celebrated actor, and a native of Dublin. Her death took place in 1832, after she had gained a great reputation as a tragic actress. According to an eminent American writer, she was "a beautiful woman and a celebrated tragedian."

The last of these famous actresses were Mrs. Warner and Mrs. Glover. The first-named was an excellent performer, and has received many high tributes from such eminent and acute critics as Dr. Westland Marston, Percy Fitzgerald, and others; she deserves to be placed very high among the actresses of the century. A native of Dublin, she excelled in severe and dignified tragedy, and till her death in 1854 held a prominent position in her profession. Mrs. Glover was born at Newry in 1781, and made her London debut at Covent Garden in 1797. It was not long before the public became aware of her histrionic powers, her Shakesperean attempts being particularly good. But it was in domestic comedy that she shone most brightly. As Mrs. Malaprop in "The School for Scandal" and as Mrs. Candour in "The Rivals" she reigned supreme. No actress approached her in those parts. She also played the garrulous Nurse in "Romeo and Juliet" inimitably; indeed, all her renderings of old women characters were of

MRS. GLOVER.

the highest order. She made her last appearance at Drury Lane on July 12th, 1850, being then in very feeble health, and played Mrs. Malaprop on that occasion with her usual carefulness and unctuousness, and died, at the age of 70, four days after (July 16th).

Before leaving this group of actresses reference must be made to Catherine Hayes (1820-1861), one of the most entrancing singers of modern times, who appeared at all the principal theatres of London in grand opera, and captivated all her audiences by her operatic singing, and no less by her magnificent rendering of Irish songs.

CATHERINE HAYES, WITH AUTOGRAPH.

Tyrone Power was the natural successor of Johnstone and Moody, and is said to have surpassed them, though that is hardly possible. Tyrone — or, to give him his true and full name, William Grattan Tyrone Power—was born near Kilmacthomas, county Waterford, on November 2nd,

1797. Owing to the death of his father, while her hero was still a child, his mother was seriously embarrassed, and as he had to earn a livelihood in some way, he chose the stage—the most fitting and the easiest occupation for him, he thought. His first important appearance was in Dublin on December 10th, 1817, and it was not till after many provincial wanderings and an American visit that he played to a London audience, which event took place on January 19th, 1824, at the Adelphi. Hitherto he had not specially distinguished himself in Irish characters; it was in February, 1825, he made his mark as an Irish comedian. At various times he played a round of the best-known and most difficult of Irish characters, and likewise "created" many original parts, specially written for him by Lover and others. Lover's "Rory O'More," with Power in the leading part, was produced at the Adelphi, and was the most successful play of the time. Like all Lover's work, this play was brimming over with genial humour. Tyrone Power met with a sad end. He had already been to America several times, and made another journey in 1840. He embarked at New York on March 11th, 1841, on the ill-fated vessel, "The President," on his return journey, but the ship and its passengers were never more seen or heard of. Power was a cultured man and wrote several clever books and some

TYRONE POWER, WITH AUTOGRAPH.

good verse. His literary ability was inherited by his son, Sir William Tyrone Power, the well-known traveller.

Another famous Irish actor of this century perished in the same manner—namely, Gustavus Vaughan Brooke, who was drowned in 1866 while journying to Australia. Brooke was born in Dublin in 1818, and, having adopted the stage as his vocation, soon won his way to a high position. His first London appearance was at the "Vic" (then the Coburg), a second-class theatre at that time, and he did not arouse any great interest. But his opportunity came later on, when Macready engaged him for Drury Lane, which was the principal stepping-stone in his eventful career. Gifted, like Spranger Barry, with a fine presence and an equally fine voice, he enthralled his hearers as Othello, and in similar parts. His unfortunate death deprived the stage of one of its most promising actors, who might have excelled, had he lived, all the other actors of his time.

Passing over many clever actors, and but briefly mentioning such performers as Charles Connor, a well-known delineator of Irish character; James Lacy, an admirable actor, manager of Drurylane for some years; John Bernard, an equally good actor; Edward Fitzwilliam and his sister, Kathleen Fitzwilliam, both of similar excellence; the well-known actor of Irish characters, Richard Malone (better remembered as Malone Raymond), who died January 14th, 1862, after a long connection with the Haymarket Theatre; and, lastly, the two celebrated ballet-masters of Drury Lane, James Byrne, and Oscar, his son, the greatest dancers of the first half of this century—we come to the four chief Irish actors of the last 70 years (leaving out of account those still living). Master Betty was born in Shrewsbury, but his parents were Irish. He went on the stage while a child, and may be said to have gained his best laurels while still of tender years. He was 12 years of age when London first saw him, at Covent Garden, on December 1st, 1804, and on this occasion, such was the eagerness to see so youthful a prodigy that several lives were lost in the crush at the doors. The scene inside the theatre during the evening was fearful; hundreds of people fainted, and the ladies in the lower boxes who had no difficulty in obtaining their entrance, were engaged all the time in fanning those beneath them, who were in a melting condition. Betty's theatrical career was really ended by the time that others are usually beginning theirs; as he grew up most of the interest in him vanished, though he always remained a good and careful actor; and, as he appreciated and accepted the altered situation, he retired from the Stage with a large fortune in 1824, aged 32, living quietly on his ample means until a few years ago, when he died at an advanced age.

The first appearance of Charles Kean in London was at Drury Lane in 1827, but it was some years before he was enrolled among the leading actors of the metropolis. Kean was born in Waterford in 1811, and died in 1868. He was a splendid all-round actor, and few failures attended his efforts. With Phelps and Macready, he shares the distinction of being among the most conscientious of the Shakesperean students and actors of the century. William Charles Macready was a greater actor than Charles Kean, and was more studious in his readings and more original in his methods. As Richelieu in Lytton's play of that name he was unequalled; his "King Lear" was a really magnificent performance, while his, "Werner" in Byron's tragedy was considered a truly marvellous piece of acting and of perfect elocution. He was also greatly admired as "Virginius" in Sheridan Knowles's play, and in the leading character of Gerald Griffin's great tragedy, "Gisippus," a work which has no superior among the dramas produced during the century.

The only actor who approached Macready as "Virginius" was the eminent actor who died in 1885—John Edward M'Cullough. He was born in Derry in 1827, and may, without exaggeration, be termed one of the greatest tragedians of latter years. He acted many parts admirably, but "Virginius" was his most famous impersonation. Finally, among the actors of more recent years Charles Sullivan occupies an honoured place. As an Irish comedian he has had very few equals, and ranks with the best of his predecessors and contemporaries.

Several eminent Irish musicians were connected with the principal theatres of London about the beginning of the century and later on, such as John Moorehead, who joined the orchestra of Covent Garden in 1798, and who composed operas for the same theatre; William Michael Rooke (or O'Rourke, which was his real name), the instructor of M. W. Balfe, who himself sang on the stage, led the orchestra of and composed operas for both Covent Garden and Drury Lane; William Vincent Wallace, whose "Maritana" and "Lurline," to mention but two of his works, are among the most tuneful operas produced in England during the last hundred years; George Alexander Osborne, Henry Grattan Cooke (son of T. S. Cooke, the composer), Mary A. C. Gabriel, and others of less note.

Sheridan Knowles, by his fine plays, "Virginius," "The Love-Chase," and "The Hunchback" naturally heads the list of Irish dramatists of the 19th century. They are now among the English classics, and may very favourably compare with some of the productions of the Elizabethan age. Knowles, who was a Corkman, was an excellent actor, and his histrionic training served him in good stead in after years, when he became a Baptist preacher. Of the other tragic writers of the same period, Sheil and Griffin have already been referred to; Maturin, in spite of Byron's and Scott's admiration for his works, may be dismissed in a line or two as a clever poet, who affected the supernatural in his dramas to a great extent; Sir M. A. Shee's "Alasco" is a good tragedy, but it was never performed, as the Lord Chamberlain thought it too independent in its teachings, and prohibited it; T. C. Grattan's "Ben Nazir" was brought out by Edmund Kean after his powers had begun to fail him, and was doomed, like the actor, to condemnation; Eugenius Roche, as the author of two good plays, may also be included; and John Banim's "Damon and Pythias" is one of the exceptions to the rule that tragedy during these last few generations has been of the dullest kind; finally, Dr. Croly's dramatic work, poetical as it is, must be considered of too gloomy and severe a type to suit the modern taste.

The early writers, like James Kenney, who did their best merely to amuse their readers, are, after all, more popular than the poets whose tragedies either fell flat or pleased only because of their poetic flavour. Kenney's "Raising the Wind" (with its ever-welcome Jeremy Diddler), " Too Many Cooks," "The World," "Oh, This Love," and other comedy-farces and farcical comedies were all extremely successful when produced, at Drury Lane, Covent Garden, and elsewhere in the early part of this century. In the same way, John Till Allingham's screaming farces, such as "Mrs. Wiggins," and the pieces of Edward Irwin, Mrs. S. C. Hall, Thomas Moore, Charles Lamb Kenney, P. P. O'Callaghan, Maurice G. Dowling, J. F. M'Ardle, William Muskerry, and many others, though sometimes amusing and successful, are not, with one or two exceptions, to be compared as literature with the serious productions of previous authors. The works of such excellent writers as Edmund Falconer (1813-1879) whose real name was Edmund O'Rourke; John Brougham (1814-1880), and Joseph Stirling Coyne (1805-1868) require a separate reference. Falconer wrote a good many plays, his most notable being "Peep o' Day," an Irish drama, which was a tremendous success when produced at the Lyceum Theatre, of which he was manager in 1858 and 1861. He was also a very clever actor, and played Danny Mann in "The Colleen Bawn" at the Adelphi. Like John Brougham, he was also a poet, and produced two volumes of poetry. To complete the parallel, he was also a native of Dublin, like Brougham. The latter, however, was a better poet, better dramatist, and better actor than Falconer. Several of his plays will doubtless stand the test of time for many years, while some of his poems are of a very high order of merit. As an Irish character-actor, he also takes high rank. Most of his latter years were spent in America, where he found few rivals. Joseph Stirling Coyne also wrote largely for the stage, many of his plays being successful at the Adelphi Theatre. He was a native of King's County, and gained a good position among London journalists, joining the staffs of several of the most important papers of the metropolis.

Foremost among the dramatists of the day, if popularity is any guide, is Dion Boucicault, who was born in Dublin in 1822. He has been a most prolific writer, and a mere list of his productions would take a good deal of space. Some of these pieces are trivial and unworthy of him, but his best pieces are unrivalled in their way. His first piece, "London Assurance," was brought out at Covent Garden, March 4th, 1841, and is an excellent comedy, and likely to be his most lasting work. The dates of his other most important plays are:—"Colleen Dawn" (September 10th, 1860), "The Octoroon" (November 18th, 1861), "Streets of London" (August 5th, 1864), "Arrah-na-Pogue" (first time in London, March 22nd, 1865), "The Flying Scud" (1866), "Hunted Down" (1866), "After Dark" (1868), "The Shaughraun" (1875). A French version of "Arrah-na-Pogue," entitled "Jean la Poste, or les Noces Irlandaises," ran in Paris for 140 nights, and everywhere "Shaun the Post" was a welcome visitor. Boucicault's powers as an actor are well known; according to the "Athenæum," he "is probably the best stage Irishman that has been seen."

The most poetic playwright of the time is doubtless William Gorman Wills, the son of the Irish poet, biographer, and divine, the Rev. James Wills. W. G. Wills is not only the author of such genuine masterpieces as "Charles I.," "Olivia," and other plays; he is also an admirable artist, and has written some fine novels and poems. He is a native of Kilkenny, and has mostly written for Mr. Irving. Other Irish dramatists of the day who have produced excellent plays are Miss Clotilde Graves (a native of Buttevant, county Cork), Percy Fitzgerald, Justin Huntly M'Carthy, Hubert O'Grady, and a few others of lesser note.

DION BOUCICAULT.

Some prominent Irish actors have yet to be mentioned before closing this account of Irish drama and acting in London. Barry Sullivan, the great tragic actor, was born in Birmingham, but made his first appearance in Cork in a travelling company, playing on that occasion the singing part of Young Meadows in Bickerstaffe's "Love in a Village." Since that time the provinces have almost wholly monopolised him, his appearances in London being few and far apart. But at Drury Lane, some years ago, he astonished London by the intensity and power of his acting, more especially in the parts of Richard III. and Beverley in "The Gamester." An actor of almost equal power is Shiel Barry, who was born in county Kildare, and made his first appearance in 1859 in Australia as Dr. O'Toole. His first triumphs were in Irish characters, but in February, 1878, he joined the company at the Folly Theatre (now Toole's), and played Gaspard, the miser, in the opera of "Les Cloches de Corneville," and made a distinct and remarkable success. The "Daily News" of September 3rd, 1878, says:—"Few who have ever heard it will forget the guttural laugh of Mr. Sheil Barry in his powerful delineation of the miser—a performance which belongs to the very highest order of eccentric comedy."

Among the comedians of the period, John Lawrence Toole, who first appeared at the Adelphi on December 27th, 1858, takes high rank. Though born in London, he is of Irish parentage, and, we believe, of Irish sympathies. Charles Groves, an excellent comic actor, born in Limerick in 1843, also comes into our survey; while other very clever actors, as Charles Coghlan, J. D. Beveridge, Dominick Murray, the late George Hodson, Harold Kyrle Bellew (son of J. C. M. Bellew), George Power, and similar performers are among the most important Irishmen connected with the Stage in very recent times. Among the Irish actresses of note may be mentioned Ada Crehan (the Irish-American actress known as Ada Rehan, a native of Limerick), Helen Barry (a good melodramatic actress, born in England), Rose Coghlan, sister of the comedian above referred to; Rose Bishop (née Egan); Kathleen Irwin, a very capable singer; Margaret and Maude Brennan (the latter of whom has played Ophelia to Irving's Hamlet); Henrietta Hodson (now Mrs. Labouchere), and her sister Kate Hodson, daughters of George Hodson; and, lastly, Kate and Mary Rorke, both admirable actresses, of Irish Catholic parentage.

Nor must we forget to mention, in completing

our review, the well-known operatic and other singers, such as Andrew John Foley (Signor Foli), Barton M'Guckin, Leslie Crotty, William Ludwig, Clara Merivale, Donnell Balfe, Helen D'Alton, Plunket Greene, and Bernard Lane; and the distinguished composers—Sir Arthur Sullivan (of Irish parentage, his father being a Thomas Sullivan and his mother a Mary Coghlan), James Hamilton Clarke (now of the Haymarket), Professor C. V. Stanford, James L. Molloy (a native of King's County), Miss Hope Temple, and others of less renown.

CHAPTER XXVI.

IRISH LITERARY MEN IN LONDON.

OR the last three centuries London has been the chief literary centre for Irishmen. Either as novelists, poets, dramatists, journalists, or historians, they have made London, if not their home, their vantage-ground, and its reading public their first study. To the majority of our countrymen the most eminent Irish writers are familiar names, but those who have helped to make English journalism the power it now is, who have been concerned in all its successes, and responsible for a considerable share of them, and who have, in a sense, consented to partly or wholly obliterate themselves in the anonymous journalism of the past and present— are little known to the general and perhaps even to the studious reader. In this and the following few chapters it will be our task to give, for the first time, a comprehensive and sympathetic account of them and their labours.

Before the introduction of the newspaper proper there were, of course, Irish literary men in London. Such were the dramatists, the Southernes, Farquhars, and others mentioned in former chapters; the poets like Denham and Roscommon, to mention but two; and one or two philosophers and divines. Novelists were, strictly speaking, unknown in England, and the only works published in those days were the political and philosophical pamphlets, the poems—no matter how short—and the dramatic works of various celebrities; all published separately, be it remembered, for want of the vehicle of a newspaper or other means of reaching the public. An aggrieved individual in those times, instead of, as now, airing his grievances in the columns of a congenial newspaper, issued his "brochure" to the world; and such was the comparative dearth of literature, that it was doubtless read. Steele found this state of things in existence when he conceived "The Tatler."

A remarkable group of Irish literary men were living at this period, including William Molyneux, the author of the splendid indictment of English rule in Ireland—"The Case of Ireland Stated;" John Leland, the philosopher, whose works, though of a heterodox nature, evidence his immense learning and ability; Dr. George Berkeley, the great propounder of the Idealistic Philosophy; Thomas Parnell, the tranquil poet; and Dean Swift, the unapproachable master of irony and of scorn. Swift has often been compared with Voltaire as a satirist, but they were as wide apart as the poles upon nearly every point. One thing they had in common, a hatred of injustice and tyranny. As satirists, they differed in their methods; Voltaire aimed to make his opponents, or

LELAND.

the abuses he satirised, as ridiculous and absurd as possible, believing in Ridicule as a mighty weapon; while Swift tried to make his objects of attack as contemptible as possible, by depicting them in the blackest colours.

Steele posed as a social censor in his "Tatler," and not as a political satirist or advocate, or as a personal satirist. But his journal necessarily referred in some way, chiefly indirectly, to the public events of the period. As previously the most common disseminator of news was rumour, news passed by word of mouth through the city, and, exaggerated by each new teller, was discussed in the various coffee-rooms by the beaux and wits over a cup of Mocha or a game of whist. "The Tatler" made its first appearance on the 12th of April, 1709. It was a single folio double-columned sheet, and was published every Tuesday, Thursday, and Saturday. The first four numbers were given away gratis; afterwards, the price was a penny. For some time it was written by Steele only, and it was not until the seventieth number or so that Addison commenced to aid the editor. The sheet was wholly taken up by delightful bantering of the ridiculous fashions of the day, by keen analysis of the theatrical performances, or by an occasional critical study of Milton or Shakespeare, and an infrequent dissertation on political events.

The venture was a great success; the circulation increased rapidly, and it became a steady source of income for Steele. When later on Addison gave the paper the benefit of his acute criticisms, moral reflections, and keen irony, it still further increased its influence and circulation.

HUGH KELLY.

But the credit of founding it, and all the innovations it contained, are due to Steele alone; and moreover, some of the finest of the essays are also his. As Austin Dobson has said—"For words which the heart finds when the head is seeking; for phrases glowing with the white heat of a generous emotion; for sentences which throb or tingle with manly pity or courageous indignation, we must turn to the essays of Steele." And the same pleasant writer remarks:—

"The whole life of the time is mirrored in its pages. We see the theatre, with Betterton and Bracegirdle on the stage, or that 'romp,' Mrs. Bicknell, dancing; we see the side-box bowing 'from its inmost rows' at the advent of the radiant 'Cynthia of the minute;' we hear the shrill cries of the orange-wenches, or admire the pert footmen keeping guard over their mistress's bouquets. We see the church with its high pews, and its hour-glass by the pulpit: we hear, above the rustle of the fans, and the coughing of the open-breasted beaux, the sonorous periods of Burnet or Atterbury; we scent the fragrance of Bergamot and Lavender and Hungary-water. We follow the gilded chariots moving slowly round the Ring in Hyde Park, where the lackeys fight and play chuck-farthing at the gates; we take the air in the Mall with the Bucks and Pretty Fellows; we trudge after the fine lady, bound, in her glass chair, upon her interminable 'how-dees.' We smile at the showy young Templars lounging at Squire's or Serle's in their brocaded 'night-gowns' and strawberry sashes; we listen to the politicians at White's or the Cocoa-Tree; we company with the cits at Batson's, and the Jews and stockbrokers at Jonathan's. We cheapen our Pekoe or Bohea at Motteu's China Warehouse; we fill our boxes with musty or 'right Spanish' at Charles Lillie's in Beaufort Buildings; we choose a dragon cane or a jambee at Mather's toy shop in Fleet-street; we ask at Lintot's or Tonson's for 'Swift in Verse and Prose;' we call for the latest 'Tattler' at Morphew's by Stationer's Hall. It is not true that Queen Anne is dead; we are living in her very reign; and the Victorian era, with its steam and its socialism, its electric light and its local option, has floated away from us like a dream."

Swift, who had used the name of Isaac Bickerstaffe, now appropriated, with his consent, by Steele, had ridiculed the almanac-makers of his day, especially one of them named Partridge. He predicted that this individual would die at a certain hour on a certain day—and when the fateful hour arrived, and Partridge did not die, Swift was not in the least disconcerted, but calmly declared that his prediction was fulfilled. Partridge protested that he was not dead, but Swift was inexorable, and the wits, seeing the joke, kept it up, with the result that elegies were written on Partridge, his last moments were minutely described, and even the Stationers' Company applied for an injunction against the almanacs that were published under the name of Partridge. It was to this humorous affair that Steele alluded when, in his introduction to the "Tatler," he said— "It is impossible for me to want means to

STERNE.

entertain—(the public), having, besides the helps of my own parts, the Power of Divination, and that I can, by casting a figure, tell you all that will happen before it comes to pass." But he adds that he will use his power "very sparingly, and not speak of anything till it is passed, for fear of divulging matters which may offend our superiors."

"The Tatler" ran to 271 numbers, and was almost immediately followed by "The Spectator," the first number of which came out on March 1st, 1711. This was in its turn succeeded by "The Guardian" (March 12th, 1713), "The Englishman" (6th of October, 1713), "The Lover" and "The Reader" (1714), "Town Talk" (1715),

"The Tea-Table" and "Chit-Chat" (1716), "The Plebeian" (1719), and "The Theatre" (1720). In some of these ventures Steele had the active assistance of Addison; but they were mainly written by their projector. His work may be easily identified: all his contributions are signed "R." or "T."; Addison's signature was one of the following letters—C., L., I., O. Steele was of a most inventive turn of mind, and all the improvements and the finest ideas of the different publications were due to him. He conceived the idea of the "Visions," which Addison worked out so successfully; he created Sir Roger de Coverley, and left his collaborator to take the credit of the invention; he was probably the first literary critic of the day, and by his short stories may be considered the true founder of the English novel; he strenuously opposed duelling, gambling, and other vices, and was the first English writer to rescue the name of woman from the degradation to which it had been brought by the writers of the Restoration, and for his chivalrous defence of them deserves, as Thackeray says, their good-will and affection.

Among the principal occasional contributors to Steele's periodicals were Swift, Berkeley, and Parnell. The latter only wrote one or two things; and Berkeley, a firm friend of Steele's, was not a frequent contributor, "The Guardian" being the journal for which he mostly wrote. Swift helped Steele in many ways, until he became a Tory, when he transferred his allegiance to other journals. To "The Examiner," a weekly sheet brought out on the 3rd of August, 1710, he constantly contributed.

HUGH BOYD.

In this paper appeared his remarkable essay on " The Art of Political Lying," which has a strange interest for the present-day reader on account of its applicability to certain statesmen. It is couched in Swift's best vein of keen irony, and one or two of its most piquant passages will be doubtless appreciated by the students of present politics. Thus, after remarking that the devil, called "the father of lies," was expelled from heaven for insubordination," where (as Milton expresses it) he had been viceroy of a great western province," he adds—"But although the devil be the father of lies, he seems, like the great inventors, to have lost much of his reputation by the continual improvements that have been made upon him. Who first reduced lying into an art, and adapted it to politics, is not so clear from history, although I have made some diligent inquiries. . . . . It has been the guardian spirit of a prevailing party. . . . . It gives and resumes employments, can sink a mountain to a mole-hill, and raise a mole-hill to a mountain; has presided for many years at committees of elections; can wash a blackmoor white; make a saint of an atheist, and a patriot of a profligate; can furnish Foreign Ministers with intelligence, and raise or let fall the credit of the nation." And again—"Some people may think that such an accomplishment (as lying) can be of no great use to the owner, or his party, after it has been often practised and is become notorious; but they are widely mistaken. . . . As the vilest writer has his readers, so the greatest liar has his believers; and it often happens that, if a lie be believed only for an hour, it has done its work, and there is no further occasion for it. Falsehood flies, and truth comes limping after it, so that when men come to be undeceived it is too late; the jest is over, and the tale has had its effect; like a man who has thought of a good repartee when the discourse is changed or the company parted; or like a physician who has found out an infallible medicine after the patient is dead."

Among the many eminent Irish writers contemporary with or succeeding Swift we may particularise Dr. Samuel Madden, the scholar and author of a notable work, "A Memoir of the Twentieth Century;" Henry Brooke, the author of "The Fool of Quality" and other admirable works; Dr. Thomas Leland, the distinguished historian; Charles Johnstone, the clever author of "The Adventures of a Guinea," an unjustly-neglected novel; and lastly, Laurence Sterne, whose everpopular "Tristram Shandy" and "Sentimental Journey" place him among the greatest of the masters of English fiction.

Oliver Goldsmith is known to the world all over as a novelist, dramatist, and poet of supreme excellence. But it is principally as an essayist— in short, a journalist—that we refer to him here. His first work in this direction began in 1757, when he reviewed books for "The Critical Review" and "The Monthly Review." In 1759 he favoured "The Bee" and "The Busybody" with some admirable essays, and some poetic attempts, including the clever imitation of Swift, known as "The Logicians Refuted," and the comic "Elegy on Mrs. Mary Blaize." His most important work in this way was his inimitable Letters of the Chinese Philosopher, famous as "The Citizen of the World," which were commenced early in 1760 in the "British Magazine," and ran on into 1761. They appeared twice a week, and Goldsmith obtained a guinea each for them. At this time he was also editor of "The Lady's Magazine," and wrote some "serious" biographies for "The Christian Magazine," edited by the unfortunate Rev. Dr. Dodd, afterwards hanged for forgery. Goldsmith's other works were published separately, and few of them equal "The Citizen of the World" for wit, vigour, and irony. In the guise of a Chinaman resident in England, he comments delightfully on English follies, prejudices, and vices, and passes shrewd and humorous remarks on their time-honoured but somewhat "played-out" institutions. Goldsmith reached almost his highest powers in some of these essays, which are too familiar to need quotation.

MADDEN.

Two of the most vigorous political writers of the period were Hugh Boyd, one of the reputed authors of "The Letters of Junius," and Hugh Kelly, the dramatist. The former has not, despite his great powers and his reputation, left any work of importance to posterity; Kelly is best known as a playwright and as a poet, but his political writings exercised considerable influence, and earned him the hatred of his opponents. He conducted a paper called "The Babbler," and in its columns fulminated with great effect against the Opposition. Arthur Murphy was more a man of letters than a journalist, yet he edited "The Gray's Inn Journal" for a couple of years. It is by his dramatic work, however, and by his classical translations and his biography of Dr. Johnson that Murphy will be remembered. The greatest journalist of that age was undoubtedly Sir Philip Francis, assuming (as we have a right) that his identity with the mysterious "Junius" is practically certain. The famous "Letters" appeared in the "Public Advertiser," a prominent journal of the time, during 1769-1772, and by their unsparing treatment of the Ministers then in power caused an immense sensation. It may be mentioned that people at the time of publication considered them to be the work of an Irishman, for Junius, in No. 29, answers a correspondent who attacked the race in attacking him, and refers to the "unremitted rancour" shown by the Governmental party towards Ireland, "a nation which we well know has been too much injured to be easily forgiven." And, in another letter (No. 35), he exclaims that "the Irish have been uniformly plundered and oppressed. In return, they give you every day fresh marks of their resentment."

CHAPTER XXVII.
IRISH LITERARY MEN IN LONDON.

EDMUND BURKE was one of the leading figures in the literary world at the time of the publication of the "Letters of Junius." His masterly works, mines of deep thought and lofty wisdom, were among the greatest productions of that era. His journalistic connections are not so well known. He first contributed to a somewhat obscure journal, entitled "The Englishman," and then to the "London Evening Post;" afterwards beginning that admirable summary of the year's events known as "The Annual Register," now a most valuable work of reference. Its earliest numbers were largely written by Burke. Many years afterwards another Irishman of note—Marmion W. Savage—conducted the same publication. But Burke was not a journalist proper, as so many great writers have been. His great works were issued separately and might not have attracted so much attention as they did were they merely republished articles. The essay on "The Sublime and Beautiful" is useless as an authority, but its fine style and the remarkably profound maxims scattered through its pages render it a valuable contribution to the literature of England. The "Reflections on the French Revolution," "Thoughts on the Present Discontents," and the "Letter to a Noble Lord" are masterpieces of subtle reasoning, eloquence, and felicitous phraseology, and are certainly his most important tracts; yet his speeches, perhaps, remain his greatest, as they are his most famous, productions.

His friend and countryman, R. B. Sheridan, did not possess the methodical habits or the powerful mind of the philosopher, or the works he has left to posterity might have been larger in extent and even more brilliant than they are. A few dazzling speeches, some sparkling witticisms, and some witty plays are his sole contributions to the world's literature. They are splendid proofs of his genius, but they are less numerous than one would wish, or than they might have been, if his inexhaustible mind had been further stimulated and more fully sounded. Had he actively followed a journalistic career he would have ac-

EDMOND MALONE, WITH AUTOGRAPH.

quired method and perseverance; but if, as has been said Genius is but "an infinite capacity for taking pains," Sheridan possessed little of it. His journalistic work was small in amount and not particularly able. Beyond a few contributions to the "Morning Chronicle," a paper which has had associated with its fortunes a remarkable number of clever Irishmen, a little assistance he rendered to "The Jesuit," a short-lived paper started by himself in 1782, with anti-Tory principles and ultra-Liberal tendencies, and a not inconsiderable number of articles in the "Morning Herald," Sheridan has contributed very little to the Press.

Towards the close of the century several Irishmen became very prominent as journalists. Apart from Isaac Jackman, who edited "The Morning Post" (commenced in 1772) for some years; William Cooke, editor of a daily paper—"The General Advertiser"—but better known as a poet and as the friend of Goldsmith; and Edward Quin, of whom we shall have occasion to speak presently —apart from these comparatively minor writers, there were George Canning, John Wilson Croker, and Thomas Moore. The last-named became, before the close of the century, tolerably well known. Once his powers were proved he joined the staffs of three newspapers—"The Morning Post," "Morning Chronicle," and "The Times"—to which he wrote numberless stinging squibs, in the form of epistles, odes, and epigrams, which were immensely successful, and earned him a pension of £300 a year from the delighted Whigs, for whom he laboured. So successful were his political satires that we find "The Morning Chronicle" saying, in September, 1815, a few days after his "Epistle from Tom Cribb" had appeared in its columns:—"We have had so many and such incessant applications for the paper which contains the exquisite 'jeu d'esprit' that we shall reprint it to-morrow."

Some of these skits will hardly bear quotation now, when the lapse of time has somewhat blunted their point; but that they are clever, let the following few lines from one of them testify: it is entitled "An Occasional Address for the Opening of the New Theatre of St. Stephen's; intended to have been spoken by the Proprietor in full costume" (i.e., The King):—

This day a new house, for your edification,
We open, most thinking and right-headed nation!
Excuse the materials, though rotten and bad,
They're the best that for money just now could be had;
And if echo the charm of such houses should be,
You will find it will echo my speech to a T
As for actors, we've got the old company yet,
The same motley, odd, tragi-comical set;
And considering they all were but clerks t'other day,
It is truly surprising how well they can play.
Our manager (he, who in Ulster was nurst,
And sang "Erin Go Bragh" for the galleries first,
But, on finding Pitt-interest a much better thing,
Changed his note of a sudden to "God Save the King").

In taking my leave now, I've only to say
A few " seats in the house " not as we sold away,
May be had of the manager, Pat Castlereagh.

Some of the other skits of the lively little poet are still better, but would require too much elucidation of their meaning to render them quotable. Moore was in such demand among editors that when Brougham, then a leader-writer on the "Times," fell ill, he was asked by Barnes, the editor, to take his place at £100 a month. But the poet refused the offer, and preferred to express his witty contempt in verse. His most formidable foes were a few Tory writers like Canning, Croker, Maginn, not to mention English "tomahawkers" such as Gifford, Hook, Frere, and others. Canning was one of those who started the "Anti-Jacobin; or Weekly Examiner," in November, 1797, a journal which lasted about nine months. It was followed by a monthly publication, "The Anti-Jacobin Review and Magazine," which lasted from 1798 till 1821. For the former Canning wrote his most inimitable squibs and parodies, including his "Loves of the Triangles," a mathematical poem in imitation of the poet Darwin, and his burlesque play, "The Rovers," ridiculing Schiller's "Robbers." To the same paper he contributed his famous Sapphic

Ode, an imitation of Southey—"The Friend of Humanity and the Knife-Grinder." The philanthropist begins by pointing out the dilapidated condition of the itinerant tradesman:—

> Needy knife-grinder! whither are you going?
> Rough is your road, your wheel is out of order;
> Bleak blows the blast—your hat has got a hole in it.
> So have your bre ches.

And, sympathising with him, he inquires how he came to this pass, and wishes to know whether he has been the victim of the squire, the parson, or the lawyer; then asks him whether he has read Paine's "Rights of Man," and finally expresses a wish to hear his sad story. The knife-grinder replies—

> Story! God bless you! I have none to tell, sir!

except that while drinking in "The Chequers" he became involved in a drunken quarrel, and was roughly handled. He adds—

> I should be glad to drink your honour's health in
> A pot of beer, if you will give me sixpence;
> But, for my part, I never love to meddle
> With politics, sir.

To which the "Friend of Humanity" indignantly responds by kicking the Knife-grinder, overturning his wheel, and departing "in a transport of republican enthusiasm and universal philanthropy, remarking before his exit—

> I give thee sixpence! I will see thee hanged first—
> Wretch, whom no sense of wrongs can rouse to vengeance—
> Sordid, unfeeling, reprobate, degraded,
> Spiritless outcast!

The object of this vigorously written journal was, to use Canning's words in the preliminary notice, "a contradiction and confutation of the falsehoods and misrepresentations . . . which may be found in the papers devoted to the cause of sedition and irreligion, to the pay or principles of France." In short, it was to combat Republicanism, or at least the French idea of it, with what Canning considered were its natural concomitants—irreligion, licentiousness, and other reprehensible things. "Of Jacobinism," he said, "in all its shapes and in all its degrees, . . . we are the avowed, determined, irreconcilable enemies."

John Wilson Croker was a far more unscrupulous Tory than Canning, and used the "poisoned dagger" often and without hesitation. As early as 1801, Croker wrote a series of letters on the French Revolution to the "Times." When the "Quarterly Review" was started in 1809, by William Gifford, Croker became the most biting critic, and the most unrelenting and envenomed partisan-writer on the staff. The famous critique on Keats's poetry, though it did not kill the poet, deeply pained his sensitive nature; and when Croker was accused of the death of Keats, he replied that he merely sprinkled a little salt over him, and that it was Gifford that added the pepper. Croker was most likely the anonymous

J. W. CROKER, WITH AUTOGRAPH.

critic of the "Quarterly" who, reviewing an excellent epic poem, declared that it was the best epic published that week. But Croker, though his ability was as conspicuous as his literary dishonesty, met more than his match in Maginn. The latter had profound contempt for the distinguished Tory, his brother-in-arms, and did not hesitate to express it on one occasion. Croker, when in the height of his career as a Tory Minister, gave a dinner to his Tory brethren, Maginn being one of the guests. Having hopes of a peerage, Croker told his guests that he was of English descent, his ancestors originally belonging to Lyncham, in Suffolk, and he thought of taking the title of Lord Lyncham. To the intense disgust of Croker, Maginn suggested, as a more appropriate title, that of Lord Penny-a-line-em.

Maginn's first journalistic experience in England was gained on a virulent Tory journal, "The John Bull," said to have defended everything that was indefensible, to which he was introduced by Theodore Hook. His great abilities were quickly recognised, and when John Murray, the publisher, started "The Representative," a daily paper, which was a disastrous failure, Maginn was appointed its leading foreign correspondent. It was not till some years had passed that Maginn finally reached the position he had so fully earned, of chief writer on several of the most important journals of England. To that part of his literary labours we shall not refer at present, leaving it till we come to deal with the periodicals in question.

Several excellent writers of the last century,

not usually considered as journalists, may also be briefly noticed here. Such were Leonard M'Nally, for some time editor of the "Public Ledger;" Colonel Isaac Barré, a trenchant political writer; and Paul Heffernan, editor of some ephemeral periodicals, and an author of ability. There were also several eminent scholars (besides the numerous minor authors) who occasionally favoured the Press with evidences of their erudition. Among

MAGINN, WITH AUTOGRAPH.

these were the two great scholars, Edmund Malone and Dr. Adam Clarke, both of whom survived into this century. The former was admittedly one of the keenest of Shakespearean commentators, while Dr Clarke, by similar labours on behalf of the Bible, is considered one of the greatest interpreters of Holy Writ that ever lived. Malone was a native of Dublin; Dr. Clarke hailed from Derry. Their labours have enormously increased our knowledge—in the one case, of early English literature; in the other, of ancien Scriptural history.

DR. ADAM CLARKE.

Towards the close of the century a group of lady novelists suddenly appeared on the scene. Maria Edgeworth, the forerunner of Scott and other "national" writers, produced her clever novels, now somewhat faded; Lady Morgan began her career as a poetess, but soon changed her role for that of the novelist; and it must be said that she is more Irish than Maria Edgeworth, who wrote like an unemotional Englishwoman; and Lady Blessington, an inferior writer, but a more captivating person, also blossomed into a national novelist in publishing her "Repealers." They were followed by Regina Maria Roche, the authoress of "The Children of the Abbey," and the two Misses Porter, Jane and Anna Maria, the first well known by her "Scottish Chiefs" and 'Thaddeus of Warsaw."

Three of the most distinguished Irish journalists of the period were Eugenius Roche, Edward Quin, and Colonel Robert Torrens. Roche was born in Paris, of Irish parents. After a sojourn in France, where he was educated, he came to London, and became prominently identified with the Press. He was a part-editor of the "Morning Post" from 1817 to 1827, and had been editor of a daily paper, "The Day," of a weekly one, "The National Register," and of a magazine entitled "Literary Recreations," and afterwards conducted "The Courier" (changed to "The New Times"). In "Literary Recreations" Byron and Allan Cunningham made their first appearance as poets. Roche was not only a vigorous political writer, but was also

EUGENIUS ROCHE WITH AUTOGRAPH.

a clever poet and dramatist, a volume of his poems being published after his death. For "The Courier" he wrote many admirable articles on economical and political matters, and at his premature death in 1829 a large amount was subscribed for his wife and children. He had embarked in a newspaper enterprise on the understanding that he was to receive £1,000 a year for his services as editor, but the project turning out a failure, he found himself liable for a large amount of money, which so affected him that his death was the result. He had been first a reporter, and underwent a year's imprisonment for libelling the Government. Among the most effective contributors to "The Courier" under his editorship was the vindictive J. W. Croker, who wrote for it some biting verses, political and personal.

"The Traveller," primarily an organ of the commercial travellers, became in the hands of Colonel Torrens and Edward Quin a powerful and influential journal. Colonel Torrens was a brilliant economical and social reformer, and a very good journalist. He was born in Ireland in

1780, and died in 1864. He had served with great distinction in the Peninsular War, and, turning his attention to politics, was counted one of the soundest reformers of the day. He became part-proprietor of "The Traveller," and wrote largely for it. It was an evening paper, and had a large circulation. Quin was its editor, and contributed many powerful articles to its columns, his knowledge of financial matters being very extensive. Several works of his, on social and economical questions, still repay perusal. It is interesting to note that J. S. Mill's first appearance in print was in "The Traveller," and that it was Quin who accepted Leigh Hunt's earliest essays "with gaiety," to use the essayist's own words, while he, as he says, offered them "with fear and trembling." Colonel Torrens afterwards abandoned "The Traveller" and started "The Globe," for which he wrote frequently and vigorously.

Apart from journalism, there were many eminent writers. Sir Martin Archer Shee published his "Rhymes on Art" and his "Alasco," the first of which was emulated in after years by another eminent artist, Henry O'Neill, A.R.A., in his "Age of Stucco" and similar poems. Maturin brought out his unearthly novels and plays, written in the ranting German style, and modelled after Kotzebue; Croly's "Salathiel"

SIR MARTIN ARCHER SHEE.

and similar eloquent romances, produced at the same time, contrast strangely with his grave and solemn historical and religious essays, and his vitriolic articles in the "Times" and other papers; and R. L. Sheil and Charles Phillips's gorgeous orations were very popular and count as literature, the latter also publishing several poems; the former also, in conjunction with William Henry Curran, the son of the great orator and wit, writing in "The New Monthly Magazine" a graphic and altogether brilliant series of articles on the Irish Bar, which alone entitles them to rank as writers of a superior order. Nor, in concluding this chapter, can we omit a reference, however brief, to Peter Finnerty (who died in 1822), and Mark Supple (who died in 1807), able reporters, both attached to the "Morning Chronicle;" Michael Nugent, of the "Times," and John O'Dwyer and Morgan O'Sullivan, of the "Morning Herald," to mention only those who have, by their undoubted ability, assisted so largely in extending the influence and improving the condition of the newspaper Press.

CHAPTER XXVIII.

IRISH LITERARY MEN IN LONDON.

ONE noticeable point in connection with the 19th century writers is that they all, in one way or another, have been contributors to one or other of the multitudinous periodicals of the century. There is no writer, no matter how high his reputation, or of what subject he is a master, who has not occasionally appealed to the reading public through the medium of a periodical publication. And probably the majority of the eminent authors of the last fifty or sixty years have kept up regular communication with some particular journal. The most famous monthly magazine of the early years of the present century was, doubtless, "Blackwood's," started in 1817, its first editor being Professor John Wilson (better known as Christopher North), a poet, critic, and novelist of great popularity in Scotland. Soon after its inception William Maginn wrote the inimitable papers styled "The Life and Adventures of Adjutant and Ensign O'Doherty," which were so highly esteemed that Maginn was invited by the publisher to join the permanent staff. For more than ten years Maginn illuminated the pages of this periodical with his inexhaustible wit, and surprised even his most learned readers by his profound erudition. Other Irish writers began to contribute to it, and their incisive articles, flashing wit, and vigorous satire greatly helped to win that immense influence which "Blackwood's" undoubtedly possessed. T. C. Croker wrote poetry and antiquarian papers for it; Dr. Croly made onslaughts on the Whigs and Radicals of the day; John Fisher Murray contributed witty sketches to its pages; the Rev. James Wills gave to the world some of his clever poems through it; Jeremiah Daniel Murphy wrote some few translations, evincing his great knowledge of the foreign and dead languages; Dr. Anster also contributed poetry to it; and Sir Samuel Ferguson not only wrote his witty "Father Tom and the Pope" for "Blackwood's," but also published therein his "Forging of the Anchor" and one or two more of his finest poems; and Bartholomew Simmons very frequently contributed his warlike ballads to its pages. Moreover, J. J. Callanan, introduced to its editor by Maginn, in whose school at Cork he had been a tutor, also wrote spirited poems for it; Samuel Gosnell sent occasional prose and poetry, including his "Daniel O'Rourke," in six cantos; Edward Quillinan some clever sketches and poems; and, lastly, Charles Lever wrote one or two of his most inimitable works for this remarkable periodical. Some differences having arisen between Blackwood and Maginn, the latter ceased to write for the magazine, and this quarrel or disagreement led to the starting in

THOMAS COLLEY GRATTAN, WITH AUTOGRAPH.

1830, by Hugh Fraser, of the magazine which still bears, like "Blackwood's," its founder's name. Maginn became editor, and gathered round him not only the most brilliant wits in Ireland and Scotland, but also authors like Dickens, Carlyie, and Thackeray. Francis Mahony commenced his famous "Reliques of Prout" in its pages, after a year or two, and, with the aid of Francis Stack Murphy, produced an unrivalled series of polyglot translations, and Dr. Kenealy likewise gave the magazine the benefit of his learning and humour in similar exercises. To it also Maclise contributed that fine collection of life-like portraits of eminent living celebrities, known as "The Fraserians," which are so astonishingly well done that if he had left only that work he would still be one of the great artists of the century. Samuel Lover, T. C. Croker, and others were among its other contributors; and in more recent times William Allingham has edited it, writing for it the admirable papers signed "Patricius Walker" also his longest poem, "Laurence Bloomfield in Ireland;" Frances Power Cobbe, one of the clearest and most convincing of living dialecticians, and a native of county Dublin, being among the most frequent of its later contributors. It succumbed a few years back, unable longer to compete with its numerous and more go ahead rivals.

The great morning dailies of the early years of the century were "The Times," "The Morning Chronicle," and "The Morning Herald." The first of these journals has an Irish record which is unrivalled for everything that is venomous, vile, and unscrupulous. Though its opinions on most other subjects have changed more than once, it has preserved its consistency so far as Irish affairs are concerned, as its opinions on Ireland and Irishmen have ever been of the most deadly hostile character. Of its early editors, the most remarkable was Edward Sterling, a native of Waterford, whose powerful articles caused great attention and earned him the title of "The Thunderer," first given to him, we are told, by Carlyle. Under the "nom de plume" of "Vetus" he wrote many acute articles to various periodicals. But, like a later Irish editor of the "Times," he was even more remarkable for his tact and business capacity than for literary ability. Among the most brilliant contributors of this once influential journal during the earlier part of the century were Dr. Croly, Vincent Dowling (a clever journalist who was born in Queen's County), his son, Vincent G. Dowling; Alexander Knox, the eminent theological writer; Sir George W. Dasent, a scholar still living, profoundly versed in Scandinavian literature and language, who was born at St. Vincent of Irish parents, and who became one of the assistant editors under Delane; the Hon. Mrs. Norton, who contributed to its columns a series of letters on the English factory system and its disadvantages; and the versatile Matthew James Higgins, who wrote very frequently for it during twenty years under many pseudonyms, including the following—"West Londoner," "Civilian," "Paterfamilias," "Providus," "A Belgravian Mother," "A Thirsty Soul," and the one by which he is best known, "Jacob Omnium." John Thaddeus Delane, its most famous editor, was born in England, but his father, William Delane, was an Irishman, and had been connected with the Press for some years before his son's connection with the "Times." During John Delane's editorship the paper reached its highest point, and since that time it has rapidly deteriorated. Delane's skill, shrewdness, and energy kept the paper ahead of all others, so far as news was concerned, and his enterprise and the perfection of its machinery combined to give it a power such as no other paper ever enjoyed. Among its special correspondents were, as is natural when hazardous work is to be done, many Irishmen. Dr. William Howard Russell, the veteran of the present day, and the "doyen" of war correspondents, wrote for it those marvellous descriptions of the events of the Crimean war, which are as realistic and as thrilling as any battle-picture painted on canvas, and which will live as valuable contributions to historic literature. Dr. Russell is a native of Dublin, and still a power in journalism. Another war-correspondent of the "Times" was P. J. Meagher, a Corkman, who had gained some fame in his native city by his poetical abilities. In later times Frank Power, a native of Dublin, chronicled in its columns the gloomy tale of the invasion of the Soudan, where he perished, and its sequel of rapine and bloodshed; and the Hon. Lewis Wingfield, son of Lord Powerscourt, described the siege of Paris for its readers.

JOHN DELANE.

Charles Roger Dod, a native of Leitrim, heads the list of the "Times'" Parliamentary reporters, and a journalist of great promise, Edward Michael Whitty, also served on its Parliamentary staff for some time. He was born in London in 1827, and was the son of Michael J. Whitty, proprietor of "The Liverpool Daily Post" and "Liverpool Journal." When only 18 or 19 he received an appointment on "The Times," and remained there for three years. He wrote several very brilliant books, including two on the scenes in several Parliamentary Sessions. He died in Australia in April, 1860, soon after his arrival in Melbourne. The only other contributors to the "Times" we propose to mention are James Godkin, a vigorous journalist, an Ulsterman, who was its Dublin correspondent for a long period; O'Reilly, its famous Paris correspondent, who unmasked one of the greatest frauds ever contemplated, for which feat the "Times" has always received great credit; Robert O'Hara, an able draughtsman in the Irish Office, who often wrote to it on the Irish land question, and who died at the age of 40 on September 14th, 1885, and William Edward

H. Lecky, the great historian, who formerly wrote an occasional article for it. The gang of anti-Irish Irishmen of the present day who have succeeded in finally discrediting this paper do not deserve to be mentioned, unless with loathing. The libels of "The Times" against the present Irish leader are not much more venomous or more unfounded than those it flung at O'Connell, against whom, his biographer tells us, it published over 300 leading articles. The worst of these libels, it is humiliating to relate, were written by an Irishman—"Father Prout."

R. R. MADDEN, WITH AUTOGRAPH.

In O'Connell it found more than its match, just as it has found a superior in more modern times.

An important rival of the early "Times" was the "Morning Herald." It was edited for some years by an Irish journalist of proved ability—Robert Knox, at one time connected with the Dublin Press, and a member of the renowned "Comet Club," formed of contributors to the libellous "Comet," a satirical and personal Dublin periodical. The "Morning Herald" had many Irishmen on its staff at the various stages of its career, including Isaac Butt, John Sydney Taylor, whose earnest denunciations of vandalism, and whose powerful appeals in favour of the preservation of many old churches and chapels threatened with destruction, were efficacious, and enable us still to admire the many fine examples of mediæval architecture in the country; Michael Desmond Ryan, a native of Kilkenny, a musician and a poet, who acted as its musical critic for some time; the Parliamentary reporters mentioned at the close of the last chapter, and two others—viz., Joseph O'Leary, author of "Whiskey, Drink Divine" and other poems, and William Bernard M'Cabe, author of some works of fiction; and, finally, John Frazer Corkran, a native of Dublin, who acted as its Paris correspondent for eighteen years, who was well known as a writer of drama, poetry, fiction, and history, and who died in February 1884.

The "Morning Chronicle" was a Whig or Moderate Liberal paper. Its best editor was a Scotchman, named John Black, who had got together a brilliant staff, including some writers then unknown, who were destined to future fame, among them being Dickens, one of the Parliamentary reporters. Its foreign editor, under Black, was Andrew Doyle, who, having married the daughter of the proprietor, replaced Black as editor in 1843. Doyle had some mistaken notions of economy, and Dickens found some difficulty in disposing of his humorous sketches, which Black had gladly accepted, and paid for at a moderate rate. By his first work Dickens made a great stir, and as he was going to Italy he offered Doyle a series of weekly letters embodying his impressions of the country, but Doyle thought Dickens's terms too high, and refused them. Annoyed at the fancied slight, Dickens wrote no more for the "Chronicle," and this refusal really led to the foundation of the "Daily News," with Dickens as editor, in 1846, where the "Pictures from Italy" daily appeared. Doyle gave up the editorship of the "Chronicle" in 1847, and was appointed to an important official post in Ireland. He died on December 14th, 1888, aged 79, leaving a son, John A. Doyle, author of a valuable work on "The English in America." Andrew Doyle's policy ruined the "Morning Chronicle," for the "Daily News" soon supplanted it. He was a convincing writer and a sound thinker, and during his connection with the paper a large number of Irishmen were on its staff. Some of the more important of them may be mentioned. One of its best foreign editors was Michael Joseph Quin, a good novelist and poet, with a wide experience of foreign countries and foreign affairs; its musical critic for a time was Michael D. Ryan, already referred to; George Sydney Smythe (seventh Lord Strangford, and son of the translator of Camoens)

J. S. KNOWLES.

wrote brilliantly for it; as also John Lalor, the author of a work on "Emigration," and a powerful writer; Thomas Wallis, the editor of Davis's poems, and one of the Academic Young Irelanders; and Joseph Pollock, son of the United Irishman and writer in the "Press" of the same name, were each of them on its staff. Besides these there were Joseph Archer Crowe, W. B. M'Cabe, and others of note among its later Parliamentary reporters; George Higinbotham (a native of Dublin, who afterwards won reputation as a lawyer and politician in Australia); Dr. R. R. Madden, who commenced his career on this paper; W. B. Sarsfield Taylor, brother of the J. S. Taylor previously mentioned in this chapter; and Martin Haverty, who succeeded Dr. Charles Mackay as assistant-editor; and some others not so distinguished also wrote for it in various capacities. Thomas Hughes, the song-writer, who died in 1849, was for some years its Spanish correspondent, and Eyre Evans Crowe, for a short time its Paris correspondent, ultimately wrote its most brilliant leaders, only rivalled by those of his colleague on the same journal, William Torrens M'Cullagh (now known as W. M. Torrens).

"The Literary Gazette" has an interest for Irish readers in that it was the paper to which Griffin wrote some of his earliest productions, and as being the first publication out of Ireland to which Maginn contributed. It was one of the first genuine reviews of the century. The "Quarterly" and the "Edinburgh Review" contained, under the guise of book-reviewing, what were really only intended as personal articles or political attacks, the former magazine being in the interest of the Tories, and the latter devoted to the Whigs. The "Literary Gazette" aimed to be, and was, a genuine critical review, irrespective of party. It was a weekly publication, and contained original articles on various subjects, as well as poetry and serial sketches. In its columns appeared some of the witty papers of Samuel Gosnell, a clever Corkman, and also the once popular "Hermit in London," by Captain Felix M'Donogh, a talented writer, of Irish parentage, whose "Irish Gentleman in London" added to the great reputation he had won by his previous work, and who died in London in 1836.

"The Athenæum," started in 1828, supplanted the "Literary Gazette," and exists in undiminished strength and influence to-day. Its chief characteristic has been its hostility to Irish literature; it has rarely said a good word for an Irish writer, and, so far as we can discover, has still more rarely spoken a generous word of praise for an Irish Catholic writer. As there have been at all times a considerable number of Irishmen connected with it, this may appear strange, but it is nevertheless true that its severest and most unjust criticisms have been directed against Irish literature. John Sterling, son of the Captain

Edward Sterling above mentioned, was its editor for many years, and Dr. Doran acted as assistant-editor for a goodly period. His contributions to it were numerous, as were those of T. C. Croker, Lady Morgan, Miss L. S. Costello, Mrs. Jameson, Sir G. L. Staunton, Dudley Costello, Daniel Owen Madden, and other well-known writers. John Banim, James Sheridan Knowles, George Darley, Frances Browne (the blind poetess of Donegal), Lady Clarke (sister to Lady Morgan), A. O'Shaughnessy, and William Allingham, have all contributed poetry to it, some of them, such as

DR. ANSTER, WITH AUTOGRAPH.

Allingham, Frances Browne, and George Darley, very frequently. The last of these was a native of Dublin, and was a very distinguished poet; one of his brothers, William Darley, also being connected with the "Athenæum" as art critic for some time previous to his death at Paris in 1857; another brother, Charles, who died in June, 1861, holding at his death the post of Professor of Modern History and English Literature at Cork. Other Irish writers to the "Athenæum" included Isaac Weld, a scientist of repute, and a Dublin man; Julia Kavanagh, the novelist; Dr. William Cooke Taylor, the historical writer; Dr. R. Madden, the well-known biographer; "Father Prout," Professor T. Cliffe Leslie, the eminent political economist; and Dr. George Alexander Richey, from 1875 till his death in December, 1883.

Unlike the two journals last dealt with, "The Examiner" discussed politics as well as literature. Marmion Savage, the delightful author of three excellent novels—"The Bachelor of the Albany," "The Falcon Family," and "Reuben Medlicott"—was its editor for a few years. In 1867 William M'Cullagh Torrens purchased the paper from Fonblanque, and carried it on till 1870, but it was a failure. Torrens had been one of its most able writers, and Eyre Evans Crowe another, when John Forster was its editor, during its palmiest days of success, Dudley Costello (a clever artist, and brother of Louisa Stuart Costello) being then its sub-editor. In spite of the fact that many of the best writers of the day, including Irishmen as distinguished as Prof. John Elliott Cairnes, an authority on political economy, and Irishwomen as clever as Frances Power Cobbe were on its staff, the "Examiner" finally perished in 1880.

Probably the two most distinguished of what are called "service" journals are, or have been, Colburn's "United Service Gazette" and "The Army and Navy Gazette." As a matter of course, where war is concerned Irishmen are always "to the fore." As editor of the first-named journal for more than fifteen years, Major T. H. S. Clerke is deserving of some notice. He was a native of Bandon, county Cork, and, after

MATTHEW JAMES HIGGINS. ("JACOB OMNIUM.")

a military career of distinction, became a military journalist, and was universally considered an accurate and very effective writer. "The Army and Navy Gazette" was projected and edited by Dr. W. H. Russell, the premier war correspondent already alluded to. It is probably the best journal of its class ever founded, and has become a valuable property to its owner. One of its contributors we should mention—namely, John Augustus O'Shea, who, without exaggeration, may be termed one of the most brilliant journalists of the day, and who wrote for it, if we are not mistaken, some of his "Military Mosaics," or tales of a similar military character. In conclusion, we may remark that in dealing with the principal writers connected with the journals touched upon in this chapter, we have referred to the most eminent Irish authors the period embraced. Our next task is to speak of the remaining portion of the contemporary Press and those of our countrymen who are or have been identified with it.

CHAPTER XXIX.

IRISH LITERARY MEN IN LONDON.

MOST Irish writers of this century, as already stated, have been connected with London as journalists, or in other capacities. Yet the fact remains that the principal members of the Young Ireland party, and others who, though not recognised members of that famous group, were greatly influenced by its teachings and example, are, as regards London, altogether out of our survey. A truly national literature, independent of English support, was founded through their efforts, and intended primarily for Irishmen alone. If they had, following the usual course, drifted to London, they would almost certainly have helped merely to swell the already immense volume of Anglo-Irish literature, written chiefly for English minds. Previous Irish writers, even those who were considered most national, instead of addressing their own countrymen, sought their audiences in England only, and in most cases deferred largely to English taste and prejudice. The writings of the men and women of 1848, considered for their lofty teachings alone, would still be immortal, just as the brilliant examples they set and the fact that

"They kindled there a living blaze
Which nothing can withstand,"

have, quite apart from their works, entitled them to the highest praise and admiration of the people of Ireland. In giving the names of the most prominent Irish journalists and other writers who have been identified with the periodical literature of the last half century or so we naturally treat of the leading Irish literary men of that period. The starting of "Punch" in 1841 gave opportunities to some of the cleverest Irishmen of the time of displaying their powers of wit and humour. Among its earliest contributors were several whose names are familiar to Irish readers. J. S. Coyne wrote for it, as did also Dr. Maginn, and to its columns Dr. Kenealy sent his well-known Greek version of "Sweet Castle Hyde." Joseph O'Leary, seeing a worthy subject of satire in the foibles of the middle-classes, worked that vein with much ability, enriching "Punch"

with many striking poems and sketches, his pet theme being that individual who is amusing rather than awe-inspiring—the English traveller and sightseer abroad. Although only 19 years of age at the time of the inception of "Punch," Richard Doyle was invited to join the staff, and he it was who designed the familiar front page or cover of the new periodical. For years his charmingly unconventional drawings graced its pages, and it was only when his religion and the head of the Catholic

HARRY FURNISS.

Church were ridiculed that he threw up his connection with it. Henry Plunkett Grattan was another of its early Irish contributors, and John Leech also executed for it some of the finest of its cartoons, then as now one of its principal features. In very recent times its Irish contributors have, we think, been fewer, and less notable. Alfred Percival Graves, whose poems evince such an intimate acquaintance with the social life of the Irish people, has written for it; and one of its present mainstays is a writer who is doubtless Irish—E. J. Milliken, well-known as the author of "Childe Chappie's Pilgrimage," and of some of the cleverest verse appearing in the leading comic journal. Finally, its present inimitable caricaturist, Harry Furniss, is a native of Wexford, and therefore must enter into this comprehensive account. He has hardly any superior among living caricaturists in the art of hitting off likenesses of the most notable Parliamentarians, who have been his chief study.

Prior to the foundation of "Punch," there was but one paper which could be compared with it for cleverness of caricature and abundance of satire. That was the "Satirist," which possessed one or two clever draughtsmen and some wits of the first order among its contributors, but which was, generally speaking, a libellous publication. Some of its best satirical drawings were done by William Henry Brooke, probably a native of

Dublin. He was a portrait painter of great merit, but excelled as a book illustrator, among his efforts in that line being his designs for Croker's "Legends of Killarney." He died in 1860. No other English comic paper has surpassed, or even equalled, "Punch" in the matter of artists. But one, still in existence, has been almost monopolised by Irish artists, resembling the leading comic paper in that respect. The best cartoonist of "Fun" was Paul Gray, a Dublin man, who was born in 1842, but died in 1866 before his powers had fully developed. As a wood-engraver and comic designer, his talent was conspicuous, and his early death deprived the world of art of a most promising genius. The most important artist, perhaps, who has been identified with "Fun" in more recent times is J. F. Sullivan, who still does the chief pictorial work of the paper. No one, it is pretty certain, has more mercilessly and more ably satirised with the pencil the abuses and red-tapeism of officialdom and the glaring misuse of power by the vested interests. His facile pencil has always keenly depicted the various little faults and peculiarities of the "British working man," and he has earned the displeasure of a section of the working class by his irresistibly comic but sometimes exaggerated descriptions of their habits.

RICHARD DOWLING.

Another paper, called "Judy," far inferior in most things, deserves mention here from the fact that one of its best-known artists, W. G. Baxter, who recently died, was an Irishman by birth, and because Miss Clo Graves, a clever young Irish writer, who has made a reputation as a poetess, is one of its leading contributors at the present moment.

Of the literary and literary-political papers several deserve slight mention. The "Saturday Review," though bitterly anti-Irish in politics, is generally impartial in literary matters. Its most prominent Irish contributors in the past and present have been George Sydney Smythe (seventh Lord Strangford), a very brilliant writer on foreign affairs, W. J. Loftie, the eminent antiquary, a native of Armagh, who has written for it for some years, and Oscar Wilde. "The Academy"

is a purely literary journal, and among its most eminent Irish reviewers may be noticed William O'Connor Morris (the Irish judge), and Sir Richard F. Burton, the great traveller and scholar; its learned correspondents including such fine scholars as Whitley Stokes, the Rev. Dr. B. M'Carthy, and Standish H. O'Grady. "The Spectator' requires little reference here, although we believe Richard Holt Hutton, its scholarly editor, is an Irishman, and although Alfred P. Graves has been one of its contributors. For the "Guardian," W. J. Loftie wrote frequently and learnedly; and to "Notes and Queries" several Irishmen of note— W. J. Fitzpatrick and John Eugene O'Cavanagh, for example—have frequently written, and it has also had the advantage of the editorship of Dr. John Doran during many years.

One or two of the old monthly magazines also demand a little attention at our hands. "Bentley's Miscellany" was edited by Dr. Doran for a time, and in its pages a large number of Irishmen contended for public approbation. "Handy Andy" first appeared in it, and the following are a few of its principal poets:—F. S. Mahony, Dr. Kenealy, J. A. Wade (the author of "Meet me by Moon-

DR. W. H. RUSSELL.

light alone" and many other popular songs), Dr. W. Cooke Taylor, Dr. Maginn, John Sheehan ("the Irish Whiskey Drinker"), and Samuel Lover; Charles Lever writing fiction for it. The "Temple Bar" of the present day is a worthy descendant of the defunct "Miscellany." "Tinsley's Magazine" is another instance of a vastly popular magazine whose success has been largely won by an Irish editor and by many able Irish contributors. Its editor for a lengthy period was Dr. W. H. Russell, and in its pages appeared his amusing novel, "The Adventures of Dr. Brady;" John Augustus O'Shea, Edmund Downey ("F. M. Allen"), Richard Dowling (the powerful novelist and essayist), James Fitzgerald Molloy, Percy Fitzgerald, T. C. Irwin, W. B. Guinee, the clever poet and novelist, and, lastly, Justin M'Carthy, being a few of its best-known Irish writers who are still living. Joseph Sheridan LeFanu, one of the most weird of novelists, and a humorist of good type, was the most conspicuous of its past Irish contributors. In

"Cornhill" appeared some of Charles Lever's ablest novels, one or two of "Father Prout's" wittiest poems, and several graceful novels by Justin M'Carthy, whose genius G. A. Sala did not much exaggerate when he described his stories as perhaps the most delightful ever written. Of present contributors to "Cornhill," Miss Mary Geoghegan is probably the most interesting to Irish readers. This clever poetess is the daughter of an Irish poet whose name is familiar to every reader of Irish literature— Arthur Gerald Geoghegan—and she bids fair to equal even his high poetical qualities. Before dealing with the Daily Press, a word or two must be spared for reference to Charles Dickens's "Household Words" and "All the Year Round." Lovers of Irish literature owe a debt of gratitude to the great novelist for his encouragement of youthful Irish poets and novelists, some of whom have since attained a great reputation. John Francis O'Donnell was one of these writers; William Allingham was another Irishman who received many kindnesses from Dickens ; and finally Rosa Mulholland wrote for his journal some of her earliest and most idyllic stories, notably "Hester's History," "The Late Miss Hollingford," "The Wicked Woods of Tobereevil," and one or two shorter works. And we cannot conclude our reference to the monthly and other magazines without mentioning in terms of praise Dr. J. F. Waller's able essays and poems in "Cassell's Family Magazine."

Among the daily papers, the "Daily News" has been most remarkable for its Irish writers. Its first number came out on January 21st, 1846. Its earliest editor was Dickens; its politics were described as advanced Liberal. The eminent novelist only edited seventeen numbers, having grown quite tired of editorial duties, and John Forster became its acting editor for a short time. Towards the end of 1846, Eyre Evans Crowe was appointed editor, and filled that post with great success. As a forcible and sparkling leader - writer he had won his reputation ; and William M'Culigh Torrens was another of its most effective contributors. Justin M'Carthy, who preceded John Morley as editor of a daily paper of some vogue at one time—"The Morning Star"—

RICHARD ASHE KING.

also joined its brilliant band of writers later on, and among other Irish writers at various times have been Lady Blessington, Thomas Wallis, Dudley Costello, James Godkin, E. L. Godkin (now an American editor), E. M. Whitty, and others. Its foreign correspondents, at one time or another, included Dr. Lardner (Paris), "Father Prout" (Rome), and at this moment its Paris correspondent is Mrs. Emily Crawford, a brilliant Irishwoman. Thackeray advised G. M. Crawford, who formerly held the post, if he ever married, to choose an Irishwoman, there being, as he said, "No such good wife as a daughter of Erin." Crawford took his advice, and married the distinguished lady who succeeded her husband as Paris correspondent. As for the famous "specials" who have served on the staff of the "Daily News," their names are familiar to all careful readers of recent events. The thrilling story of the Bulgarian Atrocities, which roused the world, was sent to its columns by J. A. M'Gahan, the son of Irish parents, but of American birth. Another of its "specials" was Edmund O'Donovan, who saw many remarkable sights in foreign lands, and through the columns of this paper acquainted the world with them. James J. O'Kelly (now M.P.) chronicled several important wars in the "Daily News," and ranks as one of the most dashing of military journalists; and John Murphy completes the list of its Irish special correspondents. Its two most prominent Dublin correspondents have been Daniel Owen Madden and Martin Haverty.

"The Daily Telegraph" has not had many distinguished Irishmen on its staff. W. H. Russell was its most notable Irish special; and two others of some repute have been the Hon. Lewis Wingfield, who described in its columns the siege of Paris and other stirring events, and Lord Dunraven, who acted as its correspondent during part of the Franco-German and Abyssinian Wars. A well-known Dublin journalist, Edward O'Farrell, was sub-editor of the "Telegraph " for some years, and W. H. K. Wilde, a clever son of Lady Wilde, is at present on its staff as leader-writer. Finally, it was to the "Daily Telegraph" that Sir Charles Russell contributed his able articles, afterwards republished as " New Views on Ireland." The "Standard" was started on May 21, 1827, as an evening paper, its chief purpose being to oppose Catholic Emancipation—or, more correctly, to oppose O'Connell. Its first editor was Dr. Stanley Lees Giffard, a vigorous writer, and a native of Ireland (whose son is now Lord

Halsbury, Lord Chancellor of England). The Irish writers connected with its fortunes since that day have been many, and we may mention the most prominent of them. Richard Brinsley Knowles, son of the dramatist, became an important member of its staff in 1857, when he was just 37 years old. His connection with it did not last long, however, for his Catholic feelings (he had reverted to his father's original faith) could not tolerate its No-Popery attitude, and he resigned his position, and was followed by the editor, Dr. Brewer, who wholly approved of his conduct and shared his sympathies. R. B. Knowles contributed to dramatic and other literature, and died on January 28th, 1882. He became before his death editor of the "Weekly Register," the "Illustrated London Magazine," and the "London Review." Other Irish writers on the "Standard" were Michael Desmond Ryan, its musical critic, who was followed in the same capacity by his son, Desmond L. Ryan, whose death occurred quite recently; Francis Power Cobbe, one of its leading writers on social questions; and John Augustus O'Shea, who was its special correspondent during the Franco-German War and Siege of Paris. Mr. O'Shea has seen a good deal more danger and has witnessed more exciting historical scenes than many more showy "specials," and for graphic narrative power is hardly surpassed by any. He is a native of Nenagh, county Tipperary, and was born in 1840. Of the present contributors to the "Standard" only two need be mentioned—Frederick Boyle, the novelist, who, we understand, is an Irishman, and Austin Kelly, one of those clever journalists whose names are not so well known to the public as they deserve to be.

JOHN AUGUSTUS O'SHEA.

The only Irishmen of ability whom we are able to connect with the "Daily Chronicle" are Charles Williams, who acted as its "special" during the Egyptian campaign, and who is a native of Coleraine, and Robert Whelan Boyle, its present editor, an accomplished writer, but unknown outside the journalistic field.

The "Morning Post" has been somewhat more lucky in its Irish auxiliaries. Besides those mentioned in the previous chapter, it has had as editor Nicholas Byrne, who immensely improved its circulation, and who, so far as business capacity went, was perhaps its best editor; as musical critic it had the services of Michael D. Ryan; and as poet, Robert Stott, of Dromore, who may be said to have succeeded Moore as laureate of the paper. R. B. Knowles was also on its staff; J. C. M. Bellew wrote occasionally for it; Frank Hugh O'Donnell was one of its recognised leader-writers for some time; Henry M. Dunphy, who died a month or two ago, was chief of its Parliamentary reporters, and was connected with it for more than 40 years; and, lastly, Miles Gerald Keon, author of some novels and other works, and an Irishman, was one of its foreign correspondents during a long period. One or two distinguished Irish journalists are identified with the "Morning Advertiser," the organ of the licensed victuallers. An Irishman named John Byrne was its editor for a great number of years, and was succeeded by his son, of the same name, who became secretary of the Newspaper Press Fund, and who died on January 6th, 1887. Its most important Irish special has been Charles Williams, already mentioned.

We may mention here that Dr. Kenealy edited for some years a vigorous paper entitled, "The Englishman," which reached an enormous circulation, but which succumbed after Kenealy ceased to write for it.

The evening papers are mostly of recent origin, and the "Globe" is, we fancy, the oldest of those now published in London. We will refer only to its Irish editors, and that very briefly. Its first editor was Colonel Robert Torrens, a well-known political and economical writer, and a soldier of distinction; but its most talented editor has been F. S. Mahony, "Father Prout" who wrote all kinds of matter, literary, political, and otherwise, for its columns, and was also its Paris correspondent for some years. One Philip (?) Moran was its best sub-editor, and the paper owed its palmiest days of success to his efforts in its behalf. He was thought to be very wealthy, yet when he died not a sixpence of his was discovered, and he appears to have had no relatives. Doubtless other clever Irishmen were in some way or other connected with the "Globe," but we have mentioned the most remarkable. The most recent of the London evening papers, "The Star," is edited by T. P. O'Connor, than whom no more brilliant writer can be found, and there are other fine writers on its staff. It is incomparably the most sparkling, the liveliest, and the best written of the evening journals, and has some real humorists among its contributors.

George Bernard Shaw, the clever author of "An Unsocial Socialist," "Cashel Byron's Profession," and other novels of equal power and brilliancy, writes some of its musical criticisms, and displays in his "pars," that thorough unconventionality and charm of style so characteristic of his more finished work. He was born in Dublin in 1856, and came to London in 1876, and is now one of the leaders of a remarkable group of Socialistic writers and thinkers, which includes some of the best and most promising writers of the day, among whom we may particularly mention H. Haliday Sparling, who is not only intimately acquainted with Ireland, her history and literature, but who is also partly Irish himself, and a clever journalist.

One of the editors of the "Evening Standard" has been Charles Williams, and its Paris correspondent for some years was J. F. Corkran, both of whom have been already referred to. Of the "Evening News" Charles Williams is at present, we think, editor; a clever sub-editor of the paper, Stephen J. M'Kenna, having died a few years back (January, 1883). The "Pall Mall Gazette" heads the list of evening papers so far as eminent contributors are concerned, John Morley having been its most notable editor. M. J. Higgins ("Jacob Omnium") was a frequent contributor to it, as were also G. S. Smythe (seventh Lord Strangford), a fine linguist and a diplomatist of great and often proved ability; and his son, Percy William Smythe (eighth Lord Strangford), an authority, like his father, on foreign affairs.

LADY WILDE.

Of recent and living contributors, two may be particularly noted—Lady Wilde and her gifted son, Oscar Wilde. Lady Wilde will be ever remembered by her spirited and splendid poems, written during the stormy era of '48. She has written much since that period that will live, and it is gratifying to be able to state that she is as National in feeling as ever. Oscar Wilde has also been a frequent writer in the columns of the "Pall Mall," his contributions being chiefly of a critical character. He was born in Dublin in 1856, and was educated at Trinity College and at Oxford. He is now the editor of the leading English journal for women, "The Woman's World," to which a large number of contemporary Irish female writers have contributed. Excepting the editor, no one of the male persuasion ever enters the charmed precincts of its pages. From 1885 to 1888 the reviewer of the "P. M. G." was G. B. Shaw.

There are many society papers that not only manage to exist in London, but some of which have immense circulation. The best known of these is, perhaps, "Truth," edited by Mr. Labouchere. It has several Irish contributors, among whom may be mentioned Mrs. Emily Crawford, its Paris correspondent; and Richard Ashe King, a native of county Clare, and author of some exceedingly clever Irish novels, such as "The Wearing o' the Green," "A Leal Lass," and others, published under the pseudonym of "Basil," by which pseudonym, it may be remarked, he is known to the readers of "Truth" as a reviewer. "The Field" is very popular among the squires and country gentlemen, and had as its editor for 30 years an Irishman named J. H. Walsh, who died in April, 1888; John Leech also contributed to it some admirable sporting sketches, which are among his happiest efforts. "Bell's Life," an important sporting paper, was edited from 1824 to 1851 by Vincent George Dowling, his son, Francis L. Dowling, succeeding him in the post, and filling it till 1867. It has been a noted supporter of the prize ring and kindred "sports." During the Chartist agitation a journal which caused great attention by the vigorous style of its articles and its persistent advocacy of the freedom of the Press was "The Poor Man's Guardian," edited for a time by a most able writer, James Bronterre O'Brien. He fought valiantly against the stamp duty, and worked manfully for other reforms which were eventually granted, and which seem no longer very wonderful or advanced now that we have got them. O'Brien wrote and published a good deal of poetry, and was a polished and cultured writer. Of the other papers intended solely for the aristocratic or the educated classes, we will mention only two—the "World" and "Nature." The former may be dismissed in a word, for beyond the fact that George Bernard Shaw is its art critic, we are not aware of any other notable Irish contributor to it; the latter journal has had a good many Irishmen among its writers. One of its most eminent contributors is or was Professor John Tyndall, perhaps the greatest living authority in England on Light, Sound, and Heat. He is a native of Leighlinbridge, county Carlow, and is one of the most eloquent and poetical prose-writers of the day. Another constant contributor is a very clever lady, an Irishwoman and a Catholic, Agnes M. Clerke, who has written some remarkable scientific works, and whose sister, E. M. Clerke, is also a clever writer in prose and verse. "Nature" is the leading scientific organ of the three kingdoms, and circulates largely among the students of science all over the world. Of the pictorial Press, the "Illustrated London News," rather than the "Graphic," comes first for our purpose. The latter has had no conspicuous Irishmen on its staff to our knowledge; on the other hand, the first editor of the "Illustrated London News" was an Irishman—F. W. N. Bayley (a clever poet, known as "Alphabet" Bayley, from the number of letters before his name); John Leech and Pierce Egan the younger (1814-1880) illustrated it for some time; Samuel Lover sent it verses and sketches now and again and John Sheehan and Joseph Sterling Coyne wrote occasional articles for it, the former writing a weekly article for some short time previous to or about 1863. The "Pictorial World" deserves slight notice, inasmuch as it was to its columns that Frank Power contributed his clever sketches and drawings of the Soudan, and as the paper in which some of Richard Dowling's finest essays and stories appeared. Dowling, it should be said, is native of Clonmel, and is, even on the evidence of a hostile critic, equal to Victor Hugo as a word-painter and in the power of vivid description. In concluding our notice of the present-day periodical literature, we cannot omit a slight reference to "Macmillan's Magazine," in which Annie Keary's "Castle Daly" and other works appeared; the "Gentleman's Magazine," which has numbered among its most important contributors James Roche, Justin M'Carthy, and Percy Fitzgerald; and the following weeklies—the "Weekly Times," to which Dr. R. Shelton Mackenzie (a native of Limerick) wrote for some years, his pseudonym "Little John" being retained by his successors; the "Sunday Times," of which J. S. Coyne was long the dramatic critic; and the "Weekly Dispatch," wherein some of Richard Dowling's most characteristic articles, &c., appeared, and whose Paris correspondent is Mrs. Crawford, already introduced into this chapter.

T. P. O'CONNOR.

There are a number of remarkable Irish men and women who might have been referred to in connection with certain of the magazines and periodicals, but whom we prefer to deal with separately. Such are Stopford A. Brooke, the eminent critic and poet; Richard Barry O'Brien, the learned historic writer; Mrs. Cashel Hoey (a native of Dublin county), Mrs. Charlotte Riddell nee Lawson, born at Carrickfergus), Mrs. Beatrice M. Croker, Elizabeth Owens Blackburne Casey (a native of county Meath, better known as Ellen O. Blackburne), May Crommelin, Alice Corkran, Letitia M'Clintock, and several other female novelists of equal power and fame; A. H. Bullen, the greatest living authority perhaps on the early Elizabethan poets, and a son of George Bullen, the head of the Printed Book Department of the British Museum; Prof. James Bryce, the distinguished writer on foreign affairs, who is a native of Belfast; James Fitzgerald Molloy, and Edmund Downey, both clever novelists, the latter a native of Waterford; Crawford, the novelist, who is a son of Thomas Crawford, the Irish-American sculptor; and others not perhaps so distinguished, but still deserving of notice did space allow.

In concluding our task of chronicling the intellectual triumphs of the Irish of London we have only to say that we have sought to make our work as complete as possible, even at the risk of excessive detail, for many of the new facts of importance contained in it would certainly have been lost for ever if not rescued at once by some more or less competent hand. In its entirety, we think that we may fairly claim that this book, despite its many imperfections, affords proofs of the most convincing character, if such were needed, that the sons and daughters of Ireland, despite grievous disadvantages, and almost unique persecution, are capable of the highest intellectual development; and whilst marvelling at the enormous share which their genius has enabled them to take in the literary, scientific, and artistic life of Britain, we may fervently hope that the day is not far distant when those brilliant attainments may be utilised for the benefit of their widowed motherland, no longer a province, but, in all its essentials—

"A NATION ONCE AGAIN!"

CONCLUSION.

CORRECTIONS, EXPLANATIONS, AND ADDITIONS.

This Series of Articles involved a great deal of research, which was continued after their publication in the "Evening Telegraph" and during their preparation in pamphlet form. A desire to secure the greatest possible accuracy, as these Articles are the first attempt to tell the history of the Irish in London, must be an apology for the following formidable list of corrections and additions.

Pages 4 and 12.
SHAKESPEARE'S CAPTAIN MACSHANE.—This is a slip for Captain "MacMorris."

Page 14.
HUGH KELLY.—Native of Killarney, not of Roscommon.

Page 20.
LETTERS OF "JUNIUS."—The date should be 1769-1772, not 1796.

Page 29.
ROYAL SOCIETY.—Robert Boyle was never President, and Carbery was probably not Irish.

Page 35.
STATUE OF J. S. MILL.—This work, it appears, was not done by Foley, but by Woolner.

Page 37.
EMINENT CORKMEN.—There are several mistakes in this list. Willis should be "Willes," and Sainthill was an Englishman, born at Exeter; whilst Arthur O'Leary and Millikin were not natives of the city itself, but of the county.

Page 39.
WILLIAM COLLINS, R.A.—His father was an author, but not the carver and modeller—a quite different William Collins.

Page 39.
G. B. O'NEILL.—His picture is entitled "The Foundling," and it may be noted, as a curious fact, that he was himself a foundling.

Page 40.
W. C. STANFIELD, R.A.—Born at Sunderland, not at Birmingham.

Page 42.
ST. PAUL'S CHURCH.—Here were also buried W. Havard and Jack Johnstone.

Page 42.
KITTY CLIVE.—More likely to have been born in London than in the North of Ireland.

Page 43.
DRURY-LANE THEATRE.—Other Irish managers were G. Falconer and James Lacy.

Page 45.
HEADING OF CHAP. VIII.—Omit "Covent Garden and its neighbourhood."

Page 49.
ST JOHN'S GATE.—Garrick's first appearance " in London," it should be made clear, took place in this building.

Page 51.
FATHER OF MRS JAMESON.—Not G. B. Murphy, but " D." B. M.

Page 57.
CASTLE-STREET.—Is close to Mortimer-street, but does not actually run out of it.

Page 65.
KILLINOE should be "Kylinoe."

Page 65.
KENSAL GREEN.—E. Palcome and R. Doyle also buried here. The fine tomb to James Ward, R.A., was executed by J. H. Foley.

Page 71.
MRS. DELANEY.—Her name was "Mary," not "Margaret."

Page 73.
ROYAL COLLEGE OF PHYSICIANS.—Sir R. A. Churnside should be "Chermside."

Page 74.
SCOTLAND YARD.—Sir C. Cowan—a misprint for Sir C. "Rowan."

Corrections, Explanations, and Additions.

Page 83.
W. M. RORKE should be W. M. "Rooke."

Page 84.
LORD CARBERY.—Was probably Welsh; his family name was Vaughan.

Page 84.
CHILLIANWALLAH.—For "Indian Mutiny" substitute "First Sikh War."

Page 90.
RICHMOND CHURCH.—F. Cotes, R.A., also buried there.

Page 92.
IRISH WORKS IN BRITISH MUSEUM.—"Nearly every book" should be "nearly every important book."

Page 93-94.
IRISH OFFICIALS.—O'Shaughnessy was of Irish blood it is certain; it is doubtful if he was of Irish birth. J. Bullin is a native of Ireland.

Page 99.
BRIEN'S HARP.—Not in R.I.A., but in Trinity College, Dublin.

Page 114.
P. TURNERELLI.—Reference to his portrait was, of course, overlooked, after portrait had been omitted.

Page 116.
POETS IN WESTMINSTER ABBEY.—For "former" read "first-named" (i.e., Congreve).

Page 122.
PARLIAMENTARY REPORTERS.—Several errors have crept in here. Sullivan should be "O'Sullivan"; Joseph Sheehan should be "John" Sheehan; Crowe's second name was "Archer"; the second name of W H Russell should be "Howard"; and "Dold" should be "Dod". Other Irish reporters should be Sir C. Russell, T P. O'Connor, Charles Phillips, and J. S. Knowles.

Page 125.
JOHN LACY.—Under portrait, "James" should be "John." He was of Irish origin.

Page 128.
DR. SHERIDAN.—Born most probably in 1684.

Page 131.
MACKLIN'S PLAYS.—They were played before they were actually published, a fact which explains the apparent inconsistency of the passage as it stands. The word "wrote" should be therefore omitted.

Page 131.
LUKE AND ISAAC SPARKS.—Luke was a tragic actor, Isaac a comedian.

Page 133.
BRERETON.—For "John" read "William."

Page 133.
MIDDLETON.—Real name James Magann; born in Dublin in 1768; died October 18th, 1790, aged 31.

Page 135.
BICKERSTAFFE.—Swift borrowed the name from a Dublin locksmith's door.

Page 141.
MRS EDWIN.—For "Obliged to return to the boards in 1821," read "Obliged to return to the boards soon after."

Page 143.
MUSICIANS.—M. A. "A." Gabriel should be M. A. "V." Gabriel. To this list should be added the names of John Field, the great violinist; Joseph A. Wade, Sir J. A. Stevenson, Virginia Balfe, daughter of M. W. Balfe; W. H. Glover, F. S. Clark, John Clegg, and F. Robinson.

Page 145.
LIVING COMPOSERS.—To these should be added Sir R. P. Stewart, Prof. Arthur O'Leary, Prof. S. Glover Andrew Levey, and Joseph Robinson.

Page 145.
JOHN "LELAND" should be John "Toland."

Page 145.
ACTORS AND ACTRESSES.—To those mentioned might be added several, one or other of whose parents were Irish, as Lester Wallack, who recently died; Lawrence Barrett, and Jennie Lee.

Page 160.
ROBERT "STOTT" should be "Thomas" Stott.

Page 162.
CRAWFORD.—That is, Frances Marion Crawford.

INDEX.

A.

Abernethy, Dr J, 45, 47, 48
"Academy," 158
Academy, Royal, 71, 101-111.
Academicians, Irish, 110
Addison-road, 61
Adelphi Theatre, 35
Admirals, Irish, 87, 115
Admiralty, 74
Agar, Archbishop, 116, 117
Aickin, F, 111, 135
Aickin, J, 111, 138
Albany, 71
Albermarle-street, 69
Albert Hall, 79
Albert Memorial, 79
Aldersgate Church, 24
Allingham, J T, 143
Allingham, W, 153, 156, 159
Amelia Place, 82
Ampthill square, 52
Anderson, Robert, 12
Anglesey, Lord, 89
Anster, Dr J, 152
Antiquities, Irish, 23, 97, 98
Apsley House, 67
Architects, Irish and Scotch, 9
Arlington-street, 52
Art, Irish, 38-40, 95-97, 99-105, 106-109, 111, 112
Arundel-street, 30
"Athenaeum," 155
Athenaeum Club, 73
Atkinson J, 134
Autographs, Irish, 95, 104, 109
Aylmer, Lord, 87, 88

B.

Babington, Dr W, 25, 26
Baillie, Captain W, 62, 86
Baker-street, 60
Balfe, Donnell, 145
Balfe, M W, 43, 65, 71, 114, 117, 143
Banim, J, 16, 69, 81, 82, 143, 156
Barker, R, 31, 88
Barnard, Sir A, 84
Barralet, J M, 101
Barre, Col, 68, 151
Barrett, G (R A', 45, 59, 62, 64, 84, 95, 101, 109
Barrett, G (jun), 71, 101
Barrett, M, 20, 49
Barrington, G, 13, 43
Barrington, J, 125, 133
Barry, E M, 35, 36, 44, 110, 111, 119
Barry, Eliz, 125, 126
Barry, Sir C, 36, 73, 110, 111, 117, 119
Barry, Helen, 144
Barry, J (R A), 25, 32, 33, 34, 45, 55, 57, 95, 103, 106, 108, 110
Barry, L, 4, 16, 124
Barry, Sheil, 144
Barry, Springer, 116, 127, 133
Bartley, Mrs, 112, 140
Battersea Park, 89
Baxter, W G, 158
Bayley, F W N, 162
Beauchamp Tower, 22
Bedford Chapel, 47
Bedford street, 33
Beefsteak Club, 32

Bell, R, 65
Bellamy, Mrs, 57, 112, 122
Bellew, H K, 144
Bellew, J C M, 47, 160
"Bell's Life," 161
"Bentley's Miscellany," 158
Beresford, Viscount, 67, 107
Berkeley, Bishop, 35, 85, 108, 110, 145, 147
Berkeley, Dr G (jun), 30
Berkeley square, 69
Bernard, J, 142
Berwick's rest, 57
Bethnal green Museum, 105-109
Betty, Master, 50, 52, 112, 142
Beveridge, J D, 144
Bickerstaffe, I, 135
Biggar, J G, 121
Billing, Dr A, 66
Bindon, F, 106
Bingham, Sir R, 115
Binns, B 16
Bion, J, 16, 23, 33
Bishop, Rose 144
Blackfriars Bridge-road, 86
Blackwood, Sir H, 87, 115
"Blackwood's Magazine," 152
Blakeney, Sir E, 84
Blakeney, Lord W, 115
Blessington, Lady, 59, 62, 68, 72, 80, 151, 159
Blood, Colonel, 22, 70, 76, 108
Bloomsbury-square, 47
Bond-street, 77
Boucicault, Dion, 35, 144
Bourke, Archbishop, 106, 116, 117
Bow street Police Court, 43, 44
Bowen, actor, 25, 126
Boyd, Henry, 134
Boyd, Hugh, 30, 148
Boyle, F, 109
Boyle, J, 75, 75
Boyle, R, 124
Boyle, R W, 100
Boyle, Robert, 35, 37, 72, 90, 110, 111
Boyne, J, 48, 100
Boyse, S, 13, 24
Brady, Dr N, 23, 29, 84, 90, 127
Brennan, Maude, 144
Brennan, Margaret, 144
Brereton, W, 143
Bridge street, 75
British Museum, 47, 91-98
Brompton Cemetery, 83
Brompton road, 81
Brompton square, 81
Brooches and Pins, Irish, 97, 99
Brook street, 66
Brooke, G, 142
Brooke, H, 18, 85, 90, 134, 147
Brooke, S A, 47, 162
Brooke, W H, 157
Brooks, J, 96
Brooks' Club, 70
Brougham, J, 32, 143
Broucker, Sir W, 49, 110
Browne, F, 156
Bruton street, 71
Bryanston street and square, 62
Bryce, Professor, 162
Buckingham street, 35
Buckingham Palace, 75
Bullen, A H, 122

Bullen, G. 94, 162
Burke, Edmund, 52, 55, 59, 70, 73, 75, 89, 108, 119, 120, 121, 148
Burke, John, 82
Burke, Rev T N, 48, 71
Burke, Thomas, 5, 96
Burlington House, 71, 109
Burrowes, Peter, 18, 65
Burton, Sir F W, 12, 108
Burton, Sir R F, 63, 158
Bury-street, 70
Butler, J (Earl of Ormonde), 26
Butler, J (first Duke of Ormond), 70, 72, 102, 107, 108, 115
Butler, T (Earl of Ormond), 84
Butt, Isaac, 141, 154
Byrne, A F, 100
Byrne, C, 45, 74
Byrne, James, 142
Byrne, John, 100
Byrne, John, 160
Byrne, John (jun), 160
Byrne, N, 160
Byrne, O, 142
Byrne, W, 4, 100
Byron, Lord, 3, 5, 36, 53, 71

C.

Cade, Jack, 4, 21
Cadogan, Lord W, 108, 115
Cadogan place, 78
Cairnes, J E, 156
Cairns, Lord, 11, 18, 46
Callanan, J J, 153
Canning, Earl, 114
Canning, G (sen), 58
Canning, Right Hon G, 69, 71, 74, 75, 81, 89, 108, 117, 120, 149, 150
Canning, Viscount S, 114
Cantillon, R, 32, 60
Carew, J E, 27, 36, 54, 65, 121
Carey street, 46
Carey, W P, 58
Carlingford, Lord, 90
Carlton terrace, 73
Carlyle, Thomas, 84
Carroll, Father A, 15
Carter, J, 96, 100
Carter, T, 43, 139
Carvel, R, 43
Casey, E O B, 162
Casey, W L, 37, 100
Cas le street, 57
Castlereagh, Lord, 67, 72, 89, 90, 114, 117, 120
Catholic Association, 30
Catholics of England and Wales, 7
Catholics of London, 7, 10
Cavendish square and street, 58
Cecil street, 35
Cemeteries, &c, 52, 54, 64, 65, 83, 89
Centlivre, Mrs, 42, 125, 127
Chalk Farm, 52
Chambers, T (A R A), 96, 110
Characters, Irish, in English Plays, 125
Charlemont, Lord, 108, 109
Charter House, 48
Chartist Agitation, 65, 88
Chelsea Church (New), 82
Chelsea Church (Old), 84
Chelsea Hospital, 84
Cherry, Andrew, 111, 112 137
Cheyne row and walk, 84
Chinnery, G L, 95, 101, 102
Chiswick Church, 81
Christ's Hospital, 24
Church street, 83
Claggett, C, 55
Clancy, Dr M, 134
Clapham Common and Park, 83
Clare, Lord, 18, 89
Clarke, Dr A, 64, 151
Clarke, J H, 145
Clarke, Lady O, 78, 156
Clerke, A M, 162
Clerke, E M, 162

Clerke, T H S, 150
Clerkenwell Prison, 40
Clive, Kitty, 42, 44, 90, 112, 132, 133
Cloncurry, Lord, 28, 48, 60
Cobbe, F P, 153, 156, 160
Cockspur street, 74
Coffee Houses, Old, 42
Coffey, C, 144
Coger's Hall, 13
Coghlan, C, 144
Cogitian, R, 144
Coins, Irish, 97
Collins, W, 33, 56, 62, 95, 100, 103, 110, 111
Colpoys, Sir J, 87
Comerford, J, 102
Commons, House of, 120-123
Compton street, 55
Concanen, M, 15, 16, 134
Conduit street, 71
Congreve, W, 18, 31, 33, 108, 115
Connor, C, 75, 82, 142
Cooke, G F, 112, 139
Cooke, H G, 143
Cook, T S, 45, 57, 65, 139, 143
Cooke, W, 68, 134, 140
Coote, Sir E, 74, 75, 108, 115
Copley, J S, 24, 26, 30, 67, 87, 95, 100, 106, 110, 111
Corkmen, Eminent, 37
Corkran, Alice, 162
Corkran, J F, 154, 161
Cornhill, 28
"Cornhill Magazine," 159
Coronation Chair and Stone, 117
Costello, Dudley, 156, 154
Costello, L S, 156
Cotes, F, 58, 87, 95, 110, 111
Cotes, S, 50, 84
Cutter, P, 45
Covent Garden, 41
Covent Garden Theatre, 43, 44
Coyne, J S, 35, 54, 143, 144, 157, 162
Crane court, 15
Crawford, actor, 133
Crawford, Dr A, 85
Crawford, Mrs E, 159, 161, 162
Crawford, F M, 162
Crawford, T, 89
Crawford, Sir T, 11
Craven street, 35
Crehan, Ada, 144
Croker, Mrs B M, 162
Croker, T H, 76
Croker, T C, 83, 104, 152, 153, 156
Croker, J W, 83, 108, 150
Croly, Dr G, 24, 27, 47, 81, 143, 152, 157
Crommelin, May, 162
Cromwell, O, 74, 75, 95, 116, 120
Crosses, Irish, 89
Crotty, Leslie, 145
Crowe, E (A R A), 78, 100, 110
Crowe, E E, 65, 104, 155, 156, 159
Crowe, J A, 122, 155
Crowley, N J, 51
Crown and Anchor Tavern, 31
Crown Jewels, 21
Crystal Palace, 80
Cumberland, R, 47, 58, 108
Cunningham, J, 134
Curran, J P, 62, 82, 89, 108
Curran, R, 84
Curran, W H, 152
Curzon street, 63

D.

"Daily Chronicle," 160
"Daily News," 159
"Daily Telegraph," 159
D'Alton, H len, 115
Danby, F, 34, 45, 70, 79, 95, 100, 103, 110
Danby, J F, 109
Danby, T, 109
Dan er, John, 125
Darley, G, 156
Dorley, W, 156
Davent, Sir G, 153

Davit', M, 20, 77
Dean, H P, 41
Delane, D, 139, 133
Delane, J T, 153, 154
Delane, W, 153
Delaney, Mrs M, 71
Delaune, T, 19
Denh m, Sir J, 71, 73, 87, 110, 116, 124
Dermody, T, 88, 89
Derrick, S, 39, 134
Despard, Col E M, 29, 86
De Vere, Sir A, 58
Devereux court, 29
Devil Tavern, 17
Devoy, John, 75
Dickens, C, 6, 122, 155, 159
Dillon, A (Archbishop), 52
Dillon, F, 109
Dillon, J (M P), 121
Dillon, J B, 121
Dillon, W (Earl of Roscommon), 116
Dobbs, F, 135
Dobson, A, 96, 146
Dod, C R, 123, 154
Doggett, T, 21, 43, 112, 126
Doherty, sculptor, 25, 48
Donnelly, Gen W, 12
Doran, Dr J, 57, 58, 65, 156, 158
Dowland, J, 16
Dowling, F L, 161
Dowling, M G, 143
Dowling, P, 84
Dowling, R, 158, 162
Dowling, V, 153
Dowling, V G, 153, 161
Downey, E, 158, 162
Downing street, 74
Doyle, A, 155
Doyle, Sir C, 58
Doyle, J (H B), 61, 95
Doyle, Sir J, 60
Doyle, R, 82, 95, 96, 101, 109, 157
Doyle, Dr T, 86
Drury lane, 32
Drury lane Theatre, 43
Duels, Irish, 42, 53, 60, 61, 64, 89
Duff, M A, 140, 141
Dufferin, Lady, 67
Duffett, T, 4, 31, 124
Duffy, Sir C G, 73, 84, 93, 105, 121
Duffy, E .wa. d, 77
Duigenan, Dr P, 75
Duke street (Piccadilly), 70
Duke street (Lincoln's Inn), 46
Dunphy, H M, 122, 160
Dunraven, Lord, 159
Durham street, 33

E.

East Sheen, 90
Eaton square and terrace, 79
Ebury street, 79
Eccentric Club, 33
Eccles, I A, 39
Eccleston square, 79
Edgeware road, 81
Edgeworth, Maria, 154
Edgeworth, R L, 74
Edwin, Mrs R, 112, 140, 141
Egan, J, 5, 96
Egan, P, sen, 43, 54
Egan, P, jun, 43, 162
Egyptian Hall, 71
Elizabeth, Queen, 74, 93
Elks, Irish, 45, 82
Ellis, J F, 95
Ellis, W (Baron Mendip), 117
Elmore, A, 110, 111
Ely Place, 48
Engineers, Irish and Scotch, 9
English Writers on Ireland, 5, 9, 12
Engravers, Irish (in British Museum), 96
Essex street, 30
Evans, Gen Sir De Lacy, 31
"Examiner," 156

"Examiner," Swift's, 147
Exchange, Royal, 27

F.

Fagan, L, 94
Falconer, E, 143
Famine, The Great, 8
Farquhar, G, 39, 125, 127
Farren, E, 66, 67, 112, 139
Fenian Prisoners, 51, 52, 76, 77
Fenian Relics, 74
Ferguson, Sir S, 153
Fetter Lane, 15
Finborough road, 82
Finnerty, P, 122, 152
Flaber, J, 100
Fishmongers' Hall, 21
Fitzgerald, Lord Edward, 95
Fitzgerald, Percy, 141, 144, 155, 162
Fitzpatrick, W J, 158
Fitzsimon, Ellen, 65
Fitzwilliam, E, 142
Fitzwilliam, H, 142
Flecknoe, R, 124
Fleet street, 13-19
Foley, E A, 55, 108
Foley, J H, 25, 27, 52, 72, 79, 80, 102, 110, 111, 114, 119, 121
Foli, Signor A J, 145
"Fontenoy, Battle of," 103
Forster, John, 154, 155
F .wke, Capt F, 9, 79, 83, 89, 95, 100
Francis, Rev F, 84, 134
Francis, Sir P, 20, 58, 72, 93, 108, 119, 148
"Fraserians," 57, 104
"Fraser's Magazine," 153
"Freeman's Journal" Office, 30
Freemasons' Tavern, 44
Frye, Thos, 25, 45, 96, 106
Fulham ro.d, 82
"Fun," 158
Furniss, H, 157
Furnival's Inn 48

G.

Gabriel, M A V, 143
Gahagan, L, 7., 75
Gahagan, S, 25, 58, 114
Gardiner, W N, 72, 96, 108
Garibaldi Riots, 63
Garrick Club, 40, 111
Garrick, D, 41, 44, 45, 112, 116, 130, 131, 132
Garvey, R, 110, 111
"Gen leman's Magazine," 49, 162
Gentleman, F, 134
Geoghegan, A G, 12, 23, 159
Geoghegan, G, 12, 29
Geoghegan, M, 159
Geological Museum, 70
Gerrard-street, 55
Giants, Irish, 6
Giffard, S L, 11, 159
Gillespie, Sir R B, 25
Gillray, J, 69, 71, 95, 105
Gladstone, W E, 49
Glascock, Capt W N, 82
"Globe," 160
Globe Tavern, 24
Glover, Dr, 14
Glover, Mrs J, 37, 112, 141
Godkin, E L, 159
Godkin, J, 151, 159
Golden-square, 58
Goldsmith, O, .4, 15, 16, 18, 29 39, 70, 89 116, 134, 147
Goldsmiths' Hall, 24
Gordon Riots, 46, 86
Gore House, 81
Gosnell, S, 153, 155
Gospels, Old Irish, 85, 95
Gough-square, 15
Granite, Irish, 45, 79
Grattan, H, 23, 59, 60, 70, 114, 117, 129, 141
Grattan, H, jun, 90

Grattan, H P, 157
Grattan, T C, 70, 143, 153
Gratton, G, 100
Graves, A P, 157
Graves, Clo, 141, 157
Gray, Paul, 159
Gray's Inn, 48
Great Portland-street, 57
Great Queen's reet, 44
Great Titchfield-street, 56
Grecian Coffee House, 29
Greek-street, 55
Green Arbour Court, 20
Greene, P, 145
Greenwich Church and Hospital, 87
Griffin, G, 29, 44, 58, 62, 64, 81, 122, 143, 155
Griffith, Mrs E, 134
Grosvenor place, 67
Grosvenor square, 66
Groves, C, 144
Guildhall, 26
Guinee, W B, 153
Gunning, Eliz and Maria, 68

H.

Half-Moon-street, 68
Hall, Mrs S C, 35, 78, 104, 143
Hall, S C, 53, 99, 102
Halsbury, Lord, 11
Hamilton, C, 135
Hamilton, H D, 72, 107
Hamilton, "La Belle," 102, 109
Hammersmith terrace, 81
Hampstead H ath, 33
Hanger, George, 53
Hans place, 8
Hardiman, J, 92
Harley street, 58
Harps, Irish, 89
Hartland, A, 100
Hartson, H, 135
Hart street, 41
Hastings, Marquis of, 74, 81
Hastings, Warren, 119
Hatton Garden, 48
Havard, W, 131, 133
Haverstock Hill, 53
Haverty, J P, 79
Haverty, M, 155, 159
Hayes, Catherine, 65, 89, 141
Hayes, Claude, 109
Hayes, E, 109
Hayes, Sir J M, 71, 73, 76
Hazlitt, J, 107
Hazlitt, W, 55, 107, 122
Healy, T M, 121
Heffernan, sculptor, 89
Henderson, J, 35, 36, 112, 115, 139
Henrietta street, 42
Hertford street, 67
Hickey, T, 88, 85, 112
Hiffernan, P, 134, 151
Higgins, B, 55
Higgins, M J, 153, 161
High road (Knightsbridge), 79
Highgate Cemetery, 54
Higinbotham, G, 155
Hodson, G, 144
Hodson, H, 144
Hodson, K, 144
Hoey, Mrs Cashel, 162
Hogarth, W, 45
Holland House, 80
Home Rule Confederation, 75, 86
Hone, C, 37
Hone, H, 37, 102, 110
Hone, N, 37, 54, 106, 107, 110, 111
Horns Tavern, 58
Houston, R, 86
Howard, G K, 134
Howard, H, 72, 90
Huddleston. Baron, 11, 46
Hughes, T M, 135
Hutton, R H, 154
Hyde Park, 63, 64

I.

India Office, 74
Irish in London—general view, 3—7, their distribution, callings, character, and voting power, 7—12
Irwin, E, 143
Irwin, K, 144
Irwin, T C, 158
Italian Church, 48

J

Jackman, I, 134, 149
Jackson, Rev W, 47
Jameson, Mrs A, 51, 53, 58, 65, 71, 109, 158
James street, 44
Jebb, Dr J, 88, 89
Jeffrey, Lord, 6, 53
Jephson, R, 131
Jermyn street, 70
Jervas, C, 38, 69, 70, 73, 106, 111
Johnson, Dr S, 5, 14, 15, 116
Johnston, Gen J, 115
Johnstone, C, 148
Johnstone, J, 112, 138
Jones, H. 40, 134
Jones, J E, 89
Jordan, Mrs, 33, 67, 78, 112, 130, 139
"Junius," Letters of, 5, 20, 95, 148

K

Kane, Gen Sir R, 115
Kavanagh, C, 85
Kavanagh, Julia, 156
Kean, C, 43, 64, 112, 140, 142
Kean, Mrs E, 140
Keary, Annie, 81, 162
Keating, Sir H S, 65
Keightley, T, 81
Kelly, Ann, 89, 140
Kelly, Austin, 160
Kelly, F R, 112, 140
Kelly, F M, 140
Kelly, Hugh, 14, 15, 136, 146, 148
Kelly, J, 133
Kelly, M, 42, 43, 73, 74, 111, 139
Kembles, The, 139
Kenealy, Dr E V, 47, 153, 157, 158, 160
Kenney, C L, 143
Kenney, J, 143
Kennington Common, 88
Kensal Green Cemetery, 65
Keogh, Judge W, 13, 121
Keon, M G, 160
Kickham, C J, 52
Kilburn, 72
King, E A, 161
King's College, 31
King street, Covent Garden, 41
King street, Westminster, 75
Kirk, T, 87
Kit-Cat Club, 17, 53
Knowles, J S, 43, 143, 155, 156
Knowles, R B, 160
Knox, A, 153
Knox, R, 154

L

Lablache, L, 46
Laces, Irish, 94
Lacy, James, 142
Lacy, John, 125
Lalor, J, 155
Lambeth Palace and Church, 85
Land League, 75, 76
Lane, B, 145
Langham place, 58
Lansdowne House, 69
Lansdowne, First Marquis of, 64, 69, 91, 108
Lansdowne, Third Marquis of, 109
Lardner, Dr, 104, 159
Law Courts, 29, 30
Lawless, J, 35

Index. 169

Lawlor, J, 79, 89
Lawrence, Sir H, 25, 28, 108
Lawrence, Lord, 73, 74, 115, 117
Lawrence, General S, 115
Lawrence, Sir W, 27
Lawrenson, T, 107
Leadenhall street, 28
League of the Cross, 11, 89
Leahy, E D, 107
Lecky, W E H, 60, 73, 93, 154
Leech, J, 14, 48, 65, 98, 101, 112, 157, 161, 162
Lefanu, J S, 158
Leigh, J, 127, 128
Leinster, Duke of, 23, 32
Leland, Dr T, 45, 147
Leslie, Prof, F C, 156
Lever, C, 55, 66, 68, 151, 158, 159
Lewis' ain Churchyard, 88
Lia Fail, 117
Ligonier, Lord, 115
Lincoln's Inn, 45, 46
Litchfield House Compact, 72
"Literary Gazette," 155
Loftie, Rev W J, 158
Londonderry, Lord, 30
London Irish Volunteers, 120
London Stone, 21
London University, 70
Long Acre, 40
Long, J S, 65
Lord Mayors, Irish, 12, 27
Lover, S, 55, 65, 108, 126, 142, 153, 158, 162
Ludgate Hill, 19
Ludwig, W, 145
Luttrell, H (painter), 108
Luttrell, H (poet), 81
Lyceum Theatre, 32
Lytton, Bulwer, 11, 78
Lytton, Lady H, 78

M.

M'Ardell, J, 37, 42, 52, 96
M'Ardle, J F, 143
M'Arthur, Sir W, 12, 28
Macartney, Lord, 65, 81, 108
Macaule, Lord, 119
M'Cabe, W G, 122, 154, 155
M'Cabe, W P, 28, 43, 48, 57
M'Carthy, Dr B, 158
M'Carthy, Sir C, 115
M'Carthy, H P, 26
M'Carthy, Justin, 93, 122, 158, 159, 162
M'Carthy, J H, 144
M'Clintock, Letitia, 162
M'Clure, Sir R J, 65, 87
M'Cormac, S.r W, 11, 85
M'Cullough, J E, 143
M'Donagh, M, 41, 54
M'Don gh, Capt F, 155
M'Dowell, P, 25, 27, 52, 57, 71, 79, 87, 99, 110, 111, 121
M'Gahan, J A, 159
M'Gee, T D, 93, 122
M'Guckin, B, 145
M'Kenna, S J, 161
Mackenzie, R S, 162
Macklin, C, 19, 41, 42, 43, 131
Macklin, Miss, 131
Maclaine, L, 20
M'Lean, J, 14, 63, 69
Maclise, D, 39, 51, 85, 78, 84, 95, 104, 108, 109, 110, 111, 112, 124, 125, 153
M'Mahon, Captain, 23, 32
M'Mann, T B, 121
M'Nally, L, 90, 135, 151
M'Namara, Captain, 19, 53
M'Nevin, Dr W J, 11, 73
Macready, W, 135
Macready, W C, 52, 65, 112, 140, 143
M'Swiney, Owen, 38, 43, 128
Madden, D O, 154, 160
Madden, Sir F, 94
Madden, Dr R R, 154, 155, 156
Madden, Dr S, 125, 147, 148

Magdalen Hospital, 88
Maginn, Dr W, 27, 46, 57, 150, 151, 152, 157, 158
Maguire, Connor, 23, 32
Mahon, O'Gorman, 62
Mahony, F S, 36, 38, 57, 59, 104, 153, 154, 158, 159, 159, 160
Mahony J, 100
Maida Vale, 61
Malone, E, 15, 58, 103, 139, 149, 151
Malone, R, 142
Marsion House, 27
Manuscripts, Irish, 85, 92, 94
Markham, Archbishop, 113
Marsden, Dr W, 35, 92
Martin, J, 93, 12,
Marylebone Church, 58
Mason, H M, 92
Mason, J M, 139
Mathew, Father, 10, 107
Mathew, Justice, 11
Matarin, Rev C R, 143, 152
Maxwell, W H, 82
Mayfair, 68
Mayne, Sir R, 12, 63
Meagher, P J, 154
Meagher, T F, 73, 121
Medals, Irish, 97, 98
Mercer's Hall and Chapel, 26
Merchant Tailors' Hall, 29
Meriwale, Miss C, 145
Middleton, James, 133
Millbank Prison, 76
Milliken, E J, 157
Mint, The, 20
Mitchel, John, 84, 93, 121
Mitre Tavern, 16
Molloy, C, 134
Molloy, J F, 158, 162
Molloy, J L, 145
Molyneux, W, 18, 31, 145
Montgomery, J, 3
Moody, J, 111, 112, 125, 137
Moore, C, 89, 108
Moore, Dr N, 11
Moore, T, 36, 53, 59, 70, 81, 82, 83, 102, 104, 108, 143, 160
Moorehead, J, 143
Morgan, Lady, 78, 83, 90, 151, 158
Morgan, M, 134
"Morning Chronicle," 149, 155
"Morning Herald," 154
"Morning Post," 160
Morris, W O Connor, 158
Mortlake, 90
Mossop, H, 84, 128, 133
Mossop, W, 97
Mossop, W S, 97, 99
Mount street, 85
Moxom, Dr W, 11, 45
Mulholland, R, 129
Mulready, W, 26, 39, 55, 63, 64, 65, 99, 95, 100, 101, 102, 104, 110, 111
Mulready, W, (jun), 103
Mulrenin, B, 105
Munster House, 82
Murphy, A, 46, 47, 81, 108, 137, 148
Murphy, D B, 51
Murphy, F S, 36, 69, 153
Murphy, G, 108
Murphy, J D, 152
Murphy, John (engraver), 95
Murphy, John (journalist), 159
Murray, D, 144
Murray, J F, 152
Muskerry, W, 143

N

Napier, Sir C J, 25, 30, 109
Napier, Sir W P, 25, 88
National Gallery, 39-40
National League, 75 76
National Portrait Gallery, 105-109
Natural History Museum, 81
Newgate Prison, 11

Newman-street, 56
Norton, Hon Mrs, 68, 70, 123, 153
Norwood, Cemetery, 89
Nowlan, F, 109
Nugent, Earl, 19, 55
Nugent, Michael, 122, 152

O

O'Beirne, Dr T L, 134
O'Brien, J B, 65, 161
O'Brien, R B, 162
O'Brien, W, 42, 137
O'Brien, W (M P) 121
O'Brien, W S, 23, 61, 63, 79, 89, 121
O'Bryen, D, 135
O'Callaghan, P P, 143
O'Cavanagh, J E, 89, 153
O'Coigly, Rev J, 23
O'Connell, D, 13, 31, 32, 43, 44, 48, 58, 72, 73, 75, 81, 89, 104, 108, 120, 122, 154
O'Connor, Gen A, 23
O'Connor, Dr B, 38, 43
O'Connor, Fergus, 64, 65, 81, 83
O'Connor, J A, 82, 104, 105
O'Connor, J, 57
O'Connor, R 36
O'Connor, T P, 160
O'Curry, Eugene, 93, 94
O'Donnell, F H, 160
O'Donnell, J F, 18, 65, 159
O'Donnell, P, 29
O'Donovan, F, 25, 15)
O'Donovan, Dr J, 93
O'Donovan Rossa J, 51, 76
O'Dwyer, J, 152
O'Farrell, E, 159
Ogham Stones, 97
O'Gorman, R, 121
O'Grady, H, 144
O Grady, S H, 158
O'Hara, Right Hon J, 84
O'Hara, Kane, 135
O'Hara, R, 154
O'Keeffe, J, 30, 107, 134, 135, 136
O'Kelly, J J, 139
Old Slaughter's Coffee-house, 37
O'Leary, Rev A, 52, 55, 57, 86
O'Leary, John, 52
O'Leary, Joseph, 122, 154, 157
O'Loghlen, Sir M, 67, 83
O'Neil, Miss E, 109, 112, 139
O'Neil, H, 110, 111, 152
O'Neill, Rev A, 65
O'Neill, D, 24
O'Neill, G B, 3)
O'Neill, Hugh (artist), 58, 96, 100
O'Neill, Hugh (Earl of Tyrone), 119
O'Neill, Shane, 74
Orchard street, 59
O'Reilly (Special Correspondent), 154
Ormond (2nd Duke of), 108, 115
Orrery (Countess of), 13
Orrery (Earl of) 13, 23
Osborne, G A, 143
O'Shaughnessy, A, 93, 97, 156
O'Shea, J A, 155, 158, 160
O'Sullivan, M, 122, 152
Oulton, W C, 135
Owenson, R, 78, 133
Oxford street, 54

P.

Paddington Churchyard, 62
Pakenham, Sir E, 25
Pall Mall, 72
"Pall Mall Gazette," 161
Park Lane, 66
Parliament (Houses of), 118-124
Parliamentary Reporters, 122, 123
Parnell, C S, 29, 75, 88, 121
Parnell, Sir H, 64
Parnell, T, 70, 145, 147
Pearson, J, 24

Peele's Coffeehouse, 16
Pennefather, General Sir J L, 83, 84
Pentonville Prison, 51, 52
Percy street, 59
Periodicals, Irish (in British Museum), 93
Peters, M W, 100, 110, 111
Petrie, Dr G, 93, 100
Phillips, C, 58, 152
Physicians, Royal College of, and its Irish members, 73
Piccadilly, 67-71
Pilkington, Mrs L, 70, 134
Pilon, F, 134
Pitt, W, 69, 90
Plunkett, Oliver, 37, 106
Poet's Corner, 75, 116
Police, Irish Commissioners of, 12, 74
Pollock, J, 155
Ponsonby, Sir W, 25
Pope, A (the Poet), 4, 127
Pope, A (actor), 68, 95, 112, 138
Pope, Mrs E, 112, 116, 138
Pope, Mrs M, 68, 112, 116, 138
Popham, Sir H R, 74
Popkins, Irish, 93, 109
Porter, A M, 26, 151
Porter, Jane, 26, 151
Porter, Sir R K, 26, 95
Portland place, 59
Portman square, 59
Power, F, 25, 154, 162
Power G, 144
Power, Tyrone, 141
Presidents of Royal Society, 110
Preston, W, 135
Prime Ministers, Irish, 12
"Punch," 22, 24, 127
Purcell, H, 117
Purcell, R, 96
Putney, 83

Q.

Queen's road (Chelsea), 84
Quilliman, E, 62, 123
Quin, E, 148, 151
Quin, J, 16, 27, 28, 33, 41, 43, 112, 126, 129, 130
Quin, M J, 135

R.

"Ram alley," 16, 124
Rathbone place, 56
Read, C A, 31
Reading Room of British Museum, 92
Red Deer, Irish, 45, 82
Redilish, S, 133
Reform Club, 74
Regent's Park, 59
Regent street, 57
Reid, Captain M, 61
Rickey, Prof G A, 158
Richmond Church, 90
Riddell, Mrs C, 162
Riots, Theatrical, 129
Roberts, T S, 100
Robertson, G, 95
Robin Hood Society, 30
Robinson, Mrs M, 112, 138
Roche, E, 143, 151
Roche, J, 101, 162
Roche, R M, 151
Rollin, L, 82
Rooke, W M, 83, 143
Rorke, K, 144
Rorke, M, 144
Rosse, Earl of, 110
Rothwell, E, 103, 107
Rowan, A H, 76
Rowan, Sir C, 74
Rowbotham, T L, 100
Royal Society, 16, 29, 110
Russell, Sir C, 12, 29, 159
Russell, W H, 1, 2, 154, 156, 158, 159
Ryan, D L, 160

Ryan, Lacy, 41, 130
Ryan, M D, 154, 155, 160
Ryves, Eliza, 51, 134

S.

Sadleir, John, 53, 121
St Ann's Church, 55
St Bartholomew's Hospital, 48
St Bride's Church, 13
St Clement Dane's Church, 30
St Dunstan's Church, 17
St Etheldreda's Chapel, 48
St George's Cathedral 83
St George's Cemetery, 64
St George's Church, 86
St Giles's Church, 38
St James's Church, 71
St James the Less, Church of, 52
St James's H ll, 71
St James's Park, 75
St James' square, 72
St James's street, 69
St John's Gate, 48
St Katherine Cree, Church of, 2
St Margaret, Church of, 76
St Martin's Church, 36
St Martin's lane, 37, 40
St Pancras Cemetery, 52
St Patrick's Chapel, 54
St Paul's Cathedral, 24-26
St Paul's Churchyard, 20
St Paul's Church, 41
St Stephen's Church, 27
St Thomas's Hospital, 35
Sardinian Chapel, 46
"Saturday Review," 158
Savage, M W, 71, 156
Savile r w, 70
Scotch in England, 5, 7, 8
Scotland Yard, 74
Sexton, I, 144
Shakespeare, W, 4, 137
Shaw, Capt E M, 12
Shaw, G B, 161, 162
Shee, Sir M A, 24, 25, 35, 39, 58, 70, 73, 81, 85, 107, 110, 111, 112, 143, 152
Sheehan, J, 122, 158, 162
Sheil, R L, 21, 37, 43, 84, 120, 122, 140, 152
Shelley, P B, 5, 70
Sheridan, M s F, 134
Sheridan, Miss, 134
Sheridan, R B, 33, 42, 43, 44, 45, 55, 59, 64, 67, 70, 71, 108, 118, 119, 12, 122, 137, 158
Sheridan, T, 33, 43, 76, 112, 153
Sheridan, Dr T, 128
Sherlock, W, 95, 102
Shoe lane, 15
Siddons, Mrs, 138, 140
"Silken Thomas," 22, 38
Simmens, B, 48, 54, 153
Simons, J, 134
Skerritt, Sir J B, 25
Sloane, Sir H, 16, 47, 73, 84, 91, 103, 110, 111
Sloane street, 78
Small, W, 101
Smith, J C, 104
Smith, Sydney, 6
Smithfield, 48
Soane's Museum, 45
Society of Arts, 33, 34
Somerset House, 31
Southerne, T, 18, 42, 73, 76, 125
South Kingston Museum, 81, 93-105
Southwark Catholic Chapel, 86
Southwark Irish Literary Club, 66
Spanish place Chapel, 59
Sparkes, I, 41, 133
Sparks, I, 131
Spalding, H H, 31, 161
"Sprolator," 158
"Spectator" (Steele's), 29, 146
Spenser, E, 4, 75
Spooner, G, 52
"Standard," 159
Stanfield, J R, 135

Stanfield, W C, 39, 40, 54, 65, 73, 74, 75, 100, 103, 105, 110, 111, 112
Stanford, Prof, C V, 145
Stationer's Hall, 19
"Star," 160
Staunton, Sir G L, 108, 117, 156
Steele, Sir R, 17, 19, 20, 31, 35, 43, 47, 53, 70, 76. 83, 95, 105, 108, 128, 134, 145, 146
Steele, T, 16, 61
Sterling, E, 79, 151
Sterling, J, 79, 155
Sterne, L, 69, 70, 72, 145, 147
Stewart, Sir H, 25, 79
Stokes, Prof G G, 110
Stokes, Margaret, 41, 95
Stokes, Whitley, 158
Stopford, W H, 109
Stott, T, 160
Strand, The, 29
Strangford, 6th Lord, 58, 63
Strangford, 7th Lord, 155, 158, 161
Strangford, 8th Lord, 161
Sullivan, Sir A, 145
Sullivan, A M, 18, 88, 121
Sullivan, Barry, 144
Sullivan, C, 143
Sullivan, J F, 158
Sullivan, L, 38, 57, 96
Supple, M, 122, 52
Surgeons, Royal College of, 45
Swift, Dean, 6, 70, 72, 73, 84, 99, 102, 104, 105, 106, 145, 146, 147
Sydenham, 89

T

Tanner, Dr, 121
Tate, Nahum, 86, 127
"Tatler," 17, 146
Tavistock Chapel, 47
Tavistock square, 47
Tavistock street, 42
Taylor, J S, 65, 154
Taylor, W B S, 155
Taylor, Dr W C, 155, 158
Temple, The, and its Irish Residents, 18
Temple Church, 15, 17
Temple, Miss H, 145
Tennent, Sir J E, 46, 72, 79
Thatched House Tavern, 69
Thomson, T C, 104
Thomson, Sir W, 110
Thurot, Capt, 46
Tierney, Right Hon G, 70, 90, 108, 117
"Times," 30, 79, 148, 153, 154
"Tinsley's Magazine," 159
Tobin, J, 137
Todd, Dr R B, 65
Toland, J, 83, 145
Tone, Wolfe, 16, 18, 19
Toole, J L, 144
Torrens, Sir A W 25, 84
Torrens, Col R, 121, 160
Torrens, W M, 155, 156, 159
Tower Hill, 21
Tower of London and its Irish Prisoners, 21-24
Trafalgar square, 36
Traitor's Gate, 22, 23
Trench, Dr R C, 79, 113
Tresham, H, 70, 95, 109, 110, 111
"Truth," 161
Turk's Head Tavern, 55
Turner, J M W, 25, 38, 107
Turnerelli, P, 29, 51, 56, 87, 114
Twickenham, 90
Tyburn, 38, 63,
Tyndall, Professor, 73, 110, 161
Tyrrell, Sir R, 87, 115

U.

United Irish Society, 48
United Service Museum, 74
Ussher, Archbishop, 18, 31, 45, 74, 108, 116

V.

"Vanessa," Swift's, 73
"Vicar of Wakefield," 15, 20

W.

Wade, J A, 158
Wall, Governor, 19
Wallace, W V, 65, 143
Waller, J F, 159
Wallis, T, 155. 159
Walmsley, T, 100
Walsh, J H, 161
Walsh, Rev P, 17
Wandsworth, 89
Wardour street, 55
Warner, Mrs, 140, 141
Warren, Sir P, 87, 113
Weld, I, 156
Wellesley, Dr G V. 82
Wellesley, Marquis of, 67, 69, 74, 79
Wellington, Duke of, 23, 25, 26, 27, 29, 58, 67, 84, 89, 99, 102, 108, 123
Westbourne Grove, 64
Westminster Abbey. 76, 113-118
Westminster Hall, 119
Westminster Hospital, 75
Westminster Palace Hotel, 76

Westminster School, 76
Whitehall, 74
Whitehall Palace, 74
Whitty, E M, 122, 154, 159
Wigmore street, 59
Wilde, Lady, 150, 160, 161
Wilde, Oscar, 158, 161
Wilde, W C K, 150
Wilks R, 42, 43, 126, 129
William street, 78
Williams, C, 160, 161
Wills, Rev J, 152
Wills, W G, 144
Wimbledon Common, 89
Wine Office court, 14
Wingfield, Hon L, 154, 159
Wiseman, Cardinal, 54, 57, 59, 65, 86
Woffington, Margaret, 43, 104, 109, 112, 133, 133
Woffington, Mary, 138
Wolfe, General, 87, 108, 115
Wood's Halfpence, 97
Wren, Sir C, 13, 24, 26, 71
Wych street, 46

www.ingramcontent.com/pod-product-compliance
Lightning Source LLC
Chambersburg PA
CBHW020304170426
43202CB00008B/493